The Complete Idiot's Reference Card

Strange Encounters of the Heroic Kind

Aviator hero Amelia Earhart gave human rights hero Eleanor Roosevelt a ride in her plane above Washington D.C. Both women were wearing evening gowns at the time.

Confederate rebel hero Robert E. Lee is directly descended from Martha Washington's father.

Baseball hero Sammy Sosa and civil rights hero Rosa Parks were both honored with applause for their achievements at President Clinton's 1999 State of the Union address.

The father of Gulf War hero H. Norman Schwarzkopf (whose name is also H. Norman Schwarzkopf) was the New Jersey police chief in charge of the investigation into the infamous kidnapping of aviator hero Charles Lindbergh's baby.

The spacecraft *Eagle*, flown by astronaut heroes Neil Armstrong and Buzz Aldrin during the first moon landing, is symbolized by an American eagle landing on the moon on the back of the U.S. dollar coin commemorating women's rights hero Susan B. Anthony.

Acting hero John Wayne got his start in show business through a deal arranged by his USC college football coach with performing cowboy hero Tom Mix. Tom Mix, an ardent fan of the USC Trojans, received tickets to football games in exchange for getting Wayne a job.

Black civil rights hero Martin Luther King and Chicano labor hero Cesar Chavez were both inspired by the example of Indian hero Mahatma Gandhi. Gandhi was inspired in turn by the heroic nonconformist Henry David Thoreau.

A notable episode of a DC comic series tells of a boxing match between comic book superhero Superman and real-life boxing hero Muhammad Ali.

Union presidential hero Abraham Lincoln and Confederate presidential hero Jefferson Davis represented opposite sides of the Civil War, but served on the same side in Black Hawk's War, named for the heroic Indian chief.

World War II hero Daniel Inouye, who lost his arm fighting with the famous "Go for Broke" Division, was the senator in charge of the inquiry into charges brought against war hero Oliver North and others involved with the Iran-Contra scandal.

During his days as an actor, presidential hero Ronald Reagan was seriously considered for the lead in the legendary film *Casablanca* that was masterfully played by actor hero Humphrey Bogart.

World War I hero General John J. Pershing led his doughboys through the streets of Paris amid cheering crowds before they stopped to salute the statue of Marquis de Lafayette, one of the many Frenchmen who fought with George Washington in the American Revolution.

alpha
books

Strange Encounters of the Heroic Kind (cont.)

Folk-singer hero Joan Baez was on hand at a candlelight vigil held on the night of the assassination of the heroic gay San Francisco politician Harvey Milk. She sang an impromptu rendition of "Amazing Grace."

Heroic birth control champion Margaret Sanger got the idea to go to France to research birth control methods from heroic labor leader "Big" Bill Haywood.

Shortly after George Washington's death in 1799, prints were sold depicting him rising into heaven. After Lincoln was assassinated, he was painted ascending into heaven as well, where he is embraced by George Washington and crowned with laurels.

John Henry, a historical figure who lived and died as a railroad worker in the late nineteenth century, teams up with the fictional characters Paul Bunyan and Pecos Bill in the Disney movie *Tall Tales, The Unbelievable Adventures of Pecos Bill* (1995).

The Sioux medicine man Sitting Bull, who defeated General Custer and was feared by whites, toured for a time with Buffalo Bill Cody's Wild West Show.

One of the first persons to appreciate Henry Ford's plan to build a gas-driven motor was fellow inventor Thomas Edison.

What do astronaut Neil Armstrong, singing idol Frank Sinatra, and CEO Lee Iacocca have in common? They've all appeared in TV commercials for Chrysler cars.

George Washington, Thomas Jefferson, Abraham Lincoln, and Theodore Roosevelt got their faces carved into Mount Rushmore in South Dakota only after plans were scrapped to make mountain-sized likenesses to commemorate local heroes, including Sitting Bull and General Custer.

George Washington and Betsy Ross sat in adjacent pews at church.

What do President John F. Kennedy and baseball great Joe DiMaggio have in common? They were both intimate with screen goddess Marilyn Monroe.

Can you name two American heroes who portrayed their own heroic exploits as actors? Buffalo Bill Cody played himself in his Wild West Show, and Audie Murphy re-created his own World War II heroism in the film *To Hell and Back* (1955).

Entrepreneur and philanthropist Andrew Carnegie bankrolled a pension for the widow of President Theodore Roosevelt.

Explorer Meriwether Lewis (of Lewis and Clark) served as Thomas Jefferson's personal secretary prior to setting off on his famous expedition to the Pacific.

First Lady Eleanor Roosevelt christened the Liberty Ship *Harriet Tubman*.

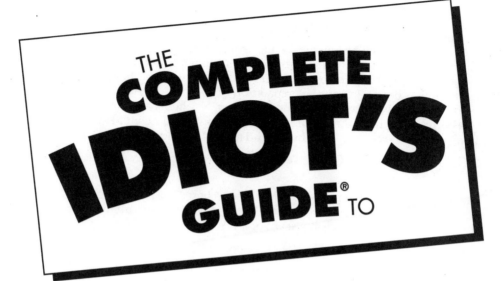

THE COMPLETE IDIOT'S GUIDE® TO

American Heroes

*by Jay Stevenson, Ph.D. and
Matthew Budman*

alpha books

A Division of Macmillan General Reference
A Pearson Education Macmillan Company
1633 Broadway, New York, NY 10019

Macmillan General Reference books may be purchased for business or sales promotional use. For information please write: Special Markets Department, Macmillan Publishing USA, 1633 Broadway, New York, NY 10019.

International Standard Book Number: 0–02863377-6

Library of Congress Catalog Card Number: 99-64049

01 00 99 8 7 6 5 4 3 2 1

Interpretation of the printing code: the rightmost number of the first series of numbers is the year of the book's printing; the rightmost number of the second series of numbers is the number of the book's printing. For example, a printing code of 98-1 shows that the first printing occurred in 1999.

Printed in the United States of America

Alpha Development Team

Publisher
Kathy Nebenhaus

Associate Publisher
Cindy Kitchel

Editorial Director
Gary M. Krebs

Managing Editor
Bob Shuman

Marketing Brand Manager
Felice Primeau

Acquisitions Editor
Jessica Faust

Development Editors
Phil Kitchel
Amy Zavatto

Assistant Editor
Georgette Blau

Production Team

Development Editor
Andrew McCarthy

Production Editor
Suzanne Snyder

Copy Editor
Keith Cline

Cover Designer
Mike Freeland

Photo Editor
Richard H. Fox

Illustrator
Brian Mac Moyerr

Book Designers
Scott Cook and Amy Adams of DesignLab

Indexer
Chris Wilcox

Layout/Proofreading
Natalie Hollifield
Ellen Considine

Contents at a Glance

Contents

Brush with Greatness

Americans are *way* into heroes. Our love for heroic people is part of who we are. Heroes are strong, unique, courageous individuals, and this is how most Americans would like to think of themselves. So we put our heroes on postage stamps, into halls of fame, made-for-TV movies, and our hearts. Other countries have their heroes too, of course, but in America heroes seem to come out of the woodwork. Brushes with greatness occur so frequently that you might think that the country is just one big fantasy camp!

It's easy to imagine getting pointers on statesmanship from George Washington, courage and dignity from Martin Luther King, valor from Audie Murphy, strength and compassion from Dorothy Day, wisdom and benevolence from Ben Franklin, justice from Susan B. Anthony, hope and endurance from Lewis and Clark, or on crushing a curve ball from Mark McGwire! Heroes are so easy to come by that it is easy to lose sight of what they actually did and what their achievements mean for the country. It is also easy to forget, when we're caught up in the enthusiasm for the hero of the moment, how many other heroes there are.

The numbers and diversity of America's heroes is perhaps the best reflection of this country imaginable. Learning about them can be a great way to learn about the cultural diversity of the country and the historical odyssey we've come through. And, who knows, it might even help you get in touch with some of your own heroic potential. So upward and onward into the wild heroic yonder, after a quick survey of the terrain!

This book is divided into five main sections:

Part 1, **The Big Ideal**, talks about theories of heroism and types of heroes, and provides background on American heroes in myth, legend, and fiction. There's a chapter on Native American myth, one on legendary American occupational heroes, and one on comic-book superheroes.

Part 2, **Questing and Nesting**, deals with the ways American heroes have established homelands, contributed to our way of life, and attempted to move beyond the spatial and technological boundaries. These are the colonists, frontier heroes, cowboys, inventors, lovers, businesspeople, and explorers.

Part 3, **Fighting Spirits**, concerns the American war heroes of all the major conflicts fought by Americans. These chapters focus on the Indian Wars, the Revolutionary War, the Civil War, World Wars I and II, Vietnam, and the Gulf War. There's also a chapter on soldier-presidents.

Part 4, **Rights Stuff**, talks about the heroic leaders of the ongoing struggle for civil rights in America. Their causes include religious freedom, minority rights, women's equality, the labor movement, and health and safety.

Part 5, **Good Shows and Good Sports**, highlights heroic actors, musicians, and athletes and explains why showtime in America is such a vital part of our way of life.

For the benefit of book browsing, there are boxes containing nuggets of information throughout all the chapters. Like heroes, they are capable of standing alone, but they also fit in with the larger picture. Here's what they look like:

Fearless Facts

Here is all manner of trivia concerned with heroes and heroism. These facts are selected more for their interest than any other reason, so you may be surprised at what you find.

Towering Tips

Here are suggestions for how you might apply heroic examples in your own life—or avoid applying them! After all, you may be called to heroic deeds yourself some day!

Worthy Words

Here are definitions for some of the heroic vocabulary used in this book, along with a little word history. Heroes have influenced the way we talk along with all the other aspects of life.

Heroic Shorts

Last but not least are these capsule biographies of some well-known and not-so-well-known American heroes. Because heroic action so often speaks for itself, you don't always need a lengthy explanation.

Special Thanks to the Technical Reviewer...

Our special thanks are extended to Cristina Beltran, who is completing a doctorate in political science at Rutgers University. Originally from California, she currently lives in Highland Park, New Jersey. Thanks, Cristina for providing insight and guidance in this project.

Part 1
The Big Ideal

Heroes are heroes because of who they are, what they do, and where they stand, but their importance depends largely on the people who admire them. The biggest heroes are the ones who have been held up as shining examples for generations to be proud of. And what people say about them down through the years says as much about those people themselves as it does about their heroes.

Heroes have a mythic stature. Although they figure into history, history doesn't always tell us everything we need to know about them, since their importance so often transcends their historical situation. As a result, heroic mythology provides an especially vivid, living picture of the ideals of the nation. In America, this mythology goes back to the Stone Age, when Native American tribes first began telling heroic legends about the doers of great deeds. And the mythology continues in the folk tales that get told about legendary American figures and in the popular myths found in that uniquely American invention, the comic book.

The first section of this book focuses on the mythological aspect of heroism in America. Chapter 1 deals with the heroic connection between myth and history, talking about what heroism is, why its especially significant in America, and how the concept of heroism has been theorized by some of the most influential thinkers on the subject. The following chapters in the section look at American legends—from Native American myth to the classic tall tales to the comic books heroes—in an attempt to provide a broad overview of what Americans look for in heroes.

Chapter 1

Lives and Legends

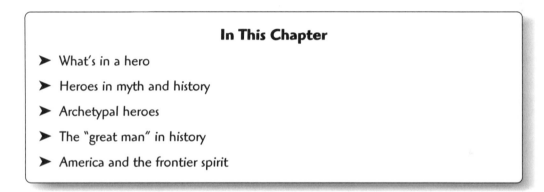

In This Chapter

➤ What's in a hero

➤ Heroes in myth and history

➤ Archetypal heroes

➤ The "great man" in history

➤ America and the frontier spirit

From the most ancient myths to the latest TV commercial, heroes across the globe have always attracted the attention they so richly deserve—and we have more than our fair share of them! Just what makes someone a hero, however, remains hard to say, and this difficulty adds to a hero's magical and mysterious hold on people. Something about a hero's personality, words, actions, and attitude strikes a chord that resonates in the imaginations of others. Identifying and describing this heroic resonance and why Americans hold it in such high esteem is not easy to do.

To make heroes still harder to get a handle on, their stories often skip back and forth between truth and fantasy. A hero's action may speak for itself, but it typically becomes exaggerated and idealized in the process of getting passed on by admiring witnesses. This makes it tough to figure out whether heroic qualities are real or whether they are just figments of people's imaginations.

As a result, we may never find the heart of the true hero underneath the stories people tell about them. This isn't a bad thing, though, because it means that the stuff heroes

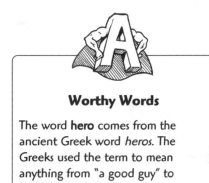

Worthy Words

The word **hero** comes from the ancient Greek word *heros*. The Greeks used the term to mean anything from "a good guy" to "practically a god."

are made of doesn't depend on genetics or geography or education or equipment. The fact that heroism has come out of all sorts of people in all sorts of circumstances suggests that it's shared by everyone. You feel it like a spark inside you every time you sense admiration for another person. However hard to pin down, this spark helps define us all as individuals and ties us together as a nation.

Where's the Beef?

All the definitions of "the hero" I've ever read seem inadequate. Heroes, after all, are heroes not because of what they have in common with other heroes, but because of how they stand apart. Each one is unique. It's true that all heroes have certain things in common, but I don't think these shared features are what make them heroes. Every hero is a hero for a different reason.

That Certain Something

Heroes seem to have a special bond with the people who admire them. Often, the specific reasons for this bond can't easily be put into words. Great athlete? Smart person? Kind and generous? Charismatic? Really good-looking? Knows right from wrong? Has done great things? There are plenty of non-heroic people with these traits all over the place, and no one is putting their pictures up on their walls or daydreaming about them. Of course, heroes certainly have these qualities, but these qualities alone don't make them heroes. Only people's admiration can do that.

Take, for example, Elvis Presley or Abraham Lincoln. Elvis was good-looking, could sing, and was a great performer. Abe was kind, honest, and accomplished great things. These qualities didn't hurt when their admirers raised them to the level of heroes (and dying before their time probably helped too), but were these the essential ingredients of their greatness? Or is all the excitement just about Abe's cheekbones or Elvis's hips? Whatever it was, it's hard to explain, especially to someone who isn't already a fan.

Even though the heroic essence remains elusive, it's important to know about heroes. You've heard the cliché that heroes helped make this country great. And it's true! But they didn't do it just by fighting the Revolutionary War, writing the Declaration of Independence, standing up for their rights, setting foot on the moon, and breaking the major league home-run record. They did it mainly by drawing attention to themselves and influencing others to be like them. That's how you get a whole country full of almost-heroes—people who may not be heroes yet, but who hope to have the opportunity to rise to the occasion someday. Americans have always been ready to follow a good suggestion!

Heroes Are Us

The idea is that there's a little bit of what made Elvis great inside everyone who loves him. Multiply this Elvis factor by a few million and you have a hunka hunka burnin' America! This principle applies not only to rock and roll, but to our other cherished ideals and institutions as well. Every hero is the source and focal point of a contagious attitude. Rules and regulations have their place in governing people's behavior, but an even stronger factor influencing how we act is the shining examples set by our heroes.

Of course, heroes don't have to be famous. There are plenty of heroes most people have never heard of. They do have to be influential in some way, even if it's merely by winning the admiration of a few people who notice something special about them. These few people will be changed, and this change might make a difference.

Fearless Facts

A dramatic depiction of the influence heroes can have on the lives of their admirers is presented in Spike Lee's documentary film *Malcolm X*. In this film, a number of children appear in sequence, each child saying, "I am Malcolm X!" A similar scene takes place in the Stanley Kubrick film *Spartacus*. This idea was picked up on in an ad for athletic shoes featuring golfer Tiger Woods and children saying, "I am Tiger Woods!"

Appreciating heroes is one of the easiest ways to learn about life. Any schoolteacher can tell you this. Learning about history in school would be a fate worse than death without heroes to bring the subject to life. In fact, you probably still associate a lot of the facts you know about American history with the stories of the heroes you heard in grade school. Chances are, the liveliness of the characters and the nobility of their spirits have stuck with you even after all this time.

It is from our earliest childhood heroes that we develop ideas about what heroism is and what sort of qualities people out to have. Here's a list of some qualities and attributes that you may want to try on for size to see if you have what it takes to be a hero. But keep in mind these qualities don't hold true for all heroes and all hero worshipers.

"My Hero," by Michael B., 4th grader at Chesterfield School, Greenfield County, Virginia

➤ **Save a life.** This is the fast track to heroism, especially if you do it in a dramatic manner. But even subtle, understated lifesaving is usually appreciated.

➤ **Be selfless.** Altruism (taking care of others before worrying about yourself) sets many heroes apart, especially for those who can be cheerful about it.

➤ **Have unswerving inner commitment to a worthy cause.** Dedication is a good way to carve out a heroic niche for yourself, especially if you combine it with selflessness.

➤ **Be a role model.** This approach becomes increasingly important as good role models become harder and harder to come by. The problem is, it's often easier to get kids to notice you by doing stupid things than smart ones!

➤ **Go above and beyond the call of duty.** Doing what you're supposed to do, only more so, may get you slated for heroism. In fact, the phrase "above and beyond . . ." comes from the official description of the military requirements for receiving the Congressional Medal of Honor.

Fearless Facts

The Congressional Medal of Honor is the highest award for valor in action awarded by the U.S. military. It was first awarded to Union soldiers during the Civil War. Over 3,400 have been awarded in the nation's history. As of the end of 1998, there were 160 living Medal of Honor recipients.

Stretching the Truth

Of course, heroes are recognized all over the world. For as long as people have been around, there have been heroes. Their deeds are recounted in the world's most ancient myths and legends. Many of the great legendary heroes of the distant past may well have started out as real people: Gilgamesh, Hercules, King Arthur—leaders and warriors who became the subjects of stories that people told to their children. As the stories accumulated, the heroes turned into magical beings.

It's the Thought That Counts

Things have changed, of course, since the days of Hercules. People tend to be more careful about keeping facts separate from fantasy. George Washington has always been a hero to many Americans, but there are limits to the stories that Americans tell about him. People say that he led and fought bravely and selflessly under adverse conditions; that, ever since he was a child, he was exceptionally honest and just; that he had a great vision for the future of this country, and worked tirelessly to bring this vision about as the first president of the United States. But no one goes around saying that he

Heroic Shorts

On January 13, 1982, a 737 passenger plane—Air Florida flight 90—crash landed in the icy Potomac River shortly after takeoff from Washington National Airport, killing 74 passengers as well as four bystanders on the 14th Street Bridge. A crowd of rubber neckers gathered at the scene on shore as police lowered rescue lines to survivors from a helicopter. Twenty-three-year-old Priscilla Tirado, partly frozen and in shock from the accident, tried in vain to hold onto the rescue line, but fell back into the freezing water. She appeared to be doomed.

Among those watching on shore was a 28-year-old assistant in Washington's Congressional Budget Office named Lenny Skutnik. He took off his boots and jacket, dove into the icy river and swam 20 feet to rescue the freezing crash victim. TV cameras were on hand to capture footage of Skutnik's heroism. He received close to 2,000 pieces of mail from admiring fans across the country in the weeks that followed. A few letters arrived at his home without an address labeled simply "Lenny Skutnik, Hero of the Potomac!"

defeated hordes of British troops single-handedly armed with only a pocket knife or that he brought chopped-down cherry trees back to life with a wave of his hand or that he crossed the Delaware River by walking on the water. People try to realize that Washington was a flesh-and-blood human being.

That's not to say that there haven't been plenty of stories told about Washington that never actually happened. Remember the story about how he chopped down the cherry tree and said to his father, "I cannot tell a lie. I did it!" This is just a tale invented by Parson Weems, one of Washington's biggest fans back in the early years of the nineteenth century. Whether young George was capable of telling a lie, Weems was definitely capable! He wanted to write about Washington in a way that would inspire readers to love their country and act virtuously in their own lives. So he invented a few anecdotes to make his hero more worthy and memorable.

Of course, even though Weems started a lot of myths about America's first president, it doesn't mean we've all been living a lie ever since. It just means that we have some sorting out to do if we want to understand Washington and his achievements more accurately. At the same time, the myths and legends that Weems and others have told about Washington are well worth knowing even if they're not all true. Not only are they good stories in their own right, but they also say a lot about the beliefs and values of the people who tell them. Washington's honesty may be more legendary than true, but it's good to know that honesty has been an American virtue for a long time, even if we don't always live up to the ideal!

Facts and Fables

This point about Washington could be made about any hero. Every hero has two sides, a mythic side and a historical side. Sometimes these two sides can be hard to tell apart. Often the legendary, mythic qualities of heroes get merged with the facts of their lives, which then become distorted or covered over entirely. What really happened can get lost beneath the larger-than-life heroic myth. Historians don't always have enough information to work with and have to fill in the gaps with speculations. And strange, amazing things sometimes really happen; so what sounds like a tall tale may actually have taken place—hey, who a few hundred years ago would have thought that a small band of rebels could win their independence from the most powerful nation on earth? Regardless of whether we're able to sort out the facts from the fables, one of the earmarks of a famous hero is that he or she has a place not only in history, but also in mythology, folklore, or popular culture.

Just what kind of place heroes occupy in myth and in history has been a subject of speculation and debate by scholars. Some have argued that heroes are not simply characters in myth and actors in history, but actually help define myth and history themselves. Stories, whether true or legendary, are what they are because heroes have made them that way, because people have had to learn how to talk about examples of the virtues they prize.

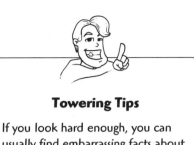

Towering Tips

If you look hard enough, you can usually find embarrassing facts about the lives of most heroes. Before the Revolutionary War, while he was still under the command of the British, Washington needlessly killed a French scout named Jumonville. He was lambasted for this deed in the Paris newspapers.

Myth Directions

Scholars point out that heroes are venerated in every culture. Many groups even attribute their origins to a heroic founder. To name a few different examples, Jesus Christ for the Christians, Mohammed for the Muslims, King Arthur for the British, George Washington for the Americans, and Henry Ford for the Ford Motor Company. And regardless of whether a hero actually founds a nation or a religion or a car company, the story of a hero's life serves as a touchstone for all those who admire the hero and care about his or her accomplishments and values. Heroes, in other words, supply a focal point for a group. They are figures everyone can identify with and emulate.

Scholars have also suggested that people have a deep, psychological need to identify with heroes. We tend to internalize the adopted characteristics of our heroes in our attitude toward life. When things get tough, we think of our heroes—or we think of ourselves as heroes—as we work through our difficulties. And everyone all over the world goes through difficulties. Everyone has to deal with hardship, with fitting into society, with resisting the temptation to do wrong, and with the confusion and

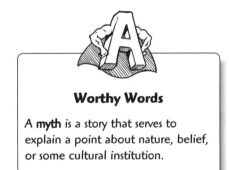

Worthy Words

A **myth** is a story that serves to explain a point about nature, belief, or some cultural institution.

displacement of changing times. Our heroes are models to show how these things should be done.

That's why stories about heroes get told everywhere. In fact, the oldest tales we know about, the myths of the ancient world, are all about heroes. Heroes are an essential element in any story. They are the main characters who get in and out of trouble as the action unfolds.

Fearless Facts

Mythology scholar Joseph Campbell became famous for his book *The Hero with a Thousand Faces* (1949), which claims that all myths about heroes from around the world treat the same essential themes. Campbell became well known to TV viewers after doing a series of interviews called *The Power of Myth* with Bill Moyers on public television.

Forever Jüng

Some see the hero not only as an essential feature of myths and legends, but also as a basic element of the human psyche. This way of thinking about heroes was pioneered by the Swiss psychiatrist Carl Jüng. Jüng identifies the hero as an important *archetype* of the human collective unconscious. The archetype recurs in mythology and dream symbolism as an expression of a basic human disposition. Jüng's work suggests that we don't simply decide to admire heroes, but that the desire for heroism is a latent tendency at work in everyone. This is why we tell so many stories and think so many thoughts about them. They may simply be what we all inwardly want to be!

As evidence of the deep psychological significance of the hero archetype, Jüng and others have pointed out that the myth of the hero is universally found in cultures all over the world and appears in the oldest known stories. They have noticed recurring themes in the hero myths of the world, suggesting that these themes represent, in symbolic form, important stages in the life of individuals and societies. The hero's deeds may be recounted and celebrated in religious rituals that have a beneficial effect on the well-being of society, helping members of the group come to terms with the psychological challenges posed by birth, maturity, sex, and death. *Hero worship*, in other words, helps people adjust to their changing circumstances as they continue through life, reassuring them that they are not alone and giving them a model to follow.

Impressive Résumé

Typically, the mythic hero is an especially powerful human or half-god who combats and overcomes an evil force such as a dragon or other monster. Mythic heroes usually have miraculous births that show how special they are even before they accomplish their heroic deeds. They often go through a period of doubt or estrangement from society, during which they may be tempted or seduced by evil beings. Eventually they return to society, however, and perform extraordinary acts that make a new start possible for everyone.

Worthy Words

In general, an **archetype** is an ideal example of something that supplies a pattern for everything like it. In Jüngian terminology, an archetype is a pattern for images that are subconsciously shared by all humans.

Hero myths generally follow this basic pattern, but scholars have identified different types of heroes. These different types evidently satisfy the psychological needs of different members of society, depending on their position in life. Here are descriptions of some main types of mythic heroes:

➤ **The Trickster**   Young children tend to relate best to the "trickster" heroes who accomplish great things by means of cunning and deception. Well-known tricksters include the Norse god Loki and the Greek god Hermes. Myths of tribal cultures often represent the trickster as an animal such as a rabbit, fox, or coyote. Brer Rabbit, the folk-tale character, and Bugs Bunny, the cartoon character, are more recent incarnations of the trickster hero. Children, especially, seem to like the trickster because he gets what he wants not through strength, but through guile. In addition, he is usually not responsible for anyone but himself, although he may form alliances with others to outwit those who have more power.

➤ **The Warrior**   Adolescents go in heavily for the warrior hero, who achieves great things through strength and courage. Typically, the warrior hero is not only strong and bold, but also selfless, doing great things for others and undergoing hardship and deprivation in the process. This type of hero appeals to adolescents because they are beginning to renounce the protection and security of childhood in order to assume adult responsibilities. The strong, selfless warrior hero provides

Towering Tips

Notice that the veneration of mythic heroes often takes on religious overtones. That's why they call it **hero worship**. Stories about religious figures may sometimes be considered hero myths. Ancestor worship, practiced in many cultures, is also a religious practice that dovetails with heroic mythology.

an ideal model for them. Mythic examples range from Beowulf to Captain America.

➤ **The Lover**   Young adults typically turn to lover heroes as their role models. Heroic lovers defy parents, society, monsters, and fate itself in order to be together. Their love can be seen as a metaphor for destiny, which they realize by obeying their inner desires while overcoming impossible odds imposed upon them by others. Romeo and Juliet and Lancelot and Guinevere are classic examples.

➤ **The Sage**   The heroes typically appropriate for older adults are the sages who understand nature and society and use their wisdom to nurture. To them is attributed the discovery of arts and sciences, as well as the guidelines necessary for preserving the harmony of society, all of which they teach to the rest of humankind. Mythic stories of sages tell of the adventures they undergo in gaining their wisdom and of their power to turn evil influences to good. Examples include the legendary Chinese ruler Fu Hsi, the wizard Merlin, and Yoda from *Star Wars*.

Of course, many mythic heroes combine some or all of these heroic types. The Greek hero Odysseus, for example, exhibits aspects of all these types, merging them into the figure of the explorer or wanderer. Often, myths that tell of a heroic quest tell of heroes who pass through several stages of heroic activity.

In Your Dreams

Towering Tips

Don't assume that a mythic character who commits evil acts is out of the running for hero status. Many myths tell of villains who transform into heroes. The Iroquois mythic hero Hiawatha, for example, starts out as an evil man who kills and eats other people. (Hiawatha is best known only as a good hero from Henry Wadsworth Longfellow's famous poem.)

Jüng and his followers believe that because these patterns of hero myth are so widespread in cultures around the world, the hero must fill an innate, subconscious need in the psychic life of all people. As further evidence for this idea, Jüngians have found that the dreams of patients undergoing psychoanalysis often contain elements of hero myths. Psychologists say these elements appear in dreams of people who are going through significant changes in their lives as subconscious responses to their situations. For example, the dreams of adolescents who are beginning to renounce childhood dependence have much in common with myths about the warrior hero type.

Often, people in psychoanalysis have heroic dreams that do not seem to match up with their position in life. An older person, for example, may have dreams that seem reminiscent of the trickster hero, which we might expect would be more appropriate to childhood. This may indicate that the dreamer is going through a frustrating time while trying to live up to adult responsibilities and is trying subconsciously to regain a childish attitude. Or it could mean that the dreamer was unable to live out a normal childhood for some reason and is compensating for this through dreams.

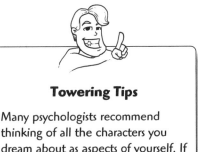

Towering Tips

Many psychologists recommend thinking of all the characters you dream about as aspects of yourself. If you dream about a fight between two people, the dream may be acting out an internal conflict.

Inside Outside

Although the theories of Jüng and his followers have been highly influential—in the fields of psychology and mythology studies as well—not everyone agrees with them. Critics argue that the Jüngian claim that myths contain universal symbolic truths obscures important differences between them. In saying that certain mythic themes are innate and universal, the theory may be imposing a misleading sense of what life is about. In addition, the theories put forward a cookie-cutter model of human development that may not hold true for everyone. Instead, life experiences may be largely different for different people.

The disagreement boils down to whether heroism comes from inside the individual or gets picked up somewhere along the way in response to life's experiences and to social influences. The question pertains not only to heroes in myth, but also to heroes in history. Similar disagreements have taken place among historians as to whether heroes in history are innately heroic or simply responding and adapting to their circumstances. So heroism may be nothing more than being in the right place at the right time.

Rising to the Occasion

Back in 1840, an English writer named Thomas Carlyle wrote an influential book called *On Heroes, Hero-Worship and the Heroic in History*. Carlyle's book says that human history results from the actions of great men. His point is not simply that historians like to write about great people, but that without great people changing the course of events, nothing worth writing about would ever happen.

Carlyle wrote his book in the wake of the career of Napoleon, the French emperor who galvanized the French people in the wake of the French Revolution and launched military campaigns throughout Europe. With Napoleon in mind as a "great man" of human history, Carlyle treated other heroes who, in his view, rose above the crowd to transform human events. These larger-than-life figures included Moses, Mohammed, Martin Luther, Frederick the Great, and Oliver Cromwell. (For whatever reason, Carlyle's book didn't talk about any American heroes.)

Since Carlyle's day, many historians have quarreled with the idea that history is shaped chiefly by the actions of great men. These historians point instead to such factors as economic conditions, technological developments, and intellectual shifts, saying that these things aren't guided by individuals acting alone, but by the combined energy of whole civilizations. People may like to think that the world's important events are spurred on by a few heroes, but it's more reasonable to say that the heroic activity of a few individuals is made possible by groups of people—some paving the way, others standing behind their heroes.

Fearless Facts

Among famous thinkers who oppose the "great man" view of history—history as being shaped by forceful individuals acting alone—are German philosopher G. F. W. Hegel, German economist Karl Mark, and British philosopher Herbert Spencer.

Most historians these days think there are limits to the ability of individuals, working alone, to change history. Even so, belief in the power of the individual is a strong aspect of the belief in heroes. This is especially true in America, where individualism has been a big part of our way of thinking all along.

Going It Alone

Many go for the idea that a hero is someone who shapes his or her own destiny, regardless of the obstacles. Many Americans have tried to live out this heroic ideal. Ever since the days before America even became a nation, people have been coming here to make their own way and get away from restrictions placed on them by others. Some sought religious freedom, wanting to practice their own faiths in their own way; and some sought economic opportunity, hoping to find jobs or get land not available in their home countries.

Of course, this doesn't hold true for all Americans. Some were brought to this country against their will as slaves. Others were here already and were nearly wiped out by the Europeans. But for a significant number of people, the colonies—and later, the United States of America—was a place to come for people who wanted to make their own rules. They believed they could do better on their own in an undeveloped country than they could as part of European society. This spirit of individualism—the belief that people ought to take care of themselves and should be free to make their own rules—helps explain the way many people think about America and American heroes.

This ideal hasn't gone away with the passing of the early settlers. Generations of Americans have been raised to think this way. After all, the entire country wasn't colonized all at once. Many generations were involved with the founding and westward expansion of the country. The American frontier was around a long time, and it's been a fixture of American consciousness for even longer. Of course, "the frontier spirit" has gradually changed and given way to other ideals, but it still influences the way many Americans think today. Some believe that the frontier never ends, that there will always be new lands to conquer—whether in outer space, inner space, or the fields of technology or commerce. These people say outside controls and regulations will only stand in the way of the heroes who will blaze the trail to new possibilities.

Towering Tips

Don't assume that the frontier spirit of individualism that inspired the early settlers and pioneers is still appropriate for today's America. Groups—like libertarians and radical militia groups—that don't try to adapt the principles in which they believe to the environment and culture in which they live, often run into conflict with mainstream society.

Different Strokes

Others, however, say that it's time for the lone cowboys to get off their high horses and learn to cooperate with others. Especially in recent decades, observers of society have pointed out that not everyone who thinks he is shaping his own destiny is actually doing so. Everybody's achievements depend in part on the opportunities available to him or her, and not everyone enjoys the same opportunities. Equality, of course, is a time-honored American ideal, but that doesn't mean that Americans have always had equal access to resources, rights, and privileges. Through no fault of their own, various groups of people have found themselves holding the short end of the stick. The playing field isn't always level.

The result is that even though we all have heroes, we don't all have the same heroes. In fact, American heroes differ widely in what they stand for—possibly more widely than any other nation. General Lee and Ulysses S. Grant fought on opposite sides of the Civil War, yet both are admired as heroes. General Custer and Sitting Bull are also American heroes, although they too fought on opposite sides. We know from history that Lee's forces lost out to Grant's, and that Sitting Bull defeated Custer; we also know, however, that the Native American nations were ultimately incorporated into the European Americans' United States. However, these outcomes don't indicate who was more heroic. That's a personal judgment call.

Stars Crossed

In addition to the heroes who actually fought on opposite sides in battle are American heroes who stand for starkly opposed ideals. Imagine these American greats locked in mortal combat. Who would win?

➤ **Samuel Gompers**, labor leader and defender of workers' rights *versus* **J. P. Morgan**, monopolist and advocate for unregulated capitalism

15

Fearless Facts

One of the all-time favorite legendary American heroes is Uncle Sam, the dapper, goateed symbol of American patriotism. Like many legends, this one is a mixture of facts from different sources, combined with fantasy and humor. Apparently, there was a real "Uncle Sam" named Sam Wilson (1776–1854). He was a meat packer living in Troy, New York, who provided meat for the army during the war of 1812. Because his shipments belonged to government, they were labeled "U.S."—but people jokingly said that the initials stood for Uncle Sam. The idea of an "Uncle Sam" representing the United States or the U.S. government has been knocked around ever since. Political cartoonists developed Uncle Sam into a full-fledged mythical being by the late nineteenth century. One of his most famous appearances was on Army recruiting posters put out during World War II where he points straight ahead and says "I Want You for U.S. Army!"

➤ **Thomas Jefferson**, "Founding Father," author of the Declaration of Independence, and slave owner *versus* **Malcolm X**, black civil rights leader

➤ **Henry David Thoreau**, naturalist and advocate of simple living *versus* **Thomas Edison**, inventor

➤ **Susan B. Anthony**, women's rights leader *versus* **Hugh Hefner**, founder of the Playboy empire

➤ **John Glenn**, outer-spaceman *versus* **Timothy Leary**, inner-space adventurer

As you can see, American heroes are as diverse a group as Americans themselves. That's one way our heroes make this country what it is—all sorts of different things to all sorts of different people!

The Least You Need to Know

➤ Heroism is hard to define. It depends on an indescribable connection between a hero and his or her admirers.

➤ Most heroic figures are combinations of historical and legendary people.

➤ Carl Jüng and his followers see heroism as a universal element in the human psyche.

➤ Thomas Carlyle propounded the "great man" theory of history.

➤ The spirit of rugged individualism associated with the American frontier is a well-known (but by no means the only) element of the typical American hero.

Chapter 2

Going Native

In This Chapter

➤ Heroes in Native American myths

➤ The sage-hero Glooscap

➤ The mighty Blood Clot Boy

➤ The trickster, Manabozho

➤ The legendary Hiawatha

In this chapter, you will read about the mythic American heroes who lived on the land long before the famous voyage of Christopher Columbus. They belonged to tribal cultures whose ancestors came to North America from Asia across the Bering Straight some time during the Stone Age between 12,000 and 40,000 years ago. No historical record exists of these ancient heroes. Stories, however, passed down for unknown numbers of generations tell of the deeds of these mythical figures of ancient America.

Ethnographers—people who study other cultures—have recorded many of these stories as important cultural artifacts. They have found that tales from diverse regions of North America often have common themes, suggesting that the stories spread from one tribe to another over the years. Because they weren't written down, there was no "official" version, and each storyteller was free to adapt and add on to the stories.

Some of them are still told today by Native Americans who learned them from their ancestors. In addition to their entertainment value, they carry reminders of ancient traditions and provide important lessons in telling right from wrong. And of course,

because they are about heroes, they are a rich source of cultural pride. In addition, some myth scholars—notably Joseph Campbell— believe that hero stories like these reveal basic universal characteristics of human nature. In any case, you may find them interesting for their own sake.

Taking Care of Business

A number of Native American tribes from the Northeastern woodlands, including present-day Main and Nova Scotia, have told myths about Glooscap—part man, part spirit. According to these myths, Glooscap controls the forces of nature, created the animals, and taught human beings to hunt, fish, and grow crops.

In addition to these accomplishments, which make him a *culture hero,* Glooscap is also a warrior hero who has defeated many of humankind's enemies, including monsters, giants, sorcerers, and cannibals. He is said to have traveled around in a miraculous white canoe that stayed afloat even though it was made out of solid granite.

Troubled Water

One of Glooscap's heroic achievements was to rescue the people from a drought that beset the land. Water was in extremely short supply, and what little water there was tasted foul and slimy. The first beings to try to do something about the problem were human-like creatures with webbed feet who lived at the foot of a mountain. Up in the mountain lived a terrible monster whose mouth was a mile wide. He was sort of like Jabba the Hut from *The Empire Strikes Back,* only bigger. This monster had built a big dam in the mountain and was keeping all the water for himself. Only a little trickle of bad-smelling, slimy water made its way down from the mountain to where the web-footed people lived.

The web-footed elders met to decide what should be done. They agreed to send a delegate to the water monster in the mountain to ask for water. A courageous young man was chosen for the job, and he set off up the mountain, slapping his way up the dry, rocky trail with his webbed feet.

The young man was determined to succeed. He told himself that life would not be worth living unless he could be the one to obtain water from the monster one way or another. As he neared the monster's dwelling, the air became cool and filled with moisture. At last he could see a large body of water off in the distance. He thought of how thirsty he was and eagerly made his way to the mountain lake.

When he arrived, he found the monster sitting in the midst of the huge lake he had made for himself by damming off the water that flowed down the mountain. He was enormous and ugly, covered with green warts. His disgusting, bloated body gave off green and yellow slime into the water, making it smell bad. The smell of the foul water and the sight of the disgusting monster made the young man a little sick to his stomach, but he overcame his queasiness and climbed the rocks up above the lake to where he could be even with the monster's head and look it in the eyes.

When he had finished climbing the rocks, he gave a shout. "Hey, monster!" The shout echoed back and forth among the rocks, and the monster turned around to face his visitor. His huge eyes bulged out of flabby face as he inspected the young man. "What do you want?" the monster demanded.

Towering Tips

We tend to think of the disgusting monsters that appear in myths as metaphors for greed and selfishness. They are grotesque and ugly because selfishness makes people ugly on the inside.

"My people don't have enough water. Give us some." The monster sneered a mile-long sneer. "No!" he bellowed, and he opened his enormous mouth. Looking inside, the young man could see all the way down into the monster's belly where there were the half-digested bodies of the monster's victims. As he looked, the bodies began to tremble and the monster let out a mighty belch so powerful it sent the young man flying down off the rocks. He landed in a pool of slime below the lake.

Weak, bruised, and nauseous, he dragged himself out of the slime and staggered back down to his village. As he retreated, the monster sang a song of ridicule. "Ho, ho, ho, you fell in the slime, better luck next time!" And the monster belched frequently as he sang. Echoing down from the mountain, the song was most unpleasant to listen to.

Monster Mash

The people were at a loss as to what should be done. Fortunately for them, the wise and mighty Glooscap knew about the situation. He grew offended with the monster and decided to take action. He painted his face with war paint and adorned his head with war feathers. He enlarged his size until he was taller than the trees so that he would be too big for the monster to swallow. Then he made himself a mighty weapon by pulling up a mountain by the roots. The mountain was formed of a single huge piece of flint, which Glooscap sharpened into a knife blade. When he was ready, he approached the monster and stood before it.

"I'm thirsty and I want lots of fresh water! Give it to me!" he shouted. The words thundered and echoed in the monster's ears. "No way!" said the monster. "I'm keeping it all to myself!" "Prepare to die, then," answered Glooscap.

At that, Glooscap and the monster waged a tremendous battle. The earth shook, the sun went black, great winds blew, pulling tall trees up out of the ground. Lightning flashed and thunder rolled. The monster grabbed Glooscap and dragged him down to the bottom of the lake where they rolled over and over in a death grip.

Towering Tips

However heroic you may be, don't assume you will always prevail over weaker opponents. One Glooscap myth tells of his encounter with a baby and how he failed to get the baby to obey his will. He was powerless to control it despite his great strength!

At last, Glooscap managed to pull his arm free and grab his enormous knife, rearing back and plunging it deep into the monster's belly. Slashing upward, Glooscap opened a gaping wound. For an instant, the monster writhed and throbbed, and then burst like a giant water balloon. The monster's body broke open with tremendous force, because it was filled with enough water to fill an ocean. The torrent of water that was set free burst through the dam the monster had built and carved out a deep riverbed down the side of the mountain. The river flowed down beside the villages where all the people lived and supplied them with as much fresh water as they needed.

Still, the monster was not dead. Glooscap held his body tightly in his mighty hands and squeezed it as hard as he could. He squeezed until the monster was reduced to only a small portion of his original size; this rendered the monster harmless. The monster became the first bullfrog, and his descendants have been singing along the banks of rivers and lakes ever since.

Fearless Facts

Myths often provide "explanations" for the way things are. Another Glooscap myth tells of how he created all the animals and then adjusted their sizes so that they wouldn't pose a threat to everyone else. The original squirrel, for example, was huge and could shred tall trees.

Make a Wish

It is said that Glooscap departed long ago from the world of human beings and makes his home in a land far to the west. The journey to this land takes seven years and leads up and down sheer cliffs of rock. Those who succeed in making the journey may ask Glooscap to grant a wish, and he always grants it. Often, however, if the wish is a foolish one, it brings trouble on the person to whom it is granted.

One man visited Glooscap and became enchanted by the beauty and serenity of the country. He asked to be granted a long life and to be able to live there the rest of his days. Glooscap granted his wish by turning him into a cedar, which took root and never again moved from the spot. Even as a tree, the man failed to find peace because the strong wind blew from time to time and broke off his branches.

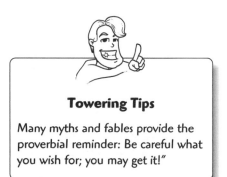

Towering Tips

Many myths and fables provide the proverbial reminder: Be careful what you wish for; you may get it!"

Another man was unhappy because he was unable to obtain a wife. He asked Glooscap to grant him many women. Glooscap gave him a little packet tied up with some string and told him not to open it until he arrived back at his village. Before he completed his return journey, however, the man was overcome with desire and curiosity and opened the packet. Out leapt hundreds of women, all smitten with love for the man. They surrounded him, clamoring to be embraced. In their desire, they piled up on the man until he was crushed and smothered. Later the women dispersed and made their way to villages where they found other husbands.

Not all of Glooscap's gifts are harmful. One man asked to have bountiful harvests to feed his family. Glooscap gave him a flute whose music helped the crops to grow. The man grew abundant crops for the rest of his life.

Blood Brother

Tribes of central North America, including the Blackfoot and the Sioux, tell stories about a great hero and buffalo hunter known as Blood Clot Boy. He gets his name from having been turned into a human being from a clot of buffalo blood. In human form, Blood Clot Boy traveled around the country helping people in need and vanquishing evildoers.

Outlaw In-Law

One of the stories about Blood Clot Boy's origin goes like this: It seems there was once an elderly couple who had three daughters, all married to the same man. They had consented to the triple marriage because the man was known as a bold and mighty hunter and they expected him to provide not only for their daughters and all of their children, but also for themselves as they continued into their old age. Sadly, however, their son-in-law proved to be lazy, selfish, deceitful, and cruel.

Fearless Facts

In many cultures it is not considered wrong to marry more than one wife at a time so long as the husband can support all of them. This has been true of the Mormons of Utah, some Islamic groups, the ancient Jews, the pre-communist Chinese, and several African tribes.

He didn't wish to provide for the elderly couple, but preferred to let them fend for themselves or starve if they were too weak to get their own food. He even tried to prevent his wives from bringing food to their parents. Only on rare occasions were the daughters able to sneak food out for their parents, hiding it under their clothing and dropping it off in secret in front of the old couple's lodge.

One day, the old man offered to go out hunting with his son-in-law to earn a share of the kill for himself and his wife. The son-in-law accepted the offer, and the old man hunted skillfully, separating a buffalo from its herd and driving it through a pass where the son-in-law lay in wait to shoot it with his bow and arrow. Thanks in good part to the old man, the hunt was successful.

Being old and hungry, however, the old man was exhausted from his efforts. The son-in-law, pleased with the kill, told him to go home and rest, saying he would butcher the meat and have his first wife, the old man's eldest daughter, bring a share to his lodge. The old man willingly returned home to wait for his share.

What's Cooking

The expected buffalo meat never arrived. The wicked son-in-law kept the whole thing for himself. When the old man questioned his son-in-law the next day, he lied and blamed his first wife, saying she must have lost the meat, eaten it herself, or given it away. When the old man complained, the son-in-law suggested they go hunting again, and this time, the old man and his wife would get their fair share.

So, again the old man and the wicked son-in-law went hunting. Again the old man hunted well, exerting himself to the utmost despite his age and declining health, and again the hunt was successful. Again the old man, exhausted, went home to rest, and the son-in-law promised to send him his share by his second wife.

The old couple waited, but still no meat came. The next day, he complained again to his son-in-law, who blamed his second wife and suggested they go hunting a third time, promising that his third wife would, without fail, bring them a share of the kill. Now, the old man was not a fool and knew that something funny was going on, but he had no other choice but to go hunting again with his son-in-law. Again they killed a buffalo and again the old man went home early, exhausted from the hunt.

This time, on his way home, the old man came across a large clot of blood lying on the ground. He picked up the blood clot and brought it home to his wife, which she put in a pot on the fire to make soup. Before long, they heard cries coming from the pot. They rushed to look and found a baby inside the pot. As if this wasn't surprising enough, they found, on taking the baby out of the pot, that it could speak like a heroic adult.

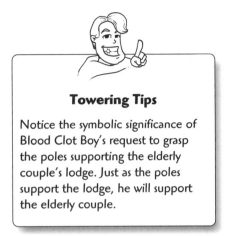

Towering Tips

Notice the symbolic significance of Blood Clot Boy's request to grasp the poles supporting the elderly couple's lodge. Just as the poles support the lodge, he will support the elderly couple.

"Hello, good and kind old people who have suffered unconscionable abuse at the hands of your wicked son-in-law! My name is Blood Clot Boy and I am here to avenge your cause! If you take me around to each of the poles that hold up your lodge so that I can grasp each one in turn, I will grow miraculously overnight into a mighty hero!"

The couple did as the baby instructed, and when they were finished, a mighty hero stood before them. Together, the three made plans to give the son-in-law what was coming to him. Meanwhile, the wicked son-in-law had come by to eavesdrop on the elderly couple, to see if they suspected the evil that he had done. When he heard the cries of the baby as it lay in the pot of water, he ran home immediately to tell his wives that the old woman had given birth to a child. The son-in law hadn't even stayed long enough to hear Blood Clot Boy speak.

Towering Tips

It's bad form to murder babies and pregnant women if you want to be a hero. Another myth tells of how Blood Clot Boy defeated a tribe of greedy bears and a tribe of selfish snakes, wiping out all of them except for a pregnant bear and a pregnant snake that pleaded for mercy. Blood Clot Boy let them live and they became the ancestors of modern day bears and snakes.

Buffaloed

Now, in his fiendish mind, the son-in-law considered that if the baby was a girl, he could have it as another wife when it grew to be a woman. If it were a boy, however, it would be another mouth to feed and might grow to be his rival, so he determined to kill it. He sent each of his wives in turn to find out whether the child was a boy or a girl.

Like the old couple, the three daughters were almost powerless against their husband, who was bigger and stronger than they were. They were smart enough, however, to know that a total creep such as he was would not be so curious about such a thing unless he had something despicable in mind. So each of the wives in turn lied and said their old mother had given birth to a baby girl. Satisfied, the husband decided to let the child live.

The next day, the old man came to his son-in-law once again to complain that he still had not received any meat. The son-in-law suggested they go hunting yet again, and promised this time to bring the meat to the old couple himself. So they went hunting. The son-in-law took his usual position at the other side of the pass to wait for the old man to drive a buffalo through.

Instead of just one buffalo, Blood Clot Boy rounded up a whole herd and drove it through the pass. Caught off guard and unable to escape in time, the son-in-law was trampled. Blood Clot Boy returned home with enough meat for everyone. "Thank you, Blood Clot Boy!" said the elderly couple. "Now you can marry our beautiful daughters and we can all be happy!"

"I'm afraid heroes like me don't have time to get married. I'm sure you'll find someone else. As for me, my work here is done, and I must travel throughout the land seeking out injustice and rescuing good people everywhere." And this, according to the stories that are told about him, is just what he did. For many years he wandered the land, fighting evil. At last, some say, he traveled up to the sky where he can be seen as a star. Others say he returned to his people, the buffalo, and still gallops with them in their herds.

Fearless Facts

Among Blood Clot Boy's other adventures is a story of how he was sucked by a great wind into the body of a giant sucker fish where he found many others who had also been sucked in. He tied a sharp stone to his head and led his fellow captives in a vigorous dance. By jumping up and down while dancing, he stabbed the fish in the heart with the sharp stone.

Manabozho, the Clown

Not all mythic heroes are wise teachers, like Glooscap, or mighty hunters and warriors, like Blood Clot Boy. Some are crafty tricksters, like Manabozho, whose stories are told among the Ojibway. Manabozho exhibits several different personalities, depending on the story. Sometimes he is wise and helpful, sometimes he is mischievous and deceitful, and sometimes he is just plain foolish. In general, however, his stories are amusing and instructive.

Crash Landing

One story tells how Manabozho desired to fly so that he could see the world from the sky. He persuaded Buzzard to give him a ride. Before liftoff, however, Manabozho made Buzzard promise not make any sudden swerves or try any other tricky maneuvers in the air that might make Manabozho lose his hold and fall off. Buzzard agreed and off they flew.

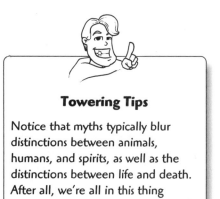

Towering Tips

Notice that myths typically blur distinctions between animals, humans, and spirits, as well as the distinctions between life and death. After all, we're all in this thing together!

Manabozho was amazed and exhilarated to be up in the sky. He gazed far and wide at the scenery below, clinging tightly to Buzzard the whole time. Buzzard, however, became restless. Flying was nothing new to him. Besides, he liked wheeling around and turning abruptly in the air. Suddenly, without warning, Buzzard swerved sharply. Unfortunately for Manabozho, Buzzard's feathers were slightly greasy, so he lost hold and plummeted to earth.

He hit the ground so hard that his back got terribly bent and twisted. It was so bent that, as he lay looking upward, his face was covered by his butt! For a long time, unable to move, Manabozho thought he had been blinded. Only gradually did he figure out why he couldn't see. At last, he recovered and straightened himself back out. Walking away, he plotted revenge against Buzzard.

Playing Dead

At last he hit on a plan. He walked into a meadow where Buzzard would be sure to notice him and turned himself into a dead deer. As he lay there ripening, he attracted insects and coyotes and other scavengers, but he didn't care about them. It was Buzzard he was waiting for. At last, Buzzard caught sight of him as he flew past. There was nothing Buzzard liked better than dead deer meat that had been lying around for a while, so he flew down to join the feast.

Buzzard found a fat, fleshy, flavorful spot just below Manabozho's rear end and began pecking away. He pecked deeper and deeper into the flesh, pushing his face eagerly into the hole he had made. The hole became deeper and deeper until Buzzard had pushed his whole head right up into the dead deer's body. Just at that moment, Manabozho clamped the flesh tightly over Buzzard's head so that Buzzard couldn't get free. He flapped and scratched wildly to get loose, but Manabozho kept a tight hold.

Not knowing what happened, Buzzard flailed desperately, terrified and unable to breathe. Manabozho stood up, still in the shape of deer, and began to prance around, shaking Buzzard violently back and forth. At last, with a painful, desperate push, Buzzard managed to pull his head free. The effort was such a tight squeeze that all the feathers on Buzzard's head were stripped off. That is why, to this day, Buzzard's descendants have no feathers on their heads.

Fearless Facts

A number of myths present Manabozho as a shape-shifter. In one tale, he changes himself into an ant so that he can crawl inside a bear skull to eat a little piece of the bear's brain. Unfortunately, he changes himself back to human form before crawling back out and gets the skull stuck on his head!

Fowl Play

Another tale relates how Manabozho captured some ducks, geese, and swans for dinner, but had to go hungry anyway. It seems the ducks and other water birds saw Manabozho hiding in the reeds with his bow and arrow to shoot them and kept their distance. So Manabozho came up with a plan to fool them. He put down his bow and arrows and picked up his drum and began to play the drum and sing.

The music was appealing to the birds. It had a good, waddling rhythm, so they came up near the shore. Still they kept a little ways off; so Manabozho said, "Dancing in a circle and singing as loud as you can to this song will bring you good luck. The spirit that is kind to water birds will draw near." Gradually, one by one, the ducks and geese overcame their fear and waddled up on shore to dance around Manabozho as he sang.

"Okay, birds," said Manabozho, "The spirit that is kind to water birds doesn't like to be seen, so you need to keep your eyes closed. Anyone who opens his eyes will have red eyes ever after. And remember to sing as loud as you can!" The birds waddled around Manabozho with their eyes closed, honking and quacking with all their might as he beat out a rhythm on his drum using just one hand.

With the other hand he reached out and grabbed the birds by the neck, one by one, as they waddled by. Of course, none of the others could hear anything except their own singing, so the squawks for help went unnoticed. One by one, Manabozho wrung their necks so that fewer and fewer were left in the dance. Finally, so few birds were left that the bird that is called the hell-diver opened his eyes to see why more birds weren't singing. He saw what Manabozho had done and sounded a warning. So warned, the remaining birds flew off. Manabozho cursed the hell-diver, which to this day has red eyes as a result.

A Bird in the Sand

Next, Manabozho turned to the pile of fat water birds he had killed. To cook them, he built a slow-burning fire that was partly buried in the ground. He heaped sand around the fire that would heat like an oven as the fire burned, and he buried the birds in the sand so that they would be roasted. Only the head and feet of a few of the birds remained visible above the sand. Tired from his work and with a long wait ahead before his dinner would be ready, he turned in for a nap on the shore of the lake. Before falling asleep, he gave his right thigh explicit instructions to stay awake and be alert in case anyone came to steal his quarry. After giving the instructions, he asked the thigh if it understood. His thigh moved back and forth, indicating no, it did not understand. So he told his left thigh to remain alert and asked it if it understood. His left thigh moved up and down, indicating agreement, and so Manabozho fell fast asleep.

As he slept, a band of travelers came upon Manabozho and smelled the water birds roasting in the sand oven he had made. Quickly and quietly, they plucked up the birds and pulled off their heads and feet, replacing them on the sand to make it look as though nothing had happened. Just as quickly, they scurried off with their plunder.

When Manabozho awoke, he was relieved to see his fire burning and his oven looking just as he left it. Imagine his dismay when he pulled at a goose foot to see whether it was done and found there was no goose attached! Outraged, he asked his left thigh what had happened. He gazed at it carefully to see whether it had grown bigger from eating all the birds by itself! The thigh moved around in circles, indicating that Manabozho had rolled over in his sleep onto his left side, so it couldn't see what happened. Manabozho went home hungry, criticizing his thighs the whole way.

Fearless Facts

Like many "trickster" myths from around the world, tales about Manabozho make him seem alternately crafty and foolish. In one tale, he looks down and sees some ripe berries and lunges for them, only to hit his head on a rock under water. Looking up, he sees the berries hanging above him. He had lunged initially at a reflection of the berries on the surface of the water!

United Nation

The mythic heroes of the Native Americans are unknown to history. At some point in the distant past, they may have existed as real people before being transformed into fabulous beings by generations of storytellers; if so, however, we will never know. Of course, there are historical Native American heroes as well—such figures as Sitting Bull and Pocahontas—whose lives and exploits are well documented. In addition, there is a well-known native hero whose existence is not recorded in history, but who seems to have actually existed. This is the legendary Hiawatha, who is credited with uniting the five tribes of the Iroquois nation sometime around 1570.

Many native legends tell of Hiawatha. Although these legends include many fabulous and miraculous events, there is evidently a kernel of truth to them. Hiawatha seems to have been born into the Mohawk tribe and to have tried to persuade his people to unite with other tribes. When at first the Mohawk rejected his teaching, Hiawatha moved to live with the Onondaga. More and more people listened to his ideas and five tribes—the Onondaga, the Mohawk, the Seneca, the Oneida, and the Cayuga—joined to form the Iroquois nation.

The Iroquois were a powerful political and military force for more than 200 years. They were joined by a sixth tribe, the Tuscarora, in 1714. Clearly the alliance resulted from the hard work and cooperation of many tribal leaders. Legend, however, gives most of the credit to the mighty leader and wise teacher Hiawatha.

Fearless Facts

Hiawatha is the subject of Henry Wadsworth Longfellow's famous poem, *The Song of Hiawatha* (1855), which adapts the legend of Hiawatha for European Americans. Longfellow combined stories from different myths and added stories of his own, including an account of how Hiawatha encouraged the natives to convert to Christianity.

The Least You Need to Know

➤ We know Native American heroes through myths that have been passed from generation to generation in an oral tradition of storytelling.

➤ Glooscap is a mythic culture hero who defeated a disgusting water monster.

➤ Blood Clot Boy grew into a generous warrior hero from a clot of buffalo blood.

➤ Manabozho is a trickster hero who is sometimes crafty and sometimes foolish.

➤ Hiawatha is the legendary unifier of the original five tribes that became the Iroquois nation.

Tall Tales

Among the most towering figures in American folklore is a group of working heroes whose stories emerged in the early decades of the twentieth century. These are the mighty workmen who were said to be the best ever at their jobs: Paul Bunyan the lumberjack, Pecos Bill the cowboy, Old Stormalong the sailor, and Joe Magarac the steel worker, among others. They filled giant-sized shoes and did their jobs with superhuman strength. In the magnitude of their personalities and escapades, they resemble the Native American mythic heroes.

These heroes bring together qualities that were especially admired by Americans at the time: hard work, inventiveness, strength, courage, and independence. These traits helped define the American spirit as European immigrants came together as a group over diverse cultural lines and industrialism spread across the country, bringing with it the hope for achievements on a giant scale. As a strong, independent, hard-working, and inventive nation, Americans believed they could do just about anything. As a result, they were drawn to stories of larger-than-life heroes who could do just about anything themselves. While these fictional heroes have served, in some respects, as role models for others in their fields, they are as humorous as they are heroic. Their stories are tall tales in more ways than one. Not only are these heroes huge, but their feats are clearly impossible. The humor often disguises the dark side of American industrialism: the danger, tedium, and competitiveness of labor. Thus these yarns are intended to make people laugh at—as well as admire—the American working hero.

Booming Voices

The larger-than-life working heroes emerged during the years following the Civil War at a time when America industry was booming and increasing numbers of workers were expected to do hard, exhausting jobs. Fictive heroes like Paul Bunyan and Joe Magarac gave people an idea of how hard the work was while making it seem easy— at least, for the hero. The working hero also gave a human face to the otherwise huge, impersonal force of industrial production. He represented the grand scale of industry in a personal way. In fact, while idealizing the work of the common laborer, tales of the working hero also provided lots of regional flavor. They also gave people an opportunity to show others that they still maintained a cultural identity while incorporating themselves into the larger American culture.

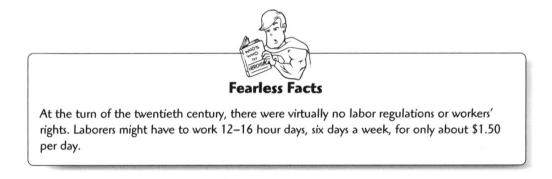

Fearless Facts

At the turn of the twentieth century, there were virtually no labor regulations or workers' rights. Laborers might have to work 12–16 hour days, six days a week, for only about $1.50 per day.

Big Laughs

The best known industrial hero is Paul Bunyan, the giant lumberjack. In some ways he resembles the traditional culture hero who achieves great deeds and teaches his people useful things. The stories say, for example, that he single-handedly cut down all the timber in the state of Maine before moving westward, that he could work for days on end without stopping to rest, and that he invented the grindstone.

These heroic qualities are also comic in their implausibility. The stories say that Paul's grindstone was so big, for example, that it took a whole week to make a single revolution. Before Paul developed this invention, the lumberjacks sharpened their axes by rolling stones downhill and running along beside them with their axes against them!

Often there is something at least a little ridiculous about Paul Bunyan's workaday world.

Even though the Paul Bunyan tales are generally whimsical, many of them deal with serious issues, especially difficult working conditions. They treat hardships in a humorous manner by exaggerating them or describing impossible solutions for them. It is said to be so cold in the northern lumber mills, for example, that steel cracks when you look at it, for example. The mosquitoes have foot-long stingers and can hold a gallon of blood. When Babe, Paul's giant blue ox, kicks the brains out of a lumberjack, the camp baker replaces them with sour dough used for bread; by the end of the week, the man was as smart as he ever was!

Towering Tips

Remember that there were no such things as cool "slackers" back in the 1920s when Paul Bunyan first caught on. Work and self-respect were closely connected.

In this way, the tales make light of the strain, tedium, and danger involved in work. While the Paul Bunyan stories laugh at hardship and recount impossible feats, however, they are not merely ridiculous stories. Despite the joking, Paul Bunyan is a serious hero when it comes to hard work. He uses both his brains and his brawn to be the best, most productive lumberjack the world has ever known. This, at least, is no joke.

A Big Lift

Paul Bunyan is a man's man, largely because he could do huge amounts of work. He could chop trees so fast that his axe blade got hot enough to set the trees on fire. It took hundreds of men to drag away the trees he could cut down in a single day. Paul Bunyan was fearless as well as hardworking. When he was still a boy, he used to run through the forest terrorizing grizzly bears. Just for fun, he chased a family of grizzlies all the way to the Arctic Circle. The bears were so frightened that their fur turned white, and their descendants are known today as polar bears! Deer, similarly, are descended from moose that Paul Bunyan terrorized and transformed into smaller, more timid creatures!

As a result of his manly strength and courage, Paul Bunyan stories were not only entertaining, but were probably good for the morale of the normal-sized lumber men who actually did clear huge tracts of northern forests. Thus Paul Bunyan may well have served as something of a role model, encouraging men to work hard and make light of hardships.

Big Jobs

One well-known story about Paul Bunyan is an account of how he and his crew managed to get enough to eat to satisfy their enormous appetites. The men sat at a table so big that it took days to get from one end of it to the other. To save time, food was served out by a big catapult that flung the food across the table. Beans were served across long distances by being shot through machine guns. Giant-sized pancakes were cooked in mass quantities on a huge griddle. Boys would grease the griddle by tying slabs of bacon on their feet and skating around on it.

Another mighty yarn tells how Paul and Babe, his blue ox, straightened out the twisty road that led from camp. The road was so winding that Paul went walking down it and met himself four times! It even twisted upside down in places. Realizing it would save time if they had a straight road instead of a twisted one, Paul harnessed Babe and hitched a chain to her harness, attaching the other end of the chain to the road. Then he called on Babe to pull until the road was completely straightened out.

Thanks to Paul and Babe, the road, which was 22 miles long when twisted, was only eight miles long when straightened out. Paul rolled up the excess 14 miles of road and sold it to the city of Chicago, where it became Michigan Boulevard! This is typical of Paul Bunyan's deeds: big, impossible, and yielding lasting benefits for everyone.

Fearless Facts

Paul Bunyan is credited with inventing the day-stretcher, a device that makes days longer. It worked so well that the surplus time could be sold second hand as Mondays!

Making Their Mark

A theme that occurs frequently in Paul Bunyan stories is the topography of America, which is said to get its shape as a result of Paul and Babe's big actions. The numerous lakes throughout the state of Wisconsin were formed from Babe's footprints. The Great Lakes were formed when Paul wiped the sweat from his brow and threw it on the ground. The Mississippi River was formed from Paul's sweat when he walked to Louisiana on a hot day.The incredible size of Paul and his achievements reflect the amazement many felt at the time about American industry. Industrial technology and mass production were transforming the world in big, incredible ways. Paul Bunyan stories present this transformation in a cozy, personal, humorous light, enabling people to feel prouder and more comfortable with American industrialization.

A Big Bill

Shortly after Paul Bunyan strode into national consciousness, a writer named Edward O'Reilly invented a larger-than-life cowboy in the Paul Bunyan mold. This cowboy was named Pecos Bill. O'Reilly not only had a great deadpan sense of humor, he also knew how to reproduce cowboy talk with the best of 'em. His Pecos Bill stories are full of colorful cowboy expressions.

Gone to the Dogs

Pecos Bill resembles Paul Bunyan in being of an indeterminately huge size, in being the best in the world at his trade, and in accomplishing many impossible feats. In addition, Pecos Bill is a good deal more ornery than Paul Bunyan. Whereas Paul Bunyan was basically a peaceable character, Pecos Bill was prone to get in fights. He also swore a good deal and drank more than is humanly possible. Of course, this doesn't detract from his heroic stature in the least. Instead, Bill's quarrelsome traits showed how strong and independent he was, and are perfectly in keeping with his being a cowboy rather than a lumberjack.

As the story goes, when Pecos Bill was a young child, he fell out of a covered wagon near the Pecos River in West Texas. By the time his family realized he was missing, it was too late to go back for him. So the young future hero fell in with a pack of coyotes. Eventually, he came to believe that he was a coyote himself. This is amusing, of course, but also shows how "real men" like Pecos Bill don't need civilized manners to make their way.

Fearless Facts

It's said that Pecos Bill's mother weaned him on moonshine and teethed him with Bowie knives and horseshoes. Don't try this at home!

When he had grown to be a young man, a traveling cowboy found him howling with the pack and asked him why he was acting like a coyote. Bill answered that he was acting like that because he *was* a coyote. "After all," he said, "I got fleas, don't I?" Eventually, however, the man persuaded Bill that he was a human being and introduced him to the world of people. No sooner did he come in contact with others, than he began drinking heavily and fighting. After this promising start, he went on to become the most successful cowpuncher in the West.

Pecos Bill is credited with several inventions that are highly valued by cowboys, including the lariat, the six shooter, and many new cuss words. He is also known a great rider, although ordinary horses were too small for him. He bred his own special giant-sized horses and also rode grizzly bears and wild cats. He even rode a cyclone from Kansas to California until it rained itself out from under him!

When there wasn't any better food around, he could eat raw cactus and drink nitroglycerine. In his later years, when even plain nitroglycerine wasn't strong enough for him anymore, he added fishhooks to give it a little more bite. This shows that Bill was cut out for the rugged life of a cowpuncher.

Take Charge Attitude

The days of the Wild West, when Pecos Bill's adventures were supposed to have taken place, were over when the cowboy hero emerged in print. Even so, Bill supplied a useful, albeit idealized, model for working men in the early decades of the twentieth century. He combined two qualities rarely seen together in real life: He was a productive worker who acted like his own boss.

Because of his size, strength, and ingenuity, he did more work than 20 ordinary men put together. He even developed ways of doing the job more quickly and efficiently for everybody. Yet he never got tied down to a single employer, and he never took orders from anybody.

One story tells of how Pecos Bill encountered a cowboy outfit he wanted to work with. He rode into their camp on a wildcat using a rattlesnake as whip. After dismounting, he immediately helped himself to a kettle full of hot beans, which he washed down with a gallon of hot coffee. Then he wiped his mouth on a prickly pear cactus and asked who was boss of the outfit. A mean looking man, seven feet tall, stood up and said, "I was the boss, but now you are!" The story shows that Pecos Bill was such a he-man that he could call all the shots, even though he did grunt work.

Employees of the Month

Pecos Bill and Paul Bunyan are the best known of the fabulous working heroes who emerged early in this century. Less well known, but equally amazing are a number of others who represent the heroic working ideal in various regions of the country. Here's a list:

➤ **Alfred Bulltop Stormalong**   Seaman who worked out of Cape Cod, Massachusetts and who loved setting out on the biggest ships he could find. He once used his skill in tying sailors' knots to tie together the tentacles of a giant octopus that had gotten hold of the anchor of his ship.

➤ **Joe Magarac**   Hungarian-American steelworker from Pennsylvania, said to be actually made of steel himself. He could lift impossibly heavy weights and fashion steel bars out of molten steel with his bare hands. He died by voluntarily smelting down his own steel body to be used for extra-high-quality steel. Clearly,

Hungarian steelworkers were able to visualize themselves in the "melting pot" of American culture!

➤ **Febold Feboldson**   Swedish-American pioneer and farmer known for his resourcefully outlandish inventions. He is said to have invented ducks by giving chickens webbed feet and broad bills so that they could fend for themselves in wet weather!

➤ **Tony Beaver**   A West Virginian version of Paul Bunyan who turned to the lumber business after time spent as a farmer growing giant-sized crops.

➤ **Annie Christmas**   Seven-foot-tall, black female riverboat pilot from New Orleans.

True Lies

These working heroes have been celebrated throughout the twentieth century as leading examples of homegrown American folklore. Numerous folklore books ("treasuries") geared toward children include tall tales about Paul Bunyan, Pecos Bill, and the others. As folklore, these heroes occupy a special place in the American consciousness. Americans like to think of their stories as "by the people, for the people, about the people."

The "folk" authenticity of these stories has been called into question by scholars—most notably Richard Dorson, who coined the term *fakelore* to describe them. Dorson claims the stories are not really folklore because they generally were not passed along by word of mouth by unknown yarn-spinners around the fire, but were concocted by professional writers to make money. Even though they are written in a folksy style, suggesting that they are based on word-of-mouth tales picked up from the working people who told them, this is all part of the fiction the tales present.

Paper Trail

Dorson acknowledges that there were some Paul Bunyan tales told in northern Midwest logging communities before the first one appeared in print. A logger turned journalist named James

Towering Tips

Even though Joe Magarac is a legendary Hungarian-American hero, it is not a good idea to call someone you admire a "magarac"—especially not someone big and strong like Joe was supposed to have been. **Magarac** is a Hungarian word meaning jackass!

Worthy Words

Fakelore is a term coined by folklorist Richard Dorson to describe written stories that get accepted as word-of-mouth folk tales. As prime examples of American fakelore, Dorson cites Paul Bunyan, Pecos Bill, and their imitators.

McGillivray heard them in a lumber camp in northern Michigan. Years later, in 1910, while working as a reporter for the *Detroit Free Press,* MacGillivray wrote a feature on the now legendary lumberjack. MacGillivray's piece told the story of the "Round River Drive" in which logs were floated for months down a river that turned out to move in a big circle! Paul Bunyan eventually dug a new channel to get the logs to lumber mills.

A few years later, a version of MacGillivray's story attracted the attention of an advertising executive named W. B. Laughead who worked for the Red River Lumber Company. He decided to include Paul Bunyan in a pamphlet given out free to his company's clients. Drawings and stories representing the hero were thus incorporated into the company's ad campaign. Laughead put a second pamphlet in 1916, and a third in 1922.

This third Paul Bunyan pamphlet was distributed not only the company's customers, but to anybody who wanted one; and, as it turned out, lots of people wanted one. By 1944, the company put out some 10 editions of the pamphlet and, in the process, helped turn Paul Bunyan into an American legend. Eat your heart out, Jolly Green Giant!

Meanwhile, newspapers across the country picked up on Paul Bunyan, contributing more stories and spreading his popularity. Paul Bunyan books appeared in bookstores starting in 1924. Dorson says that almost none of this flood of Bunyan lore actually came from stories told in lumber camps. Yet that's the pretense that has always gone along with them. Writers would make up stories and write them as if they had been told for years around a campfire.

Fearless Facts

According to Dorson, authentic Paul Bunyan "folklore" differs from "fakelore" in being less suitable for family reading and more apt to be vulgar and bawdy. One folktale, for example, tells of a lumberman who was stranded in a tree. Paul Bunyan told him to urinate. The piss froze in the cold weather, and the man climbed down on the frozen stream! Stories like this don't make it into the "folklore treasuries" for young readers!

Dorson says it is these written stories that made the giant lumberjack popular and that have defined his character for the nation as a whole, not the few Paul Bunyan stories that were actually told in lumber camps before the written ones were published. As for the other working heroes known around the country, they have even less of a folklore background; these other working heroes first appeared in stories published in magazines and children's books. Edward O'Reilly invented Pecos Bill. Joe Magarac is the work of Owen Francis. Febold Feboldson is the brainchild of Paul Beath. Margaret Montague brought Tony Beaver to life. And Lyle Saxon dreamt up Annie Christmas.

Big Bigotry

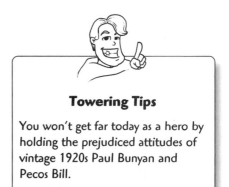

Towering Tips

You won't get far today as a hero by holding the prejudiced attitudes of vintage 1920s Paul Bunyan and Pecos Bill.

Pecos Bill, Paul Bunyan, and the other working heroes stood tall for ideals harbored by many Americans all over the country. One was the ideal of progress. Many were eager to see industry tame the country and turn its resources into useful products. Going along with this ideal is the ideal of hard work, since it takes work to make progress. Working heroes represent American working-class ideals laboring all around the country in many different jobs. To some extent, this ideal includes different ethnic, as well as regional groups. The big story told by all these tall tales put together is that Americans from all over were working hard and making progress.

Joe Magarac, in other words, isn't the only American in the melting pot. Everyone can pitch in and become part of the American dream of progress. Unfortunately, however, not all groups are included in the American ideals touted in these hero tales. In fact, many Paul Bunyan and Pecos Bill stories of the 1920s have a crude and ugly side to them. Some of these stories contain bigoted, racist representations of Native Americans, Black Americans, Mexicans, and French Canadians as lazy and stupid.

While representing hard work as a heroic ideal, the early stories about Paul Bunyan and Pecos Bill represented laziness as unmanly. Neither Paul nor Bill showed much respect for people who didn't work hard; and in the stories, these people were typically minority groups. Thus stereotyped, these groups were despised by the hardworking and inventive Paul and Bill, who showed them up with their strength and intelligence, set them to work doing menial jobs, and even tricked them out of their fair pay.

Paul Bunyan, for example, hired some Mexicans to haul lumber (the story explains that no "better" workers were available) and, at the end of the job, paid them off with lumber, which they had no use for. Seeing their dismay at being given something that they didn't want, he offered to take the lumber off their hands, free of charge. Of course, he turned around and sold the lumber to a lumber mill with the rest of the load. Clearly offensive by today's standards, this tale qualified as heroic for white readers of the 1920s when racism was widespread.

Thankless Task

Stigmatized as lazy—not only in tall tales, but in real life, too—minorities were frequently denied good jobs and paid substandard wages for the work they could get.

Even so, minority labor has accomplished a huge, Paul Bunyan–sized amount of the work that established American industry as a world leader since around the end of the Civil War. The cheap labor of poor immigrants and recently freed slaves helped make industrial progress possible, even though they didn't always stand to gain from that progress.

One working hero stands out as a case in point. This is John Henry, a mighty black railroad worker who, like Paul Bunyan and the others, was big and strong and was said to be the best ever at his job. Unlike Paul Bunyan, however, John Henry really existed. A former slave, he evidently worked in digging out the Big Bend Tunnel in West Virginia around 1870. This physically demanding work involved drilling holes in solid rock by driving steel rods into it with a hammer. A "shaker" would hold the rod with a pair of tongues and twist it around so that it wouldn't get stuck in the rock. Once the holes were drilled, the rock would be blasted out with dynamite.

According to legend, John Henry was many times stronger and faster than anyone else was at hammering steel. He was so strong and fast that he even competed with a steam-powered drill and won the contest. The story says a man wanted to sell a steam drill to John Henry's boss, saying it could work longer and faster than could any man alive. John Henry's boss replied that he didn't think the steam drill could beat John Henry, and they put it to the test.

The story has become a well-known folk song, which describes the outcome:

> The man who invented the steam drill thought he was mighty fine,
> But John Henry hammered 15 feet and the steam drill only made 9.

John Henry's great strength and his victory over the steam drill are only part of what makes him a hero. Another contributing fact is that he died as soon as the contest was over. Thus John Henry is a tragic hero in contrast to the other, comic working heroes. In addition to the message conveyed by all these worker tales—that Americans are strong and hardworking—is another message the other tales don't convey: Hard work takes its toll.

Fearless Facts

John Henry, Paul Bunyan, and Pecos Bill bury the hatchet in the live-action Disney movie *Tall Tale: The Unbelievable Adventures of Pecos Bill* (1995), in which the three heroes team up to help out a kid in trouble.

The Least You Need to Know

➤ Larger-than-life working heroes like Paul Bunyan and Pecos Bill provided popular images of American industrialism.

➤ Legendary working heroes represent several different regions of the United States.

➤ Although the stories of working heroes made themselves out to be word-of-mouth folk tales, they can be seen as literary examples of "fakelore."

➤ Paul Bunyan and Pecos Bill stories of the 1920s include numerous racist anecdotes.

➤ The story of John Henry is based on a real person who may actually have participated in a contest against a steam drill.

Chapter 4

Caped Crusaders

In This Chapter

➤ Comic book superheroes

➤ Super powers and secret identities

➤ Costumes and crime fighting

➤ Escapist fantasy and social relevance

➤ Continuity

When it comes to heroes, those of the comic book variety don't pull any punches. They're *superheroic*. (Now you know why we call them superheroes!) Superhero fans don't waste time with ordinary heroism. And who can blame them? So long as we're looking for heroic ideals, why not endow them with superhuman strength, the ability to fly, x-ray vision, and spandex jumpsuits?

Superheroism just goes on and on. If there are limits to the heroic deeds superheroes can accomplish, they are only so there will still be more deeds left over for later. And best of all, superheroes are easy to relate to because they are so mysterious; they could be just about anybody (who happens to become endowed with strange superhuman powers, that is).

Of course, there's the widespread impression that superhero comics are for kids, and that because they're comics, they aren't particularly deep and meaningful. And there's no doubt that superheroes have had a special appeal for youngsters for as long as they've been around. But there are plenty of grownup superhero fans too who take their comics seriously. In fact, comic book superheroes have a lot to tell us about what it means to be alive in the twentieth century.

Imagine That

No book on American heroes would be complete without grappling with comic book superheroes. Not only are they superheroic, they're also super American. Although comic books have spread across the globe and many American superheroes are recognized all over the world, the first superheroes were invented in the United States, where they quickly became super-popular. They've been larger-than-life fixtures in pop culture ever since. Some (namely Captain America and Wonder Woman) stand for patriotism and American might. These heroes got started during World War II as heroic symbols of the American war effort. They and Superman not only stand for American values like hard work, moral responsibility, discipline, and generosity, but they wear the red, white, and blue and work in tandem with the American government.

Fearless Facts

The first comic books were promotional freebies businesses gave to their customers. As an experiment, someone put a 10 cent price tag on a bunch of these giveaways that were left over and put them in stores. They sold quickly and people wanted more.

Of course, not all comics have a patriotic mission. In fact, they deal with all sorts of issues, sometimes by dramatizing them in superhero fashion and other times by escaping from them into bizarre fantasies. Comics are a place where the imagination often runs amok, yielding all kinds of results: extravagant, silly, exciting, sometimes cliched, sometimes poignant, and often experimental. Even so, there are conventions within the world of comic book superheroes that help make sense of all the imaginary mayhem.

First in Flight

Perhaps the most obvious features that set comic book superheroes apart from other heroes are super powers, secret identities, and showy, skin-tight costumes. Back before there were superhero comic books, there were (non-super or semi-super) heroes who appeared in Sunday comic strips and on radio shows. Among the most popular of these were Buck Rogers and Tarzan. Nothing against these heroes, but they don't exactly qualify as super since they don't have super powers or secret identities or skin-tight costumes (unless you count Tarzan's leopard skin loin-cloth). Even so, these heroes pushed the concept of heroism in the super direction and partly inspired the caped crusaders who were to come.

The first full-fledged superhero, Superman, is also the best known and most popular. He was dreamed up by a couple of high school kids in Cleveland—Jerry Siegel and Joe Schuster—who were Sunday comic hero fans and wanted to do their own strip. Jerry did the words and Joe did the pictures. They came out with the idea for Superman in 1932 and sent out samples to all the comic strip publishers they could find, but no one gave them a chance.

They actually had to break into the comic business doing other things before they could get their own invention published. This was right around the time when the first comic books were printed. At first they were no more than collections of strips re-printed from the Sunday papers. Before long, however, people got the idea of publishing adventure stories written especially for comic books.

Towering Tips

If you invent what turns out to be a world famous, super popular icon like Superman, be sure to hold on to the publishing rights! Superman creators Jerry Siegel and Joe Schuster sold the rights to their creation to the first company who agreed to publish their work. Instead of becoming billionaires, they worked as ordinary employees at DC comics.

Superman finally appeared in print in 1938 and was an instant hit. In fact, he dominated comics throughout the 1940s—a period referred to by comic historians as "the Golden Age." Rivals and imitators sprung up immediately. Some were so similar to Superman in concept and appearance that they were sued and shut down. Others became established superheroes in their own right. Two others, Batman and Wonder Woman, have been in continuous print ever since they got started, along with Superman.

Heroes Are People Too

Super powers, a secret identity, a mission to fight crime, and a flashy, tight costume all work together to make superheroes what they are. But it isn't all just fun and games for superheroes. Because their powers set them apart from ordinary mortals, they don't exactly fit in with everybody else. Let's face it, superheroes are weird. It's hard to relax and be buddies with someone who has X-ray vision and superhuman strength.

To get around this problem, most superheroes adopt two identities: one for normal, everyday use for things like going to work and running errands to the grocery store; and another for fighting enemies so evil, twisted, and powerful that conventional crime fighting is inadequate to control them. Of course, the secret identity not only serves a practical purpose for the hero, but makes for a lot of cool story lines.

The secret identity is a special secret that must be preserved at all costs; otherwise, villains might be able to get at the hero through friends and loved ones! Only the reader and perhaps one or two of the superheroes most trusted friends are let in on the secret. A big source of superhero excitement, in addition to the parts where they blast their enemies and rescue humanity, are the parts where they deal with maintaining the façade of having two totally different lives.

Fearless Facts

Some superheroes are mutants who are so unusual that they have no hope of fitting into society and must live as outcasts. Heroically, some mutants choose to devote themselves to defending the very society that rejected them. Others seek revenge. Some even waffle back and forth between good and evil. The Incredible Hulk is a well-known example.

Inside Stories

The whole identity thing makes the superhero easy to relate to. After all, we all know, deep down inside, that each of us is a totally unique and awesome individual. Often we have to hide our real selves from the world and put up false fronts in order to fit in. Often we are misunderstood or are forced to play a subordinate part when the time isn't right for us to show our true colors. Even if you don't have a tailor-made set of neon-colored tights hanging in your closet, you probably sometimes feel that you're capable of bigger things than you're actually accomplishing. The superhero fantasy says "yes, you can be totally, amazingly great even though you lead an ordinary, boring life, or are misunderstood or rejected by others."

Kid Power

This has been a gratifying message to generations of comic-book readers, especially adolescent boys looking ahead to white-collar careers in their futures. For kids in the 1940s, the thought of putting on a suit and tie to go to work everyday like Clark Kent must have been easier to take when they could imagine having that spandex jumpsuit on underneath like Superman! In fact, superhero comics are traditionally set in the contemporary big city, where people's working lives and inner, private lives can be totally different.

To enhance the superhero appeal to youngsters, many superheroes (especially during the 1940s) had sidekicks—junior versions of the adult hero who shared in his adventures and learned the superhero ropes. The most famous sidekick, of course, is Robin, who, as an orphan named Dick Grayson, was adopted by Bruce Wayne, alias Batman. Green Arrow's sidekick was named Speedy. Captain America's sidekick was named Bucky. (Superboy was actually not Superman's sidekick, but was Superman as a boy. The fact that Superman and Superboy are one person, however, hasn't stopped them from teaming up to fight crime together, thanks to the wonders of comic book time travel!)

Fearless Facts

The comic book industry was faced with intense public criticism in the early 1950s in response to a growing trend toward publishing graphic horror stories. There was even a congressional hearing to investigate connections between comics and juvenile delinquency. As a result, most publishers voluntarily adopted the Comics Code, a strict set of guidelines preventing the depiction of excessive sex and violence and the glorification of antisocial behavior.

People Power

Even though super powers often need to be disguised, they are essential to the heroism of the superhero. Their powers allow them to take up the battle against evil where ordinary humans fail. In addition, the nature of a hero's powers may say something about who he really is, reflecting or symbolizing aspects of his personality.

A famous example that shows how meaningful super powers can be is the series that helped get Marvel Comics off the ground. Marvel (along with DC) has been one of the two main superhero comic book publishers of the century. Marvel's first big success was the Fantastic Four. It seems a group of four freelance astronauts and scientists built their own rocket and blasted off for the moon. The rocket crashed, however, and they were all accidentally zapped with cosmic radiation that endowed the four with super powers.

Each of the four got different powers, reflecting each one's individual personality. The leader, Reed Richards, was highly ambitious, but also tried hard to accommodate the needs of others. He became the super stretchy Mr. Fantastic, a genius with an elastic body. The group's pilot, Ben Grimm, was a truculent, stubborn hardhead. He acquired a big, ugly body that looks like it's made of lumps of stone and became known as the Thing. Reed's fiancée, Sue Storm, was the self-effacing type. She acquired the power to turn invisible as the Invisible Girl. Sue's hot-tempered little brother acquired the power to burst into flames and fly and became known as the Human Torch.

Towering Tips

See if you can visualize your own personality defects and peccadilloes as the source of undiscovered super powers. See if you can imagine how to use these powers for good instead of evil!

Fantastic Four comics not only show the heroes battling bad guys, but also show them engaging in personal conflicts among themselves. Because their powers have a personal, psychological slant, their adventures have a special appeal beyond the hackneyed good-versus-evil scenarios. In fact, the personal problems and situations of the superhero are important in many comic book stories. Often, there's an important connection between the superhero's special powers and his or her personal problems.

Far-Out Warriors

Of course, not all superheroes have super powers that reflect existential truths about their personalities. The appeal of super powers and their acquisition is often simply that they are amazing and imaginative. Here are just some of the far-out super powers in the comic book arsenal. Watch out, bad guys!

Talent Pool

➤ The Metal Men are made of metal and can form their bodies into all kinds of shapes, including tools, wire, walls, weights, globules, and sheets. There's Lead, Tin, Gold, Platinum, Iron, Mercury, and others working as a team.

➤ Swamp Thing has the power to regenerate himself like the plants of which he is made. He can foil his enemies by tangling them up in vines and branches.

➤ Medusa is a mythical monster turned superheroine who can entangle bad guys with the snakes that are her hair.

➤ Banshee has a sonic scream.

➤ Animal Man can take the form of any animal.

➤ Wolverine has metal claws that spring out of his fists, a metal-encased skeleton. He also has super healing powers, and can therefore recover from virtually any injury.

➤ Hawkman and Hawkgirl can fly and talk to birds.

➤ Negative Man is made of negative energy. Just think of the possibilities!

➤ Robby Reed is a teenager who finds a telephone from another planet. The telephone turns him into a different hero every episode, including Radar-Sonar Man, Quakemaster, Baron Buzz-Saw, and Velocity Kid.

➤ Metamorpho, the Element Man, has the powers of a walking chemistry set.

Fearless Facts

Ever since the 1960s, many superheroes and super villains have been deliberately outlandish and campy. During this time, Batman appeared as a TV show to do battle with such oddball villains as the Penguin, the Joker, the Riddler, and King Tut.

Supe Yourself Up

Each superhero gets his or her powers in a particular manner. As a result, every super-hero has a special origin story that explains who he is and how he got that way. In general, though, there are a few basic approaches to becoming a superhero. Here are some tried and true techniques for becoming a superhero. Good luck and remember, the world needs you!

➤ The most straightforward way is through hard work, study, and by just being a strange guy. This is how Batman got started. His powers aren't, strictly speaking, super powers, but he qualifies as a superhero anyway because he's got a first-rate costume. In addition, he's incredibly athletic and has superior detective skills. Both of these traits are augmented by his flair for invention—he has his famous utility and souped-up Batmobile. He has no trouble paying for all his crime-fighting gizmos, because in private life he is millionaire Bruce Wayne. Of course, this approach to becoming a superhero can take a lifetime and is clearly not for everybody. In fact, in his later years, Batman has turned into something of a psycho. He is emotionally consumed by his hate of evil and he often goes too far in his zeal to punish wrongdoers.

➤ A much quicker method of becoming a hero is to have a freak accident. The Flash, for example, acquired the ability to run super fast when he was electro-cuted while covered with spilled chemicals. Spiderman was bitten by a radioac-tive spider and acquired "spider strength." If you decide to go for the freak accident approach, be careful! Freak accidents can be dangerous. Even so, they're a great way to unleash the inner you and change your personality flaws into super powers.

➤ A safer way to become a superhero is to be born on another planet where they have special abilities that we Earthlings don't have. This is how Superman and a bunch of others did it. He was an ordinary kid on the planet Krypton. Here on Earth, he's a superhero. I would recommend trying this approach first and going for the freak accident only as a last resort. After all, this is the approach that first got superheroes off the ground with the first Superman comic in 1938. The downside of coming from another planet is that Earthlings may not understand you. Even so, it's important to stay humble despite your super powers and keep fighting evil for the benefit of humankind.

Fearless Facts

Some say the whole idea of extraterrestrially acquired super powers was first invented by the pulp-fiction writer Edgar Rice Burroughs, the inventor of Tarzan. In addition to Tarzan, Burroughs created a science-fiction hero named John Carter who went to Mars where, because the planet has less gravity than Earth does, he was super strong. It was left to Superman to bring super powers from the planet Krypton to Earth.

➤ Another good way to become a hero is to be born as a mythical being like Thor, a Norse god, and Wonder Woman, an Amazon. This way a lot of your story will already have been written in ancient mythology. Be sure to update your mythic powers for the modern world with a sleek, flashy costume and revved-up super powers!

➤ Becoming an adept in occult arts is the way to go if you're the mystical type. Unleash an ancient magical force or tame an assortment of wandering spirits. Be prepared for a swirling future of magical battles! The esoteric Dr. Strange popularized this approach with the addition of James Bond–good looks and debonair style.

➤ Genetic mutation is a popular approach but, as with coming from another planet, you may have a hard time fitting in with ordinary humanoids. As a mutant, you can battle evil and stand up for mutants' rights at the same time.

➤ And of course, if you're into high tech, you'll want to become a cyborg. You'll have to deal with malfunctions, meltdowns, short circuits, and "vegematic" jokes. But if you're handy with a soldering gun, you can always make repairs and improvements.

➤ Of course, feel free to experiment with any combinations of these suggestions. You might hit on the superhero to end all superheroes!

To Be Continued

Once you're a superhero, don't expect to live happily ever after. Your story will never end until you're discontinued by your publisher! Comic adventures are published serially, telling sequences of continuous stories. These stories are episodes that link together indefinitely. In fact, many superhero fans look for continuity from story to story and even from hero to hero. In general, the traits (and "history") of a super-hero will be about the same from episode to episode, unless something happens in one of the episodes that changes things. What's more, different superheroes often cross paths and even share a common "history." In other words, their ongoing stories intersect.

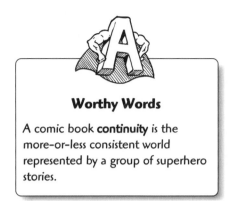

Worthy Words

A comic book **continuity** is the more-or-less consistent world represented by a group of superhero stories.

A convention most comic publishers adopt is to treat groups of their stories as a kind of imaginary history that more or less hangs together. The idea is for the various superhero stories and series published over time to be consistent with one another. The stories are part of a *continuity,* an imaginary world that remains basically consistent from issue to issue.

Consistency within a comic book continuity means that, in effect, all the writers of superhero comics who work within the continuity are all working on the same big, ongoing story made up of hundreds of little stories and maybe dozens of heroes. Readers can appreciate the little stories right away. Once they get hooked on a super-hero, they may get interested in the larger story and start buying other comics in the same continuity.

This means that superhero comics have some of the appeal that soap operas have. Part of the fun is keeping track of all the stuff that goes on and how it fits together. It also means that, in addition to the usual blasting of bad guys and rescuing decent folks everywhere, superheroes can go through big, special, once-in-life-time changes to keep readers interested and on their toes.

Parallel Lives

The desire for continuity doesn't prevent comic publishers from experimenting with alternative versions and spin-offs of their superhero stories. Parallel worlds, alien galaxies, time warps, strange new dimensions, and other odd nooks and crannies in time and space allow different versions of the same superhero to coexist within a single continuity. If the new version catches on, it can supercede the old version or continue in a parallel world or dimension. If not, it can fade away or go out with a bang, with no harm done to the original concept.

Comic publishers are always trying to keep their readers happy by giving them the kind of heroes and stories they want. If sales of a certain hero drop, the writers may change the hero in an attempt to make that hero more interesting and appealing. Heroes may even disappear from comics altogether and reappear decades later. In fact, many heroes discontinued in the late 1940s and early 1950s were revived in the 1960s.

Fearless Facts

The Marvel Comics hero Captain America was popular during World War II, but he faded and was eventually discontinued. Decades later, Marvel began reissuing Captain America comic books to a new generation. His disappearance from the comics was accounted for in the stories themselves, which explain that he got himself frozen in the Arctic ice for a few decades. He was finally found and revived and given the opportunity to stand and fight for everything America holds dear!

Hero Today, Gone Tomorrow

Superman, for example, has been through numerous big changes over the course of the century. When he first appeared, he was super strong, but he couldn't fly and he didn't have X-ray vision. These things came later. That's why they used to say he can "leap tall buildings in a single bound." This actually meant something before he could fly!

Also, Superman used to have a super weakness. His super strength became sapped whenever he became exposed to kryptonite, elemental material from his home planet, which exploded and sent out meteors all over space shortly after he left. After he got over the kryptonite thing, he could only be weakened by especially powerful and strange cosmic forces.

Not long ago, Superman went through an especially dramatic change: He died! He met his end in a battle with a mighty costumed menace named Doomsday who crossed the nation leaving a wake of destruction in his path. In the end, Doomsday was destroyed, but the battle cost our hero his very life. To make his death even more tragic, he was finally getting ready to marry Lois Lane after all these years!

His tragic comic book death no doubt reflects a death inflicted by the lack of interest on the part of comic book readers who got tired of him! Ironically, Superman publishers killed him off in order to revive him in the hopes of attracting readers back to the series. After he died, he was cosmically reincarnated as four different super beings, each with his own comic intended to appeal to different sorts of readers.

These four new incarnations of Superman are drastically different from one another and from Superman as he was before he died. One is a teenage punk-type in a leather jacket. Another is a black scientist and construction worker. There's also a cyborg Superman, and a bossy version of Clark Kent.

The comic book readers of the 1980s and 1990s were a bit more sophisticated and generally more jaded than the readers of earlier decades. The simple superhero with simple motives and simple powers started to make room for the more psychologically complex anti-superheroes, who usually have more personal battles than brawls with bad guys. (The writers of Batman were able to keep the hero alive through the years by begging the question of whether he was a good guy or just a psychopath.)

Towering Tips

Don't miss the parallels between the story of Superman and the story of Christ! Both are superior beings sent by their fathers to Earth to help humanity. Both died in their struggle, but were reborn. Notice, though, that Superman pretty much just blasts bad guys while Christ atones for the sins of all who believe in him.

The Least You Need to Know

➤ Superhero comics first emerged in 1938 with the appearance of Superman.

➤ Super powers, a secret identity, a flashy, tight costume, and a mission to fight crime are all typical features of the superhero.

➤ Super powers may cause or reflect a hero's personal problems, which readers can relate to.

➤ Super powers may be campy, fantastic, and imaginative rather than symbolic or dramatic.

➤ Comic publishers preserve continuity while experimenting with their heroes by introducing parallel worlds and dimensions and alternative time frames.

Part 2
Questing and Nesting

Two complementary and crucial venues for heroism are traveling: the journey, the quest, the migration, the pilgrimage; and building: laying the foundation, putting in roots, taking care of business. These heroic strains are about establishing and moving beyond the way we live. Of course, to establish a new way of life, you have to move beyond the old one; so the process of branching out and hunkering down keeps going on and on. It isn't every day that this process results in a powerful democracy like America, however.

This process is vital to heroism in general, but especially as far as America is concerned, because so many Americans had to come so far to get here, explore so much to figure out where they were, and build so much to make the country what it is today. As a result, America has more than its share of questing and nesting heroes. And because we all need to keep living and looking for new ways to live, it helps to have heroes like these to show us how it's done.

This section deals with homeland heroes, starting with the first colonists and moving through the settlers and frontier heroes, cowboy heroes, heroic lovers, inventors, businesspeople, and explorers—the most admired figures who have come from far away, put the country together from the inside out, and kept on looking for something more. The section is only loosely chronological, though, because searching and settling are just two sides of the same coin.

Brave New World

The first heroes in U.S. history were here long before the United States actually became a country, helping to make possible the nation as we know it today. Some came over on ships from Europe; others were here to meet them when they arrived. In either case, they faced the difficult task of dealing with people and situations that were entirely unknown and almost completely unpredictable.

These days, it's easy to miss just how strange and unpredictable things must have seemed at the time. By now, our heroes have been turned into stock figures. From an early age, we're taught to recognize the Puritan pilgrim settler with his high-buckled hat and blunderbuss along with the Indian wearing a feathered headdress and bow and arrows heading out into the woods together to hunt Thanksgiving turkey. And then there's the New World frontiersman, wearing a buckskin suit and a coonskin cap and carrying a Tennessee long rifle for "huntin' bar."

Of course, many people were involved in the series of complex events leading up to the founding of our country, but only a select few have been turned into heroes.

These early heroic figures represent an appealing side of the sometimes ugly process of starting up a whole new country on somebody else's land.

Group Efforts

Ever since before this country became the United States of America, all sorts of people have been interested in the land for all sorts of reasons. (Some things never change!) There were Dutch, English, French, and Spanish colonists. Some were after military conquests, some wanted economic opportunities, and some wanted religious and political freedom. There were also the Indians. They lived in numerous tribes, some of which were receptive to trade and interaction with the colonists, some of which were not. What's more, the tribes also had alliances and disputes with one another that often influenced the way they dealt with the colonists—just as the colonists' problems with each other influenced the ways they dealt with the Indians.

Basically, between the Indian and the colonists, there was a whole panoply of racial, national, political, military, religious, and economic groups involved in shifting alliances and conflicts. And they all had different interests and resources. One result of all this is that historians are left with a complex and confusing situation to try to sort out. Making their job still harder is the fact that comparatively few records that chronicle the events of the time are left, and those that exist are not always reliable.

Historians may never agree on which stories are true, but that hasn't stopped people from regarding some of the more exciting and colorful figures of the time as heroes. Prominent among them are Captain John Smith, the adventurer who helped protect the struggling British colony of Jamestown, Virginia, and Pocahontas, the high-spirited Indian girl who is said to have rescued Smith from having his brains beaten out by her tribesmen. Both are celebrated for their exciting stories and for enabling the Virginia colonists to keep their slender toehold in the New World.

Getting Settled

Captain John Smith was among a group of settlers who arrived in Virginia in 1608 to establish Jamestown, the first permanent English settlement in the New World. The journey was funded by a stock company that sought to make profit through trade. The settlers, however, were more concerned with survival than with sending goods back to London. Smith responded brusquely to his backers when they wrote him to demand immediate profit, saying that additional investments of workers and resources would be necessary before the New World could be turned into a money-making enterprise.

John Smith. (Dictionary of American Portraits)

Because the colonists weren't able to live off the land and their provisions were running out, that winter Captain Smith led a party upriver in hopes of trading with the Indians for food. There they met the chief known as Powhatan, leader of an alliance made up of several Algonquin tribes. Smith and Powhatan arranged for an exchange of European goods for food and agreed to maintain peaceful relations; the peace did not last, however, and the fighting began again.

Hostilities were eventually smoothed over again, however, thanks in part to Powhatan's daughter, Pocahontas, who formed a friendship with the settlers and even sailed to England with an Englishman, John Rolfe, as his bride. Evidently, Powhatan restrained his desire to make war on the settlers for the sake of Pocahontas.

Maid in the Shade

Just how Pocahontas got hooked up with the settlers isn't certain, although the most famous account—told by John Smith himself—has been widely accepted as true. In any case, it is a well-known story. Smith says he was captured in battle and brought before Powhatan to be executed. Held by numerous Indians, his head was placed on two stones as an Indian prepared to break his skull with a club. At this point, Pocahontas sprang to his side and placed her head on top of his, urging Powhatan to spare his life. Smith was spared and returned to Jamestown and, eventually, went back to England.

Pocahantas. (Rutgers University Special Collections and Archives)

Fearless Facts

Smith said Pocahontas was only about 10 years old at the time, but suggested she was intrigued by him. As the story was retold by others, it was turned into a love story, with Pocahontas as a young woman instead of a young girl. The recent Disney film *Pocahontas* is only one of many dramatic renditions of the legend.

Some historians have cast doubt on Smith's story of his rescue by Pocahontas. They point out that when he first told it, Pocahontas had already become a celebrity in London. She had been introduced to the queen, on whom she made a powerful impression. John Rolfe, her husband, was a wealthy tobacco trader, so he could afford to show off his unusual bride at court where she would be noticed and talked about. (Although she was married to an Indian named Kocoum when she set sail for England, her Indian marriage wasn't recognized by the whites.) It seems possible John Smith came out with his story at this time simply to get a little recognition.

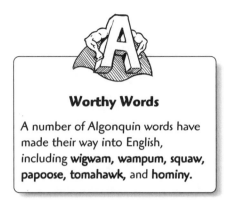

Worthy Words

A number of Algonquin words have made their way into English, including **wigwam, wampum, squaw, papoose, tomahawk,** and **hominy.**

Those who doubt Smith's story also point out that he had fabricated adventures for himself in the past to bolster his image as a dashing and gallant adventurer. Others claim, however, that Smith's story seems consistent with the available evidence and with Indian customs. Chances are, neither side will ever be proven for certain.

Although the story did a great deal to bolster the fame of Smith and Pocahontas, it's quite possible that both figures would have achieved hero status even without it. Pocahontas exhibited impressive poise, courage, and initiative in choosing to sail to London to see how the English lived, and the eventual success of the Jamestown colony may well have been made possible by the placating influence she had with her father Powhatan.

Captain Smith was also crucial to the success of the colony—and to British colonialism in general—in a number of ways. He not only traded with the Indians, but he also explored widely. He named New England and discovered Plymouth, Massachusetts, where the *Mayflower* landed years later. In addition, he served as a spokesman for settlers in dealing with England, recommending additional investment in the colonies.

Harvest Hero

In 1620, 12 years after Captain Smith and his group of colonists first arrived in Virginia, the *Mayflower* arrived in Plymouth, Massachusetts, which Smith had scoped out as a suitable site for future settlement. Like the Virginia colonists, the *Mayflower* pilgrims were ill prepared for survival in the New World and many died that first winter. Life improved for those who made it through, thanks in part to Tisquantum, better known as Squanto, an Indian who acted as interpreter, teacher, and benefactor for the Plymouth pilgrims. As a result of this help, Squanto has been regarded as an American hero for generations. Many school kids look to him as the Indian who helped make the first Thanksgiving possible.

Worthy Words

Indentured servants were not paid wages. Instead, they worked only for food, clothing, and shelter for a stipulated period of time. Many people were so poor that indentured servitude was their only legal means of support. An indenture is a cut or fold made in the edges of a contract; so the term *indentured servant* means "bound by contract."

Learning the Hard Way

Squanto, who belonged to the Pawtuxet band of the Wampanoag Indian tribe, spoke fluent English and was familiar with white people. In fact, prior to the arrival of the *Mayflower* in 1614, he had been kidnapped and sold into slavery by an English explorer named Thomas Hunt. Squanto was taken to Spain where he was rescued from slavery by some Spanish friars. Unable to return home immediately, he made his way to England. From England, he accompanied an exploration voyage to Newfoundland in 1617. He may have made the journey as an *indentured servant*.

Although Squanto returned to England with an exploring ship, he sailed again for America soon after; finally, in 1619, he made it home to stay. Unfortunately, however, he found his village wiped out by disease—possibly the plague or smallpox, brought from Europe to the New World by colonists. Squanto fell in with one of the other Wampanoag bands in the vicinity of his former home.

Chief of all the Wampanoags was Massasoit. Although Squanto joined with Massasoit, they may have had an uneasy relationship. In any case, Squanto's home had been destroyed, and his loyalties may have been divided uncertainly between the Wampanoags and the colonists.

Squanto came to the Plymouth colonists in the spring of 1621 to arrange a meeting with Massasoit. The meeting, with Squanto acting as interpreter, resulted in a famous peace treaty between the colonists and Wampanoags. Not only did the Indians allow the pilgrims to live in peace at Plymouth colony, but they also taught them techniques of planting corn, trapping, and fishing (without which they may not have survived). Squanto, in particular, was a valuable teacher to the colonists, who said he was "sent from God."

Fearless Facts

The first Thanksgiving took place in December 1621, when the pilgrims invited Massasoit to a harvest feast. Massasoit arrived accompanied by some 90 Indians—too many for the settlers to feed. Luckily, the Indians contributed food as well, so there was plenty for everyone. Washington declared a one-time-only national holiday in honor of the event, observed November 26, 1789. Many people continued to celebrate the event, although it was not made an official national holiday until 1863 under President Lincoln.

Thankless Tasks

Sadly, relations between the settlers and the Wampanoags gradually deteriorated. Part of the problem may have been due to a difference in attitudes toward land. The peace agreement granted the pilgrims use of a specified tract of land, which individual settlers took over as their own private property. Indians found hunting, fishing, or trapping on this land could be regarded as trespassers and shot.

This concept of private ownership of land, however, was foreign to the Wampanoags, who thought they had a right to use land occupied by the settlers. Massasoit was able to maintain an uneasy peace, despite numerous unpleasant incidents. Finally, war broke out under the Wampanoag chief Metacomet, whom the settlers referred to as King Philip. After leading repeated attacks against the colonists, King Philip was killed in the summer of 1676. His head was cut off and displayed on a pole in Plymouth for many years afterward. Remaining Wampanoags were hunted down and killed or sold as slaves to work in the West Indies. King Philip's wife and son were among those sold.

Bad Habits

Although it isn't pleasant to think about, most people know that the "Indians," or Native Americans, were decimated by the whites during the approximately 200-year period since the American colonies got started. The colonies at Plymouth and Jamestown established a pattern that was repeated many times as white settlers pushed westward. Relations between Indian and whites moved from treaties to uneasy peace, open conflict, and finally extermination and relocation all across the continent.

Heroes have emerged from both sides of this struggle. Later chapters will say more about heroic Indian warriors and Indian fighters. Clearly heroism is a morally complicated state of affairs. People guilty of helping to periodically wipe out the Indians have been, and still are, admired as heroes. This is partly because many felt it was necessary to defeat the Indians in order to establish a white society in America.

Company Man

The struggle between whites and Indians was not simply political and military, of course, but economic. Not all whites felt an overwhelming desire to conquer the Indians out of pure racial hatred or for the sake of conquest itself, but many whites felt they had the right—and even the duty—to pursue economic opportunities in the New World. As a result, many tolerated, condoned, or actively pursued aggression against Indians insofar as they seemed to stand in the way of economic progress.

This is true even of whites who aren't usually associated with trade. Even while pursuing the ideal of "freedom" into the virgin wilderness of the New World, many whites retained economic ties with the countries of Europe whose trading companies sought profit in America. This is true of one of America's greatest heroes, Daniel Boone. The people who admire Daniel Boone don't generally think of him as being funded by

Daniel Boone. (Rutgers University Special Collections and Archives)

European trade. After all, he was independent, lived off the land, and sided sometimes with Indians and sometimes with whites (as he thought best). Much of the exploring Boone did, however, was for the Transylvania Company, which sought profit from land and resources.

Well Traveled

Daniel Boone was one of the best and best known of the so-called long hunters—men who went out hunting and stayed away a long time. He was a frontiersman even back in the days before the Revolutionary War, often surviving alone out in the woods and building homes for his family in places where no other white people had ever been. He seemed to prefer a largely self-sufficient existence in the wilderness to the comforts of civilization and the company of large groups of people. Ironically, in moving farther and farther westward away from white civilization, he made it easier for more whites to follow in his footsteps and establish settlements.

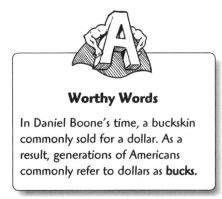

Worthy Words

In Daniel Boone's time, a buckskin commonly sold for a dollar. As a result, generations of Americans commonly refer to dollars as **bucks.**

Daniel Boone grew up close to the frontier and learned at a young age to hunt and trap game. When he was about 15 years old, his family moved from Pennsylvania to less-settled land in North Carolina. The French and the British governments were fighting over the territory and both sides made alliances with Indian tribes to help them in battle. This is known as the French and Indian War, which was not simply a war over American territory, but an extension of a conflict going on in Europe.

The young Daniel Boone volunteered to serve as a teamster—a driver of a team of horses—carrying supplies. As a teamster, he was involved in the famous attack on Fort Duquesne led by British General Edward Braddock. (A young George Washington also fought in this battle as a major in the colonial militia.) The British forces were easily defeated as a result of Braddock's decision to attach the fort in broad daylight in regimental formation. The British soldiers made easy targets and many were shot, including Braddock himself.

Boone was more fortunate and made it back home safely. Shortly afterward, he married and moved to Virginia. Married life did not stop him from joining a team of explorers to Florida to assess the area's suitability for future settlement. (The explorers found Florida too hot and swampy for convenient colonizing!)

Claims to Fame

Boone later explored the Cumberland Gap leading from Tennessee to Kentucky and helped build the Wilderness Road so that settlers could make the journey. He helped establish the town of Boonesborough, which was originally little more than a fort. Boone moved to this fort with his family and helped to defend it against Indians.

At one point, Boone was kidnapped by the Shawnee tribe and was adopted by the Shawnee Chief Blackfoot. He was named Sheltowee, which means "Big Turtle." He lived with them four months before escaping and returning to Boonesborough. By this time, his wife and children had enough of the wilderness and returned to North Carolina.

Fearless Facts

Shortly after the Revolutionary War, in 1778, Boone was arrested as a British spy. He was not only acquitted, but was made a major in the United States militia.

Boone continued to explore unsettled territory, often in the pay of land companies. He established claims of his own for thousands of acres, but was swindled out of them (because he had no experience or interest in real estate law). Fortunately, his children had better success securing land. Boone accompanied his son Daniel to Missouri where he lived many years until his death.

Fictive Feats

By the time he died in 1820, Boone had already become an international legend. A school teacher named John Filson wrote a idealized memoir called *The Adventures of Col. Daniel Boone* based on accounts reported to him by a land speculator who knew Boone (and swindled him out of some land). Readers were quick to latch on to the wilderness hero who lived off the land, made few enemies, and accomplished adventurous deeds in the wilderness. Boone's story was even translated into French and German.

While he was admired in Europe, he was idolized in America. He had a huge funeral. Twenty-five years after his death, his body was claimed by the state of Kentucky, which had it dug up and escorted in state to be buried in the Kentucky town of Frankfort. Almost 100 years later, in 1937, the state of Missouri tried unsuccessfully to get the hero's remains back to their original resting place.

Many legends have been told over the years about Daniel Boone, wilderness hero. I wouldn't swear to any of these events:

➤ As a child, Boone was quarantined to keep him from catching smallpox. He hated the confinement of quarantine so much, he deliberately exposed himself to the disease and got sick.

➤ His father had a policy, when his children did wrong, to beat them until they asked for forgiveness. Young Daniel, however, was too stubborn to ask for mercy, preferring to be beaten.

➤ Boone was forever being chased by Indians. He put them off the trail by running backward, swinging on vines, and other wilderness trail tricks.

➤ Boone was once kidnapped by Indians, but escaped after they drank his whiskey and fell asleep. He then burned through his ropes by holding them against hot coals in the fire.

➤ Boone put three notches in a tree with a tomahawk way out in the middle of the wilderness. Some time afterward, the tree was identified as a boundary of a land claim. Twenty years later, the bark of the tree had grown over the notches, so no one knew where the boundary was. Boone was called in to help and was able to identify the tree and locate the notches under the bark through his superior powers of wilderness recollection.

➤ Boone's daughter Jemima was kidnapped by Indians. She helped her dad follow the trail by leaving deep footprints and tearing off bits of her dress. Boone caught up with her three days later and rescued her without a fight.

➤ Boone was supposedly found dead beside his rifle, which was propped up on a log and pointed in the direction of a deer, which was also found dead from the shot of Boone's rifle.

Fearless Facts

Among those to idealize Boone for his rugged, outdoor way of life were the English Romantic poet Lord Byron and the American naturalist J. J. Audubon. Boone also provided much of the inspiration for the heroes of the famous *Leatherstocking Tales* of James Fenimore Cooper, including *The Deerslayer* and *Last of the Mohicans*.

King Davy

A frontiersman of a later generation cut from much the same mold as Daniel Boone was Davy Crockett (1786–1836). In addition to being a celebrated hunter, marksman, and pioneer, Crockett was also a popular politician, serving in the Tennessee State Legislature and later, as Tennessee's U.S. Congressman. He was among those who died defending the Alamo.

Crockett got his start doing odd jobs, including farming and cattle driving before distinguishing himself as a marksman. He often won prizes in shooting contests as a teenager. He enlisted in the Tennessee militia and led a battalion against the Creek

Davy Crockett. (Rutgers University Special Collections and Archives)

Indians in 1813–1814. His military experience led to a political career and eventually he became a congressman, becoming noted for bringing frontier ways to Washington. It was as a pioneer congressman that Davy Crockett first began to attain legendary status.

Fearless Facts

Like Daniel Boone, Davy Crockett is often pictured wearing a coonskin cap. These caps were popular among settlers and also became trendy in France after Benjamin Franklin arrived there as a diplomat sporting one of them. Older readers may remember the coonskin cap fad of the 1950s, which was triggered by the popularity of the TV show *Davy Crockett*, starring Fess Parker.

Crockett's status as an American hero was confirmed by the Alamo. This was a fort that was originally a mission in Texas at the time when the territory was part of Mexico. Though Texas belonged to Mexico, the majority of settlers who lived their were American colonists. Violent conflicts between Americans and Mexicans in Texas were frequent. In the midst of one bloody clash in 1836, an outnumbered force of 187 American militia men took a stand in the San Antonio de Valero Mission, better known as the Alamo, named for *los alamos*—a grove of cottonwood trees nearby.

Holed up in the Alamo, the American militia held off a force of some 5,000 Mexicans for 10 days, hoping in vain for support from the U.S. army. Help never came, and the Mexicans broke through the mission walls and killed all the Americans inside, including Davy Crockett. "Remember the Alamo" became a rallying cry in the Texas Revolution that resulted in Texas territory becoming a U.S. State.

Legend has it that Crockett died fighting. Recently, however, evidence has emerged to contradict this legend. A diary by a Mexican officer who fought at the Alamo reveals that Crockett was captured and later died under torture after pleading to be set free. The diary, which appears to be genuine, recently sold for $350,000 at an auction.

Free Spirit

Another frontier hero whose life story is permeated with legend is John Chapman (1775–1845), better known as Johnny Appleseed. Unlike the frontier fighters Boone and Crockett, Johnny Appleseed is famous for his peaceful co-existence with people, animals, and plants. Little is known about his life. He was a land owner who cultivated apples and sold or gave apple trees to settlers. These trees proved to be an important part of the frontier diet for many people and

Heroic Shorts

Johnny Appleseed was a follower of the Swedish mystic visionary, Emanuel Swedenborg. He spread Swedenborg's teachings as he traveled the countryside.

Fearless Facts

One of the biggest heroes of one of the biggest states of the Union is Sam Houston (1793–1863) who commanded the Texas colonial militia in the Texas Revolution against Mexico. Houston was a U.S. Congressman and later Governor of Tennessee who spent many years living with the Cherokee Indians, whom he befriended. He later moved to Texas where he became active in colonial politics, eventually taking command of the colonial army. He led his troops in a decisive victory over the Mexicans at the Battle of San Jacinto not long after the Alamo in 1836. Later that year he was elected 1st president of the Republic of Texas. (Texas didn't become a state right away after winning independence from Mexico. Instead it became a separate country.) Houston later became governor of Texas after it became a state in 1845.

some of them are still bearing fruit a century and a half later. He lived close to nature and spent much of his life traveling around Pennsylvania, Ohio, Kentucky, Illinois, and Indiana.

Much more well-known is the Johnny Appleseed of legend. This is the kindly, ragged wanderer who owned nothing but a bag of appleseeds and a cooking pan which he wore on his head. They say he could survive outside in the cold with nothing and melted snow for drinking water with his feet. He carried no gun or knives, but lived peacefully with humans and animals, enjoying the respect of white settlers and Indians alike.

Much about this legend may be true, since it began to emerge during his own lifetime as pioneers expressed admiration for his outdoor existence and his unselfishness as well as his apple trees. He died of pneumonia at the age of seventy and was buried beneath a marker inscribed with the words, "He lived for others." Many more monuments have since been put up throughout the Northeast and Midwest to the legendary folk hero.

The Least You Need to Know

➤ Pocahontas married tobacco grower John Rolfe and sailed to England where she was introduced to royalty.

➤ Captain John Smith may have made up the story that he was saved from execution by Pocahontas.

➤ Squanto acted as teacher and interpreter for the benefit of the *Mayflower* pilgrims and arranged a treaty between the pilgrims and Wampanoag Indians.

➤ Daniel Boone helped open up the wilderness of Kentucky to early settlers.

➤ By the time of his death in 1820, Boone was admired in Europe and idolized in America.

➤ Davy Crockett served in Congress and died at the Alamo.

➤ Johnny Appleseed owned land but did not settle on it.

Western Stars

Perhaps no other heroic figure has had such a deep and prolonged influence on so many Americans as the cowboy. Originally, being a cowboy meant having the not-very-prestigious job of making sure big herds of half-wild cattle made it safely on foot from the range to the stockyards. Today, even though there are still people who handle cattle for a living who think of themselves as cowboys, the term "cowboy" refers more to an image than to a profession.

The cowboy mystique has left its mark on many generations of Americans. Chances are, even if you're from back East, you have felt the call of the open prairie deep down inside, and have enjoyed many a pleasant daydream of tumblin' along with the tumblin' tumbleweeds somewhere out in the wide open spaces. And even if you don't have cowboy boots, a stetson hat, or a snakeskin belt, you probably have at least one pair of blue jeans.

Thanks to the stories and traditions—and the advertising—that have perpetuated the cowboy image, there's a little cowboy inside every American. Whether we particularly like it or not, the land that framed them and the loud voice of their (maybe gruff) independent, no-nonsense, and head-on approach to life is part of what formed us as Americans. These days, it usually works best if we keep our inner cowboys inside where they belong. If we let them out, they tend to raise hell and get us into trouble! Time was, though, when trouble was just part of a cowboy's job description, and the appropriate way to do the job was to act a little wild and crazy.

Having a Cow

Believe it or not, the first cowboys were not professional actors, singers, or male models. All that came later. The first cowboys started off as guys who got paid to handle cows. No, they weren't dairy farmers, but cattle drivers. Pretty much all the money to be made in the cowboy business came from the sale of cattle for beef and leather. This means there would never have been any cowboys without lots of cows that needed to be driven from the mostly unpopulated desert to a place where they could be loaded onto trains and taken to people who wanted to eat them.

Fearless Facts

Among the cowboys known to history are several African-American cowboys like Nat Love, also known as "Deadwood Dick," who wrote in his memoirs that he considered himself lucky in sustaining only 14 insignificant gunshot wounds.

Bustin' Loose

The first cattle in America—and the first horses, for that matter—were brought over by the Spanish (Mexican cowboys are known as "vaqueros"). As the Spanish colonized Mexico and Texas, they brought the cattle along, which went forth and multiplied. In fact, the cattle did so well in their new environment that before long, there was more cattle than anyone could use. The herds outgrew the ranches where they were kept and began wandering around the range, free and half wild.

Cattle accumulated in especially large herds in Texas, where they had been brought by Spanish missionaries. When the United States took over Texas, the cattle came along with it. At the time, Texas was basically just a big cattle range with a few settlers trying to make a living there. No one really had any serious plans for the cattle until after the Civil War. By that time, Texas boasted more than 6 million cattle.

Cow Town

Every once in a while, some ranch hands got together and organized a cattle drive north out of Texas in order to sell them. One early cattle trader was Jesse Chisolm, a mixed-blood Indian who drove the cattle on a route that came to be known as the Chisolm Trail. This became one of the main routes north out of Texas to Kansas.

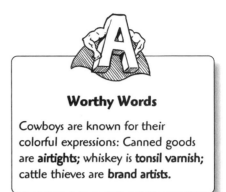

Worthy Words

Cowboys are known for their colorful expressions: Canned goods are **airtights**; whiskey is **tonsil varnish**; cattle thieves are **brand artists.**

One day, an entrepreneur named Joseph McCoy got the idea of building a stockyard right beside a railroad depot where the cows could be kept prior to shipping them all over the country—especially west to California where the gold rush was taking place. All the miners ate meat, and they could be supplied with Texas cattle. McCoy built his stockyards in Abilene, Kansas at the end of the Chisolm Trail. This helped kick the cattle industry into high gear; and for several decades afterward, there was a big demand for Texas cattle and for cowboys who could drive them north.

Unsung Heroes

A cowboy's job was demanding and required skill, strength, and endurance. In particular, cowboys had to put up with hardships such as inclement weather, hostile Indians, and uncooperative cows as they drove the cattle up the trail for days at a time, stopping only to eat and sleep out under the open sky. Apart from dust storms, rainstorms, snowstorms, Indian attacks, and stampedes, however, there wasn't a whole lot going on in a cowboy's life. In fact, some historians have ventured to suggest that being a cowboy was basically pretty boring. Cows, after all, are not known for their engaging conversation.

Perhaps partly for this reason, cowboys were not considered particularly special back during the late 1800s in the days of the big cattle drives. They were ordinary schmoes who had to do hard, menial, boring work for other people. It was only later that cowboys became glamorous. In fact, there really weren't any famous cowboys during this time. And certainly no one saw cowboys as heroes. There were famous explorers, famous scouts, famous soldiers, famous outlaws, and famous lawmen, but no famous cowboys—at least no one whom most people have ever heard of.

Bringing Home the Buffalo

The first person to make the cowboy seem glamorous to the public was William Cody, better known as Buffalo Bill. Cody may have done a little cowboying in his younger days, as well as many other things, but he is best known as a showman. Prior to this, he was a scout—someone who acted as guide for military and private expeditions into Indian country in the days following the Civil War. He also hunted buffalo for the

Buffalo Bill. (Dictionary of American Portraits)

Kansas Pacific Railroad to supply the workers with meat. He contracted to bring in 12 buffalo per day for $500 dollars per month. This was good money in those days. The job paid well because it was dangerous.

Feathers in His Cap

During and after Bill's railroad years, a number of things happened that boosted his fame in the eyes of the world. One day in 1868, some cavalry officers arranged a buffalo shooting contest between Buffalo Bill and another buffalo hunter named Bill Comstock. The contest was attended by many wealthy spectators who are said to have consumed large amounts of champagne at the event. Buffalo Bill won handily with a tally of 69 buffalo to 46.

Fearless Facts

It was while working as a buffalo hunter for the Kansas Pacific Railroad that William Cody got the nickname "Buffalo Bill." In fact, this was a popular nickname, shared by at least five other rugged individuals of the Old West.

The following year, two white women were kidnapped by Cheyenne Indians, and Bill (while acting as a scout for the U.S. Army) was part of the rescue party. The women were killed, but Bill turned the situation to his advantage by claiming to have killed Tall Bull, the Cheyenne chief. This boosted his reputation with folks back East, especially since a pulp-fiction writer named Ned Buntline got hold of the story and turned it into a fictional feature for the *New York Weekly*. The story became the first part of a series called *Buffalo Bill, King of the Border Men*.

Towering Tips

If you want to be a hero, it wouldn't hurt to invent stories of your heroic exploits. If people like your stories enough, they just might believe them!

As a scout, Buffalo Bill got the opportunity to fraternize with some wealthy men who wanted to hunt buffalo for sport. One vacationing hunter who hired Buffalo Bill, along with the famous cavalry general George Custer, was the Grand Duke Alexis of Russia. All these things contributed to the growing Buffalo Bill legend. In fact, Buffalo Bill himself cultivated his image as a western hero in ways that Easterners could appreciate. He wore fancy western clothes and wore his hair long so as to look dashing and gallant. He encouraged writers like Ned Buntline to write stories about him, and even wrote stories of his own.

I'll Be Buffaloed

Here are just some of the stories Buffalo Bill told about himself. Some of them are certainly false; others are only probably not true.

➤ As a boy he rode for miles at night with a fever to warn his father of approaching killers.

➤ He killed his first Indian at the age of 11.

➤ He rode as a courier for the pony express.

➤ He stole horses from Confederate troops in the early days of the Civil War until his mother told him to stop.

➤ He woke up in the morning after a night of hard drinking, failing to remember what happened the previous night, but finding himself enlisted in the Union Army.

➤ He served in the Union Army as a spy.

➤ He obtained the rank of colonel.

➤ He killed the Indian chiefs Tall Bull and Yellow Hand.

Buffalo Bill was showy and boastful and liked to make the most of his accomplishments. He even collaborated with Buntline by starring in a stage show, *The Scouts of the Plains,* dramatizing western adventures. The show played in numerous big cities around the country, including Boston, Cincinnati, Chicago, and, of course, Buffalo. From then on, Buffalo Bill gave up the rugged life on the prairie to become a showman.

Fearless Facts

While touring with his Wild West Show, Buffalo Bill exhibited what he claimed was the scalp of Yellow Hand, an Indian chief, which he had taken himself to avenge the death of Custer.

Big Show Offs

In 1883, Buffalo Bill started up a Wild West Show, featuring Indians, animals, as well as rope, gun, and riding tricks. Touting himself as an authentic western hero reenacting his exploits, he hired Indians to stage terrifying attacks on a stage coach and a mock-up log cabin and emerged in the arena in time to save the day. Chief Sitting Bull, who previously led the Sioux against Custer at the Battle of Little Big Horn, toured with the show for a while. In addition, the show featured the first real cowboy to become a star. This was Buck Taylor, "King of the Cowboys."

Towering Tips

Don't believe everything you see on Broadway. In the Broadway musical version of the life of Annie Oakley, *Annie Get Your Gun* by Rogers and Hammerstein, Annie deliberately loses the shooting match with her future husband in order to get him to marry her. In reality, she won.

Buffalo Gal

The show's biggest star, however, was Annie Oakley, a farm girl from Ohio turned western sharpshooter. She once challenged a traveling sharpshooter to a shooting contest and won. Rather than taking his defeat badly, he married her and she became part of his act. Oakley applied to perform with Buffalo Bill's show when the previous sharpshooter—a man—suddenly quit. Buffalo Bill had reservations about hiring a woman, but she turned out not only to be a great shot but a great crowd-pleaser as well. Oakley's husband worked as her assistant; her stunts included things like shooting cigarettes out of his mouth.

The Wild West Show was such a success that Queen Victoria invited Buffalo Bill to bring the show to England. The show went on to tour all over Europe before returning

Annie Oakley. (Dictionary of American Portraits)

to play at the Chicago World's Fair before an audience of 6 million people. Buffalo Bill remained a showman almost right up until his death in 1917, despite a drinking problem and repeated financial trouble. Despite the show's phenomenal success, Buffalo Bill was able to spend or lose as much or more money than he made. He was buried in a bronze casket near the top of Lookout Mountain overlooking Denver, Colorado.

Career Moves

Ever since Buffalo Bill first popularized them, cowboys have turned into show people. Cowboys sing, act, compete in rodeo, tell jokes and stories, write poetry and homespun philosophy, and even cavort in the ring as professional wrestlers. They also advertise things, especially tobacco products, pickup trucks, beer, and blue jeans.

From Rodeo to Radio

Cowboy heroes were extremely popular during the early days of radio. Famous cowboys of the airwaves include Roy Rogers, Gene Autry, Tom

Towering Tips

If you want to tap into the legacy of the old west while hosting a meeting, party, or some other get-together, hire an old-time cowboy re-enactor to come and do rope tricks, tell stories, or lecture on cowboy history. You might be surprised at how well the old entertainments hold up!

Mix, Red Ryder, Sky King, Buck Jones, and Hopalong Cassidy. Several of these went on to get their own TV shows and some, notably Gene Autry and Roy Rogers, were singing stars as well.

In fact, singing is one of the few activities performing cowboy stars do in common with the original cowpunching cowboys. Cowboys used to sing out on cattle drives to soothe the cattle. A significant number of cowboy folk songs have been passed down, thanks partly to this practice. Among the first professional cowboy singers were Otto Gray and "the Oklahoma Cowboys" who appeared on the scene in 1923.

Fearless Facts

Roy Rogers mounted his horse, Trigger, many times during his popular TV show. After Trigger's death, he was mounted one more time—stuffed and mounted, that is! The famous horse was put on display at the Roy Rogers Museum in Apple Valley, California.

Happy Trails

The performing cowboys of the first half of the twentieth century worked conscientiously to clean up the cowboy image and make themselves good role models for kids. Cowboys like Roy Rogers cultivated a friendly, common-sense attitude, suggesting that being a cowboy was good, clean fun. Sure, they had adventures and got into scrapes with bad guys, but that didn't stop them from promoting fair play and family values.

The TV and radio cowboys were effective spokesmen for all kinds of products aimed at kids, including toys, models, watches, and so on. Tom Mix endorsed Ralston cereal, and Roy Rogers lent his name to a fast-food franchise. Their sponsors wanted to use the cowboy mystique to make their products look good and seem good for you. The idea is that cowboys are big and strong and know how to be healthy. More important, advertisers wanted to make products seem consistent with the cowboy spirit, if not exactly the cowboy way of life. No, cowboys didn't stop to eat at fast-food restaurants along the Chisolm Trail. You would think that if they did, however, they would probably stop at the one named for a cowboy rather than the one named for a clown!

Sagebrush Sagacity

A big part of the appeal of the twentieth century cowboy image is that it suggests plain, ordinary folks can be heroes. The ideal cowboy is his own boss, even though he may work for somebody else; therefore, he represents independence and individualism.

Whatever his responsibilities to others may be, the cowboy always seems free to think and act for himself—as he must, since he's dealing with the forces of nature most of the time and unpredictability goes along with his trade! And he's not intimidated by the snobbery that sometimes goes along with wealth, education, or social background.

This appeal differs from the attraction of Buffalo Bill, who presented himself as a dandy and was popular among high-society types and to ordinary schleps who admired high society. Since Buffalo Bill's day, the fashion among cowboy heroes has mostly been to wear their hair shorter and not put on airs. The twentieth century cowboy's job is not to suggest that the privileged classes can look dashing and elegant on the prairie as well as in the parlor, but to suggest that refinement is unnecessary.

This attitude lay at the center of a popular way of looking at things that replaced social snobbery with a common-sense, down-to-earth view of right and wrong. A famous and popular advocate for this practical, unassuming outlook was cowboy hero Will Rogers, a cowhand turned vaudeville performer turned homespun philosopher. Rogers spoke for the ordinary guy in a way that had even world leaders listening.

Fearless Facts

Will Rogers was unusual among public figures in that he succeeded on so many fronts. He was not only a vaudeville, radio, and movie star, but he also wrote a popular column in the papers.

Will's Ways

Will Rogers was born in 1879 of mixed white and Cherokee Indian blood. He learned fancy rope tricks from a freed slave before dropping out of high school to join a cattle drive. Despite a lack of formal education, he learned a lot through experience and talking to people. He made the famous remark, "Everybody is ignorant, only on different subjects."

He was very interested in current events and suggested that it was more important to know what was going on in the world than to become an expert on anything in particular. Another of his famous comments is "All I know is what I read in the papers." He had a friendly, unassuming manner and liked people. In fact, his most famous remark is "I never met a man I didn't like."

Eventually, he became a vaudeville performer, telling jokes and stories as well as doing rope tricks. He went on to star in movies and to write books and essays filled with his witty, common-sense observations. He saw people as basically good, but with a tendency to be corrupted by bureaucracy. In keeping with this view, he blamed war not on conflicting national interests, but on diplomats who were putting their jobs above the desires of the people. Not surprisingly, his optimistic way of looking at ordinary folks as good, fair, honest, and sensible made him extremely popular with those ordinary folks.

Will Rogers was a popular philosopher, but not a leader. He went to the White House as an honored guest, but not as an elected candidate. Even so, many politicians have since tried to imitate his affable and witty good sense. He helped give the cowboy a reputation for practical wisdom and promoted that kind of wisdom among Americans in general.

Girls Take the Reins

The cowboy appeal worked for adults as well as kids, and for women as well as men. If a cowboy can be his own man regardless of where he stands in relation to others, the cowgirl can be her own woman. All she needs are courage and independence, and maybe a pair of jeans that show her figure to advantage. At any rate, this is the idea behind cowgirl heroism as it is portrayed in popular culture through such figures as Dale Evans (Roy Rogers' co-star), Barbara Stanwyck, who played Victoria Barkley in the TV series *The Big Valley*, and Gail Davis, who starred in the TV series *Annie Oakley*.

Fearless Facts

Women were popular in rodeo throughout the early decades of the twentieth century, despite sporadic restrictions placed on female competitors by rodeo organizers. As the sport became more tightly organized, women were phased out until, in 1941, they were banned from the professional rodeo circuit altogether. The Girls Rodeo Association (now called the Women's Professional Rodeo Association) was formed in 1948 to bring women back into the sport.

Rootin' tootin' cowgirls of the comics include the fictional Buckskin Belle, K Bar Kate, and Rhoda Trail. Dale Evans also had her own comic series. In short, cowgirls do everything cowboys do, including singing, acting, modeling, advertising things, and competing in rodeos. Historically, however, the cowgirl trail wasn't an easy one to blaze. For many cowgirls at around the turn of the twentieth century, straddling a horse, rather than riding sidesaddle, was considered unfeminine and an act of defiance. To ride this way, it helped to wear pants or split skirts, thereby bucking the fashion trends that called for long skirts. Eventually, however, the cowgirl image came to be accepted as suitably clean-cut and feminine, and riding side-saddle went out of style.

Smoking Guns

Since the days of Roy Rogers and Dale Evans, cowboys have tended to downplay their cheerful, happy-camper spirit to tap into the hard, no-nonsense aspect of their image. Less friendly and more macho, cowboys in spaghetti westerns and cigarette ads are strong, silent types who seem to make their own rules and don't seem to care what anybody thinks of them. They are often alone and at odds with the rest of society, but this is because they prefer to live life on their own terms rather than compromise with others.

This macho cowboy image has been irresistible, especially to adolescent boys and young men who are uncertain of their place in society—or else certain they will end up no place in particular. As a result, this image has been incredibly effective at selling tobacco products. As an advertising strategy, the cowboy creates an association between tobacco use and the freedom, autonomy and vigor of the cowboy lifestyle. The strategy has roped in young smokers quicker than a cowhand can rope cattle.

Of course, we now know that tobacco is addictive and causes cancer. Sadly, this knowledge has been withheld and distorted for the sake of the tobacco industry. Tobacco has long been associated with the cowboy lifestyle and the cowboy image and many cowboy-types have ended their careers and their lives battling cancer. Here's a list of some famous cowboy models, actors, and singers whose deaths were hastened by tobacco.

Fearless Facts

Perhaps not surprisingly, the models who represented the Marlboro man in advertising lost their lives to tobacco-related illness. Lilo McLean, widow of Marlboro man David McLean, has sued tobacco company R. J. Reynolds for the wrongful death of her late husband.

➤ **David McLean**   Marlboro man of TV commercials of the 1960s who died of lung cancer at the age of 73 in 1995.

➤ **Wayne McLaren**   Marlboro man of billboard and magazine ads who died of lung cancer at in 1992. He was 51 years old at the time of his death.

Towering Tips

Don't be roped into smoking by cowboy imagery (or any other kind of imagery). Smoking is neither inherently macho nor inherently feminine, but can be made to seem that way through advertising. In fact, Marlboro cigarettes were originally aimed not at macho men, but at women. During the 1920s, their slogan was "Mild as May."

➤ **David Millar**   Early Marlboro man who died of emphysema.

➤ **Michael Landon**   Star of the hit cowboy series *Bonanza* (1959–1973) who died of pancreas and liver cancer in 1991.

➤ **Doug McLure**   Star of the hit cowboy series *The Virginian* (1962–1970).

➤ **Chuck Connors**   Star of *The Riflemen* who died of lung cancer.

➤ **John Wayne**   Hollywood icon who died of complications from lung cancer and heart disease at age 72 in 1979.

➤ **Ernest Tubb**   "The Texas Troubador" who died of emphysema at age 70 in 1984.

➤ **Tex Williams**   Country-western singer who died of lung cancer in 1985.

A special cowgirl hero is Amanda Blake, who played Miss Kitty on the hit series *Gunsmoke*. After smoking two packs of cigarettes a day for many years, she developed a malignant tumor on her tongue at age 48. After the tumor was removed, she had to learn to talk all over again. She overcame the challenge of speaking in order to campaign for the American Cancer Society, which awarded her their Courage Award in 1984. She died five years later of throat cancer at age 60.

The Least You Need to Know

➤ "Real" cowboys of the post–Civil War era drove half-wild cattle north out of Texas. The cattle descended from stock brought to America by the Spanish.

➤ Buffalo Bill was a showman who glorified and exaggerated his accomplishments as a buffalo hunter, scout, and Indian fighter. Annie Oakley was a sharpshooter who starred in Buffalo Bill's Wild West Show.

➤ Cowboy heroes of the first half of the twentieth century such as Will Rogers, Roy Rogers, and Dale Evans set an upbeat, clean-cut example.

➤ Three models hired to portray the Marlboro man died of tobacco-related illnesses.

Larger-Than-Life Lovers

The heroic lover is an archetype—an ideal that affirms the importance of love above all other things, including wealth, society, and even life itself. Because heroic lovers often see love as more important than life, they are often tragic heroes. Romeo and Juliet chose to die rather than live apart. Cyrano de Bergerac (who had an heroically prodigious proboscis—in other words, a big nose) chose to conceal his love for Roxanne throughout his lifetime because he believed she couldn't possibly love him back.

Heroism in love is not always sad; it may be comic or adventurous instead. Love can kill you, but it can also make you laugh and take you to new heights. Casanova went from lover to lover, ennobling their lives as well as his own. Mozart's Don Giovanni exhibited an almost noble independence in his dedication to the wooing of women. The fictional character Tom Jones from the novel by Henry Fielding also underwent many amorous exploits while inviting us to laugh at him and at his society.

Heroic Shorts

Perhaps the most legendary of American Latin-lovers is Rudolph Valentino (1895–1926), the famous idol of silent films. He started off his career as a dancer in cafes before taking bit parts in plays and movies while living as a playboy. His lifestyle helped him get exotic starring roles in major films, most notably *The Sheik* (1921) in which he plays an Arabian chief who falls in love with an Englishwoman. Valentino became legendary as "sheik" and "sheba" became popular expressions for lovers. Other famous films in which he smolders on the silent screen are *Blood and Sand* (1922), in which he plays a bullfighter, and *The Four Horseman of the Apocalypse* (1921), which first made him famous.

Love has been a predominant theme in the stories and legends of the world for about as long as stories and legends have been around. Ancient mythology, chivalric romance, and modern novels are full of heroic lovers. Perhaps not surprisingly, it's often difficult to find these ideal types in real life, especially in America where people tend to keep busy doing other things. There are, however, some notable real-life American variations on the theme.

Love Lost

For better or for worse, Americans are not generally known as great lovers. The really famous heroic lovers tend to be European: Camille was French; Don Juan, Spanish; Casanova, Italian. Americans go in for a pragmatic, no-nonsense approach to life that usually precludes the idea that heroism in the arena of love is a virtuous pursuit. This is not to say that Americans haven't gone to heroic lengths for the sake of love, but they have tended to see love as a practical problem to be worked out together with other priorities rather than as a romantic ideal to be exalted above all others. Perhaps our democratic roots haven't afforded us the kind of leisure and dedication to pleasure that these other heroic lovers have cultivated.

On the Side

Traditionally, most Americans have focused their energies in other directions. Things such as opening up the frontier, conducting business, developing new technology, and fighting for civil rights have tended to occupy the heroic spirits and capture the ennobled imaginations of this country more than great and beautiful lovemaking. Those great Americans who have concerned themselves deeply with love have not generally been lovers for love's sake, but have worked to make lovemaking more convenient and practical. A look at a few historical highlights reveals some heroic figures, but shows how Americans have tended to focus on the practical aspects of love and sex.

➤ The Puritans who came over on the *Mayflower* believed deeply in loving God, but were not great believers in the value of human sexual love. In fact, they sometimes went to heroic lengths to make sure that people didn't get too carried away with love. Many Puritans believed sex should be strictly for procreation.

Fearless Facts

History records two famous cases of bestiality that took place in the early Puritan colonies. Bestiality was considered a heinous offense and the guilty men were executed after being made to witness the death of the animals they had copulated with. In one instance, a whole menagerie was slaughtered: a horse, a cow, two calves, two goats, five sheep, and a turkey!

➤ No doubt there was something heroic about the boomtown pioneers who advertised for mail-order brides and the women who answered those ads, knowing that settling the frontier also meant settling for whatever they could get in the way of a love match. It was a real sellers' market in those days! This sort of heroism hasn't really set anyone apart in the annals of history, though. Who wants to remember the person who put up with the ugliest or most bad-smelling partner for the sake of posterity and companionship?

➤ There have been heroic experiments in love and sex undertaken by a variety of American utopian communities. A range of alternative approaches includes the celibacy of the Shakers, who discouraged even marital sex, and the open sexuality of the Free Lovers. These experiments, however, did not involve heroic lovers so much as heroic attempts to deal with the problem of sexual desire in new ways.

How It's Done

Many heroic Americans have left a permanent mark on American sexuality, but you probably wouldn't think of them as heroic lovers. They made a name for themselves in ways that show something of the unique sexual character of America: progressive, practical, and eyes wide open.

➤ Radical activist Margaret Sanger promoted birth control during the 1920s and fought to legalize contraception. She saw that reproductive rights would enable women and men much greater control over their lives. This far-left radical idea has since

Towering Tips

Don't allow your personal style to be limited by old stereotypes like the one that says Americans are the best inventors, Italians are the best lovers, French are the best cooks, Germans are the best mechanics, and Britons have the best manners. Many Americans are great lovers and lousy inventors!

become accepted by the mainstream. But although she went down in history as a modern hero, her own love life was unremarkable; so she hardly qualifies as a heroic lover.

➤ Inventor Henry Ford opened up the world of sexuality to young people who were old enough to borrow the family car. In pioneering the automobile in America, Ford also pioneered running out of gas and the back seat, thus providing a portable nesting ground for generations of young lovers. But because Ford's real interest was driving down the highway rather than flying someone special to the moon, you certainly wouldn't call him a heroic lover.

➤ Sex researchers Alfred Kinsey, William Masters and Virginia Johnson, and Shere Hite opened America's eyes to sexuality on a whole new scale. They provided the vital statistics on sexual behavior in America that Americans were dying to know and also revolutionized the way we understand sexuality—especially with regard to homosexuality and women's orgasms. But since these are professional researchers who did not get personally involved with their test subjects, you wouldn't call them heroic lovers—at least, not unless you have a thing for people wearing lab coats!

Towering Tips

If you have a cause that is vitally important to you that others regard as crazy, dangerous, or just plain wrong, you might consider eliminating any other radical or eccentric beliefs from your life in order to show people how solid and sensible you are. Others will then be more inclined to take your cause seriously. In fact, this is what Margaret Sanger did with birth control. She started out with many radical views, including socialism. After she became convinced of the importance of birth control, she backed away from socialism in an effort to encourage non-socialists to accept her views on contraception.

It Takes All Kinds

Where love and America are concerned, the predominant theme is "different strokes for different folks." The people and ideals some folks admire are precisely what other see as reprehensible. There have been many different groups who care deeply about the political significance of sexuality, and each of these groups has its own heroes who are reviled by other groups.

New Wrinkles

A number of public figures in the 1960s helped bring about a wide-ranging sexual revolution. These figures can be considered heroes insofar as many Americans have admired them, believed in what they stood for, and sought to emulate their lifestyles. The "sexual revolution" generally focused less on love relationships per se than on the political attitudes that influence them.

➤ Radical feminists of the 1960s such as Kate Millet argued that sexuality is deeply political and warned that conventional sexual relationships of the time failed to recognize the rights of women. Her book, *Sexual Politics,* became a groundbreaking bestseller.

➤ Gay and lesbian activists such as Frank Kamany and Barbara Gittings fought for gay and lesbian civil rights, arguing that homosexuality should not be regarded as a crime, a psychological problem, or a sin.

Fearless Facts

For many years, gay nightclubs were routinely raided by police and gay patrons arrested. Gay rights made it into the national spotlight in 1969, when violence erupted during a raid on a gay bar in Manhattan's Greenwich Village. Patrons resisted arrest, onlookers threw rocks, and someone set fire to the bar. A riot ensued that continued sporadically for days. Soon afterward, New York gays and lesbians organized the Gay Liberation Front.

➤ Publishing stars Hugh Hefner, who started *Playboy* magazine, and Helen Gurley Brown, of *Cosmopolitan* magazine and author of *Sex and the Single Girl,* championed promiscuous sex and helped perpetuate a revolution in sexual attitudes that was also fueled by the countercultural movement of the 1960s.

Back to the Drawing Board

In the wake of the sexual revolution came a right-wing moralist backlash in the 1970s and 1980s, led by some high-profile conservatives that became heroes in the name of traditional family values. These so-called moral majority leaders denounced what they saw as the moral decay of the nation, and blamed it on liberals and liberal sexuality. Sexual equality, homosexuality, abortion, and pornography were the main evils they targeted, and they succeeded in curbing legislation in support of these things.

➤ Anita Bryant, a former Miss Oklahoma, professional singer, and spokeswoman for Minute Maid orange juice led a campaign to squelch gay rights in Florida. The campaign attracted national attention and fueled gay opposition in other states. On the flip side, she galvanized gay rights sympathizers into concerted political action in response.

➤ Jerry Falwell, a Baptist preacher and televangelist, spearheaded the moral majority movement and helped raise millions of dollars for right-wing political efforts.

➤ Attorney General Edwin Meese launched a commission on pornography that attempted to show that porn inflicts severe damage on the fabric of American society.

Days Gone By

Certainly there has always been plenty of star-spangled sex, sex breakthroughs, sex scandals, sex policing, and sex salesmanship. In all this fervor, a recognition of the importance of the interpersonal bond formed in a love relationship often gets lost. Even so, many of the expectations we have for the public figures involved in these sexy doings stem from—and depart from—attitudes nourished long ago by legends of love handed down since before the days of TV and radio—legends that focus on the importance of the bond between two people.

Fearless Facts

Since the sexual revolution, lesbian and gay rights activists have largely retreated from the idea that there is something inherently wrong and oppressive about a long-standing, monogamous, heterosexual union. Similarly, fewer single people, whether straight or gay, see promiscuous sex as more healthy and liberating than monogamy. Whatever their sexual orientation, more people agree that a strong bond between two people is important.

Colonial Coupling

The line of legendary lover-heroes in America goes back to John Smith and Pocahontas. Their love was probably only legendary and nothing more, because many historians doubt Captain Smith's story of his dramatic rescue by Pocahontas and Smith did not say the two were lovers. That idea got started later. Another love legend set in early colonial times is the story of Captain Miles Standish of the Plymouth colony. He loved the fair maid Priscilla, but didn't want to court her in person himself. He made the mistake of asking the young John Alden to woo Priscilla in his place. The two fell in love, and the older Captain Standish was out of luck.

Although Captain Standish was a real person (he was nicknamed "Shrimp Standish," possibly because he was not very tall and had a pinkish complexion), his love story was the invention of poet Henry Wadsworth Longfellow. Part of Longfellow's point was to represent Puritan sexual morality in a negative light. Longfellow suggests that

Standish, like the Puritans in general, was too strict and proper for his own good and should have been warmer and more personal in his pursuit of Priscilla.

All or Nothing

In addition to inventing the legend of Captain Miles Standish and Priscilla, Longfellow also retold the old story of another legendary lover named Evangeline. Evangeline was the young daughter of a wealthy farmer in the French colony of Acadia (now Nova Scotia). She agreed to marry the blacksmith's son, young Gabriel. Unfortunately for them, right after their engagement, the whole colony was broken up by order of King George II of England, who had taken over the territory from the French. The colonists' land and property were confiscated and they were dispersed.

Evangeline and Gabriel were separated, but the noble Evangeline never forgot her promise to her betrothed. She spent many years searching all over the country, but never found him. Still, she never married or loved anyone else. Finally, an old woman, she abandoned her search, moved to Pennsylvania, and became a nun.

At that time, a plague broke out, and Evangeline took on the job of tending to the sick. One day, she went to the almshouse and found a poor beggar who was dying of the plague. The old man turned out to be Gabriel. She was glad to find him, but it was too late for the pair to live happily ever after. Gabriel died before he was able to muster the strength to say her name. This unfortunate turn of events didn't weaken Evangeline's resolve a bit. She lay down in the grave beside her intended.

Fearless Facts

A number of steep, scenic overlooks in the world have the name "Lover's Leap," implying that some disappointed lover once took his or her life by jumping over the edge. There are at least two Lover's Leaps with verifiable historical significance (or at least, verifiably appropriate names) in the United States and one in Jamaica. The original Lover's Leap is in on the island of Leucas in the Ionion Sea, where the ancient Greek poet Sappho is said to have taken her life in despair over the love of a young boatman named Phaon.

Same Old Song and Dance

If we take Evangeline as a model of heroic love, it's easy to see why there aren't too many heroic lovers in America: Their love is unrequited, and they die early. She remained true to her promise all her life, but she wasn't very practical, and didn't have

Worthy Words

Antiheroes are admirable in spite of their blatant misdeeds and short-comings. Of course, since different shortcomings are tolerated more or less by different people at different times, there is often only a blurry distinction between hero and antihero and between antihero and villain.

much fun. In fact, a big part of the reason she has been looked to as a heroine is because of an old-fashioned mania for female purity and fidelity. Back in Longfellow's day, women were expected to be irrationally devoted to their men, regardless of the circumstances.

Stories like *Evangeline* suggest that women who remain true to their men no matter what are virtuous and those who don't are bad. Variations on this theme can be found in many old songs and stories about sailors or soldiers who leave their wives or sweethearts and return years later. Typically, the man pretends to be somebody else and tries to make time with the woman. The woman says she must remain true to her man, even if he's dead or has married somebody else. That's the sign that she's a really good woman and the cue for the man to reveal his identity and claim her as his own.

On Shaky Ground

Traditionally, there's a double standard at work in the whole business of heroic love. Women are heroes if they are especially devoted to their men. This goes all the way back to the very earliest Greek poetry: Homer's *Odyssey,* in which Odysseus' wife Penelope lies to a whole group of very pushy suitors for 20 years so that she wouldn't have to compromise her fidelity. Traditions change, of course, and this sort of heroism doesn't go over as well as it used to. And even back in the old days, there were alternatives, although these alternative heroes were also cautionary examples to avoid.

Under the Gun

These negative examples were the *antiheroes* of the old murder ballads popular before the days of radio. (Antiheroes are people we admire in spite of their unsavory actions or qualities.) Rather than die for their true loves, these horrible heroes made their true loves die for them. Clearly this is a terrible thing, but for many people it isn't that hard to understand—and maybe even relate to—someone so in love and so angry and frustrated they resort to murder. Murderous lovers tend to hold a fascination that wavers between horror and admiration.

One of the most famous and distinctively American legendary love stories is Frankie, whose man, Johnny, "done her wrong" in the murder ballad, "Frankie and Johnny." Not only was Johnny generally not very nice or respectful of Frankie, he also took her money and spent it on other women (in particular, on that slinky Nellie Bly). Frankie fixed Johnny by plugging him with a Colt 44. She was arrested, found guilty of murder, and executed. Being put to death didn't bother her as much as the pain she suffered at seeing Johnny cheat on her and then seeing him dead after she shot him.

The Good with the Bad

You can look at Frankie as a fiend for killing a man and as a fool for loving such a heel, but there's a strangely heroic quality to her love since it drove her to take such extreme, forceful action in response to the situation. This complex mix of feelings you get from the story is what gives murder ballads their appeal. And there was a slew of them, all recounting tender but gruesome tragedies.

Of course, whether you look at a love crime as heroic depends partly on how badly you've been hurt yourself. If your man has done you wrong, you may well be inclined to look up to Frankie. What's more, different sides in a war have different sets of heroes, and this is true of the war between the sexes.

People feel a similar fascination toward some of the love crimes that make front-page news in our own day. Lorena Bobbitt won the admiration of many Americans for cutting off her husband's penis in 1993 in retaliation for his abusive behavior. She is a bizarre kind of hero and admiration for her was deeply mixed with both shock and amusement. The story may be amusing because it expresses in extreme form something of the sexual conflicts many Americans have experienced in one way or another. As a result, just about everyone was fascinated by the whole thing. Someone even published on the Internet a humorous song about the Bobbits to be sung to the tune of "The Beverly Hillbillies!"

> **Towering Tips**
>
> Keep in mind, sexual politics being what they are, one person's hero is often another person's snake. This was true in the case of the popular woman buddy-movie *Thelma and Louise,* in which the friends lash out heroically against male oppression. Shortly after seeing the film, a man with a two-headed snake named his bifurcated pet Thelma and Louise!

American Dream

Of course, love can be stormy, passionate, and even a little dangerous without involving death or dismemberment. This is the kind of love romance novels and soap operas are made of—good clean passionate fun with endless fascination for a country that, for the most part, doesn't have much time or energy for prolonged sexual adventures, but has plenty of interest in fantasizing about them. And, of course, the best fantasies are the ones that are true. That's why one of America's greatest love heroes is someone who has lived a fantastic, soap opera–style life, complete with heartbreak, jealousy, passion, romance, and decades of tabloid attention.

Heroic Shorts

It's become a common practice among celebrities to go through numerous lovers over the course of their careers. Admirable exceptions are Paul Newman (1925–) and Joanne Woodward (1930–) who have remained together through decades of movie-making success. The two actors met in 1952 as little-known members of the cast of the Broadway show *Picnic.* Soon they became stars before getting married in 1958. The same year, Joanne Woodward earned an Oscar for her starring performance in *The Three Faces of Eve,* while Paul Newman starred in the highly successful *Cat on a Hot Tin Roof* with Elizabeth Taylor. Since then, Newman and Woodward have appeared together in 11 films. Newman has also directed 5 movies starring Woodward, including *Rachel Rachel* (1968), for which Woodward received an Oscar nomination. In addition to acting, both have done a great deal of work for charity. Newman started making *Newman's Own* salad dressing in 1982, donating all the profits to a variety of causes.

Always On

Of all of America's glamor queens, Elizabeth Taylor has had the longest and most eventful reign. While she's been a beautiful and spell-binding actress, she has also attracted rapt audiences for her doings off the screen. As Hollywood goddesses go, she is surprisingly human and three-dimensional, yet continuously larger than life. She's been married eight times to seven husbands—and of course, that's just the marriages!

Along with this hectic love life has gone some of the usual joys (four children) and some unusual sorrows (numerous bouts of addiction to sleeping pills, pain killers, and alcohol), and health problems including surgery for a brain tumor. On top of all this, she started up her own line of perfume and her own foundation for AIDS research. Her doings are reported in the tabloids so often that it's no wonder she seems to many Americans like a famous member of the family.

Imitating Art

Part of the attraction for Liz Taylor has to do with the way her private life and acting career have been strangely intertwined. She set herself apart from the run-of-the-mill Hollywood starlets for good by seducing pop singer Eddie Fisher, who was married at the time to the spunky actress Debbie Reynolds. Having established herself as a bona fide major league femme fatal, she was a shoe-in for the title role in the epic spectacle film *Cleopatra* (1963). With this, she became the first person to earn a million dollars for acting in a single film.

Fearless Facts

Much of the inspiration behind the film *Cleopatra* came from the idea that Liz Taylor and the historical Cleopatra had a lot in common: most notably wealth, exotic beauty, and the ability to treat love as a dangerous sport. Sadly, the film didn't measure up to its provocative potential in the minds of most critics, who found it dull and pretentious.

Cleopatra spelled the end of Liz's marriage with Eddie Fisher and the beginning of a torrid relationship with the film's Marc Antony, Wales-born actor Richard Burton. The co-stars married, got divorced, married, and divorced again. Meanwhile, the pair starred together in Taylor's best film, *Who's Afraid of Virginia Woolf* (1966), as a couple entangled in a sinister and spiteful co-dependency.

In addition to her heroic feats of psychosexual interaction on and off the screen, Taylor has been decorated for heroism in other ways. She was awarded two Oscars (one for *Who's Afraid. . .* and another for *Butterfield 8*), was inducted into the French Legion of Honor, received the Jean Hersholt Humanity award for AIDS activism, and also received the American Film Institute award for lifetime achievement.

Staying Power

Clearly heroic American lovers are a breed apart. Still, you wouldn't exactly say they have succeeded in making love seem particularly worthwhile. There's so much fighting and falling out that this chapter could just as well fit into the section of war heroes! Yet not all the battles in the American love wars are bitter ones. Many American couples have spent the better part of a lifetime together and wouldn't want things any other way.

A particularly noble and uplifting example of the strength of the bond between two people is the true story of Isidor and Ida Straus, a nice Jewish couple who were vacationing in Europe back in 1914. They had a rich, full, hard-working life together (Isidor was one of the founders of Macy's Department Store in New York City), but it was about to come to an end after 40 years of marriage. For their return trip, they booked first class passage on board the *Titanic*.

As the ship started to sink after its hull was torn open by an iceberg, the first class passengers made for the lifeboats. First Ida stepped into a boat, and then Isidor started to get in beside her, but was prevented by the officer in charge who was enforcing the "women and children first" rule of abandoning ship. Seeing that Isidor was an elderly gentleman who would have little chance of fending for himself on a sinking ship,

Towering Tips

Look for a reenactment of the final moments of Isidor and Ida Straus in the 1958 Titanic film *A Night to Remember.* Their story got left out of the recent blockbuster *Titanic,* so that it wouldn't overshadow the young lovers.

some of the passengers objected and said he should be let on the lifeboat. But Isidor said no, he would not get in a boat if other men weren't allowed to go. At that, Ida gave up her seat on the lifeboat, choosing to stay with Isidor on the doomed ship.

They died together, along with about 1,500 other passengers. A plaque above an entrance to Macy's and a park on Broadway and 107th Street memorialize the couple.

The Least You Need to Know

➤ Americans are not generally known for being great lovers.

➤ Puritans and other religious groups, pioneers, politicians, and sex researchers in America have tended to focus on the practical aspects of sex rather than on romantic bonding.

➤ The sexual revolution of the 1960s brought with it an awareness that sexuality is political. In the process, a sense of the importance of personal bonds often got lost.

➤ Because sexual politics is such a hotly contested subject, it can be impossible to tell the difference between heroic, antiheroic, and villainous lovers.

Chapter 8

American Know-How

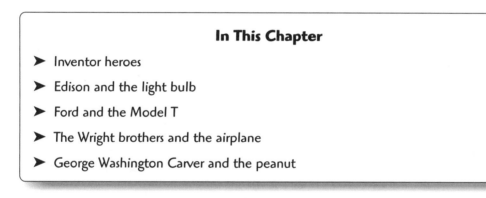

In This Chapter

➤ Inventor heroes

➤ Edison and the light bulb

➤ Ford and the Model T

➤ The Wright brothers and the airplane

➤ George Washington Carver and the peanut

In America, you can be an ordinary schmoe like a farmer or a bicycle mechanic with not much formal education and still become a rich and famous hero. All you need is loads of determination and inventive genius. At least that's how it was for a handful of gifted souls around the turn of the twentieth century when the industrial revolution was at its height.

Americans are especially proud of their inventors. We have a lot of them and they have taken us a long way. The pride is not simply due to who they are and what they've accomplished, but to what they stand for and what they say about American attitudes. Americans have a reputation for being hardworking, practical, and resourceful. As a result, we can figure out how to accomplish big things. This attitude stands behind the American inventor heroes of the turn of the twentieth century.

A number of big inventions are closely associated with the American way of life, partly because they have had such a profound influence on everyone's lifestyle. The light-bulb, the gas engine, and the airplane, to name a few, all arise out of, and contribute

Towering Tips

Don't let it get to you when people laugh at your ambitions. Remember the old cliche: They laughed at Edison! They laughed at the Wright Brothers!

to, a way of living that stresses movement, efficiency, production, and convenience. The desire for these things inspires the inventions, and the inventions make whole new levels of movement, efficiency, and production possible, which in turn inspire a new set of inventions.

For some, this is a vicious cycle that results in the American rat race. For others, however, it's a recipe for opportunity, enabling everyone to get in on the action of working and expanding. Americans invent, make the inventions, and earn the money to buy the inventions—transforming their lifestyles and creating the need for new inventions. This way of doing things has not only made America what it is, it has transformed the world.

Making Things Tick

Thomas Alva Edison (1847–1931) is the biggest inventor hero of a country, with many inventions to his credit. Everyone knows that he invented the electric lightbulb, but he also had scads of other inventions. In fact, he took out patents for about 1,000 of them. An early invention (1869) was the electric stock ticker, a machine that could transmit stock prices with almost no time delay. Naturally this item appealed to investors; J. P. Morgan snatched the gadget up.

Towering Tips

Notice that the lightbulb is not only one of the most important American inventions by one of the most important American inventors, but also a widely recognized symbol for "the bright idea." When we talk about "a lightbulb coming on in someone's head," we are referring to the sort of inventiveness that Edison stands for.

Edison sold many of his other inventions as well and used the money to open a big workshop with lots of assistants. In effect, he started his own invention factory. He didn't always make money, but he seemed not to worry too much about that. He was unusual in that regard and in being totally absorbed in his work. He claims to have slept only about four hours per night so that he could have as much time as possible to invent things.

A Bright Idea

He is widely regarded as a genius. In fact, he's the one who said that "genius is 1 percent inspiration and 99 percent perspiration." This formula provides a pretty apt explanation of how he invented the electric light. He figured out the basics: a glass bulb with a vacuum inside and a filament made of stuff that would burn

Thomas Edison. (Rutgers University Special Collections and Archives)

for a really long time while charged with electricity. The only problem was finding the stuff that would burn a really long time. He spent days testing fibers in search of the right material.

A Sound Concept

Edison is said to have invented the phonograph by handing a sketch to an assistant and asking him to build the contraption represented by the drawing. The assistant built the thing without even knowing what it did. When it was finished, he brought it to Edison.

99

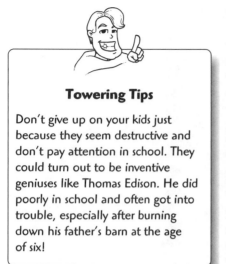

Towering Tips

Don't give up on your kids just because they seem destructive and don't pay attention in school. They could turn out to be inventive geniuses like Thomas Edison. He did poorly in school and often got into trouble, especially after burning down his father's barn at the age of six!

For "recording," the phonograph had a tube for speaking into attached to a rubber diaphragm, which was in turn attached to a needle that could be pressed onto a cylinder wrapped in tinfoil. Speaking into the tube while rotating the cylinder by turning a crank caused the needle to vibrate as it etched into the tinfoil. To replay the recording, you simply placed the needle back into the groove that had been etched out while recording. Turning the crank made the needle vibrate, which made the speaking tube resonate, reproducing the recorded sound.

When the assistant brought Edison the phonograph machine, the inventor tried out the new invention, making the first sound-recorded message. He took the opportunity on that auspicious occasion to utter these undying words: "Mary had a little lamb, its fleece was white as snow!" (Obviously times had changed since Samuel F. B. Morse sent the first telegraph message quoting a passage from the Bible on "what God hath wrought.")

Early Signals

Edison had his own particular style: grungy. Of all American heroes, Edison was probably the biggest slob. He couldn't care less about his appearance. He was too busy thinking about all the things he was going to invent. This shows something of how committed he was to his work.

Edison started out his working life at age 12 when he got a job selling newspapers on a train, the Grand Trunk Railroad. Selling papers wasn't enough to keep him busy, however, so he started up his own paper for the train workers in one of the empty cars, the *Grand Trunk Herald*. In addition, he started up a chemistry lab in one of the other cars. Unfortunately, a stick of phosphorus fell to the floor as the train was rattling around. It ignited and set the car on fire. And speaking of fire, that's what they did to young Edison as a result!

Edison went on to teach himself Morse code and got a job as a telegraph worker. One day when the telegraph wires were damaged and couldn't be repaired because of the weather, he came up with the idea of sending messages to the next town by blasting out Morse code signals on a train steam whistle. It took a while for people to realize why someone kept tooting a train whistle, but someone eventually recognized the dots and dashes of the code and the messages were received.

Fearless Facts

Edison nicknamed his two children Marion and Tom "Dot" and "Dash" after Morse code signals.

Big Plans

Critics of Edison have suggested his fame is due largely to his skill in business rather than simply to his inventiveness. They point out that he took out patents for a number of inventions that were developed by other people. It seems clear, though, that he was not especially motivated by greed, but in an interest in useful things in general. He started large workshops and employed dozens of workers to develop ideas. To some extent, he has taken credit for work done by others, but he also helped create an atmosphere where people could work together.

In fact, they say Edison never liked saving money. Even in his younger days, he would spend money quickly on things like books or experimental materials. Inventing, then, was not something he did up on cloud nine somewhere, isolated from the reality of other people, but something that related to a whole way of life focusing on material things, practical improvements, hard work, and free spending. This way of life, of course, has a distinctly American flavor, and goes a long way toward accounting for Edison's popularity.

Driving Ambition

Invention and business go together in the life of Edison, and even more so in the life Henry Ford, whose genius lay not only in inventing, but in making his invention practical and affordable. In fact, he is not credited with inventing the automobile as many assume. What he did was to develop the gasoline-driven car and figure out how to build it economically through mass production.

Finding the Road

Ford grew up on a farm in Michigan, where he quickly came to appreciate machinery for its ability to make farm labor less physically difficult. He was well into his twenties, however, by the time he decided he wanted to design a horseless carriage. At first he tried steam power, which was then being used successfully to drive ships, boats, and turbines for industrial uses. After a number of failed attempts, he found that a steam engine wasn't practical, because it was too heavy and required too much heavy fuel.

Henry Ford. (Dictionary of American Portraits)

Fearless Facts

Ford did not intend for cars to be used as farm machinery, but they turned out to be a convenient source of power during their early days. Farmers sometimes attached one of the rear wheels of the Model T to hand-operated farm machinery, such as threshers and mills, to speed up the work.

Through his reading, he learned about the recently developed gasoline engine and figured this was what would work to drive a car. At the time he was working on his farm, and, when he had time, working as a mechanic and clock repairman. After reading about the gas engine, he moved with his wife to Detroit where he bought one for himself and began work on designing a car. He took a job as chief engineer in the Edison plant in Detroit and worked on his car during off-hours. At one point, he told Edison about his plans. Even though Edison was more involved with electricity than gas, he liked the idea.

Back to the Drawing Board

Ford wasn't the only inventor interested in making an automobile. Other Americans, and Europeans too, had been working on them. Everything they came up with was experimental and, for the most part, auto inventors were happy leaving their inventions at the experimental stage. They were amusing contraptions that ran for a little while and quickly broke down. Some had gas engines, some had electric motors, and most were steam driven. To take the automobile to the next level—to improve it for public use—would require a considerable investment in time and money. Few people at the time thought automobiles were worth it. Cars were just hobbies for a few eccentric people who liked machines.

Ford wasn't interested in cars just as a hobby, but wanted to make them and sell them. He got together with a group of investors to form the Detroit Automobile Company. Ford was part owner as well as chief engineer. The company disbanded, however, as backers began to doubt their prospects, leaving Ford to continue experimenting.

He also found a way to attract investors. He decided to try to drum up interest in his car by organizing a race between his model and another inventor's. Ford's car won. He then built an even faster car and challenged another car-builder to take him on. Ford's car ran on four cylinders with 80 horsepower. He hired a bicyclist to drive it for him. The race wasn't even close. Immediately afterward, Ford started up the Ford Motor Company.

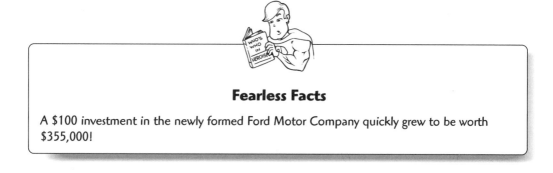

Fearless Facts

A $100 investment in the newly formed Ford Motor Company quickly grew to be worth $355,000!

Affordable Fords

Sales were slow starting out. The first cars cost about $1,000 each, so only rich people could afford them. Ford decided to try to increase sales by reducing the price as much as possible, and the company started making cars that sold between $600 and $750. Sales improved, encouraging Ford to attempt to cut costs still further. To do this, he decided to build just one model and to mass produce the cars. In 1908 he began to develop the famous Model T and began also to develop a system for turning out the car in large quantities. By 1916 he managed to bring the price down to $360. That year he made more than 730,000 Model Ts, or "Tin Lizzies" as they were nicknamed.

Demand for the car increased, enabling Ford to build them in even greater quantity at even less cost per car. Meanwhile, he started paying his employees a minimum wage of $5 per day, an unprecedented practice that helped compensate workers for the monotony of working on the assembly line. He also limited the work day to eight hours and introduced profit sharing. News of the policy made the front pages of papers around the country and Ford became a hero of the working class. It also didn't hurt Ford's reputation that his Model T spurred commerce and construction by making everyone more mobile and creating a need for better roads and highways. Ford's popularity was even eclipsing Edison's. After all, it's easy to feel you have a personal relationship with your car. Lightbulbs, on the other hand, just don't have much personality.

Ford's employment policy wasn't motivated purely by benevolence. He needed to do something to attract workers, because there was an extremely high turnover rate at his factory. The work was so repetitive that few people could stand to do it for long unless they could feel really good about their compensation. This philosophy of the workplace has been standard in corporate America for decades: Make workers specialize so as to be maximally productive and pay them enough so they'll put up with the tedium of their jobs.

Although Ford was willing to pay high wages, he resisted workers' efforts to join the CIO (Congress of Industrial Organizations). At first, employees who tried to unionize were fired. When this became illegal, they were sometimes brutalized—not necessarily according to Ford's orders, but in keeping with his desire to keep unions out. He wanted as much control as possible over labor decisions and acquiesced to unionization only gradually and reluctantly.

Fearless Facts

Ford cars sold so well that the company continued manufacturing straight through the Depression. Jobs in one of Ford's factories were so highly in demand that dozens of unemployed workers stormed the gates. They were resisted with fire hoses.

Wrong Turns

Ford was widely revered for his accomplishments, his policies, his power, and his wealth. To many, he seemed like a magical figure who could do anything. Certainly, his cars and his methods of producing them continuously in huge quantities had a tremendous influence on the American way of life. He also attempted to use his power and prestige to influence society in more direct ways. His deliberate attempts to bring about social change, however, were generally unsuccessful and sometimes misguided.

Ford's talents definitely lay in inventing rather than in social activism. Here are some examples of Ford's attempts to tinker "under the hood" of society:

➤ He launched a failed crusade against cigarettes for which he was accused of arrogance.

➤ He sponsored a "Peace Ship," which sailed on a diplomatic mission to Europe in a quixotic attempt to end World War I. The mission turned out to be dead in the water, and Ford booked separate passage back home to the States.

➤ He started his own magazine, *The Dearborn Independent,* and endorsed an alarmist anti-Semitic article that claimed that Jews were conspiring to take control of the world. Seven years went by before he was called to account, at which point he issued a retraction and apology. The incident gave rise to a myth that Hitler kept a picture of Ford on his desk.

➤ He offered to buy the Tennessee Valley Power Plant from the federal government, implying that he would revitalize the region economically. The government turned him down.

➤ He appeared as a witness in a libel suit and gave testimony that revealed a surprising ignorance of history. He excused his ignorance with the infamous remark: "History is bunk!"

➤ He made no effort to squelch a short-lived grass-roots movement to make him President of the United States, despite his ignorance of history, law, and government. He looked on with satisfaction as "Ford for President" clubs sprang up around the country.

A Flight Of Genius

People had always thought about flying (including, for example, Leonardo da Vinci, who designed flying machines he never tried out). And there have been many attempts at human flight—enough so that the prevailing scientific opinion at the time of the Wright Brothers' flight at Kitty Hawk was that it was impossible. In fact, doing the impossible is almost a sure-fire way to get to be a hero—or, at least famous.

The Wright brothers were not only inventor heroes, they discovered a whole new line of heroism: aviation. Since they first got off the ground, flying has been seen as a heroic enterprise and fliers have reaped the admiration of humanity. Even so, they were about as unassuming as they come—just two guys from Dayton, Ohio named Wilbur and Orville.

Clearing for Takeoff

Wilbur and Orville Wright were bicycle mechanics who believed they could build a self-propelled flying machine and devoted years of study and practice to the endeavor. Like Ford and Edison, they disliked schoolwork and preferred learning about the world in their own way. As kids, they built things, including kites and machinery. An important discovery they made that helped them get off the ground was that air pressure on moving things could be measured. They figured that flight involved the right amount of pressure pushing in the right directions.

The studied the work of a German inventor named Otto Lilienthal who built and flew gliders, hoping to learn from his successes and mistakes. They especially wanted to avoid one of Lilienthal's biggest mistakes, which was to die in a crash landing. Wanting to find an optimal spot for testing their machines, they wrote the U.S. Weather Bureau asking if it knew of a place with steady winds, low hills for takeoff, and sand for cushioning the landings. The Weather Bureau recommended Kitty Hawk, North Carolina, the name we all know as the birthplace of modern aeronautics.

Heroic Shorts

A pioneer named Ezra Meeker made the long journey across the country over the Oregon Trail to the state of Washington in 1852. He was 21 at the time and the trip took six months by ox-cart. Seventy-two years later, in 1924 at the age of 93, he made the same journey. The second time he took a plane and made the trip in a single day!

This End Up

So, the brothers packed up their equipment for Kitty Hawk and began their trials. In 1900 they built and flew a glider, shaped like a big box kite, capable of supporting human weight. The next step was to attach a motor. They went back to Ohio to work on their motor plane and returned again to Kitty Hawk three years later.

During that time, the Smithsonian Institute sponsored a flight project involving trained scientists, state-of-the-art equipment, and lots of money. Earlier in the same year as the Wright Brothers' famous flight, 1903, the Smithsonian plane was cleared for takeoff along the shores of the Potomac. The machine remained earthbound, leading many of the scientists involved or looking on to conclude that motorized flight in a heavier-than-air craft was impossible.

Fearless Facts

The Wright Brothers decided which of them would get the first chance to try out their plane by flipping a coin. Wilbur won the toss, but the plane fell over on its side after only three seconds off the ground. Orville took the pilot's seat for the second try and became the first person to fly.

In fact, people were so convinced that flight was impossible that many newspaper editors refused to print reports of the first successful flight, believing they were fabricated. Actually, the first flight was only a hop, skip, and a jump by modern standards. But the brothers kept working on their plane. Two years later, in 1905, they made their first extended-distance flight, this time near their hometown of Dayton, Ohio.

The world was a little slow to catch on to their achievement at first, especially since many continued to refuse to believe that heavier-than-air flight was possible for human beings. Gradually, however, the accolades started to pour forth. They have been honored with numerous medals and prizes, including the John Fritz Medal, the John Scott Medal, the Albert Medal from England's Royal Society, the gold medal from the French Academy of Sciences, and the French Michelin Prize. They are also honored by a monument that stands at Kitty Hawk.

Cultivated Spirit

Many mythic stories have been told about the great American inventors, but the most legendary of them all is George Washington Carver, who has become the patron saint of peanuts. Although he is credited with hundreds of inventions and three patents, his deepest influence is perhaps more spiritual than technological, and he is perhaps more important for what he represents than for what he invented.

A Hard Row to Hoe

Carver was the son of slaves, born in Missouri just before the end of the Civil War. Shortly after his birth, his father was killed in an accident while hauling logs. While still a baby, Carver and his mother were kidnapped by outlaws. A rescue attempt failed to recover his mother, but he was brought back to his owners, the Carvers, who raised him until he was about 10 years old.

At this time, he set off on his own, managing to get some formal schooling while doing odd jobs. He applied for admission to Highland University, but was denied

George Washington Carver.
(Dictionary of American
Portraits)

entrance because he was black. He later made his way to Iowa and applied to Simpson College, which he entered in 1890. Shortly afterward he transferred to what is now the Iowa State University College of Agriculture. After he graduated, he stayed on to complete his master's degree.

Back to the Land

In 1896 he was invited by Booker T. Washington, head of Alabama's Tuskegee Institute, to serve as head of agricultural studies there. This was an important opportunity not only to help educate other blacks, but also to work toward improving Alabama's agricultural economy, which was close to ruin in the aftermath of the Civil War and almost entirely dependent on cotton.

Towering Tips

If you're thinking about becoming a famous inventor, consider the economic and environmental impact of your inventions. Can they be manufactured out of recycled materials? Will they be fun and profitable to use and make?

Cotton was an important crop because it was in demand, especially by northern industries. Unfortunately, it depleted the soil of nitrogen. As a result, fields where cotton had grown were often left to erode as farmers sought new fields for growing more cotton. In his research, Carver discovered that the peanut plant replenished nitrogen in the soil. He encouraged farmers—both black and white—to rotate their crops, planting cotton one year and peanuts the next. Many took Carver's advice, especially since cotton crops were being invaded by the boll weevil, a voracious beetle.

Crop rotation was a big success; the peanuts were so good for the cotton that soon all the Alabama farmers were growing them. Suddenly there was a big peanut surplus. The locals ate peanuts and fed them to their livestock, but there wasn't nearly as much demand for them as there was for cotton. So Carver set to work trying to find a way to deal with the surplus.

Branching Out

In fact, he explored many solutions. For one, he looked for other plants that would replenish the soil's nitrogen that had been sucked out by the cotton plants. He found some, including pecans and sweet potatoes. He also successfully lobbied Congress to impose tariffs that would promote peanut sales.

In addition, he developed hundreds of new uses for peanuts, and later, about a hundred for sweet potatoes. Carver's inventions showed you could do just about anything with the peanut plant. It could be turned into stains, cosmetics, milk substitute and other synthetic foods, paper, shaving cream, charcoal, and much more. Right there in Alabama were the materials necessary for a vital industrial and consumer culture. All that was needed was for people to manufacture the products, market them, and put them to use.

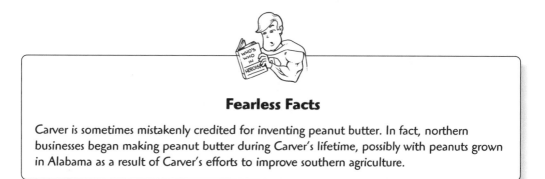

Fearless Facts

Carver is sometimes mistakenly credited for inventing peanut butter. In fact, northern businesses began making peanut butter during Carver's lifetime, possibly with peanuts grown in Alabama as a result of Carver's efforts to improve southern agriculture.

Unfortunately, this never happened on a large scale. Peanuts continued to be used chiefly as peanuts. Even so, Carver became a hero. In recognition of his work, he received an honorary doctorate from Simpson College, and the Spingarn medal from the NAACP. After he died in 1943, he was buried in Tuskegee beside Booker T. Washington. His birthplace in Diamond, Missouri was declared a national monument.

Balancing the Books

More importantly, he is hailed as a hero in the history books, especially in books for young readers, where he serves as an inspiring example of a peaceful, honorable, and creative African-American inventor who succeeded under adverse circumstances. Typically, though, these books tend to cover up the significant differences between Carver's achievements and those of inventors like Ford and Edison.

Towering Tips

Don't overdo it with the peanut butter sandwiches. Even though they taste good and are good for the peanut farmers, they're loaded with cholesterol!

Carver's approach to inventions did not involve the domination of the environment through technology, but an attempt to accommodate technology to the environment. Northern industry has always been slow to consider its environmental effects, often with disastrous results. The car and the lightbulb, used everyday by billions of people, place a tremendous burden on the environment, both in terms of pollution and depletion of natural resources.

This is not to say that Ford and Edison are to blame for our environmental problems, but they helped set a dangerous precedent for regarding natural resources as limitless. Carver, in contrast, invented things from materials that needed to be used up. In doing so, he was thinking about technology and "progress" on a whole other level.

The Least You Need to Know

➤ Edison opened workshops and had dozens of assistants working under him, producing and perfecting inventions.

➤ Ford introduced mass production as a way of making the automobile cheap and practical. America itself has been cheap and practical ever since!

➤ The Wright brothers discovered the ability to measure air pressure on moving objects, enabling them to accomplish what many authorities believed was impossible.

➤ George Washington Carver invented hundreds of new uses for peanuts in an effort to improve the economy of the poor South.

Chapter 9

Taking Care of Business

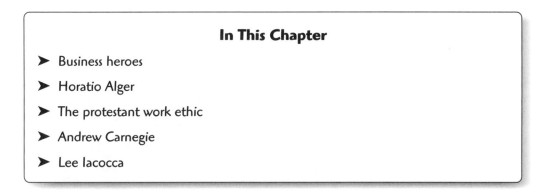

In This Chapter

➤ Business heroes

➤ Horatio Alger

➤ The protestant work ethic

➤ Andrew Carnegie

➤ Lee Iacocca

The American dream isn't just about getting rich, but riches play a big part of it. Believe it or not, Americans accomplished something new when they came up with a philosophy that says, "It's okay to want to get rich." Prior to that time, the prevailing advice was, "Don't be greedy; don't try to change your lifestyle or position." The idea was that society had gotten itself all sorted out already, with aristocrats at the top and peasants at the bottom. Aristocrats didn't need to get rich; they were born that way. And peasants were supposed to be content with their lot.

Naturally, plenty of people wanted to get rich even though they weren't supposed to. It took Americans, though, to turn greed into something to be proud of. Money is not a dirty word in the United States. Americans will do just about anything to get it, and once they've got it, they'll do just about anything to flaunt it. And of course, even if they don't have it, they'll borrow and try to live like they do.

It makes sense that a society that values money so highly should make heroes out of people who have lots of it. The biggest money heroes are the ones who not only knew how to get it but also what to do with it. They came on the scene at a favorable time in American history, when industrialization was just getting under way. At that time, there were lots of ways to get incredibly rich and few laws to stand in their way.

All That Glitters

A handful of Americans became fabulously wealthy during the *Gilded Age* when the industrial revolution started bearing its first fruits. Along with wealth, some gained admiration. The wealthiest and most admired of all was Andrew Carnegie, a working kid from Scotland who made his pile in the steel business. The story of his rise to fame and fortune is a crucial part of the larger story of the industrialization of America. It also amounts to a real-life approximation of the popular American myth of going from rags to riches.

Alger Rhythms

Millions of Americans indulge themselves in the rags-to-riches dream every time they buy a lottery ticket. And the dream goes way back before state lotteries caught on.

Andrew Carnegie. (Rutgers University Special Collections and Archives)

America has always been seen as a land of opportunity, especially during the industrial age when people loved to imagine what the trip down the path to riches would be like. The fantasy usually follows a familiar pattern.

You start with a poor waif with patches on his patches and nothing to his name besides a sick mother, a heart of gold, and the determination to succeed. You set him loose in America where some wholesome manly challenges and opportunities come his way and pretty soon he's vice president of a big company, married to the president's daughter, and bringing mom home a life-time supply of rheumatism tonic.

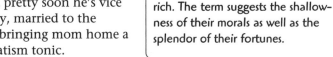

Worthy Words

The **Gilded Age** refers to the late nineteenth and early twentieth centuries in the United States, when many Americans became incredibly rich. The term suggests the shallowness of their morals as well as the splendor of their fortunes.

This familiar story (and dozens more exactly like it) was made famous by Horatio Alger (1834–1899), a writer of pulp stories for kids. Alger wrote the stories of "Ragged Dick," "Tattered Tom," "Plucky Paul," and many others to encourage young folks along the road to success. The outstanding quality of the young heroes of Alger's stories is their courage in the face of hardship. They are always ready to try and do their best, despite their humble circumstances. Of course, they are also ambitious, and Alger's heroes are one reason Americans tend to regard ambition as a virtue.

Fearless Facts

Horatio Alger wrote 135 novels—most of them on the rags-to-riches theme. They sold some 20 million copies.

Carnegie fits the mold of the Alger hero quite well. He came from a very poor family and started working early out of necessity. While he worked hard, he also kept his eyes open for new opportunities. As a result, people admire Carnegie for the same reasons they admire Alger's "Plucky Paul." Both figures stand as proof that America is a place where anyone can succeed. Of course, in real life, there's a lot more behind Carnegie's rise to wealth besides "luck and pluck."

Worthy Words

The **protestant work ethic** is sociologist Max Weber's phrase for describing the values he says are largely responsible for American enterprise. These values can be found in the writings of the early American hero Ben Franklin, who advocates thrift and hard work.

Puritans' Progress

Carnegie was just one of a number of extraordinarily wealthy Americans of the Gilded Age. The way was paved for these mega-millionaires by Americans before them who were only moderately well off, or even poor, but wanted to be prosperous. These included the Puritans who threw themselves into business dealings with religious zeal back before the industrial revolution. They believed that hard work was a Christian virtue, and felt that God had blessed them if they made an honest profit. What's more, the Puritans tended to be reluctant about spending their money; they lived frugally and saved their money. This combination of hard work and thrifty living characterizes what sociologist Max Weber calls the *protestant work ethic*—a set of values that helps account for the traditional American obsession with money.

The early American Protestants worked hard and lived frugally in order to reassure themselves that God liked them. Their lifestyle had earthly consequences in the form of big piles of money lying around that could be invested in big projects requiring lots more hard work. And so the cycle continued and America became settled and industrialized.

Turning the Wheels

Starting in the eighteenth century, a whole set of ideas about freedom and progress took Europe by storm and helped the protestant work ethic to lay the groundwork for American industrial capitalism. Throughout Europe many were getting tired of the old aristocratic regime in which political power largely depended on what family you happened to be born into. This "ancient regime" was particularly oppressive in France, where radical new ideas about government, science, and trade were on everybody's minds. These ideas became a driving force behind the French Revolution at the end of the eighteenth century.

Meanwhile, America was just getting started and many Americans—most notably the "founding fathers"—were deeply impressed by the new thinking. True, they had to fight off the British government and wage the American Revolution for the chance to try it out, but that was a small price to pay compared to the bloodshed and turmoil that went on in France. America got in on the ground floor with the ideals of freedom and progress, and even added an extra dose of independence to boot.

Freedom, progress, hard work, thriftiness, independence. Naturally, everyone wanted to see how these ideals panned out, hoping something special would happen. What happened was the industrial revolution. People discovered they could make lots of money by manufacturing goods in factories in large quantities. Manufacturing got a boost from technology as machines became increasingly useful in building things, as steam-powered transportation enabled raw materials to be shipped to factories from suppliers, and as more raw materials (especially fuel such as oil and iron and coke for steel) were discovered and processed.

Soldiers of Fortune

Of course, like any other time, the industrial revolution was a time when people had to figure things out as they went along. And there was a lot to figure out: new discoveries, new techniques, new possibilities, and, perhaps most important, new money. The only thing they didn't have to figure out were new rules. Rules came later, only after people realized the whole thing was getting out of control. Business people (especially in America) were free to try to make money just about any way they thought possible, short of outright stealing.

Have a product that people will pay high prices for? Make an agreement with your competitors to keep the prices high so that all of you can make huge profits. Someone doesn't want to join in on your price-fixing scheme? Drive him out of business by selling your products way below cost. If you can survive longer than the other guy can—if you're the only one left standing after a price war—you'll have a monopoly and will be able to charge whatever you want. Need an extra advantage over your competition? Make deals with suppliers and clients; give them kickbacks and form trusts, leaving your competitors out in the cold.

All these things were common practice back around the turn of the twentieth century, when fortunes were made in a big way. There weren't any laws against them. Of course, people complained once they figured out what was going on, but most people weren't looking for this kind of trouble. Instead, those American ideals of freedom, progress, hard work, and independence were in the back of people's minds when they looked at big business. Instead of getting angry, people got a warm glow of pride for their country!

Lone Sharks

So people started looking up to wealthy entrepreneurs as heroes, choosing to believe that they got their money through hard work, progress, thriftiness, and independence. As Americans, they congratulated themselves on living in a country where you could get ahead if you possessed these qualities. It often didn't seem to matter whether a wealthy person's

Towering Tips

Don't rely on the business practices that made Andrew Carnegie rich. They wouldn't work in today's highly regulated economy. Carnegie is one of those American heroes of days gone by who didn't play by the rules. This was partly because the rules hadn't been made yet. Heroes of today have to figure out which rules are made to be broken and which ones to live by.

Towering Tips

It's worth thinking about "independence" as it applies to doing business. Even though they have been largely responsible for many of the more exploitative business practices conducted in America, "independence" and "individualism" are traits Americans tend to admire in their business leaders. Like many other Americans, businessmen often like to think of themselves as "rugged individualists," despite the fact that their job is to make deals with other people. Because, in an industrial society, these other people tend to be strangers, it's easy to feel alone. This feeling is easier to deal with for people who believe they are "independent," even if they are not in fact completely self-reliant.

actions were good for other people. Because Americans had always valued independence, there was a widespread every-man-for-himself attitude, and the men who came out ahead were thought to deserve admiration.

Independence, of course, is important in the arena of democratic politics where the right to think for yourself is important. For many people of the time, that political right also became a rationale for economic opportunity. This may seem kind of paradoxical, since economics always involves exchange and interaction with other people. Compromise, cooperation, agreement, and group organization are necessary in any economic system. This holds true not only for the highly regulated consumer capitalism of today's America, but also for the unregulated industrial capitalism of the Gilded Age. Back then, the cooperative aspects of economics were a big part of the practice (often, the dirty practice!), but not the theory of capitalism.

In fact, the belief in the value of economic independence was a key feature of "social Darwinism," an influential economic theory put forth by English philosopher Herbert Spencer. Social Darwinism applies Darwin's ideas about biological evolution to economics. Just as individual plants and animals compete for resources and "succeed" if they pass their genes along to their offspring, individual businessmen compete for profit and succeed if they make money. According to Herbert and many who agreed with him, unregulated economic competition was a good thing because it would allow for "the survival of the fittest."

Although this way of thinking is blind to the way every person depends on other people, it helped make unregulated big business seem like it was fulfilling the American values of freedom, hard work, thrift, and independence. At the same time, however, the system was deeply involved in trusts, cartels, monopolies, kickbacks, and price fixing. It also helped Andrew Carnegie come off as heroic.

Dream Come True

So Carnegie (1835–1919) was this American dreamer-type who pulled himself up by his bootstraps. (Of course it helped a lot that he fell in with the right people at the right time.) He came to America from Scotland at the age of 13 with his family, who were looking for a better life. They moved to Pittsburgh where he started working right away, first in a textile mill and later as a messenger. Then he learned telegraphy and became a telegraph operator; after that, he studied bookkeeping.

Fearless Facts

Carnegie's father was a Scottish weaver who worked at a hand loom and was put out of work by power looms that revolutionized the textile industry in the mid-nineteenth century. With unemployment rampant in Britain, he was forced to come to America to look for work. Although he found work in a textile mill in Pennsylvania, he did not keep the job long and never made a comfortable living.

Carnegie's knowledge of accounting and telegraphy suited him to work as a personal secretary to a railroad executive named Thomas Scott, who taught him about business. Scott rose through the ranks of the railroad business until he was appointed Assistant Secretary of War. Carnegie went along for the ride. During this time, Carnegie went to Europe to sell railroad securities, which were used to finance the railroad industry in the wake of the Civil War. Thus he got a chance to see where big money came from and where it went. He also made big commissions for himself, which he invested with the help of his boss, and was soon rolling in dough.

Man of Steel

He wasn't stinking rich yet; that came later. First he parted ways with Thomas Scott and moved to New York City where he invested heavily in iron. Iron, of course, is important in making steel, which is important for building railroads. Eventually, he put up the money for a steel refinery, which made him filthy rich. Even so, he still wasn't stinking rich.

Before he became really rich, the railroad boom that had made steel such a lucrative business

Towering Tips

If you think things are tough at your job, consider the situation at Carnegie's Homestead steel mill in 1892 when armed guards (called Pinkertons) battled a small army of picketers armed with makeshift weapons in a failed attempt to keep the picketers locked out. The purpose of the lockout was to defeat the Amalgamated Association of Iron and Steel Workers who were fighting for their union. The workers managed to force their way into the mill, but the union was defeated in court. As a result, steelworkers had to put in 12-hour days, 7 days a week, and faced hazardous conditions. Obviously, Carnegie was not a hero to everyone!

came chugging to a halt. Carnegie saw the slowdown coming and shifted his focus from railroad steel to construction steel. He kept his competition at bay by making an agreement with oil magnate John D. Rockefeller. That agreement provided him access to iron on Rockefeller's land. He also undercut the competition by buying his own ships to transport the iron and using his own railroad to transport his steel. And he smelted, refined, and shaped the steel in his own factories. The whole process, from mining to finished product, was under his control. And yes, now he was stinking rich. His steel business alone made $40 million a year. His personal cut was more than half the pie: $25 million—at a time when that kind of money was unheard of.

Easy Come, Easy Go

In 1901, Carnegie made a dramatic deal with financier J. P. Morgan: He sold his steel company for $492 million. Morgan renamed it United States Steel, the name it is still known by today. Ever since, bankers have exerted a great deal of control over corporate finance.

Carnegie retired to his castle in Scotland and spent the rest of his days giving away his money. As a result of his many philanthropic acts, there are all sorts of things named Carnegie, including a number of foundations, a famous auditorium in New York City, and a species of dinosaur. In all, Carnegie gave away about $350 million to various causes. Here's a list of some of them.

➤ $10 million went to a Hero Fund. Looked at as a hero himself, largely for his philanthropy, he set up a fund awarding medals to people who committed acts of heroism.

➤ $60 million went to building 2,811 public libraries.

➤ $29 million went to the Carnegie Foundation for the Advancement of Teaching.

➤ $10 million went for an endowment for international peace.

➤ $6 million bought 7,600 church organs for the Episcopal Church

➤ $4 million went for pensions for steelworkers.

➤ $280,000 went toward a program to simplify the way words are spelled.

➤ He also supplied pensions for former President Taft and for the widows of Grover Cleveland and Theodore Roosevelt and for those who worked as telegraphers during the Civil War. For many years, he also paid to supply the White House with high-quality Scotch whisky!

Fearless Facts

At the turn of the twentieth century, the Philippines were fighting a revolutionary war against the United States for their independence. Carnegie disapproved of the resistance on the part of the United States to grant the Philippines independence, so he offered to buy the entire country from the U.S. government for the sum of $20 million in order to liberate it.

Lee's Loan

Not all business heroes make scads of money and then give it away. In fact, a recent hero who worked as chairman of a huge corporation became famous for asking for money. And he worked for a salary of only $1 a year! This was Lee Iacocca, head of Chrysler Corporation.

Before joining Chrysler, Iacocca worked for Ford, where he was instrumental in bringing out the Ford Mustang. He took over at Chrysler in 1979 when the company had been slumping badly for several years. The big losses were due to many factors, including recession, inflation, high interest rates, gas rationing, and over-expansion on the part of Chrysler. In addition, the American car industry in general was losing money to Japanese companies, which were building quality cars for less money.

Chrysler was on the brink of going under. To save the company, Iacocca appealed to Congress for a bailout loan. He persuaded enough congressmen that Chrysler's demise would spell big trouble throughout the country in the form of unemployment and loss of business. He asked for $1.2 billion.

Time for a Tune-up

With extra cash in hand, Iacocca presided over a drastic restructuring of Chrysler, making it leaner and more competitive. He took a huge pay cut, down to $1 a year. (He was able to live on a pension he collected from Ford for his work there.) The pay cut went straight to the hearts of many Americans, who were disgusted by the huge salaries of many CEOs who seemed to be

Towering Tips

When you need help, only take as much help as you need, regardless of the amount you are offered. When Iacocca asked for a loan of $1.2 billion, Congress offered to shell out $1.5 billion. Iacocca scored points with the public by making due with only what he asked for and by repaying the loan with interest well ahead of schedule.

willfully unconcerned about the current recession. Iacocca was taking the woes of his company seriously and was personally involved in doing something about them.

In fact, Iacocca became a persuasive spokesman for his company, the value of Chrysler cars, and the economic importance of American industry. He appeared in a series of impressive TV ads making a personal appeal to Americans to buy Chryslers. His appeal alluded to the tendency of many Americans to buy Japanese cars, which enjoyed a reputation of being reliable and inexpensive. Although he didn't exactly blame people for buying Japanese cars, he insisted that it was a mistake to think that Japanese cars were better than Chryslers. He claimed Chryslers were as good, if not better, than any other cars and suggested that he felt his personal integrity was at stake in the quality of Chryslers.

Wrapped in the Flag

The ads brought Iacocca acclaim and made him a celebrity. He used his celebrity status to continue campaigning for Chrysler, playing up the argument that American products were good for America. Not only do American cars mean more jobs for Americans, but they also mean more tax revenue for the country.

Many Americans were frustrated by the recession and became convinced that a big part of the problem had to do with Japan's trade policies. While exporting huge quantities of consumer goods to America, the Japanese imported very little of anything from the United States. Iacocca's appeal struck a patriotic note, and Americans responded with enthusiasm, both by buying cars and by admiring the Chrysler chairman.

Fearless Facts

Iacocca's autobiography *Iacocca,* published in 1984, became a bestseller.

Iacocca's serious, straightforward appeal was a big success. In fact, the company began turning a healthy profit within the next four years—after Iacocca had requested the government bailout. Chrysler repaid the loan seven years ahead of schedule. In saving his company, Iacocca kept faith with the government and established rapport with car buyers. In fact, he turned out to be extremely good at two things he claimed to be reluctant to do: asking Congress for money and appearing in TV commercials for Chrysler.

Would You Buy a Car from This Man?

Iacocca is probably the first person to become a hero by appearing in a TV ad campaign, with the possible exception of Morris the cat. Most of the big names in commercials are famous before they start. Here are other celebrities who appeared in Chrysler ads right around the time Iacocca first took over as head of the company. It should give you an idea of the sorts of people who drove Chryslers!

➤ Astronaut Neil Armstrong

➤ Baseball star Joe Garagiola

➤ Football star Walt Garrison

➤ Singer Frank Sinatra

➤ Actor Ricardo Montalban

The Least You Need to Know

➤ Horatio Alger wrote dozens of popular stories about poor young Americans working their way up the ladder.

➤ The protestant work ethic helps account for the American fixation with economic success.

➤ Andrew Carnegie came from an impoverished family and became one of the richest and most powerful men in the world.

➤ Lee Iacocca took over as head of Chrysler Corporation during a recession and made the company profitable again by making personal appeals on TV ads.

Chapter 10

Out There

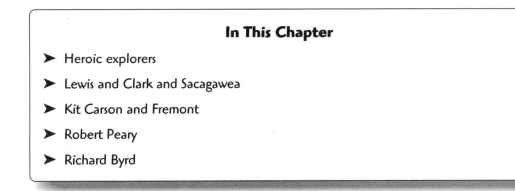

In This Chapter

➤ Heroic explorers

➤ Lewis and Clark and Sacagawea

➤ Kit Carson and Fremont

➤ Robert Peary

➤ Richard Byrd

One of the quintessential heroic types is the wanderer, a mythic figure like Odysseus who has adventures in strange lands and returns home to tell about them. The fact that this type of hero appears in the myths and legends of virtually every culture suggests that exploring is part of what being a human being is all about. These mythic heroes have real-life counterparts in the famous explorers of history.

It's easy to see why explorers are widely admired as heroes. It takes courage, endurance, and determination to face the hardships and dangers involved in venturing into the unknown. And the work of explorer heroes, if successful, often brings us to a new level of progress or discovery. There's a sense that all of society benefits from explorers' achievements because they expand the limits of what we know, where we've been, and what we can do. Somehow, everyone shares in an explorer's success.

What's more, explorers generally have a reputation of working for unselfish reasons. The chief motivation for exploring may be glory, or sometimes even greed, but it is often simply curiosity and the desire for adventure—things everyone can relate to.

And explorers rarely do harm to anyone. Even if they are intruding on someone else's territory, they aren't invaders, but are just having a look around. Although almost everyone appreciates exploring, Americans are especially prone to explore and to admire explorers. This may be because there was such a lot of exploring that took place in the process of settling the country. When you are faced with something as vast as the American frontier, it's only natural to develop explorative habits and to look to the greats in the field as heroes.

Plenty of Room in the Back

The U.S. government sponsored much of the exploration of the American interior for a number of reasons. Scientific and geographic discovery were among them. In addition, as Europe fell on difficult times, more and more immigrants made the journey to America and eastern cities became increasingly crowded. The government encouraged exploration as a way of expanding the country and providing more room for settlers.

Far-Reaching Plans

Even before the immigrants started pouring in from Europe, back before anyone with white skin had ever made it all the way to the western side of the North America, Thomas Jefferson realized that the United States had a lot of potential for growth. So, in the early nineteenth century, he commissioned one of the most important expeditions in U.S. history, led by Meriwether Lewis and William Clark, to explore the vast terrain west of the Mississippi. The expedition had no overt political, economic, or military agenda, but was intended to discover more about the West (which, at the time, was a mystery).

The epic journey is one of the classic real-life adventure stories of American history. Equipped only with flint-lock rifles and the tools they could carry with them, a team of 23 volunteers known at the time as "the Corps of Discovery," spent two years and four months trekking from the northern Mississippi River to the shores of the Pacific Ocean and back. The purpose of the trip was to map the territory west of the Mississippi River along the Missouri and Columbia Rivers as far as the Pacific Ocean. They were also expected to make scientific reports of plants and animals and make peaceful contact with the Indians.

Esprit de Corps

Lewis had served as Jefferson's personal secretary and aide de camp before he was offered the chance to lead the expedition. Lewis invited his friend Clark, whom he had

*Meriwether Lewis.
(Rutgers University Special
Collections and Archives)*

served briefly with in the army, to join him as co-captain. Together they assembled a crew of hunters and woodsman, many of whom had useful skills such as carpentry and blacksmithing. The full contingent consisted of 23 men and Lewis's dog, named Seaman.

The crew was assembled in the fall of 1803, and they built a winter camp prior to their departure where the Missouri flows into the Mississippi. That winter they bought supplies and kept busy conducting military drills. At last, in May 1804, they assembled in St. Charles, an outpost village along the Missouri. On the 21st of May, the expedition set off in three boats, traveling west up the Missouri as the villagers of St. Charles gathered along the banks and cheered.

Fearless Facts

Jefferson promised a promotion to captain for both Lewis and Clark as leaders of the expedition, but Congress failed to promote Clark, who remained a lieutenant. Despite this failure, the two explorers agreed to serve as co-captains and shared equal authority, never telling their crew members that Clark was not officially a captain.

The trip was expected to take two years, and, as it turned out, took two years and four months, covering 7,500 miles to the Pacific and back. Much of the journey was by boat, because one of the objectives of the expedition was to evaluate the possibility of river passage to the Pacific. Clark was an experienced boater and took on the job of mapping the Missouri River as they traveled. Meanwhile, Lewis made much of the journey on foot nearby, observing and collecting plant and animal specimens. The group's hunters also traveled on foot, up ahead of the others. Their job was to shoot game and prepare it for cooking, and then hang the dressed meat in a tree along the river where the rest of the party would find it.

The team was remarkably successful in working together through the many difficult situations they encountered, including food shortage, bad weather, rough terrain, and long, dull winters with little to do. Surprisingly, only one member of the group was lost—Sargent Charles Floyd, who probably died of a ruptured appendix in August 1804. Throughout the journey, both Lewis and Clark kept journals. These journals are the basis of most of what we now know about the expedition.

Help Along the Way

After less than six months, the weather turned cold and the team built a winter camp not far from a cluster of Mandan Indian villages in what is now western North Dakota. Here they were visited occasionally by Indians and by fur traders. One fur trader was Toussaint Charbonneau, who came with his two Indian wives. Charbonneau failed to make a good impression on the explorers, but when they learned that his younger wife, named Sacagawea, or "Bird Woman," had been kidnapped by the Shoshone, they suppressed their dislike.

Lewis and Clark hoped to lead the expedition safely through Shoshone territory farther to the west. In fact, they wanted to arrange a trade with the Shoshone for horses for the return trip back east. They realized Sacagawea could act as an interpreter, so they offered to hire Charbonneau as a guide on the condition that Sacagawea would come too. Thus, the group picked up its famous Indian member, who turned out to be a great help in many ways.

A series of amazing events brought Sacagawea to cross paths with Lewis and Clark. As a child, she was kidnapped from the Shoshone by the Hidatsa tribe, who adopted her, and she was married as a young girl to a Hidatsa tribesman, who already had another, older wife. Charbonneau the fur trader encountered the Hidatsa and won both wives in a wager. As Lewis and Clark soon learned after joining up with Charbonneau and Sacagawea, the young Indian, who was only about 16 years old at the time, was already six months pregnant.

Sacagawea has been romanticized as a guide who showed the expedition the way over the Rocky Mountains to the Pacific. Actually, the team followed the Missouri and Columbia Rivers the whole way as they planned. Even so, Sacagawea became a highly valued member of the team. She was familiar with the territory and could tell the others what to expect of the way ahead. She also knew about wild edible plants that provided an important source of nourishment. She was able to interpret for many of the tribes they met along the way. In addition, it was an advantage having a woman as part of the expedition, because it helped show the Indians they encountered that they had peaceful intentions.

Fearless Facts

Not long after joining the team, Sacagawea gave birth to a son, named Jean Baptist, or Pompey. Clark later adopted him and saw to his education. Eventually he traveled to Europe, learned many languages, befriended the German Prince Paul of Wurttemburg, and became Mayor of San Louis Rey, California.

What's more, Sacagawea helped arrange a deal for horses between the expedition and the Shoshone. As it turned out, her brother, Cameahwait, whom she had not seen for years, had become chief of the tribe. They had a tearful reunion, but Sacagawea decided to stay on with the explorers rather than rejoin her tribe.

Years Later . . .

The group made it successfully to the Pacific on November 7, 1805, and set up a winter camp nearby before starting the return trip in the spring. They arrived at their original point of departure on the Mississippi River on September 23, 1806 and were hailed as heroes. Each member was given twice the salary he was promised and the leaders received big spreads of land of more than 1,000 acres each. Soon afterward, Lewis was made governor of Louisiana Territory and Clark was made Brigadier General of the militia.

Clark married Julia Hancock and had many children. Lewis found himself unhappily burdened by his responsibilities and shot himself on October 11, 1809. Sacagawea lived to be an old woman, but was not rewarded for her valuable service to the government. She drifted from place to place for many years by herself, unable to fit in either with whites or with Indians. It was only after her death that her heroism was recognized.

Fearless Facts

Before setting off on his famous journey, Clark met Miss Hancock, his future bride, and made plans to marry her. During the course of his travels, he named a tributary of the Missouri, the Judith River, in her honor. This gallant gesture misfired, however, because the woman's name was not Judith, but Julia!

Kit and Caboodle

The job of exploring the country was taken up years later by Colonel John Fremont, a scientist who traveled throughout the Rocky Mountains doing surveys for the Army Corps of Topographical Engineers. Fremont mapped out the West and opened up the Oregon Trail for settlers who came after him. Although Fremont's fame has faded since his own time, he helped confer lasting fame on the man who served as his guide, the rugged and courageous Kit Carson (1809–1868).

Carson was a trapper who lived in Taos, New Mexico, but traveled all over the West in pursuit of beaver and other fur-bearing varmints. He met Fremont in 1842 and was hired on as guide for $100 a month. Carson turned out to be handy to have along, thanks to his wilderness experience. Fremont's expedition suffered near-starvation and other dangers. In Fremont's official report, Carson was described as brave, scrupulously honest, loyal, and skilled in outdoor survival.

Fremont's report became popular reading and thousands of copies were printed up for the public. Carson quickly became a hero, known as "the king of the mountain men." He became the subject of legends and inspired "dime novels" like those written about Buffalo Bill. Thus Carson is remembered as a legendary frontier hero, along with Daniel Boone and Davy Crocket.

Part of the myth surrounding Carson has to do with an unofficial, but politically important, aspect of Fremont's expedition. The government hoped to be able to solidify claims to the territory for U.S. settlement and believed that Fremont's map would help legitimize their claims. At the time, British and Mexicans were also interested in the land. In the minds of his admirers, the heroic figure of Kit Carson came to represent the stuff Americans were made of—the sort of people who could tame the country and who were worthy of possessing it.

While his work as a guide brought him his greatest fame, Carson was involved in many other historic events. He fought in the Civil War and in western colonial battles against Mexicans and Indians. As a result, he is seen as a villain by many Native Americans, Mexicans, and Chicanos (Mexican-Americans). Most notably, he was responsible for an economic war waged against the Navajo, destroying their crops until they were forced to surrender. This led up to the famous 300 mile "Long March" of 8,000 Navajo from Arizona to Fort Sumner, where they were kept as prisoners of war.

Towering Tips

Remember, U.S. colonial conflicts were not always fought along racial lines. Contributing to the defeat of the Navajo were the aggressions of their traditional tribal enemies, including the Utes and other tribes. In fact, Carson (who aided the government in displacing the Navajo) was himself married at various times to two Indian women and a Mexican.

Swashbuckling Scientist

Scientific inquiry has long been an important motive for exploration and the scientist-explorer hero has become a popular figure for many Americans. This figure combines the courage and determination of the frontier explorer with the penetrating intelligence of the scientist. This sort of hero has been dramatized in the *Indiana Jones* adventure films. In fact, the character, Indiana Jones, is modeled in part on a real life scientist and explorer named Roy Chapman Andrews (1884–1960).

Andrews was a naturalist who began his career at the American Museum of Natural History. He loved natural history so much that he was willing to do anything for a job at the museum—so he started off scrubbing floors. He gradually moved on to other kinds of work, helping with exhibits and collecting specimens. He developed a specialization in cetology—the study of whales—and he collected the marine mammals on expeditions throughout the Pacific. His travels took him to the Far East, which he explored extensively. He later wrote popular books about his experiences.

His most famous expedition took place in 1922 when he led a team to the Gobi Desert in search of fossils of extinct creatures. He hoped to find evidence that early Man, the famous "missing link" came from East Asia. Although he failed to find human fossils, the team made other important finds of even older fossils. These included fossil remains of dinosaurs and ancinet mammals.

In the Flaming Cliffs region of the Gobi Desert, Andrews' team found a new species of triceratops that is called *Protoceratops andrewsi* after its discoverer. The team was also among the first to find dinosaur eggs. While these discoveries were important, the public was especially drawn to Andrews' swashbuckling image. He later wrote about run-ins with desert bandits and reports frightening them off with gunfire. Among his books are *The Ends of the Earth* (1929), *All About Dinosaurs* (1953), and *All About Whales* (1954).

Fearless Facts

Andrews distinguished himself as an explorer and specimen collector for the American Museum of Natural History and was promoted to museum director in 1934. His real talent was field work, however, and he proved not to be a particularly fine director. He resigned the post in 1941.

Ice Guys

With the settling of the American frontier, explorers had to look elsewhere for new lands to discover. Pretty much all that was left were places where human life was extremely difficult: the poles of the globe. The icecaps were the last earthly unchartered frontier that remained above the surface of the ocean. These were discovered and explored at different times by two American navy men, Robert Peary (1856–1920) and Richard Byrd (1888–1957).

Heading North

Robert Peary explored the northern reaches of Greenland and was the first to make it to the North Pole after numerous failed attempts. Although he was in the navy, the navy did not sponsor his expeditions. Instead, he had to obtain leaves from his duties to go on his own.

In 1886, the first time he went exploring in the frozen north, he simply booked passage on a whaling steamship bound for the Arctic and made his way north as far as he could go until he and his Danish guide ran out of food. At one point, the two found themselves walking in deep slush as the glacier on which they traveled began to melt in the sun. This was the first of seven Arctic expeditions.

Cold Hard Facts

In subsequent expeditions, Peary befriended Eskimos who taught him survival skills, including how to build igloos. As a trophy from one of his trips, he brought back a

Robert Peary. (Dictionary of American Portraits)

1,000 lb. meteorite from Greenland that had long been known to the Eskimos and had been discovered by whites some 75 years previously. On another expedition, he got severe frostbite and had to have eight of his toes amputated.

Fearless Facts

Peary's wife Josephine accompanied him on some of his expeditions as far as the northernmost settlements of Greenland. There, at a shelter in Bowdoin Bay at the start of the third expedition, she gave birth to a child.

With each trip, he made it closer and closer to the pole. In 1903, he came within 343 miles; in 1906, he got as close as 174 miles. By this time, he was attracting attention. Because it was clear he was determined and experienced, he had no trouble raising funds for his later expeditions. Finally, on his seventh and final trip, on April 6, 1909 at the age of 53, Peary arrived at the pole. With him were five sledges, 38 dogs, and five men, African American Matthew Hanson and Eskimos Seegloo, Ootah, Eginwah, and Ookeah. On returning home, Peary was promoted to rear admiral.

Byrd on the Wing

Richard Byrd is known as the first to reach the North Pole by plane. Although this accomplishment has been disputed, he had a distinguished career as a pioneer aviator and explorer. He led numerous missions to the Arctic and Antarctic regions and mapped out large expanses of polar territory. In the process, he spearheaded the founding of the Navy Aeronautics Bureau and became a national celebrity.

Off the Ground

Byrd's promising career in the navy was literally hobbled due to a series of foot injuries. He injured his right foot playing football. Then, he re-injured the foot in a fall doing gymnastics. Later, he injured the same foot once again in a fall on board ship. As a result, he wound up with a steel pin in his foot and a naval desk job.

Byrd became restless behind his desk, so in 1917 he persuaded the navy to let him undergo flight training. This was back in the early days of aviation and Byrd was among those who appreciated the potential importance of flight to the navy. He was crucial in establishing the Navy Aeronautics Bureau and became a skilled pilot. He developed a technique for landing a seaplane on the surface of the ocean at night.

Heroic Shorts

The first woman to reach the North Pole by dogsled was Anne Bancroft (1956–), who joined an expedition as a photographer. She was the only female member of an eight-person team. She later led an all-woman expedition to the South Pole on skis. The team reached its destination on January 14, 1993. Before becoming an arctic explorer, she got a degree in physical education from the University of Oregon. Before that she started up the first girl's basketball team at her high school.

From an early age, Byrd had been interested in polar exploration and he got his chance as a navy flyer. Early in his career, he volunteered to lead a unit of three seaplanes to explore Greenland. A foot expedition was already being organized, however—led by Donald MacMillan and funded in part by the National Geographic Society. Byrd's team served as an airborne escort for MacMillan's expedition. The trip was marred by conflicts between Byrd and MacMillan, both of whom wanted total control.

On the Spot

Afterward, Byrd made plans and raised money for his own trip, deciding to explore the North Pole by plane, a feat which had never been accomplished. He arranged to get time off from the navy for the purpose, and raised funds on his own. At the same time, another explorer, Roald Amundsen of Norway, was planning a trip to reach the Pole by dirigible and, as it turned out, the two explorers were ready to set off at nearly the same time, May 1926. For some reason, however, Amundsen's balloon flight was delayed, enabling Byrd to make the attempt first.

Norwegian Roald Amundsen was an explorer who had accomplished many things in his career. He was the first man to reach the South Pole and the first to sail a ship through the Northwest Passage from the Atlantic to the Pacific across North America. It may be that he simply decided to let someone else have some of the glory that he already enjoyed. In any case, his mission to fly to the pole was unexpectedly delayed, allowing Byrd a head start. On May 9 at around 2:00 a.m., Byrd took off from the Norwegian island of Spitsbergen in a Dutch-built Fokker tri-plane, headed for the North Pole.

Fearless Facts

In preparing for his expedition to the North Pole, Byrd had to choose between two planes, a tri-plane designed by Dutchman Anthony Fokker and a plane built by the American Ford company. He opted for the Dutch plane, which he named the "Josephine Ford" after the daughter of Ford chairman Edsel Ford.

Byrd reached the pole later that morning at 9:02 and returned to Spitsbergen at 4:30 p.m. after a 15-hour flight of 2,500 miles. His success was disputed, however, by the Norwegians and the Italians, who had built Amundsen's dirigible. They claimed that Byrd could not have flown so far in such a short period of time. Their objections were apparently motivated by the desire to have the Norwegian Amundsen capture the glory of being the first to fly to the pole in his Italian-built airship.

Historians have also questioned Byrd's success. Not the American public, however, and his return to the states was celebrated with a tickertape parade in New York City. Congress was also satisfied and awarded Byrd and his co-pilot, Floyd Bennett, the Medal of Honor.

South for the Winter

Byrd's exploring days were only just beginning. He went on to put together a trip to the South Pole, financed in part by the National Geographic Society. The expedition established a scientific base in Antarctica on the Ross Ice Shelf and nicknamed the outpost "Little America." Along on the mission were 41 men, 4 planes, and 94 sled dogs, as well as exploration and scientific equipment.

On the morning of Thanksgiving Day, November 28, 1929, Byrd began his flight to the South Pole, arriving at 1:14 p.m. and returning at 10:00 that evening. In the course of the flight, he was able to answer the unresolved question of whether the Antarctic

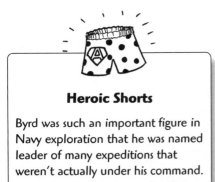

Heroic Shorts

Byrd was such an important figure in Navy exploration that he was named leader of many expeditions that weren't actually under his command.

consisted of single continent or a group of islands connected by an ice cap. (It's all one land mass.) He was later awarded the Navy Cross for heroism and promoted to rear admiral.

Byrd returned to "Little America" in 1934, in preparation for spending the winter in Antarctica by himself. (Winter in Antarctica, by the way, happens when it's summertime in the Northern Hemisphere.) He lived in a meteorological hut 120 miles from the nearest human beings, surrounded by snow and frigid temperatures. He planned to monitor the weather and study the southern auroras.

Unfortunately, he became extremely sick near the beginning of his stay as a result of a carbon monoxide leak from his camp stove. He kept his illness to himself—partly because he wanted to complete his mission, and partly because he didn't want others to risk their lives to rescue him in frigid winter conditions. He was finally rescued in August, after a rescue attempt launched in July but aborted due to temperatures of 80 degrees below. Byrd wrote an account of the ordeal, *Alone,* which became a bestseller.

Underwater Hero

A heroic figure of undersea exploration is Robert Ballard (1942–), a pioneer in the use of deep-sea exploring equipment who discovered the wreck of the *Titanic* in 1985. Ballard is a scientist as well as an explorer, who got a Ph.D. in marine geology and geophysics before serving in the navy for five years as an officer. He later became head of the Deep Submergence Laboratory of the Woods Hole Oceanographic Institute on Cape Cod, Massachusetts. Up until the time when Ballard found the wreck of the *Titanic,* many other explorers had searched in vain for the famous sunken ship. Ballard succeeded with the help of the latest in high tech equipment, support from the navy, the National Geographic Society, and the French government, in addition to lots of know-how and determination. Ballard and his crew located the wreck approximately two miles below the surface of the ocean in the North Atlantic after sweeping the ocean bottom with a video camera. A remote controlled submersible robot, equipped with a video camera, was later used to explore the wreck.

> **The Least You Need to Know**

➤ Lewis and Clark led the first expedition across the country and reached the Pacific Ocean in November 1805.

➤ Sacagawea, hired by Lewis and Clark as an interpreter, was neglected in her time, but is remembered today as one of the biggest heroes of the expedition.

➤ Robert Peary led the first expedition to reach the North Pole, arriving in April 1909.

➤ Richard Byrd was an aviator as well as an explorer. He is credited with being the first person to fly over the North Pole.

Chapter 11

Sky High

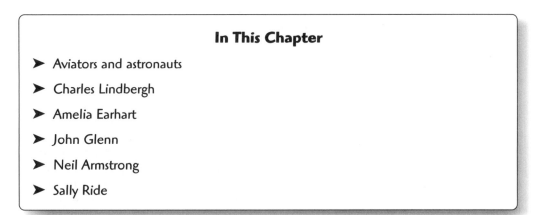

In This Chapter

➤ Aviators and astronauts

➤ Charles Lindbergh

➤ Amelia Earhart

➤ John Glenn

➤ Neil Armstrong

➤ Sally Ride

One of the things that makes heroes heroic is their ability to do things that ordinary people can't do. This includes magical things like flying. Ever since the Wright brothers made the first airplane flight in 1903, aviator heroes have been American favorites. Aviator heroes include inventor heroes such as the Wright brothers, explorer heroes such as Admiral Byrd, and war heroes such as Eddie Rickenbacker. But they also include heroes who fly just for the sake of flying and to help advance aviation technology.

Flying heroes are especially courageous, even though the great things they have done are things that ordinary non-heroic types have gone on to do as well. Lots of people fly these days and it's no big deal. But the reason flying is no big deal is because early aviators had the guts to take to the air before all the bugs had been worked out of flight technology. They risked—and sometimes lost—their lives because they felt the thrill of flying was worth the chance.

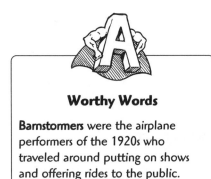

Worthy Words

Barnstormers were the airplane performers of the 1920s who traveled around putting on shows and offering rides to the public.

Of course, the same urge to get off the ground that inspired the early aviator heroes applies to the astronauts. Their way into space was paved by people in leather helmets driving go-carts with wings. And space travel today poses the same challenges and dangers faced by the pioneer aviators—and reaps similar rewards of glory and technological advancement.

Hero Crossing

The biggest aviator hero in American history is Charles Lindbergh, a winsome adventurer who thrilled the nation by coming out of nowhere and surpassing a field of famous competitors to become the first to fly solo nonstop across the Atlantic from New York to Paris. The acclaim and adulation he received was unprecedented for an aviator. Fans all over the world clamored to find out all about the young flyer the papers called "Lucky Lindy." Unfortunately, the attention had tragic consequences, as it led to the kidnapping of Lindbergh's infant son.

Up and Coming

Lindbergh became enthusiastic about airplanes just as they were first getting off the ground. He dropped out of high school to go to flying school—where he was the only pupil. When his teacher closed the school in 1922 and sold the only plane, it looked like Lindbergh was out of luck. The man who bought the plane was a *barnstormer,* someone who flies around in rural areas attracting attention by performing airplane stunts and offering onlookers airplane rides for a fee. Lindbergh wanted the barnstormer to take him on as an assistant, and even offered to pay his own way.

Lindbergh proved he had unusual courage as a barnstormer, doing things like walking out on the wing while his partner was flying the plane, and skydiving with multiple parachutes—cutting the strings of one before opening the next. Meanwhile, he was learning about aviation and mechanics, greedily absorbing how planes worked and how to fly them.

As aviation technology improved, the barnstorming business took a nosedive, so Lindbergh bailed out and enrolled in army training as an air cadet. After graduating at the head of his class, he took a job with an airmail service flying mail between Chicago and Saint Louis. Meanwhile, a number of more famous aviators were making preparations to fly across the Atlantic.

Flight Path

The French, like the Americans, were avid aviators. In 1919, Frenchman Raymond Orteig offered a prize of $25,000 to the first person who could fly nonstop between

Paris and New York. Among the many famous aviators preparing to make the attempt was Admiral Richard Byrd, the polar explorer, and French World War flying ace Rene Fonck. Hearing of the prize and the hoopla surrounding it, Lindbergh decided he wanted to make the attempt too. He arranged for financial backing from St. Louis business and for a plane built to his specifications by a small company in San Diego.

Lindbergh thought he would have the best chance of success flying alone in a small, single-engine plane. In fact, others failed with larger, more powerful planes. Some even lost their lives in the attempt even as Lindbergh was making preparations for his own flight. When his plane, *The Spirit of St. Louis,* was ready, Lindbergh flew it from San Diego to St. Louis and then to New York. In the process, he set a record for the fastest flight across the country.

Partly because of a recent series of spectacular failed attempts to make the flight, and partly because of his dramatic cross-country flight to New York, Lindbergh was swamped with media attention as he made final preparations for the intercontinental voyage. He lifted off from New York at 7:52 a.m. on May 20, 1927 on a flight of more than 3,500 miles that would last 33 hours.

Fearless Facts

The night before his famous transatlantic flight, Lindbergh was kept awake by reporters assigned to his story. They were staying at the same hotel playing cards late into the night!

Of course, as a solo pilot, Lindbergh had to stay awake the entire journey. He faced the added challenge of flying through sleet and fog for much of the way. Even so, he managed to stay right on course and arrived in Paris where tens of thousands of cheering French waited to greet him. Back in New York, Lindbergh was awarded two medals by President Calvin Coolidge: the Flying Cross and the Congressional Medal of Honor. And New Yorkers turned out in droves for the largest tickertape parade up to that time. Of course, he was front-page news across the country.

Unlucky Lindy

The hero proceeded to go about trying to live happily ever after. He went on tours to promote aviation and other causes, including goodwill between the United States and Mexico. In fact, after speaking in Mexico at the request of the U.S. ambassador, he married the ambassador's daughter, writer Anne Morrow. They had a baby boy and named him Charles Jr.

All the while, Lindbergh was continually hounded by the press, which couldn't seem to get enough of him. He became something of a national treasure, and people wanted to keep tabs on him and his doings. This continued through March 1, 1932, when kidnapper(s), hoping to profit from Lindbergh's fame, used a ladder to climb into the room of his 20-month-old son, took the baby, and left a ransom note.

Fearless Facts

The man in charge of the Lindbergh kidnapping case was New Jersey State Police officer Colonel H. Norman Schwartzkopf, father of General H. Norman Schwartzkopf, who led U.S. forces during the Gulf War against Iraq.

The kidnapping was touted as the crime of the century. Despite paying the ransom, the Lindberghs never recovered their son. The baby's body was found, long dead, almost two months later. Bruno Hauptman was later arrested for the crime, convicted, and sent to the electric chair. Another suspect committed suicide, and a third died of tuberculosis shortly after the kidnapping.

Airborne Earhart

Lindbergh's flight across the Atlantic caused such a frenzy of admiration that promoters soon began hatching schemes that would help them cash in on aviator heroism. One such promoter was George Putnam, who was working for a woman who had bought a tri-motor plane from Admiral Byrd and wanted to sponsor a heroic transatlantic flight of her own. She wanted a woman on board to draw attention to the flight and to promote awareness of female aviators, so she asked Putnam to find a female pilot who would go along for the ride. He called on a student pilot named Amelia Earhart, who turned out to be eager to go as far as she could as an aviator.

Getting Her Wings

Earhart had earned her pilot's license only shortly before and had been employed as a social worker, flying only in her spare time. Prior to that she had been a nurse's aid during World War I. The flight, made in June 1928 in a Lockheed Vega, was successful. Although she did not pilot the plane herself, she caused a sensation as the first woman to cross the Atlantic by air and acquired a reputation with the public—cultivated by Putnam the promoter—of being a great pilot. She became a popular speaker, going on lecture tours around the country appearing in front of clubs, organizations, and colleges to talk about aviation. She also became an associate editor of *Cosmopolitan* magazine, where she published articles on flying.

Fearless Facts

In 1929, an organization of female flyers called the Ninety Nines was formed. Amelia Earhart became its first president, serving from 1930–1932. The name refers to the number of original members of the group.

Although she was the most famous woman aviator, she wasn't the best. Despite her passionate love of flying and her interest in promoting aviation, she did not have a great deal of experience as a pilot. Because of her lecturing, she wasn't able to spend as much time flying as she would have liked. She also promoted products such as spark plugs and gasoline. In addition, she promoted her own Amelia Earhart brands of luggage, clothes, and stationery. She improved with practice, however, and in 1932 flew by herself across the Atlantic. The feat confirmed the reputation she already had as "Lady Lindy," a premier pilot.

World Class

In subsequent years, she laid even loftier plans to fly around the world at the equator. Flying straight through the whole way would have been impossible, so the journey was planned in numerous stages with stops to rest and refuel. On May 20, 1937, she took off from Oakland heading southeast in a Lockheed Electra, accompanied by navigator Fred Noonan. They made it to South America and then across the Atlantic to Africa. They crossed Africa and India, flew southeast over Indonesia to Australia, and continued northeast to New Guinea.

They had gone a good three quarters of their journey with only three long legs remaining: to the Howland Islands in the South Pacific, then to Hawaii, and then back to Oakland. They took off from New Guinea on July 2nd and were never seen again. Earhart last made radio contact more than 20 hours after leaving New Guinea. She was unsure of her position, but she was somewhere near the Howland Islands. Then she disappeared without a trace. Searches by the United States and Japan were unable to turn up any sign of the plane.

Fearless Facts

In 1932, the year Earhart made her solo flight across the Atlantic, she also made a pleasure flight with Eleanor Roosevelt on an aerial tour of Washington D.C. Both women were dressed in evening gowns at the time.

Heroic Shorts

Another *Right Stuff* hero is Chuck Yeager (1923–), who was a test pilot who became the first person to break the sound barrier. He was a World War II flying ace before working after the war as a test pilot, when he broke the sound barrier in a Bell X-1 rocket. On October 14, 1947 he reached the speed of 670 mph. This feat helped him become a leading test pilot as well as one of the main heroic figures in Tom Wolf's book, *The Right Stuff*. His best selling autobiography, *Yeager* was published in 1985.

Hotshots

Air travel has become routine, but America's frontier spirit still finds room to wander out beyond Earth's upper atmosphere. In fact, space travel became a matter of national pride in the 1960s as the United States vied with its Cold War rival, the Soviet Union, for supremacy in space. To millions during those days, the space race was more exciting and important than any sporting event. The two world superpowers were competing for the honor of taking humanity out of this world.

Elder Statesman

Patriotic American space buffs were mortified by Russia's early victories in space. In April 1961, cosmonaut Yuri Gagarin was the first human to go into orbit, making NASA scientists dizzy with envy. Astronaut Alan Shepherd accomplished a great feat in becoming the first American in space, but was only playing catch-up to the Soviets. At that time, May 1961, American rocket science was not yet ready to orbit the planet. NASA officials thought that an orbit mission would be too dangerous. Meanwhile, the Soviets continued to fly rings around the Americans. In July of the same year, cosmonaut Gherman Titov orbited the Earth 17 times on a single mission. The United States had yet to take its first spin.

Preparations were quickly being made, however. NASA culled and rigorously trained a select team of seven astronauts for Project Mercury: Alan Shepherd, Gus Grissom, Scott Carpenter, Wally Schirra, Donald Slayton, Gordon Cooper, and John Glenn. Their story was told by Tom Wolfe in the best-selling book *The Right Stuff* (made into a movie of the same title in 1983).

At last NASA officials thought they were ready to send an American into orbit. They selected the oldest of the original seven astronauts: Lieutenant Colonel John Glenn. Glenn had already amassed stellar credentials as a Marine Corps combat pilot and as a test pilot. As a fighter pilot during World War II, he flew 59 combat missions against Japan. He flew 90 combat missions in the Korean War. As a test pilot, he set a new speed record in 1957, flying from Los Angeles to New York in 3 hours and 23 minutes.

Fearless Facts

Among John Glenn's many noteworthy accomplishments prior to becoming one of the original seven astronauts was his appearance as a contestant on a TV game show, *Name That Tune.*

Spin Cycle

Glenn blasted into orbit on February 20, 1962 in the *Friendship 7* with 1,500 reporters and photographers on hand—the largest gathering of newspeople in America ever up until that point. The *Friendship 7* circled the earth at a speed of 17,500 mph, making three orbits before splashdown. On returning to Earth's atmosphere, the spacecraft caught fire, but Glenn was unhurt. Four million people were on hand in New York City for the largest tickertape parade ever, featuring John Glenn riding in state with President John F. Kennedy. Kennedy thought Glenn's importance as a national icon was so great that he refused to allow him to return to space. Glenn was grounded to avoid the risk of losing him in another dangerous mission.

With his days of "pushing the envelope" over, Glenn had to find other things to do to keep busy. He retired from NASA and became an executive for a soda-pop company. He later ran for the U.S. Senate from the state of Ohio and was elected in 1974, and reelected in 1980 and 1986. During this second term, his heroics as an astronaut again appeared in the spotlight, thanks to Tom Wolfe's book. But he had another curtain call to make.

Years later, NASA selected him for another mission, making him, at 77, the oldest person ever launched into space. His return brought national attention to NASA once again. On October 29, 1998, Glenn blasted off on board the *STS-95* shuttle as part of a seven-person crew. Among the many missions of the flight were to launch a satellite from space and do radiation tests on parts to be installed in the Hubble telescope. Glenn was the subject of experiments done on aging and space travel. The shuttle returned successfully to Earth after almost nine days in space.

Moonwalk

As important and memorable as it was, John Glenn's accomplishment in orbiting Earth was outdistanced by a still more "giant step" into space. This step was taken by Neil Armstrong (1930–) when he became the first human being to set foot on the moon. The image of Armstrong planting the American flag on the lunar surface has been bringing lumps to the throat of patriots ever since and has been commemorated on coins, stamps, buttons, pennants, plates, medals, and even shower curtains.

Making Light of Things

Neil Armstrong began flying at an early age. In fact, he got his pilot's license at age 16—before getting an ordinary driver's license. He went to Purdue University to study aeronautical engineering, but took time off from his studies to fly as a navy pilot during the Korean War. After he finished his degree in 1955, he became a test pilot at NASA's Edwards Air Force Base.

One of the things that makes space flight such a dangerous proposition is that the unexpected can happen. When things go wrong, it isn't always easy to set them right again out in space with limited tools, time, fuel, and air to breathe. It helps to have an astronaut who can keep cool and improvise. This is a big part of the excitement of such space-disaster movies as *Marooned* and *Apollo 13*. Armstrong has had a few near-disasters in his career, but managed to pull through.

On the strength of his work as a test pilot (most notably with the famous *X-15* jet), he was selected to become an astronaut. In 1966 he orbited Earth aboard the *Gemini 8*, and docked temporarily with another ship that had been previously launched. When the ships uncoupled, the *Gemini 8* went into a dangerous end-over-end spin at the rate of one revolution per second. Armstrong was able to keep down his cookies and pull out of the spin. Unfortunately, however, he used extra fuel in maneuvering out of the somersault, so he had to splash down early. The good news was that he made it back to Earth alive and was able to return to space as a member of the famous *Apollo 11* space mission.

Destination Moon

Armstrong was selected for the first manned lunar landing together with Michael Collins and Edwin "Buzz" Aldrin. Only Armstrong would have the honor of walking on the moon. His selection was somewhat controversial, because, unlike the other astronauts, he wasn't a military pilot at the time. He may have been selected instead of one of the others to emphasize the peaceful intent of the historic mission. Although the mission was indeed peaceful, a good amount of national pride was at stake.

In fact, just three days before the *Apollo 11* blasted off, an unmanned Soviet spacecraft, *Luna 15,* landed on the moon. The space race was a close one, and the United States was only just catching up after a relatively slow start. NASA prepared carefully. Armstrong and the others spent some 400 hours each in low-gravity space-simulation areas so that they would be able to deal with the space routine as well as with unexpected problems.

Apollo 11 was launched on July 16, 1969 at Kennedy Space Center in Florida in front of a million tailgaters and millions more watching on TV. Liftoff was successful, and the *Apollo 11* made it safely into orbit around the moon. As Collins remained inside, Armstrong and Aldrin left the ship in the lunar module, *Eagle,* and headed for the Sea of Tranquility.

The plan was to let *Eagle's* automatic pilot mechanism take care of the landing. As it turned out, however, the site selected for landing was covered with boulders. Aldrin and Armstrong had to steer the module by hand to a suitably flat spot on the moon. Safely parked, they radioed the famous message back to Earth: "The *Eagle* has landed!" Armstrong descended from the *Eagle,* took the first steps on the moon, and planted an American flag.

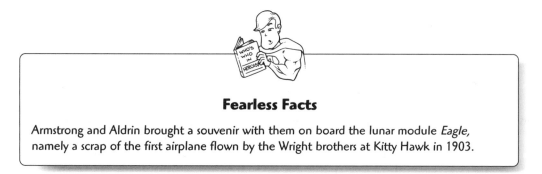

Fearless Facts

Armstrong and Aldrin brought a souvenir with them on board the lunar module *Eagle,* namely a scrap of the first airplane flown by the Wright brothers at Kitty Hawk in 1903.

The mission came off without a major hitch. As Armstrong and Aldrin prepared to launch the *Eagle* from the moon on its flight back to the mothership, *Apollo 11,* they found that a switch had broken. They fixed the problem by replacing the switch with the casing from a ballpoint pen! Talk about rocket science! Armstrong made no more space flights after his moon landing. He took an administrative job with NASA, becoming a professor of aerospace engineering at the University of Cincinnati in 1971.

Unlucky 13

The moon landing was undoubtedly the biggest success in the history of American space travel. Another exciting Apollo "success" resulted from an aborted mission, leaving NASA officials and onlookers beside themselves with joy simply because the

Towering Tips

Ever wonder how you get to be an astronaut? One way is to look in the classified ads for an opening. That's how Sally Ride did it; she answered an ad placed by NASA in her campus paper at Stanford University asking for scientists who wanted to train as astronauts.

astronauts made it home safely. This was the famous *Apollo 13* flight of April 1970, in which astronauts James Lovell, John Swigert, and Fred Haise found themselves without light or electricity as their oxygen supply leaked out into space.

Internal power went out when one of the ship's oxygen tanks exploded, ripping a leak in another tank. As the oxygen supply dwindled, the obvious course of action was to scrap the rest of the mission immediately and head back to Earth. Unfortunately, the ship's navigation system was damaged in the accident. The crew had to navigate the ship by hand, attempting to follow a suitable course for reentry and splashdown. This real-life cliff-hanger was made into the hit movie *Apollo 13* (1995), directed by Ron Howard.

Ride, Sally Ride

The first American woman ever to be launched into space was Sally Ride (1951–), who got her Ph.D. in physics from Stanford University and used her scientific training to launch herself into space. Because of the scientific nature of many of their space missions, NASA wanted to use scientists as astronauts. Out of a pool of 8,000 applicants, Ride was one of only 35 selected for training and one of only six who were women.

While training as an astronaut, she worked in NASA labs doing research on X-ray physics for several years. At last, she got the call to join the crew of the space shuttle *Challenger,* which was launched on June 27, 1983. The shuttle crew spent six days in space, launching two satellites and recovering a satellite that had been launched previously. Ride made a second *Challenger* flight in 1984 and was scheduled for a third in 1986 when the biggest disaster in NASA history took place.

In January 1986, six astronauts and a civilian schoolteacher were to be launched into space on the *Challenger's* 25th mission. The teacher, Christa McAuliffe, was to be the first civilian ever launched into space. She prepared two lessons that she intended to tele-teach from space while orbiting the Earth. Only a minute and 15 seconds after launching, nine nautical miles in the sky, the shuttle exploded into fragments and a burst of smoke and flame.

Unexpected disaster is always hard to take, but the *Challenger* tragedy was especially sobering because the shuttle carried the first civilian and so many people were eagerly watching the launch. A NASA investigation revealed that one of the shuttle's O-rings, which forms a pressure seal, did not seal properly. A contributing factor was the intense cold of the days leading up to the flight. The tragedy took the wind out of

NASA's sails like nothing else could have. Sally Ride's upcoming flight was never rescheduled and she served on the team investigating the accident.

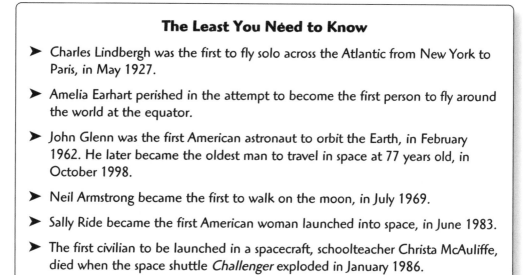

The Least You Need to Know

➤ Charles Lindbergh was the first to fly solo across the Atlantic from New York to Paris, in May 1927.

➤ Amelia Earhart perished in the attempt to become the first person to fly around the world at the equator.

➤ John Glenn was the first American astronaut to orbit the Earth, in February 1962. He later became the oldest man to travel in space at 77 years old, in October 1998.

➤ Neil Armstrong became the first to walk on the moon, in July 1969.

➤ Sally Ride became the first American woman launched into space, in June 1983.

➤ The first civilian to be launched in a spacecraft, schoolteacher Christa McAuliffe, died when the space shuttle *Challenger* exploded in January 1986.

Part 3
Fighting Spirits

For many people throughout history, the epitome of heroism has been the conquering soldier. One of the most basic, perhaps instinctual, of human desires is the desire for victory—and victory on the battlefield has often seemed like the ultimate fulfillment of this desire. People have always made war, and have always made heroes out of their warriors. This is actually a very simple, and perhaps obvious thing. Yet coming to terms with war is always one of the most difficult and wrenching experiences you could ever go through.

Many patriotic Americans point out (rightly, I believe) that we wouldn't be here today without the sacrifice and heroism of those who have gone to war for this country. Many other Americans—every bit as patriotic—are also right when they say we won't be here tomorrow if we continue to regard war as a justifiable activity. This is an important (perhaps THE important) question, but I'm not going to fight about it here!

Thinking about the people whose experiences and achievements are the subject of this section fills me with powerful, profound, and conflicting feelings: pride, sadness, anger, disgust, fear, pity—the whole human megillah.

Chapter 12

Home of the Braves

You have to appreciate the heroism of all those who battles against the odds as an underdog to protect themselves, their families, their homes, their way of life, or their rights, even if, ultimately, they lose in the end. Of all the heroes of the first 200-plus years of American history, the Indian leaders stand out as the most noble and tragic. They mustered the forces of scattered, low-tech tribal cultures against a highly coordinated and competitive society intent on taking over.

The battles were waged on political, economic, and military fronts. On all these fronts, the Indians were severely overmatched. As a result, the whites who conquered them often chose to regard them as inferior and without human rights. To the Indians, in contrast, white society often seemed evil, incomprehensible, and even insane. The difficulties of their struggle were compounded greatly by the strangeness of their enemies whose attitude toward the land, toward people, and toward life differed completely from theirs.

In their own day, the Indian leaders in the wars against the newcomers were admired and often romanticized by the whites, but also feared and despised. American settlers

Towering Tips

Whenever you read about the battles between whites and Indians, be aware of the inevitable tendency among historians to make one side seem morally better than the other side. As a result, different historians recounting the same event often provide different versions of the story. A famous example is the "Battle" at Wounded Knee, said by some to be provoked by shots fired in desperation by Indians and said by others to have been set off by trigger-happy U.S. soldiers.

usually worried about protecting themselves and securing land first and about heroism and justice afterward. Today, we see the Native American war heroes as committed leaders of their people in a struggle for everything they held important and recognize the tragedy of their defeat.

Downward Spiral

The stories of the Indian war leaders, different as they are from one another, are all variations on a theme. Typically, they responded to white encroachment on their land in a number of ways: They argued with the Europeans, rallied Indians into an organized force, and led a resistance effort. Although they won many battles, they all lost out in the long run. This scenario was repeated again and again as the white settlers moved west and encountered different Indian tribes in succession.

For King and Country

The first Indian leader to organize a military force against the white newcomers was the Wampanoag chief King Philip, mentioned in Chapter 5. The colonists of Massachusetts, Connecticut, and Rhode Island saw King Philip as a terrifying, bloodthirsty savage to be stopped by any means necessary. He attacked their settlements and, when he could, burned them to the ground before disappearing into the woods to plot more attacks. In hindsight, however, his motivation was most likely not savage cruelty but the defense of the rights of his people and of other Indian tribes who were being cheated and kept off the land where they hunted and grew their crops.

Some East Coast Indians signed treaties with the colonists relinquishing ownership of the land to the newcomers. One reason they did this was because land ownership didn't mean much to the Indians. They didn't see the land as property, but as a common resource. As a result, they were willing to sell the land, especially since the agreements often guaranteed them the right to continue to use it. Once the colonists took possession, however, they were unwilling to let the Indians hunt and grow crops on land they saw as theirs.

So, King Philip mobilized an Indian force and attempted to take the land back. This was no easy feat for a number of reasons. The problem they faced was an unfamiliar one. Most Indians had no idea of what the colonists were doing or how white society worked. Not all Indians regarded them as a threat, especially since they offered new economic opportunities; so they were unwilling to go to war. This meant that King

Philip could not focus all his attention on battle, but had to spend much time and energy trying to persuade potential followers and allies to help him. In fact, all the other Indian leaders who mounted resistance to the newcomers faced the challenge of playing military leader and diplomat at the same time.

Fearless Facts

Indian war leaders were sometimes aided in the task of mustering support by Indian priests and medicine men. Tecumseh joined forces with another man known as "the Prophet." Pontiac formed an alliance with the Delaware Prophet. The most famous pairing of a chief with a medicine man is Crazy Horse and Sitting Bull of the Sioux.

Detroit's Finest

One of the most successful Indian war leaders—for a time, anyway—was Pontiac, an Ojibwe (Chippewa) chief born around 1720. Pontiac played a major role in the French and Indian War between British and French colonialists in the Great Lakes Region. Indians fought on either side, making Pontiac's efforts to organize an Indian force especially difficult. Pontiac sided with the French—not out of any special loyalty to them, but because he felt an alliance with the French would give his people the best chance of victory. In fact, early in his career, he came to see that economic independence was important for the Indians. By relying on trade with the whites, many Indians were sacrificing political autonomy.

Pontiac aided in the famous defeat of General Braddock at Fort Duquesne in what is now Pittsburgh. Braddock led a force of British soldiers and colonial militia, including the young George Washington, who marched on the fort but were put to rout. Eventually, however, the tide of war shifted in favor of the British. The French surrendered and agreed to turn over to them a number of forts east of the Mississippi. Soon afterward, Pontiac met with British Major Robert Rogers who had been commissioned to take over the French forts, letting him know that peace with the French did not necessarily mean peace with him and his people. He demanded that the British respect Indian hunting and farming rights. His demands were rejected, so Pontiac continued his war against the British. The French, meanwhile, indicated they would help him fight.

With a force that included Ojibwe, Ottowa, Huron, Mingo, Delaware, and Seneca Indians, Pontiac took many forts held by the British, including Fort Sandusky, Fort

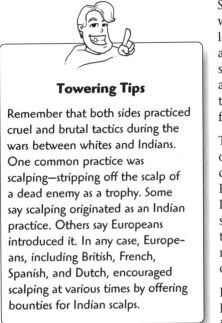

Towering Tips

Remember that both sides practiced cruel and brutal tactics during the wars between whites and Indians. One common practice was scalping—stripping off the scalp of a dead enemy as a trophy. Some say scalping originated as an Indian practice. Others say Europeans introduced it. In any case, Europeans, including British, French, Spanish, and Dutch, encouraged scalping at various times by offering bounties for Indian scalps.

Saint Joseph, Fort Miami, and Fort Wayne. Pontiac was a zealous fighter, an inspiring and respected leader, and a shrewd tactician. His warriors deployed a successful ruse to take Fort Michilimackinac: They started up a game of lacrosse outside the fort walls and let the lacrosse ball roll through the gates. As they started chasing after it, they pulled out guns from under their cloaks and waged a surprise attack.

The British deployed some unusual tactics of their own over the course of the war. Captain Ecuyer, the commander of Fort Pitt (the same fort known to the French as Fort Duquesne) made a present to some Indians of blankets that had been infected with smallpox. Indians ever since have deeply resented this, because entire tribes were decimated by the resulting epidemic, including, of course, women and children.

Pontiac himself was not stricken by the disease, but his task of maintaining a powerful force became increasingly difficult as his followers died or became discouraged. Pontiac's war effort, already seriously weakened, collapsed completely when the French, who had promised assistance, announced they wouldn't help. Many of Pontiac's followers abandoned the cause at this time. A Peoria Indian named Black Dog finally assassinated Pontiac in the spring of 1769.

Drawing the Line

Among the most respected of the Indian chiefs—respected by both whites and Indians alike—was Tecumseh (1770–1813), a Shawnee leader who traveled throughout the Mississippi basin urging Indians to join together in resisting the newcomers and asking U.S. officials to call a halt to westward expansion. In fact, he garnered a reputation as a great orator as well as a warrior. He was staunchly opposed to the land deals that the whites were making with the Indians.

Tecumseh's nemesis was Brigadier General William Henry Harrison, who later became president. Harrison made a deal to buy 3,000,000 acres of land from the Indians for about $10,000. Tecumseh argued that the Indians who agreed to the deal did not represent all Indians, and certainly didn't represent the best interests of Indians in general. As far as he was concerned, the land wasn't theirs to sell.

Harrison refused to listen to Tecumseh's arguments, so Tecumseh prepared for war. At this time, the British were also preparing to renew hostilities with the Americans. Tecumseh asked the British for guns and supplies and stockpiled them at Tippecanoe,

Tecumseh. (Dictionary of American Portraits)

in what is now Indiana. He then traveled south to persuade other tribes to join him against Harrison. Realizing that something was going on, Harrison decided to provoke Tecumseh's followers into battle in his absence. He marched his troops up to the vicinity of Tippecanoe and built a fort, which he named Fort Harrison after himself.

As Harrison had hoped, the Indians attacked the fort before Tecumseh had returned from his travels. Harrison and his men retaliated and raided the stockpile at Tippecanoe. Tecumseh was frustrated by the setback, but did not give up. He continued fighting against U.S. troops and negotiating with the British—who were eventually so impressed with his abilities that they made him a brigadier general in charge of British as well as Indian troops. Thus, Tecumseh fought on the side of the British in the War of 1812.

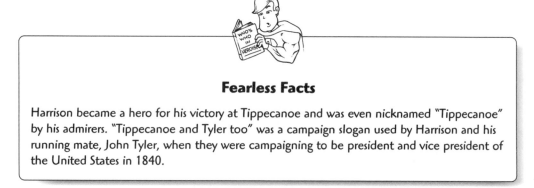

Fearless Facts

Harrison became a hero for his victory at Tippecanoe and was even nicknamed "Tippecanoe" by his admirers. "Tippecanoe and Tyler too" was a campaign slogan used by Harrison and his running mate, John Tyler, when they were campaigning to be president and vice president of the United States in 1840.

Tecumseh and his men laid siege to Fort Harrison unsuccessfully, but they met with success elsewhere. Among his many victories was the capture of the command post at Detroit. He managed to induce the captain of the fort to surrender without a fight through a clever bit of deception. He had his warriors muster for battle right outside the fort in a noisy show of strength, and then he had them slip away quietly back into the woods. Immediately afterward, the same warriors would put on the same show of strength, pretending to be a whole new group. After repeating the act several times, Tecumseh made the captain think his force was several times larger than it actually was!

Tecumseh is remembered as a brilliant and courageous military strategist who worked well with his British counterpart, General Isaac Brock. Brock respected Tecumseh highly, often consulting with him and following his advice. Unfortunately for Tecumseh, Brock was killed in battle and replaced by Colonel Henry Proctor, who disliked Indians and had limited talent as a soldier and commander. Tecumseh came to despise Proctor, suspecting him of cowardice.

Despite many impressive early successes, Tecumseh was eventually defeated and killed while fighting alongside the British in an impossible battle. Not long afterward, the British capitulated and the Americans won the War of 1812. Tecumseh's work, however, had repercussions after his death. His reputation as a courageous fighter and his efforts to gather support among the Indians galvanized tribes to the south, making them highly cautious in their dealings with whites.

Close to Home

Twenty years after Tecumseh's death, Black Hawk (1767–1838), the Sauk chief, became embroiled in a war that is named after him: Black Hawk's War. Like Tecumseh, Black Hawk refused to accept a land deal signed by other chiefs, believing they had no right to sell the land. The treaty in question, negotiated by the man who fought Tecumseh, General Harrison, called for the Sauk and the Fox to move west of the Mississippi, allowing them to use the land to the east only until it was settled by whites.

When the other Sauk and Fox moved, Black Hawk and those loyal to him stayed on. When the settlers came, he burned down their cabins and demanded that they leave. The military was called into action and sent out a force many times bigger than the one Black Hawk was able to raise. The two sides met in battle in August 1832, but there was never any doubt of the outcome. Yet, despite clear defeat, Black Hawk managed to escape.

Towering Tips

Don't assume that your only option in defeat is to go out in a futile blaze of glory. Consider dignified surrender instead. Admitting defeat is not the same as sacrificing your principles, and you may even gain respect and sympathy for your lost cause. This happened in the case of the Sauk leader Black Hawk.

Black Hawk. (Dictionary of American Portraits)

Soon afterward, Black Hawk surrendered in state to U.S. General Henry Atkinson. He continued to believe fully in the justice of his cause and expected that, in defeat, he would be permitted to join what remained of his people on the other side of the Mississippi. Instead he was taken prisoner and eventually sent to Washington where he spent close to a year behind bars.

Strangely, after his release, he was taken on a tour of the eastern United States, where he was hailed as a celebrity. No one seemed to regard him as a dangerous threat or even as an enemy. He attended many banquets in his honor, chatted with officials, and received gifts from admirers. Afterward, he returned to his homeland; there his reception was very different. People remembered the bloodshed he had caused and held him responsible. He was burned in effigy in Detroit, and government troops had to protect him from angry mobs. He died in 1837, disillusioned and in despair over the plight of his people. His grave was later vandalized. After that, the governor of Iowa acquired his remains and put them on display in his office.

Without Reservations

Not all heroic Indian leaders were warriors. Similarly, not all Indians resisted assimilation into white society. The Cherokee became especially successful at adapting to the new ways. Although they were forced to live on a reservation in Georgia, they prospered as farmers and keepers of livestock. They lived in houses, went to schools, learned to read, and started their own newspaper. They were familiar with white laws and government and had a well-organized governing body of their own led by Chief John Ross (1790–1866).

157

John Ross. (Dictionary of American Portraits)

Heroic Shorts

Suzette La Flesche (1854–1903) was an Omaha Indian who toured the country lecturing on injustice perpetrated against Native Americans. She attended the Elizabeth Institute in New Jersey before becoming a teacher on her reservation. In 1879 she went on a lecture tour with Thomas Tibbles, a journalist working for the *Omaha Herald*. She married Tibbles in 1881. In promoting awareness of the abuses of Indian rights she was instrumental in the passage of the Dawes act of 1887, which made concessions to Native Americans.

Unfortunately, this rare success in the history of Indian assimilation didn't last. As the white population of Georgia grew, settlers wanted the Cherokee out so they could have the land for themselves and so they could mine for gold in the Appalachian hills. They clamored for the government to take action, which it did. Congress voted to have the Indians put out and offered them a paltry $30,000 to leave. The Cherokee council, led by Chief John Ross, strongly opposed the offer of money for their land. The council passed a resolution not to accept payment of any kind.

The whites responded with intimidation and bribery attempts. When offered money to sell out his people, Ross publicly denounced the scheme. Meanwhile, the Georgia state government took measures. The legislature passed laws dividing up Cherokee land into lots and denying the Cherokee rights to the land. In addition, laws were passed denying the Cherokee the right to defend themselves. The laws had nothing to do with justice, but were simply designed to steal the land of the Cherokee reservation. All the while, white settlers grew increasingly violent, terrorizing the Cherokee.

Fearless Facts

The Cherokee were part of the Iroquois civilization that pre-existed the coming of the white man and followed democratic procedures for choosing leaders and passing laws. Some historians have suggested that Iroquois ideas of government were incorporated by the founding fathers into the U.S. Constitution.

Ross still refused to see his people put off their land. He was familiar with the concept of "justice" that seemed to be such an important part of the American legal system, and knew that justice was on his side. So he took his cause to the Supreme Court. This was the first time Indians ever made such an appeal. The Supreme Court heard the case and rendered a decision in support of the Cherokee. Neither Congress, nor the Georgia state legislature, nor the white settlers had any right to the land or any right to pass special laws limiting the rights of the Cherokee.

Sadly, no one in the U.S. government was willing to stand up and assert the rule of law against the bogus rulings of the Georgia legislature and the selfish demands of the white settlers. President Andrew Jackson made no attempt to uphold the rights of the Cherokee. John Ross's house was confiscated. Not long afterward, the Cherokee were rounded up and forcibly led to a new settlement in Oklahoma. Many perished of disease and exposure along the way. The trip has come to be known as the Trail of Tears.

Fading in the West

The last organized effort mounted by Indians to resist the westward expansion of the whites was organized by the young Sioux chief Crazy Horse

Heroic Shorts

Chief Joseph the younger (1832–1904) of the Nez Perce was a renowned Indian chief, warrior, military strategist, and orator with a reputation for wisdom and justice. He assumed charge of the Nez Perce in 1871 when his father, Chief Joseph the elder, died. He led his people in a retreat across thousands of miles through mountainous terrain while being chased by the army. The Nez Perce stopped to fight on numerous occasions, avoiding defeat thanks to Chief Joseph's ingenious tactics. He and his people were finally defeated just short of the Canadian border after six days of fighting when Chief Joseph surrendered and was taken prisoner. He made and kept a famous vow never to fight again.

Sitting Bull. (Dictionary of American Portraits)

(1850–1877) and the older Sioux medicine man, Sitting Bull (1835–1890). The Sioux were buffalo hunters who occupied the Great Plains until the western railroads were built. The railroads interfered with their hunting and they, in turn, interfered with the railroads. Eventually they were moved to a reservation in the Black Hills of the Dakotas.

Fearless Facts

Sitting Bull participated in a sacred—and, to many whites, grisly—Sioux ritual known as the Sun Dance. His upper body was pierced in many places to permit thongs to be strung through his flesh. The thongs were suspended from a pole, allowing him to dance around the pole while the thongs tugged at his body. The Sun Dance went on for days until Sitting Bull had a vision of destroying the white enemies.

The Sioux found this to be a tolerable arrangement, because they regarded the Black Hills as sacred ground and were therefore willing to live there. The whites were satisfied too, because the rough terrain was not particularly desirable for their settlements.

The territory is known as the Dakota Bad Lands, where, due to highly alkaline soil, there is almost no vegetation. Unfortunately for the Sioux, however, gold was discovered in the Black Hills in 1873 and a gold rush quickly followed. Bands of greedy miners descended on the Sioux reservation, digging up the sacred ground and showing no regard for the rights of the Sioux to the land.

Crazy Horse, a chief of only 25 years, retaliated with violence and the army was called in to deal with the situation. Crazy Horse was married to a Cheyenne woman and easily won the support of many Cheyenne tribesmen. Sitting Bull was widely respected for his wisdom and power and succeeded in enlisting many more warriors. The two leaders commanded a force of more than 3,000 men.

Whipped Custer

The U.S. military force that rode out to confront them was led by General George Crook, who had considerable experience in dealing with Indians; the Indians respected him for his honesty. He was in charge of 10 troops of cavalry and 2 more troops of infantry. An additional division, the 7th Cavalry, was led by Field General George Custer, a zealous Indian fighter who had gained a heroic reputation in battle early in his career (only to tarnish it later with reckless conduct). He was eager to try to win back some of his fame.

In an initial encounter, Crook met with Crazy Horse and battled to a standstill after a full day of fighting. That night both sides retreated. It was Custer, leading the 7th

General George Armstrong Custer. (Dictionary of American Portraits)

Cavalry, who later encountered the bulk of the Indian forces encamped on the bank of the Little Big Horn River in June 1876. Custer was eager for fight and hungry for glory. He chose not to bring along the Gatling guns he was supplied with, not wanting to be slowed down by the heavy artillery. He also chose to ignore his instructions to wait for reinforcements, preferring to lead an advance immediately.

Towering Tips

Don't let concern for your public image cloud your judgement in dangerous situations. This kind of vanity may have been a factor in Custer's defeat at Little Big Horn. He tried to cultivate a dashing public image and even went so far as to bring a newspaper reporter along with him on campaigns!

In fact, Custer was so eager for battle that he led his troops on the Indians' trail all night. After coming up to them in the morning, he spurred his troops into battle with insufficient rest. Finally, Custer made the mistake of grossly underestimating the strength of his adversary. He led 600 men against an encampment of some 10,000 warriors. Of these 600, Custer took 212 around to the side of the encampment, leaving the rest under the command of Major Marcus Reno and Captain Frederick Benteen, who were to attack from the front and side, respectively.

Custer charged into the thick of the encampment and Crazy Horse, Sitting Bull, and their warriors were ready for him. His force of 212 men were wiped out in less than an hour. This was Custer's "Last Stand," the famous defeat of the 7th Cavalry at the Battle of Little Big Horn. Reno and Benteen managed to retreat to strategic ground on a hillside and hold off the Indians, who struck camp the next day and moved off. But, as they realized, the hiatus in fighting was only temporary. Enraged at Custer's defeat, General Brock was determined to defeat the Indians and kill or capture their Sioux leaders.

To increase their chances against the campaign they knew was coming, Sitting Bull and Crazy Horse divided up their forces into small bands and dispersed throughout the territory. Soon afterward, in January 1877, Crazy Horse was captured and taken prisoner. He drew his knife attempting to escape and a scuffle ensued, leaving the young chief dead, killed by his own weapon. It's uncertain whether he was murdered, committed suicide, or died by accident.

Sitting Bull escaped to Canada, where he stayed for several years until he and his followers found themselves unable to keep living off the land. He returned to the Dakotas and surrendered in July 1881. He returned to the reservation, reconciled to living out the rest of his days there. He did not die a peaceful death, however, because although he put up no further resistance, his reputation made the whites fear him and he was shot in an event leading up to the famous massacre at Wounded Knee.

Seeing Ghosts

The Wounded Knee incident is sometimes called a battle, but it was really the mass killing of a nearly powerless Indian settlement by an anxious military force. They were concerned in part because of a strange religious movement called ghost dancing that had sprung up among the Indians in recent years. The instigator of the movement was a Paiute medicine man named Wovoka.

Wovoka had a prophetic vision and declared that the Indians who had been killed by the whites would return to life and the whites would be destroyed. The slaughtered herds of buffalo would return and the Indians would live in peace. The hopeful message spread to the Sioux reservation where Indians began performing the ghost dance to welcome the return of the dead. It was said that anyone wearing the shirt in which he performed the ghost dance could not be harmed by a white man's bullet.

Fearless Facts

Wovoka's prophetic vision came in 1890 during a solar eclipse. Many Indians saw this eclipse as a sign of a coming cataclysm.

Ghost dancers danced themselves into a frenzy and kept on dancing until they collapsed in exhaustion. The movement provided a focus for Indian frustration and resentment and offered hope that it would come to an end in the near future. Although it was harmless in itself, whites began to worry that it would result in an attack of some kind. And they assumed, whatever was going on, that the dreaded leader Sitting Bull would be involved, so they ordered his arrest.

On December 15, 1890, a small army of Indian police arrested Sitting Bull. Looking on were a number of ghost dancers. One of the ghost dancers fired on the police, who then shot the Sioux leader (following instructions to shoot rather than allow Sitting Bull to escape). He was shot through the body by an Indian named Bull Head, and shot in the head by an Indian sergeant named Red Tomahawk.

In the wake of Sitting Bull's death, a number of Sioux escaped the reservation, just as U.S. troops were preparing to crack down to prevent an uprising. A band of about 200 were captured by the cavalry and ordered to return to the reservation. As they were getting their gear together, the troops surrounded them and trained their guns on the group, including some heavy artillery. Meanwhile, troop leader Colonel James Forsythe ordered the Indians to surrender their weapons.

Not satisfied with the number of guns the Indians turned in, Forsythe ordered a search that revealed additional guns. As the search continued, resentment on the part of the Indians increased until someone began firing. In no time, the entire camp came under fire as troopers and Indians shot at one another from point-blank range with the heavy guns blazing behind them. Those Indians who weren't killed right away were hunted down. The troopers killed 143 Indians and wounded 33 more. Many were women and children. On the other side, 30 U.S. soldiers were killed and 34 were wounded.

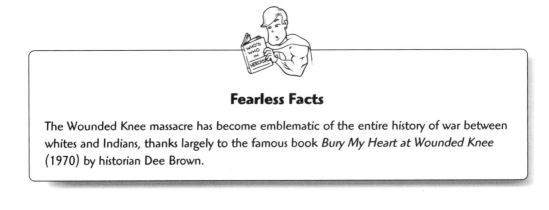

Fearless Facts

The Wounded Knee massacre has become emblematic of the entire history of war between whites and Indians, thanks largely to the famous book *Bury My Heart at Wounded Knee* (1970) by historian Dee Brown.

Geronimo!

The collapse of the war effort led by Crazy Horse and Sitting Bull marked the end of large-scale Indian resistance. Only small, scattered renegade bands occasionally escaped the reservations to terrorize ranches and military outposts. One of these bands was led by a chief so wily and tough that he managed to avoid capture for close to two years in

Geronimo. (Dictionary of American Portraits)

Fearless Facts

In his later years, Geronimo became a member of the Dutch Reformed Church.

1885–1886, despite the fact that he was pursued by thousands of troops. This was the Apache leader known as Geronimo (1829–1909).

Geronimo led a group of about 80 Indians known as the Chiricahua band. They avoided pursuit by crossing back and forth between the United States and Mexico. Although Mexican troops came after them too, no one knew where the band would turn up when they crossed the border. Finally, Geronimo was captured and agreed to return to the Apache reservation. He quickly changed his mind and escaped, however, and the chase continued. At last, he was captured a second time and lived out his days on the reservation to the age of 80.

Raider of the Southwest

Among the great chiefs of the Apache is Cochise (1812–1874), leader of a band of raiders and warriors in the Southwest. He was able to continue raiding as a way of life by playing different sides against one another through various conflicts. During border disputes between the U.S. and Mexico, he allied with Mexico for a while in order to get safe haven in Mexico while raiding U.S. settlements. Then he made agreements with the U.S. that enabled him to make raids in Mexico. Later, during the Civil War, he resumed his raids in the U.S. while the military was preoccupied. And while Mexico was in conflict with the French, he continued raiding there. He finally signed a treaty with the U.S. in 1872, agreeing to stop raiding in exchange for land use and supplies.

The Least You Need to Know

➤ History reveals a succession of Indian leaders who rose to defend their lands and rights and were defeated by whites.

➤ Pontiac fought on the side of the French in the French and Indian War.

➤ Tecumseh served as a British general in the War of 1812.

➤ Black Hawk was welcomed as a hero in the eastern United States and reviled as a villain in his homeland in the Mississippi basin.

➤ Chief John Ross won a victory for the Cherokee in the Supreme Court, but the ruling was not upheld by the U.S. government.

➤ Crazy Horse and Sitting Bull defeated General Custer at the battle of Little Big Horn in 1876.

Chapter 13

Fearless Leaders

In This Chapter

➤ Soldier-presidents and presidents at war

➤ Washington and the Revolutionary War

➤ Jackson and the War of 1812

➤ Lincoln, Grant, and the Civil War

➤ Teddy Roosevelt and the Spanish-American War

➤ Dwight D. Eisenhower and World War II

History shows that if you want to become president of the United States it doesn't hurt to be a war hero first. And if you want to go down in history as a great president, it's not a bad idea to lead the country in a victorious war as commander in chief. Ever since the days of George Washington, who first made the transition from general to president, the ideal of the great soldier and statesman has loomed large in the hearts and minds of the American people.

Many voters like to think of the president as someone who has paid his dues in the service of the country by facing the dangers and deprivations of war. They often assume that someone who has survived, succeeded, and excelled as a leader on the field of battle will do the same as a political leader. And successful military leaders seem to have an aura of competence and power that people like to see in a president.

What's more, the job of commander in chief of the military has always been a crucial part of the office of president in the minds of many Americans. This is largely because

Worthy Words

A **mercenary** is a professional soldier hired to fight someone else's battle. Few people in England were passionate about the cause of suppressing the Revolutionary War in America, so most of the troops enlisted to fight for the British were German mercenaries known as Hessians. England's King George III hired some 30,000 German soldiers to fight his war.

the traditional American values of freedom and independence don't leave much room for compromise with opposing powers. Instead, these values need to be maintained and preserved continuously with military preparedness. That's why the country's highest office tends to seem like the right desk job for the country's greatest war heroes.

General Considerations

George Washington (1732–1799) set the pattern for all the heroic soldier/presidents who came after him. He acquired military experience early as a major and later a colonel in the colonial militia in the French and Indian War, serving under the defeated General Braddock. Of course his real heroism emerged later as a Revolutionary War general. This heroism was based not only on his courage and skill as a military leader, but also on his commitment to the revolutionary cause. He wasn't just some tough guy with a gun, but he believed in what he was doing. His ability to spread this belief to his men enabled him to succeed.

Midnight Crossing

Prior to the Revolution, Washington was a delegate to the First Continental Congress, which met to air grievances of the colonists against the British. When war broke out in 1775, he took command of the Continental Army and, the following year, drove the British from Boston. He was later defeated in battle on Long Island and things began to look bad for the Revolution. The revolutionaries did not have the wealth and power of their British enemies or the experience in battle of the soldiers who fought for the king. Most of these soldiers were German *mercenaries*—professional fighters whose only interest in the conflict was their pay.

As the war wore on with few successes, many began to criticize Washington for being too cautious. When it looked like he couldn't win a battle, he retreated to save his troops. Although Washington kept casualties of war to a minimum, hardships mounted for his troops, because they were often inadequately supplied with food and clothing. Finally, it was the willingness of his forces to undergo hardship that led to victory.

At a crucial juncture in the war, Washington decided to strike the city of Trenton, New Jersey, which was held by British forces. He chose to attack on the day after Christmas, when the British troops and German mercenaries would be sleeping off the party of the night before. While the enemy was carousing and later sleeping it off in warm beds, he and his men were on the march through the cold. Some men wore shoes that were so worn, shards of ice poked through and drew blood from their feet.

George Washington crossing the Delaware. (Rutgers University Special Collections and Archives)

This is how Washington got the drop on his enemies: On Christmas night, 1776, he and his men quietly ferried across the Delaware River into Trenton. When morning came and the British forces were getting out of bed, the Americans had cannons set up in the street. Groggy and unprepared for battle, the enemy surrendered after a few brief exchanges of fire. Nine hundred and twenty enemy soldiers surrendered to Washington. Ninety had been wounded and twenty-five were killed. On the American side, only four were wounded and none were killed in battle. In fact, the only American soldiers lost were two who froze to death!

Forge-ing Ahead

Washington spent the following winter holding his troops together at Valley Forge, Pennsylvania during a long, cold winter with inadequate supplies and ebbing morale. And the war dragged on for years after that. At last the Americans and their allies, the French, took the opportunity to cut off and lay siege to a British battalion at Yorktown, Virginia, where Lord General Charles Cornwallis waited with close to 7,000 troops. In a coordinated surprise maneuver, Washington led his forces to Yorktown on a sudden march from New Jersey while a French fleet sealed off Chesapeake Bay.

Cut off by land and sea, Cornwallis waited in vain for reinforcements. For close to two weeks, he endured the siege as supplies dwindled and casualties mounted under American artillery fire. At last, on October 19, 1781, Cornwallis surrendered to Washington after the battle that marked the end of the Revolution. Washington emerged unequivocally as the greatest hero of the war, having led continual, grueling campaigns from the beginning.

After the war, he returned to his plantation in Virginia. Although his power and popularity would have enabled him to take the helm of the young country, he refused to fill the power vacuum that ensued after the war as a military dictator. Years later, in 1789, he was unanimously elected as the nation's first president.

Hatchet Job

As president, Washington was conscious of the awe and respect Americans had for him and did his best to live up to his reputation and the importance of his office. He took care to preserve his dignity and deal with others in a straightforward way. His dignified reserve made it easy for people to idealize him as the epitome of courage and honesty. He was touted as a virtuous role model for young people in a widely read biography written in 1800 by Parson Mason Weems.

Weems, who simply invented anecdotes about the life of the hero, is responsible for a number of myths about Washington, including the famous story about the cherry tree. Weems says that when young George Washington was six years old, he was given a hatchet, which he used to chop down a cherry tree belonging to his father. When his

Fearless Facts

Washington made a heroic effort to preserve his dignity while sitting for his portrait painted by the noted artist Gilbert Stuart. At the time, all of Washington's teeth had recently been pulled and was wearing a badly fitting pair of false teeth! Needless to say, the first president didn't feel like saying "cheese." Stuart's portrait shows him with a grim, sour expression.

father asked about the tree, little George resisted the urge to lie and get himself off the hook. The little story illustrates Washington's uncompromising honesty.

Americans have celebrated this mythical quality in their first president ever since. His dignified portrait on the dollar bill suggests that the U.S. Treasury has put its money where its mouth is in issuing bank notes that are sound and reliable. The connection between money and Washington's honesty often gets alluded to when stores run Presidents' Day sales and feature George on the dollar bill or with his hatchet by the cherry tree.

Change for a Dollar

For millions of Americans, the ideal of honesty in business and personal dealings has gone together with the ideals of freedom and independence that inspired the patriots fighting the Revolutionary War. Parson Weem's fables, however, are no longer required reading in American grade schools. Instead, historians are coming to terms with the fact that Washington and the patriots did not live up to all that they have come to stand for. The country, after all, has grown and changed tremendously since those days.

When Washington was elected president, only a small percentage of Americans had the right to vote: only land-owning white men in most states. Washington himself owned slaves. Although all kinds of Americans shared in the hardships and even died in the Revolution, not all shared equally in the victory. "The People" referred to in the Declaration of Independence were not originally taken to include blacks by all those who signed it, and included white women only indirectly through their fathers and husbands.

Fearless Facts

Revolutionary forces under Washington included hundreds of African-American slaves who fought in exchange for freedom from slavery.

If this seems surprising or ironic, it may be because the force of the ideals of freedom and independence has grown since Revolutionary War days. They continue to seem important and worth fighting for, even if that means acknowledging that our heroic founding fathers did not fight the entire battle themselves. What they did was set an example for others who have battles of their own.

Action Jackson

Whereas Washington bore himself with aloof, gentlemanly dignity, the big hero of the War of 1812, Andrew Jackson, was a rough, rowdy, frontiersman from Tennessee. Jackson is remembered for his uncompromising toughness and courage. A story that is often told about Jackson is that when he was still in his early teens he helped out in the Revolutionary War and was captured by British soldiers. A British officer ordered him to wipe off his boots, but he refused; whereupon the officer opened a gash in Jackson's head with his sword.

As a grown man, he frequently got into quarrels, in part because he was touchy about the honor of his wife, Rachel, who had been married previously to another man. He had just fought a duel over Rachel (and been badly injured) when he was called to lead a force of volunteers against the Creek Indians. He led his men to victory with his arm in a sling and the bullet still in the wound. It wasn't removed until 19 years later. When it was finally taken out, Jackson offered to give the bullet back to the man who shot him!

Andrew Jackson. (Rutgers University Special Collections and Archives)

Fearless Facts

Andrew Jackson's wife, Rachel Donelson, had been married to a man named Robards before becoming engaged to the future president. Rachel believed that Robards had filed for divorce by the time she and Jackson got married, but it turned out he had not. The divorce was not legalized until two years after her marriage to Jackson. When Robards objected to Rachel's marriage to Jackson, Jackson threatened to cut his ears off!

Jackson's men were backwoodsman who admired his fierce pride and stubborn determination. Because he was tough and lanky, his men called him Old Hickory. The Indians called him Sharp Knife because he was such a formidable and ruthless opponent. After defeating the Creeks, he imposed harsh terms of surrender, knowing they had no choice but to accept.

Jackson's most heroic victory during the War of 1812 took place when the war had technically already ended. Unfortunately, the news of the peace agreement was slow to travel. The war concerned trade disputes between America and Britain and possession of territory that had not yet become part of the United States, including the rich port city of New Orleans. Jackson and his men were stationed in this city to protect it late in the war.

Jackson thought that the British would be crazy to attack New Orleans directly, because it would be more effective to make war on outlying settlements. As a result, he was caught unprepared by a British assault that was lured in part by the city's wealth. Even so, he acted quickly to minimize the advantage gained by the British in surprising him. He went out to meet them in their camps outside the city the night of their arrival—when they were tired from traveling—and attacked. This was only the first night of weeks of fighting, but it started things off badly for the British. They were able to advance only a little farther and not into New Orleans itself before surrendering in January 1815.

In fact, the War of 1812 settled almost nothing. Both sides realized that the disputes between the United States and Britain would have to be worked out a little at a time. But the war established Jackson as a major American hero. He was especially popular with southerners and westerners who admired his roughness. In the Northeast, however, he was generally considered too wild to be a good statesman.

In 1824, Jackson ran for president and won a majority of popular votes, but failed to win a majority of electoral votes. The presidency was decided by Congress, which elected John Quincy Adams. The following term, however, Jackson and his supporters were not to be denied, despite a determined anti-Jackson campaign that featured a derogatory pamphlet titled "An Extract from the Catalogue of General Jackson's Youthful Indiscretions Between the Age of 23 and 60." Not only was Jackson elected decisively, he was reelected the following term. And these days, his tough, lanky looks are more striking than ever with the minting of the new $20 bill!

Towering Tips

Make the most of your supporters, even if they don't seem important or powerful. It was his popularity with voters—rather than the endorsement of Congress—that won Jackson the presidency. He was the first president to be elected in spite of serious congressional opposition.

Honest Abe

Perhaps the greatest American president of all was in office during the most terrible American war. Abraham Lincoln led the struggle to preserve the union as president during the Civil War. In the process, he declared an end to slavery. In coming from a poor working family and keeping in touch with ordinary people, he embodied the ideals of democracy. More than any other president, he's been looked upon as a wise, modest, patient, and benevolent leader.

Cabin Boy

Everybody knows that Lincoln was born in a log cabin. (Some of his more ardent admirers have even suggested that he built this cabin with his own hands, but this is doubtful!) Much of his political popularity stemmed from his roots as an ordinary working man. His supporters pointed to his days in Illinois splitting rails on his homestead and working in a store. In fact, he was always at home among ordinary folks and liked to talk with them even as president.

He had a reputation for honesty and was often called "Honest Abe." One legend says that he walked for miles to return a few cents he had mistakenly overcharged a customer in his store. He's also known for educating himself. He had only about a year of formal schooling, but read everything he could get his hands on. Another Lincoln legend says that he borrowed Weems' life of Washington from a friend. After he accidentally left it out in the rain, he worked off the cost of the book. The point of these legends is that his integrity helped him rise to greatness from his humble circumstances.

Abraham Lincoln.
(Rutgers University Special
Collections and Archives)

Fearless Facts

Some of the many legends told about Lincoln as a boy seem to contradict one another. Some say he was physically lazy and would do anything to get out of work in order to read books. Others say he was so strong that he did the work of three or four men. Some say he was so sensitive and kind to animals that he couldn't stand the sight of the blood of any creature. Others say he was a great shot with a rifle and loved hunting.

Holding It All Together

When he became president in 1860, seven states had already announced their secession from the Union. Soon after he took office, four more states seceded. Determined to preserve the Union, Lincoln declared war on the Confederate States after shots were fired on U.S. Fort Sumter in Charleston, South Carolina on April 12, 1861. One of the key issues in the struggle was slavery, to which growing numbers of people in the North were strongly opposed. Slavery was an important part of the southern economy, however, and southern states refused to give it up.

Unlike northern abolitionists who called for an immediate end to slavery, Lincoln favored a gradual phasing out of slavery, after southern growers had a chance to find ways to work their plantations without slaves and after schools could be built for the freed slaves. The Civil War, however, didn't provide the right climate for the gradual progress Lincoln had in mind. In hopes of restoring the Union and ending the war, he used emancipation as a threat to the Confederate States, saying that unless they returned to the Union, he would declare an immediate wholesale end to slavery.

His efforts to negotiate were unsuccessful and the war raged on. In 1863 on New Year's Day, he signed the Emancipation Proclamation, which declared freedom for the slaves throughout the nation—including the Confederate States. The first official step to secure freedom for the slaves had finally been taken. (The 13th Amendment to the Constitution, abolishing slavery, was passed into law by the southern states themselves in 1865.)

Fearless Facts

Although the Emancipation Proclamation was signed on January 1, 1863, it took several months for the news to spread. Many slaves in Texas did not learn they were free until the following June. As a result, "Juneteenth Day" is an official state holiday in Texas. The holiday is recognized elsewhere in the U.S. as well.

Lincoln continued to regard the preservation of the Union as his immediate priority. Three and a half months after the decisive battle of Gettysburg (Pennsylvania), Lincoln delivered the Gettysburg Address, stressing the importance of Union within the United States to preserve the ideals of democracy. This has become the most famous speech ever given by a president.

Last Act

Early in Lincoln's second presidential term, on April 9, 1865, General Robert E. Lee surrendered to General Ulysses S. Grant by the Appomattox River in Virginia and the Civil War ended. It had been the most harrowing struggle in U.S. history—especially for Lincoln. Despite the pressures of war, he was habitually mild in tolerating the verbal abuse that was heaped on him by his many detractors who held him to blame for the bloody struggle and the economic plight of the defeated South.

Lincoln turned his attention to piecing the Union back together after the war, but was not able to get far in his plans. Deeply frustrated by the fall of the old South, an actor from Maryland named John Wilkes Booth planned to kidnap the president and hold him in exchange for Confederate prisoners of war. The war ended before he could put his plan into action, but his deep resentment didn't subside. Just five days after the Confederate surrender, on April 14, Booth walked into a theater where Lincoln was attending a play, crept up behind him, and shot him in the back of the head. Lincoln died the next morning.

Towering Tips

Don't combine vainglory with treachery and murder. After shooting Lincoln, actor John Wilkes Booth leapt from Lincoln's box onto the stage shouting "*Sic semper tyrannus!*" ("Thus ever to tyrants"). During his dramatic leap, however, he tripped on some bunting and landed wrong, breaking his foot. He then hobbled from the stage after his final appearance and worst performance.

Union General

The big Civil War hero for the North was Ulysses S. Grant. He started out his military career as a reluctant cadet, entering West Point Military Academy against his own wishes. He graduated as a mediocre student and became an undistinguished military officer assigned to California, far from his family. He later became homesick and gave up the military to return to his family and try his hand at other things. As it turned out, however, he wasn't very good at other things. He tried farming, shopkeeping, and real estate, all without success.

When the Civil War broke out, he applied for duty as an officer and turned out to be just what his country needed: a trained, dependable, solid, experienced officer who was finally determined not to fail. There was nothing particularly flashy about Grant, but there didn't need to be. The North had more troops and more supplies, so the odds were in his favor. He led his men with determined good sense and usually won his battles. He entered duty as a colonel, but before long was made general, and shortly after that he had command of the whole Union Army.

Worthy Words

A *jingo* is a pro-war patriot who is overeager to provoke conflict with foreign powers out of pride for his or her own country. The meaning of the term stems back to a song by G. W. Hunt popular in England during the late nineteenth century. The song includes the words, "We don't want to fight, but by Jingo if we do, we've got the ships, we've got the men, we've got the money too!" Historians use the term jingoism to describe Roosevelt's attitude during the Spanish-American War.

Grant served two terms as president, starting in 1869. Unfortunately, although he was not corrupt himself, many of the Cabinet members he appointed were, so his administration was mired in graft and scandal. Although Grant is honored as a war hero, his term in office was not a particularly productive time.

Rough Rider

One of the more dynamic personalities among presidential war heroes is Theodore Roosevelt (1858–1919). He was the sort of person who loved outdoor adventures. One of the first things he did when he stepped down from the presidency, for example, was go on a safari in Africa. His enthusiasm for vigorous outdoor activity emerged early in his life as a response to the asthma from which he suffered as a boy. He overcame a sickly constitution by keeping active outside whenever he could.

Roosevelt made time for his outdoor life as well as his political career. He studied law and served on the New York legislature before moving to his ranch in the Dakota Territory. He later returned east and became Assistant Secretary of the Navy. During this time, the United States entered into war with Spain over control of Cuba. Roosevelt was a *jingo*—someone whose patriotism takes the form of eagerness for war—and threw himself enthusiastically into the war effort.

Theodore Roosevelt.
(Rutgers University Special
Collections and Archives)

The Maine *and Spain*

Many Americans, including Roosevelt, didn't like the fact that Cuba belonged to Spain and were interested in provoking war to gain possession of the island. Spain wished to avoid war and adopted a conciliatory policy toward the United States, but refused to simply relinquish control. The war the American imperialists were hoping for was touched off when the U.S. battleship *Maine* was sunk in Havana Harbor on February 15, 1898. The sinking of the *Maine* remains a mystery, because the Spanish government wanted to avoid war with the United States at almost any cost. Nevertheless, the sinking was officially regarded as an act of aggression by the Spanish, and war ensued. "Remember the *Maine*" was a rallying cry of U.S. troops as they fought for control of the island.

Roosevelt organized a volunteer cavalry regiment that came to be known as the "Rough Riders." At a decisive point in the conflict, he led the Rough Riders in a daring charge up San Juan Hill, a strategic position where Spanish forces were occupied. In what was literally an uphill battle, the Rough Riders were fired upon from the hilltop as they advanced. Despite their unfavorable position, they made it to the top and routed the Spanish. Soon after, the Spanish surrendered and the United States took control of Cuba.

Big Deeds

The charge up San Juan Hill made Roosevelt a hero and helped him go on to become governor of New York and later vice president under William McKinley in 1901. When McKinley was assassinated, Roosevelt took over as president and was reelected the following term. As president, he was especially energetic, developing vigorous new domestic and international policies.

He launched a campaign of "trust busting," developing legislation to make big commercial trusts illegal. He promoted conservation of natural areas to prevent them from being exploited by industry. He helped negotiate peace between the Russians and the Japanese in the Russo-Japanese War, for which he received the Nobel Peace Prize. He also spearheaded the building of the Panama Canal, one of the most ambitious and economically significant engineering feats in history. For this he has been immortalized in the famous palindrome, "A man, a plan, a canal, Panama!" (A palindrome is a phrase that is spelled the same way backward and forward). And he is one of the four presidents whose face is carved on Mount Rushmore.

Fearless Facts

Mt. Rushmore, in Keystone, South Dakota, was made into a huge presidential memorial by American sculptor Gutzon Borglum. This memorial features the faces of Washington, Jefferson, Lincoln, and Roosevelt carved in solid granite. The project was originally planned by a South Dakota resident as a monument to regional heroes, including Custer and Sitting Bull, but Gutson insisted the grand work be devoted to national heroes. The work took six and a half years, done intermittently, of labor between 1927 and 1941. Gutzon employed 400 local miners who blasted the mountain roughly into shape with dynamite.

D.D.'s D-Day

One of the most popular presidents of the twentieth century got to be that way by successfully leading American forces in Europe during World War II. Eisenhower was a career military man at the time America entered into the war and was soon put in charge of the American effort in Europe. This meant, among other things, developing a plan of attack in coordination with the other Allied powers, especially Britain.

He started in North Africa, in November 1942, where German tank divisions were creating havoc. He then coordinated the American invasion of Italy in the summer of 1943. Then he took over as commander of the entire Allied force in Europe for one of the most famous military assaults in modern history: the invasion of Normandy on *D day*, June 6, 1944—the largest amphibious invasion ever undertaken, involving about 150,000 men

Eisenhower planned the attack, coordinated it with other Allied leaders, and chose the date and the place. The whole thing was crucial to the Allied war effort, enabling thousands of troops to get involved where they were needed most. At the same time, it was extremely risky, because the Germans were expecting an invasion of France from across the English Channel and had stationed heavy artillery all along the French coast.

The heaviest concentration of German guns was in Calais, where the French coast is closest to England. In fact, Eisenhower and the Allied leaders wanted the Germans to expect an invasion at Calais. They maintained a phoney headquarters in Dover, right across the channel from Calais. They also flew many phoney surveillance missions over Calais and leaked false leads to German spies about an invasion of Calais. Meanwhile, the real assault was planned for Normandy, where the defense was less heavily concentrated. The invasion was costly, claiming the lives of large numbers of soldiers. It succeeded, however, and led, ultimately, to an Allied victory in Europe on May 7, 1945.

Cold Warrior

Worthy Words

D day is a name that can be applied to the day of any big military operation in order to keep the date secret. The *D* simply stands for day. The most famous D day, of course, is the day Allied forces invaded Normandy, June 6, 1944.

A controversial hero of the cold war between the U.S. and the Soviet Union was the charismatic John F. Kennedy (1917–1963), who has become an American legend since his mysterious assassination in 1963. At the time of his election, Kennedy was the youngest president elected to office and the only Roman Catholic. His youth gave him a special appeal with Americans, especially in light of his marriage to the worldly and attractive first lady, Jacqueline.

Kennedy served as a Navy officer in the South Pacific during World War II on a PT boat that was rammed and sunk by a Japanese destroyer. He led his men to safety despite being injured. Years later, in 1955, as a congressmen recovering from back surgery, he wrote the Pulitzer Prize–winning book, *Profiles in Courage.* He became the Democratic candidate for president in the election of 1960 and became popular with the nation largely as a result of his performance in televised debates with the Republican candidate, Richard Nixon. On becoming elected, Kennedy made his famous inaugural address, which included the words, "Ask not what your country can do for you, ask what you can do for your country."

Kennedy took office during a time of potentially catastrophic global instability. Before leaving office, his predecessor, President Eisenhower, made plans to invade Cuba, hoping to rally Cubans to overthrow Fidel Castro's communist regime. Kennedy approved the plan and the U.S. launched the infamous Bay of Pigs invasion in which U.S. forces suffered an embarrassing defeat in April of 1961, failing to elicit substantial support from dissatisfied Cubans. Still worse, the following year, air reconnaissance revealed that the Soviets had installed nuclear missiles in Cuba, posing a severe threat to the safety of the entire Western Hemisphere.

Kennedy responded by imposing a naval blockade of Cuba, preventing foreign ships from entering Cuban ports. In addition, he announced that the U.S. would retaliate with nuclear force against any missiles fired in the West. Many historians believe that, at this point, the world came as close as it ever has to nuclear holocaust. Fortunately, the Soviets backed down and removed their missiles. A nuclear test ban treaty between the U.S. and U.S.S.R. was signed the following year.

That same year, on November 22, Kennedy was shot while being driven through Dealey Plaza in Dallas, Texas. Lee Harvey Oswald was arrested and charged with the assassination. Oswald never stood trial, however, but was shot two days later by Jack Ruby. The killings triggered one of the most famous and fascinating controversies in American history. The Warren Commission determined that Oswald was mentally disturbed and acted alone in killing the president. Scores of other theories have been put forth, however, including the popular claim that Oswald acted as part of a conspiracy involving the CIA. A version of this conspiracy theory is dramatized in the Oliver Stone film *JFK* (1991), starring Kevin Costner.

The Least You Need to Know

➤ Washington refused advice to assume power as a military dictator years before being elected as the nation's first president.

➤ Andrew Jackson was the first president to be elected despite major opposition by Congress.

➤ Lincoln passed the Emancipation Proclamation in 1863 to make good a threat to rebel states that unless they ceased their opposition to the Union he would free their slaves.

➤ Teddy Roosevelt, a life-long rugged outdoorsman who led the Rough Riders cavalry unit in the charge up San Juan Hill, turned to exercise as a child to compensate for poor health.

➤ Eisenhower assumed command of the Allied forces during World War II and planned the D-day invasion of Normandy.

Freedom Fighters

Many Americans look to the Revolutionary War as one of the most heroic causes in history, both because it transformed the American colonies into the United States of America and because it was fought for the sake of the lofty ideals most people think of as "American." These are the heroes who made America possible and they did it at a time when the odds often seemed against them. They shared a vision that enabled them to fight and work together and to take history in an entirely new direction.

Their basic motivation was independence from the oppressive economic policies of mother England, so much of the heroism that went on involved fighting the British redcoats. But the challenge also involved forging a compromise among the many different constituents of the Revolutionary cause. As a result, Revolutionary War heroes often seem to have been fighting the British on one hand and making friends among themselves on the other.

Worthy Words

The **minutemen** were the members of the colonial militia who fought for the American Revolution. The name stems from the idea that they would need to get ready at a moment's notice to combat any sudden action on the part of British troops. This idea developed out of the militia system instituted to guard colonial settlements against sudden Indian attacks.

America's Revolutionary War heroes got in on the hero business on the ground floor, when the country was just getting started. They made the rules that heroes would follow generations later, fighting to establish what later heroes would fight to defend. And they were a whole new breed of hero; they came from all walks of life to fight for common ideals. In fact, Revolutionary War heroes are a mixed crowd, including people of many different nationalities, professions, and talents. Their ability to join together says a lot about what America is all about.

Networking

The American effort for independence involved military action, of course, but also involved public relations. The success of the Revolution required getting the word out—communicating with allies and persuading more people to join the cause. As a result, some of the most important Revolutionary heroes were not soldiers, but communicators, people who spread the lofty ideas behind the Revolution and who reported Revolutionary developments as they took place. Among the standout word-spreaders for the patriotic cause back in the days of the Revolution are Thomas Jefferson, Thomas Paine, Benjamin Franklin, and Paul Revere.

In fact, in many ways, a successful revolution took place before the Revolutionary War actually got started. The policies of England with regard to the colonies were so unpopular that the local colonial governing bodies banded together to resist them, driving loyalists from power. It was this revolutionary political organization that enabled military resistance to take shape in the form of a colonial militia known as the *minutemen*—ordinary citizens prepared to drop everything at a moment's notice to assemble for battle. This militia system was already in place when Paul Revere began his famous ride on the eve of the first battle of the American Revolution.

A Name to Revere

Paul Revere (1735–1818) was a silversmith who became the quintessential spreader of news from the Revolutionary period as a result of his famous midnight ride from Boston to Lexington in April 1775 to warn the minutemen that the British redcoats, or *regulars*, were on the march. He was a key part of an intelligence network. This network managed to find out that the regulars were sailing across the bay and gave word for the signal lamps to be hung in the steeple of the Old North Church from where other Revolutionaries could see the lamps. He then set off on his horse to spread the news. Riding at the same time on the same mission but by another route was a less well-known Revolutionary named William Dawes.

Paul Revere. (Rutgers University Special Collections and Archives)

PAUL REVERE.—[1735–1818.]

The redcoats wanted to keep their actions secret, because war had not yet broken out and tensions were high on both sides. Their main objective was to arrest the Revolutionary leaders John Adams and John Hancock, who were staying in nearby Lexington. They may also have had plans to march on to Concord, where the Revolutionary forces kept a supply of arms. A surprise raid on the Revolutionaries' guns and leaders would have nipped the Revolution in the bud. In addition, the redcoats also wanted to make trouble for any Revolutionaries they found on the way. In any case, Revere knew what they were up to and was doing something about it.

187

Towering Tips

Don't turn your admiration for Paul Revere and the minutemen into an effort to justify lax gun control and independent militant militia organizations in today's America. Militia groups of today who use Paul Revere as a figurehead may be confusing love for their guns with love for their country.

Revere rode to Lexington, spreading the news along the way that the British regulars were on the move. The minutemen responded, getting out of their beds to assemble in Lexington to meet the British. Meanwhile, Revere had a number of near misses with British troopers and was almost captured on his way to Lexington. He arrived in Lexington around midnight and roused Hancock and Adams, who were staying at the home of Reverend Jonas Clark, and warned that the British were coming to arrest them. An hour later, the leaders escaped to Philadelphia.

Revere rode on toward Concord and was captured on the way by a group of six British officers. They grabbed his bridle and ordered him to dismount at pistol point. They threatened to kill him, but set him free just before dawn—and just before the first shots were fired in the first battle of the war in Lexington, where eight minutemen were killed. Meanwhile, fighting erupted in Concord as well, with casualties on both sides before the British returned to Boston.

Tea Time

Paul Revere played an important part in events leading up to the war. He was among those who participated in the famous Boston Tea Party of December 16, 1773: A band of colonialists dressed up as Mohawk Indians and crept on board a ship at anchor in Boston Harbor. The ship had a cargo of tea belonging to the East India Tea Company. Britain had awarded this company a monopoly on the tea trade to the colonies. In protest, the tea party dumped bales of tea overboard.

Fearless Facts

Ben Franklin was on a diplomatic mission to Europe at the time of the Boston Tea Party. In an effort to prevent war from breaking out, he offered to pay for the tea dumped overboard out of his own pocket, if King George III of England would be willing to call an end to the tea monopoly. The offer was refused.

Even before the Boston Tea Party, Revere was active as a Revolutionary. He copied and published a well-known drawing of the infamous Boston Massacre of March 5, 1770, in which an angry mob was fired at by British troops. The mob was resentful of British colonial policy and of efforts to police the colonies with British troops, so they threw rocks and snowballs and brandished clubs, provoking the shooting. Revere's drawing was widely circulated and served as inspiration for the Revolutionary cause.

On the Same Page

Not long after Paul Revere's ride, as the fighting between the British and the Revolutionary colonists was just beginning, the Continental Congress met to discuss the situation. Representatives from each of the original states met to debate whether to support independence for the colonies. A Virginia delegate named Henry Lee drafted a statement, which justified American independence from British rule. Before Congress met to debate whether to adopt the statement as a resolution, it was given to Thomas Jefferson (1743–1826) to revise. Jefferson was known for his literary talent and his knowledge of political philosophy.

I Declare

In fact, Jefferson's reworking of Lee's resolution was substantial. The result was the Declaration of Independence, which drew on current progressive philosophical views regarding

Heroic Shorts

Among the first to be gunned down in the Boston Massacre—and hence among the first to die in the revolutionary cause—was an escaped slave named Crispus Attucks (1723–1770), who was part African and part American Indian. Although little is known about him, he is thought to have been an escaped or freed slave who was among those throwing rocks and snowballs at British guards outside the state house in Boston. The soldiers were unpopular because they enforced and symbolized British rule with its unfair taxation policies. The British soldiers fired on the crowd, hitting 11 and killing 5. Attucks was among the first to fall and the only one whose name is widely known among those who died in the infamous Boston massacre. His statue was unveiled in Boston Common in 1888. He quickly came to be regarded as a martyr for the revolutionary cause.

government and human nature. The main ideas, borrowed from British philosopher John Locke, were that government should be consensual and should promote individual rights. Whenever a government fails to uphold these rights, the people have the right to institute a new government.

This was radical stuff at the time—especially for colonies belonging to England, where the king still possessed a great deal of power. After drafting the declaration, Jefferson showed it to John Adams and Ben Franklin, who suggested minor changes, and then presented it to Congress for discussion and emendation. Although some delegates opposed independence, every state but New York, which abstained, eventually agreed. On July 4th, 1776, the congressional delegates signed the Declaration of Independence and the nation was born.

Fearless Facts

Recent DNA tests have confirmed that Thomas Jefferson or a male family member may have had sexual relations with one of his females slaves, Sally Hemmings, who lived at Monticello, Jefferson's estate. A descendent of Hemmings' youngest son, Eston Hemmings, has DNA that matches Jefferson's. Although Jefferson could have been Eston's father, it seems more likely that another man closely related to Jefferson, was responsible. Jefferson had many close relatives who lived near him. He himself was 65 years old when Eston was born.

Thomas Paine.
(Dictionary of
American Portraits)

A Royal Paine

Although it was based on the political philosophy of John Locke, the Declaration of Independence wasn't simply a head-in-the-clouds statement of belief; it reflected the fact that the power structure of the colonies was very different from that in England, where a social hierarchy had been in place for centuries. Of course, not everyone in England was satisfied with this social hierarchy, and many of England's malcontents came to America for a new start.

One heroic British immigrant was Thomas Paine, who had been fired from his government office in England for his writings. In those writings, he had protested the plight of the poor and other problems that he ascribed to unfair social conditions. Jobless, he came to the colonies in 1774 to escape being thrown into debtors' prison. Here he found a much more enthusiastic audience for his writings. In fact, he became a famous pamphleteer and a leading exponent of the Revolution.

Towering Tips

Be careful the revolution you support doesn't end up going too far. After doing his part in furthering the American Revolution, Thomas Paine went to France where he fed the fires of the French Revolution with his work *The Rights of Man*. He was imprisoned, however, for opposing the execution of French royalty.

In January 1776, Paine published *Common Sense*, a pamphlet calling for a free, democratic country and unity among the Revolutionaries. In effect, the pamphlet was a great Revolutionary pep talk, encouraging rebels to stand up to the hardships they faced and take the opportunity to build a new country. *Common Sense* was just one of many pamphlets by Paine. A later work, *The Crisis*, was read by George Washington to his troops before the famous crossing of the Delaware and invasion of Trenton. Paine's Revolutionary propaganda was a valued asset to the Revolution and he was voted a stipend by Congress for his work.

Big Ben

One of the most colorful and beloved heroes of the Revolution was Ben Franklin, a writer, printer, and inventor-turned-diplomat. Franklin made a big splash in France, where he sought military and financial support for the Revolutionary cause. A warm, brilliant, and eccentric elder statesman, he succeeded in cementing an invaluable alliance between the French and the Revolutionary American government.

Despite suffering from gout, Franklin made himself a lovable character with his witty good sense and rustic, frontier-style fur cap. In the process, he secured financial backing from the crown and personal military assistance from two men who later became heroes of the Revolution. One of these was the Marquis de Lafayette, who helped Washington win the battle of Yorktown that sealed the Revolutionary victory. The other was Friedrich von Steuben, a Prussian officer and self-styled aristocrat and military expert, who drilled the ragged troops at Valley Forge, thereby improving discipline and morale at the same time.

Ben Franklin.
(Rutgers University
Special Collections
and Archives)

Franklin is remembered as one of the most creative, energetic, and resourceful Americans of all time. Before serving as a diplomat to France, he wrote and published the famous *Poor Richard's Almanac*, containing innumerable nuggets of Early American wisdom. He invented the storage battery, the odometer, and the glass harmonica, and designed his own bifocals. He also founded the American Philosophical Society, helped instigate the U.S. postal system, and drew the first known American political cartoon—a snake representing the colonies divided into separate pieces with the caption "Join or Die."

And that's only a portion of Franklin's accomplishments. In addition, he wrote the constitution of Pennsylvania with help from Thomas Paine and designed the Great

Seal of the United States along with Thomas Jefferson and John Adams. What's more, Franklin alone, of all the founding fathers, signed each of the documents that made the United States an official nation: the Declaration of Independence, the treaties with France and with England, and the U.S. Constitution.

Ringing Words

Some of the best-known utterances in American history were made during the Revolutionary War. You may already know who said "Give me liberty or give me death." And how about, "I have not yet begun to fight"? And of course there's "My only regret is that I have but one life to give for my country." If you don't know who made these noble statements, or what the circumstances were in which they were made, then you had better keep reading so you will know about three American heroes who had just the right words when they found themselves on center stage in American history.

Towering Tips

When your moment of truth arrives, you might want to have an appropriate sound bite ready so you'll be remembered for generations to come. It is by virtue of their famous remarks that Nathan Hale, Patrick Henry, and John Paul Jones are best remembered.

Patrick Henry (1736–1799) was one of the leading statesmen of Revolutionary Virginia and an ardent patriot. He was said to be "a Quaker in religion, but the very devil in politics." He bitterly opposed the Stamp Act, risking punishment for treason by the British. As a delegate to the Virginia Convention in 1775, he galvanized the Revolutionary cause in a stirring speech that included the famous line, "Give me liberty or give me death." Fortunately for him, and for America, he got liberty.

Nathan Hale (1755–1776) was a teacher from Connecticut who joined the Revolutionary militia and rose through the ranks to captain in charge of a division fighting in New York. The war in New York City was going badly, with the British firmly in control of the city. Hale volunteered to go behind enemy lines as a spy in hopes of gaining useful information that would turn the tide. So, he went under cover as an unemployed schoolmaster.

Unfortunately, Hale was caught, possibly because he was identified by an informer. The British were not kindly disposed toward Hale. In fact, they looked upon spies as despicable lowlifes who lacked the nobility of real soldiers. So, they sentenced him to be hanged, a less glorious way to die in the eyes of the British than being shot. Legend has it, however, that Hale preserved his dignity by uttering some of the most famous last words of all time: "My only regret is that I have but one life to give for my country."

John Paul (1747–1792) was a Scottish captain of the British merchant marines trading in the West Indies. He left the merchant marines and came to America after killing a mutinous member of his crew. To escape detection, he adopted Jones as his last name. This wasn't the last British sailor he put an end to. In fact, he became the most deadly captain of the Revolutionary Navy. As captain of the sloop *Providence*, he sank or captured 40 British ships.

193

John Paul Jones. (Dictionary of American Portraits)

He won his most famous naval victory as captain of the *Bonhomme Richard* in a battle in the North Sea off the British coast in 1779. He became literally tied up with the larger, more powerful ship *Serapis* when he lashed his ship together with his adversary's for a point-blank shoot out. Things looked bad for John Paul Jones when two of *Bonhomme Richard*'s cannons exploded. At that point, the captain of the *Serapis* called to him to surrender. The moment prompted this memorable machismo: "I have not yet begun to fight." In fact, Jones kept fighting, eventually boarding the *Serapis* with his crew and taking over as his own ship sank.

Fearless Facts

The *Bonhomme Richard* was named for Ben Franklin's fictive sage, Poor Richard (called Bonhomme Richard in France). The ship was an old French merchant ship converted to naval duty and obtained from the French with the help of Ben Franklin. John Paul Jones' famous victory made him a hero in France before it was known in America.

Women's Work

Women have been ardent patriots as long as men have, but relatively few women of the Revolutionary period had a chance to contribute in a memorable way to the patriotic cause. You can tell it was a man's war from the fact that the best-known female hero is remembered for making the first American flag. Even so, women got involved in other ways too, including actual combat.

According to Betsy Ross herself, the woman who sewed the first American flag, she was approached by General George Washington with the assignment in May 1776. It seems that Betsy had a pew in church right next to George and Martha's, and the future president often paid social calls. Betsy Ross was a natural choice to sew the flag because she ran her own upholstery business. Washington came with a plan for the Stars and Stripes with stars that had six points, because he thought they would be easier to cut out. Betsy made a convincing case for using five-pointed stars, showing that she could cut them out with a single snip of the scissors.

Betsy Ross. (Rutgers University Special Collections and Archives)

A Revolutionary heroine of a different stripe was Mary Hays McCauley, the wife of an artillery gunner. McCauley and her husband weathered the long, cold winter at Valley Forge before she became famous under the nickname of Molly Pitcher as a result of her valued service to a troop of artillery men at the battle of Monmouth on June 28, 1778. There she carried water for some 30 soldiers on a hot day. The water was used for cooling overheated artillery as well as for drinking. Between trips with the water, she tended to wounded soldiers. At one point, she rescued a wounded man by carrying him bodily away from the British line of fire.

As they battle took its toll, the patriot force was depleted. Eventually, Molly's husband was wounded. Legend says that Molly filled in for her wounded hubby, manning—or womanning—the cannon for the duration of the battle. George Washington is said to have shown his gratitude by making her a noncommissioned officer. Her heroism is memorialized at her grave in Carlisle, Pennsylvania by a cannon and flagstaff.

Fearless Facts

One of the largest and longest-standing women's organizations is the Daughters of the American Revolution, founded in 1890 with the purpose of fostering patriotism and promoting historical knowledge. Since its founding, the group has engaged in ultraconservative politics. Originally, members were required to show evidence of ancestors who fought in the Revolution.

Far-Flung Heroes

A lot of the action during the war was centered around the eastern seaboard, the areas that were already pretty well settled. Important fighting also took place in less-settled areas to the south, north, and west. Battles on these fronts produced regional heroes, who expanded the boundaries of the nation even as it was being born—General Nathaneal Greene in the south, General George Rogers Clark to the west, and Ethan Allen in the north.

Nathaneal Greene (1742–1786) led the Revolutionary forces in South Carolina and Georgia, where the British had the run of things. Greene thought that he was insufficiently supplied with men and that the forces he had were insufficiently supplied with food and ammunition. In fact, Greene suffered a number of defeats, but the defeats weakened the British forces considerably. Eventually, the British fell back to Yorktown, Virginia, where they were defeated after a siege led by George Washington.

Fearless Facts

Nathaneal Greene was a Rhode Island Quaker who was kicked out of his meeting group when he joined the militia. Many Quakers are pacifists, and Greene defied his faith in fighting for his country.

George Rogers Clark led a force down the Ohio River with the stated objective of defending settlements in Kentucky, but with an actual purpose of attacking British outposts. On the way, he established a settlement on Corn Island that later became Louisville, Kentucky. The town is named after King Louis XVI of France, who entered into an alliance with the Revolutionaries during the early days of the settlement.

Clark went on to take the British-held forts of Kaskaskia on the Mississippi River, and Vincennes on the Wabash. He succeeded in taking Fort Vincennes despite having only a tiny force. Clark fooled the fort commander into thinking that he had many times the number of men actually involved by having the men change their clothing and only showing them briefly. The trick (which was not necessarily new) was successfully

George Rogers Clark. (Dictionary of American Portraits)

used years later by the Shawnee chief Tecumseh. Clark's victory secured territory that later became the states of Ohio, Indiana, Illinois, and Michigan. He and his men were paid for their efforts in tracts of land in the new territory.

Ethan Allen (1738–1789) was a homesteader in Vermont who led a battle for independence years before the Revolutionary War officially started. In 1760 he commanded a militia force, known as the Green Mountain Boys, made up of settlers who occupied land through grants controlled by the governor of New York. The homesteaders had to pay stiff taxes to New York or face having their land confiscated until their resistance effort, led by Allen, won them control of the land. During the Revolution, Allen led an attack on Fort Ticonderoga in New York, taking the strategic fort from the British, along with its valuable supply of guns and ammunition.

The Least You Need to Know

➤ Paul Revere rode out into the night in April 1775 to warn the colonists that British troops were on the move.

➤ Thomas Jefferson wrote the Declaration of Independence (1776), drawing on the political philosophy of English thinker John Locke. Thomas Paine gave popular expression to similar ideas in *Common Sense* (1776) and other writings.

➤ As a diplomat to France, Benjamin Franklin secured invaluable military and financial assistance.

➤ Patrick Henry, Nathan Hale, and John Paul Jones are best remembered today for famous remarks at critical moments.

➤ Betsy Ross sewed the first U.S. flag. Molly Pitcher manned a cannon left vacant by her wounded husband.

➤ Nathaneal Greene, George Rogers Clark, and Ethan Allen are regional heroes of the Revolution.

Chapter 15

Split Personalities

NORTH -VS- SOUTH

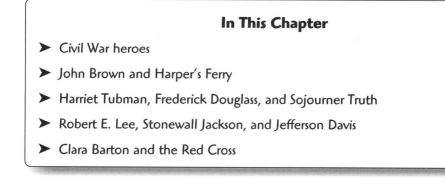

In This Chapter

➤ Civil War heroes

➤ John Brown and Harper's Ferry

➤ Harriet Tubman, Frederick Douglass, and Sojourner Truth

➤ Robert E. Lee, Stonewall Jackson, and Jefferson Davis

➤ Clara Barton and the Red Cross

The Civil War was the greatest national tragedy in American history. A conservative estimate puts the combined death toll for both sides at over 540,000. It was certainly the largest and most costly conflict ever fought on American soil. Losses on both sides were huge. In some of the bloodiest battles ever fought, armies numbering tens of thousands each faced each other in open fields and decimated one another with no clear victory for either side.

The terrible casualties resulted from an unlucky distribution of strength between the two sides. The South possessed better generals and military tacticians and more determined and motivated fighters, but the North possessed more troops, weapons, and supplies. To ensure victory, northern leaders were willing to battle to a stalemate and incur huge losses, knowing that the North could sustain heavy casualties longer than the South. The deadly trade-off strategy worked for the North in the long run, but the price was devastatingly high.

Civilians, too, especially in the South, were ravaged by the war. In addition to losing husbands, sons, and brothers, many lost homes and belongings, which were confiscated or destroyed. Near the last days of the war, the entire city of Atlanta was burned to the ground. This was the culmination of strife that had been building since the days of the Revolution concerning the issue of slavery. Against this bloody, smoldering backdrop, a variety of heroic figures emerged. Some fought; some worked and spoke out for their cause; others did what they could to heal the many wounds opened by the war.

Great Divide

The issue of slavery was at the heart of the Civil War. Southern states saw slaves as a crucial feature of the southern agricultural economy and plantation-based way of life. Abolitionists, most of whom were from the North, regarded slavery as an unconscionable, dehumanizing institution. Growing numbers were speaking out against it. President Lincoln opposed slavery, although he was not an abolitionist in the sense of wanting an end to slavery at any cost. Nevertheless, his election in 1861 prompted the first of the Confederate States to secede from the Union.

Brown's Battle

Lincoln thought that the divisive issue of slavery had to be decided on a national level. He didn't think that the nation could be strong with some free, and some slave states. Animosity between abolitionists and pro-slavery factions had come to a head shortly before his election when John Brown (1800–1859), an ardent abolitionist agitator, raided an arsenal at Harper's Ferry, Virginia in October 1859.

Fearless Facts

A song remembering John Brown the abolitionist was sung by Union troops during the war and contained the words "John Brown's body lies a–molding in the grave . . . , his truth is marching on."

Brown's plan was to start an uprising and free slaves by force with the help of the armaments stored at Harper's Ferry. Brown and his followers succeeded in taking the arsenal, but were surrounded and eventually caught by a militia force led by Robert E. Lee, who would later command the Confederate forces in the Civil War. Many of Brown's followers were killed and he himself was wounded.

John Brown. (Dictionary of American Portraits)

In well under two months, Brown was tried, convicted, and hung for murder, treason, and conspiracy. Throughout the proceedings, he maintained an impressive dignity, never wavering from his conviction that his cause was just. His death made him a martyr and hero to other abolitionists who were inspired by his bravery.

The pro-slave side had other feelings about Brown, regarding him as a fanatic. Many remembered an incident that took place in Kansas territory in May 1856. At that time, Brown was part of the Free-Soil militia, which fought to prevent slavery from becoming legal in Kansas. Incensed at an attack by pro-slavers on the town of Lawrence, he retaliated by attacking a band of unarmed homesteaders, brutally killing them and mutilating their bodies. Therefore, while abolitionists regarded Brown as a saint, pro-slavers saw him as a devil. The split typified the tension that erupted in the Civil War soon after Brown's execution.

Freedom Train

For many, the war against slavery began long before the Civil War began. Among those most dedicated to the cause of freeing slaves before and during the war years was Harriet Tubman (1820–1913). Born into slavery in Maryland, Harriet escaped to Canada and freedom along the *underground railroad*, a secret network helping slaves to escape. She later returned to lead hundreds of others along the same path.

Harriet Tubman.
(Dictionary of
American Portraits)

Born Harriet Ross to slave parents, she was seriously injured at the age of 12 when she was struck in the head for refusing to tie up a fellow slave who had been caught trying to escape. Some believed the injury produced a condition known as narcolepsy, causing Harriet to fall deeply and uncontrollably asleep at various times throughout the rest of her life. This explains why she sometimes stopped suddenly and slept at the side of road while leading slaves to freedom.

At about 25 years of age, Harriet married a free black man named John Tubman. Five years later, she escaped by herself along the underground railroad. While starting a new life in Canada, she maintained her ties with the underground railroad, most notably with the white "station master" William Still, who wrote about Harriet's courage and determination in his history of the underground railroad. Before long, Harriet became a "conductor" for the organization.

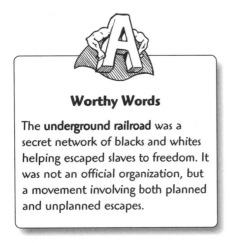

Worthy Words

The **underground railroad** was a secret network of blacks and whites helping escaped slaves to freedom. It was not an official organization, but a movement involving both planned and unplanned escapes.

Before the war, it was illegal to help slaves to escape, so the entire underground railroad was at risk. Harriet helped protect the secrecy of the organization by adopting a strict policy of refusing to let anyone she was conducting to freedom turn back on the way. She threatened to shoot those who had second thoughts. The policy made her an extremely effective conductor who led some 300 passengers in her career with the underground railroad.

During the Civil War, Harriet continued her secret activity, serving as a spy for the Union army. At her death she was buried with military honors. Her home in Auburn, New York has been preserved as a museum and historical center.

Fearless Facts

Years after Harriet Tubman's death, a ship named in her honor, the *Liberty Ship Harriet Tubman*, was christened by Eleanor Roosevelt.

From Slave to Statesman

Perhaps the most revered African-American leader of all time, with the exception of Martin Luther King, is Frederick Douglass (1818–1895), an escaped slave who went on to become a great statesman, an advisor to President Lincoln, and an internationally recognized exponent of civil rights for blacks. His autobiography, first published in 1845, is recognized as a minor classic. As a national political figure, he extended his personal struggle for freedom into a struggle for the rights of all blacks.

Frederick Douglass.
(Dictionary of American Portraits)

Born in Bondage

A slave, Douglass was born to a black mother and a white father; his father was unknown to him. It was rumored that he was the illegitimate son of his owner, farmer Aaron Anthony. If so, he received no special treatment from his father, who was generally not a very kind or caring master. Douglass tells in his autobiography that he and the other slave children were fed corn meal in a trough as though they were animals.

As a boy, Douglass learned the alphabet and the rudiments of reading from a white mistress who was later cautioned against teaching slaves to read. Slave owners correctly realized that the ability to read could sharpen a slave's dissatisfaction with slavery, so they discouraged literacy among slaves. Douglass acquired a taste for reading after his early experience and practiced reading, on the sly, whenever he could. Gradually he taught himself to read books that awakened him to the possibilities of freedom.

Towering Tips

When you stand up for yourself, you're actually doing your oppressors a favor too by showing them what a worthy adversary or valuable ally you can be.

Meanwhile he suffered mistreatment that increased his personal dislike for slavery. He openly resented bad treatment and was often punished. At one point in 1834, he was loaned to a farmer named Edwin Corey who had a reputation for his ability to break the spirit of unruly slaves. When Corey threatened to beat him, he resisted by grabbing Corey's neck. To his surprise, Corey left him alone afterward. He evidently didn't want to harm his reputation as a strong master by acknowledging Douglass's resistance. The incident gave Douglass confidence in his ability to stand up for himself.

Moving and Shaking

While still a slave, Douglass was apprenticed to a ship caulker and eventually became skilled at caulking ships. His master was paid for Douglass's work. Not surprisingly, Douglass was unhappy with this arrangement and, in 1836, he planned an escape along with several other slaves. Word of the plan leaked out, however, and Douglass was jailed for plotting to escape. A second attempt, made two years later, met with better success. In 1836, disguised as a seaman with forged papers saying he was free, he boarded a train from Maryland to the free states.

In the following years, he studied, published his autobiography, worked for the underground railroad, and lectured widely on abolition. In 1859, two years before the war broke out, he gave lectures in England on civil rights. During the war, he continued lecturing in the United States. He also met with the president to air his concerns about continued slavery in the South.

Fearless Facts

Douglass enjoyed great popularity as a lecturer and included anecdotes of his experiences as a slave in those lectures. His popularity ebbed as his grammar and vocabulary improved and he lost his southern accent. His audiences found it hard to believe that such an educated speaker could have lived through the experiences he described!

One thorny wartime issue in which Douglass was involved was the question of whether black troops should fight for the Union cause. Congress finally gave the okay to black enlistment in 1863 and Douglass was active in recruiting black troops, most notably the Massachusetts 54th Regiment, the first black unit to fight in the war. In all some 200,000 blacks fought—about 10% of the Union force. Of these, 38,000 were killed or wounded. The story of the 54th Regiment is dramatized in the award-winning movie *Glory* (1989), starring Matthew Broderick and Denzel Washington.

Despite their large contribution to the war effort, blacks were most often inadequately trained and supplied and received only about half the pay white soldiers received. Moreover, they faced more than their share of danger, because blacks were typically shot when captured by rebel troops (unlike whites, who were taken prisoner). When Douglass learned of these conditions, he ended his recruitment efforts.

He remained politically active, however, and met with Lincoln a second time in 1864, when Lincoln asked him to prepare a plan to evacuate slaves from the South in the event of a Confederate victory. After the war, Douglass campaigned for black suffrage. His work bore fruit in 1870, when the 15th Amendment was passed. This amendment gave blacks the right to vote. In addition, he served as president of the Freedman's Savings and Trust, edited the *New National Era*, and served the nation as U.S. Marshall and as Consul General to Haiti.

Truth Will Set You Free

Still another heroic black civil rights activist of the Civil War era was Sojourner Truth (1797–1883), who made her mark through the force of her irrepressible personality. She was born Isabella Baumfree into slavery in upstate New York and, as an adult, simply demanded and received her freedom from her Dutch-American master years before slaves were liberated in New York. Soon afterward, she sued to recover her son who had been sold in Alabama and won her case.

Fascinated by spirituality and alternative lifestyles, she became involved in several radical religious sects—a free-love sect, a millennial sect, and a utopian society—

eventually taking the name Sojourner Truth in 1843 to reflect her religious searching. She told the story of her life to writer Olive Gilbert, who published *The Narrative of Sojourner Truth* in 1845.

Thanks in part to the attention she received as a result of the book, she became widely admired by northern white women. A second edition of her book appeared with an introduction by Harriet Beecher Stowe, the famous author of *Uncle Tom's Cabin*. Meanwhile, Sojourner Truth became a sought-after lecturer, promoting civil rights for blacks and for women. She also spoke in support of temperance and women's rights and against capital punishment. She gave her famous "Ain't I a Woman?" speech to a women's convention in Akron, Ohio in 1851. In that speech, she exposed the hypocrisy of men who affected gallant behavior toward white women—treating them as weak and delicate creatures—while expecting hard labor and endurance from black women. She claimed to be able to work as hard and endure as much hardship as any man.

Fearless Facts

The abolitionist movement suffered a major setback in 1850 with the passage of the Fugitive Slave Act, making it legal for slavers to travel north to repossess escaped slaves. Legally free blacks as well as escaped slaves were sometimes kidnapped into slavery after the passage of this legislation.

Southern Soldiers

What was for the North a war to end slavery and preserve the Union was, for the South, a war to preserve the way of life and the autonomy of the Confederate States. Adhering to ideals that hearkened back to the aristocratic codes of honor of the Old World, southern leaders fought with pride, determination, and spirit unmatched by the more pragmatic military leaders of the North. The Confederate leaders, especially Jefferson Davis, Robert E. Lee, and Thomas "Stonewall" Jackson gave the Old South hope of surviving and resisting the pressures of the coming industrial age. In the end, the odds against them proved to be too great. They are, however, remembered as the greatest of soldiers.

Rebels with a Cause

The greatest Confederate general was Robert E. Lee (1807–1870), the son of "Light Horse" Harry Lee, a distinguished cavalry officer of the American Revolution. After

Robert E. Lee. (Rutgers University Special Collections and Archives)

graduating from West Point, Lee served in the Mexican War, during which he was promoted to colonel. His reputation as a leader and military strategist was so great that, at the outbreak of the Civil War, he was offered command of the entire Union Army. His loyalties lay with the South, however, so he refused the command and resigned to fight for his native state as commander of the Army of Northern Virginia.

The second greatest Confederate general was Thomas Stonewall Jackson (1824–1863) who, like Lee, a fellow Virginian, had also served in the Mexican American War as a lieutenant before taking a professorship at the Virginia Military Institute. At the start of the war, Jackson was promoted to Confederate general and soon earned his nickname in the war's first big battle: the Battle of First Manassas, also known as first Bull Run. (Bull Run is a creek near Manassas railroad junction in Virginia.)

Despite being outnumbered nearly two to one, the Confederate troops withstood a Union charge, thanks largely to the bravery and discipline of General Jackson and his troops (who refused to budge). Their firmness rallied the rest of the rebel force, who proceeded to rout the more powerful Union army. Jackson became known as Stonewall and has been so called ever since. He and Lee would go on to team up for some of the South's greatest battles, often against seemingly unbeatable odds.

Fearless Facts

Lee was an enthusiastic student of the tactics of the French Emperor Napoleon, who was known for his daring strategies in battle.

Lee led his army against the Union forces led by General McClellan in the famous Seven Days from June 26 to July 2, 1862. McClellan was an over-cautious leader and Lee took advantage with daring aggressive assaults that drove McClellan back almost out of Virginia. Both sides suffered heavy losses (especially all the Confederate rebels) but Virginia—and, most importantly, the city of Richmond—was saved (at least for the time being).

A second assault on Virginia, led by Union General John Pope, was quelled by a combined effort led by Lee and Stonewall Jackson at the Battle of Second Manassas, or Second Bull Run. Stonewall and his men did most of the fighting, demolishing the Union supply depot, surrounding the Union troops, and driving them out of Virginia, but it was Lee who drew up the battle plans. The decisive rebel victory made the Union question its chances for victory. Soon afterward, Lee was put in command of the entire Confederate force.

Lee and Jackson teamed up for their greatest victory in May 1863 at Chancellorsville, Virginia, not far from Fredericksburg, where Union General "Fighting" Joe Hooker waited with a larger force. Supremely confident, Hooker and his men dallied outside of Fredericksburg savoring the anticipation of certain victory. As night fell, they were surprised by a sudden rebel attack that left them weakened for the next day's battle.

In a daring move the following day, Lee divided up his smaller force to surround the Union soldiers. He even deployed some of his troops to defend Fredericksburg. Nearly surrounded, Hooker's army was unable to strike effectively and Hooker took the first available opportunity to retreat. Approximately 17,000 Union soldiers were killed next to 13,000 Confederates.

Stonewall Jackson.
(Rutgers University Special
Collections and Archives)

Fearless Facts

Lee's estate was located in Arlington, Virginia and later became a museum as well as the most famous cemetery in the country, Arlington National Cemetery. The first to be buried there were Civil War soldiers—Union and Confederate dead were often buried side by side. Since then, the cemetery has been used as the resting place of many war heroes and other figures of national significance, including the unknown soldiers of the major American wars. More than 200,000 are buried at Arlington.

Unfortunately for the rebel cause, Stonewall Jackson was among those wounded in battle. He was shot in the arm by one of his own men. His arm was amputated and, before he could recover, he caught pneumonia and died. After that time, the tide of war turned against General Lee. Finally, after a decisive battle at Appomattox, Lee surrendered to General Grant on April 9, 1865, marking the end of the war for all practical purposes.

Fearless Facts

Jackson was a personal friend as well as a valuable subordinate to Lee. When he learned that Jackson's arm had been amputated, he said, "He has lost his left arm, but I have lost my right."

Rebel Chief

Just as Abraham Lincoln bore a heavy burden in the knowledge of the loss of tens of thousands of Union soldiers, the burden of southern leadership rested on Jefferson Davis (1808–1889). Like Lincoln, Davis served in the Black Hawk War and like Lee and Jackson, he fought in the Mexican War. He also served as a congressman and later as senator from Mississippi before taking an appointment as Secretary of War. As the first southern states joined in seceding from the Union, Davis made plans to lead rebel forces as a general. Instead, he was elected president of the Confederacy and was inaugurated on February 18, 1861.

Davis has been faulted for taking too much responsibility on himself and for adhering too rigidly to his principles. He was reluctant to delegate authority over military matters, yet also reluctant to impose his will on the states whose war he was fighting. He refused to impose taxes or appropriate supplies in order to bolster the war effort, because the war was being fought in defense of states' rights.

While Davis's ideals actually stood in the way of a Confederate victory, they appeared to his advantage in defeat. He refused to surrender and attempted to rally his scattered forces until he was captured in May 1865 by Union cavalrymen in Georgia. He was put into prison and indicted for treason, but was never tried. He was released after two years. Convinced that he had done nothing wrong, he refused to ask for a pardon. As a result, he was barred from public office for the rest of his life. He published his book *The Rise and Fall of the Confederate Government* in 1881.

Heroic Healer

Perhaps the most beloved Civil War hero of all lived through many of the bloodiest battles—not as a soldier, but as a nurse. Clara Barton, (1821–1912) tended wounded Union soldiers at the Virginia battles of Cedar Mountain, Second Manassas, and Fredericksburg, and at Antietam (in Maryland) where she became known as "the angel of the battlefield." After the war, she became founder and president of the American Red Cross.

Before she was able to start taping up wounded soldiers, she had to cut through the red tape of the Union army. She had to petition the army for permission to collect medical supplies and to nurse soldiers as a private citizen. And eventually this is just what she did, showing up at battlefield hospitals with supplies she had collected herself. She worked all day nursing the wounded, and into the night by the light of candles she furnished herself.

Clara Barton. (Dictionary of American Portraits)

Fearless Facts

Other well-known Civil War nurses include novelist Louisa May Alcott, poet Walt Whitman, and the head of the Union nursing corps, Dorothea "Dragon" Dix, who refused to accept volunteer nurses unless they were plain and over 30 years old.

Clara developed the knack for nursing at an early age by tending to her brother who had taken a bad fall from a barn. It was two years before he recovered, during which time young Clara was able to perfect her bedside manner. Before the war, she was one of the first women to become a government employee—working as a clerk in a patent office.

After the war, she was active in helping to identify and account for Union soldiers missing and dead. She later worked for the International Red Cross during the Franco-Prussian War. After returning to the United States, she applied for funds to start the American Red Cross, becoming the organization's first president. Under her leadership, the organization shifted its focus from war relief to natural disaster aid.

The Least You Need to Know

➤ More than 540,000 soldiers lost their lives in the Civil War.

➤ Abolitionist heroes include John Brown, Harriet Tubman, Frederick Douglass, and Sojourner Truth.

➤ Heroic leaders of the Confederacy include Generals Robert E. Lee and Stonewall Jackson and President Jefferson Davis.

➤ Clara Barton, founder of the American Red Cross, got her start as a nurse in the Civil War using medical supplies she collected herself.

Chapter 16

Wars of the World

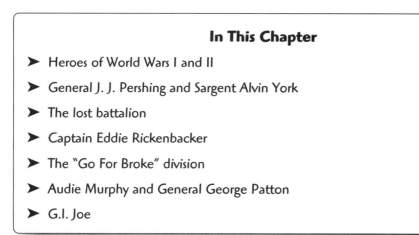

In This Chapter

➤ Heroes of World Wars I and II

➤ General J. J. Pershing and Sargent Alvin York

➤ The lost battalion

➤ Captain Eddie Rickenbacker

➤ The "Go For Broke" division

➤ Audie Murphy and General George Patton

➤ G.I. Joe

Americans have always been proud of the part played by U.S. forces in World War I and World War II. The historical significance of both conflicts is enormous because never before had war been waged on such a large scale. In both cases, democratic countries of Europe were under attack from military dictatorships when American soldiers came to help out. They fought well and made a big difference in the fate of the world. And they established, without a doubt, America's position as a global power.

Both wars were "popular" wars in the sense that the majority of the American people were behind them and believed in the cause. Americans made big sacrifices on the home front as well as in combat for the sake of the war effort. Both wars also drew on technological developments—weapons of mass destruction—that made fighting in them even more deadly. Yet, unlike the "smart bombs" of today, these weapons had to be deployed at close range to be effective, so soldiers really had to stick their necks out to do their jobs.

All these things made the two world wars virtual hotbeds of heroism. Heroism was simply expected of practically everyone. As a result, not just individuals, but also the entire generations of those involved, are remembered as heroic.

Deeply Entrenched

World War I had been raging since June 1914 before the United States, under President Woodrow Wilson, decided to get in on the action in April 1917. Prior to that time, the nation maintained its neutrality despite political opposition to Germany and Austria-Hungary, who were making war on the Allies (Britain, France, and Russia). America stood aloof also despite outrage at the death of Americans on board the British passenger liner *Lusitania* and the U.S.S. *Housatonic*, which were sunk by German U-boats.

The last straw was the infamous Zimmerman note——a telegram sent in code to the German ambassador in Mexico proposing a military alliance against the United States between Germany and Mexico. The Zimmerman note, combined with German shipping interference and sympathy for the Allies, galvanized Wilson to enter the fray. France and Britain couldn't have been happier with the decision. They had been hoping for years that the United States would enter the war and looked forward to an end to the bitter stalemate.

Fearless Facts

Popular support for World War I was fueled by a public relations campaign that cast suspicion on many political activists and German–American citizens. Among those jailed during the war were an ex-conductor of the Boston Symphony Orchestra, Dr. Carl Much, socialist presidential candidate Eugene Debs, and "Wobbly" labor leader "Big" Bill Haywood.

By the time the Yanks arrived, the war had literally entrenched itself in the French countryside. Both sides were exhausted and demoralized, yet neither side was willing to give up. The Allies hoped the Americans would turn the tide of battle. The first U.S. forces to arrive in France were given a hero's welcome. Led by General John. J. Pershing, they marched through the streets of Paris amid cheering crowds and stopped to salute the statue of Marquis de Lafayette, one of the many Frenchmen who fought with George Washington in the American Revolution.

Coming Through with the Dough

J. J. "Black Jack" Pershing (1860–1948) commanded the American Expeditionary Force of the World War I. He was known for his strict, by-the-book discipline which he enforced by maintaining control over his troops. He rejected the demands of British and French commanders to incorporate the Americans as replacements into their divisions, insisting that he remain in charge of an army that fought as Americans. In so doing, he bolstered the pride and fighting spirit of his men.

Worthy Words

Soldiers of the American Expeditionary Force were popularly known as **doughboys**—both because their khaki uniforms bread-like color and because they were "fresh," inexperienced troops newly come to a war that had been dragging on for years.

Although the Germans hoped that the U.S. troops would turn out to be lukewarm fighters, they proved themselves to be intent and spirited, despite their inexperience. The American *doughboys*, as they were called, maintained a high level of morale and patriotism that enabled them to perform bravely as soldiers, despite sometimes heavy losses. Among the worst of the campaigns in terms of American casualties were the

General John J. Pershing. (Dictionary of American Portraits)

battles fought in the Meuse-Argonne offensive that continued up until the very end of the war on November 11, 1918. It was out of these battles that some of the biggest doughboy heroes emerged.

Hotshot

The Meuse-Argonne battles were uniquely suited to individual heroism because the plan of attack drawn up by the U.S. commanders called for a splintering of forces that were to drive separately into enemy lines. The terrain was so rugged and obstructed by barbed wire, trenches, and shell craters that action as a large unit was extremely difficult. Smaller, more mobile forces had a better chance of inflicting damage. Of course, small forces were similarly more likely to suffer damage as well—and many did. In fact, some 10% of the Americans who took part in these final battles of the war were lost.

On separate occasions, heroic doughboys of the Meuse-Argonne campaign managed to take out a number of German machine-gun installations and snipers. One was Sergeant Alvin York, a sharpshooter from Tennessee who was part of a detachment that made it partway around a cluster of machine guns before surprising a German battalion. Many of his comrades were killed in the skirmish that followed and the rest were pinned down by enemy fire. Meanwhile, the machine gunners began to swing their guns around to finish off the intruders.

York found a spot behind a tree in some underbrush that was on an elevation looking down into the machine-gun nests. From there he was able to shoot—one by one—each gunner of each machine gun, along with the soldiers who manned the guns in their place, until each gun was knocked out. Eventually, a German officer figured out where the one-man assault was coming from and moved to attack York with a band of six men, including himself. Many of the rifles used in the war fired five times before they had to be reloaded, so the Germans must have thought their chances were good that at least one of them would get to York.

Fortunately for York, however, his rifle fired six shells at a clip. As the crew advanced single file toward him, York shot each of them in turn, beginning with the man in the rear and ending with the officer in front. The marching order prevented the men from scattering as they might have done had their leader been shot first. After continuing his sniper fire a few minutes more, he called on the German major in charge to surrender. The major blew his whistle and his men emerged with their hands up. In the end, York and the dozen or so of his men who remained standing captured 132 German soldiers!

Fearless Facts

Another sharp-shooting doughboy hero is Captain Samuel Woodfill, who took out four German machine guns. Shortly afterward, when out of ammunition, he vanquished a pair of enemy soldiers with a pickax.

Land of the Lost

As it was penetrating into enemy lines, an entire U.S. division was surrounded and cut off. This was the famous "lost battalion" (not actually a battalion, but the 77th Infantry Division led by Major Charles Whittlesey). They remained holed up a solid week, holding out long after running out of food and medical supplies under continual enemy fire.

Whittlesey was able to make his position known back at the U.S. command post by sending messages via carrier pigeon. As a result, the trapped division quickly became a military objective in its own right, yet repeated rescue attempts met with failure and couriers were unable to get to the isolated soldiers with supplies. Still, American Major General Robert Alexander refused to allow heavy shelling of the area, convinced that Whittlesey had not yet surrendered.

Fearless Facts

One of the aviator heroes of World War I is *Cher Ami*, a carrier pigeon that brought word of "the lost battalion" to the U.S. command post despite getting hit by shrapnel and losing an eye and a leg. *Cher Ami* was later preserved and put on display at the Smithsonian Institution.

Towering Tips

Volunteering for hard jobs can pay off in many ways, including personal satisfaction, public recognition, and valuable experience. This is true during peace time as well as in war.

In fact, the lost battalion did suffer "friendly" fire from American comrades and French allies as well as "unfriendly" fire from Germans. The German commanding officer sent a note asking Whittlesey to surrender. Whittlesey was said to have replied, "Go to hell." The 77th held on until, at last, reinforcements fought their way through with food and medical supplies. Of 550 soldiers in the division, all but 195 had been killed or wounded.

Flying Aces

At the start of the war, planes were used primarily for observation. Bombing was a new and developing concept, and no one had yet figured out how to attach machine guns to a one-man plane that could be fired by the pilot in mid air. The Germans were the first to design a one-man plane equipped with effective machine guns. The firing was timed so that the bullets shot between the whirling blades of the propellers.

Eventually the Allies managed to shoot down a German fighter plane and learned the secret of German air superiority. This happened in time for the spring of 1918 and the first missions flown by the newly formed American Air Service. Flyers who shot down five or more enemy planes were known as "aces" (as in "Snoopy, the World War I flying ace"). In fact, Snoopy's nemesis, "The Red Baron," actually existed. This was the German ace Baron Manfred von Richthofen.

The Americans had a planeload of aces of their own. The "ace of aces" was German-American Captain Eddie Rickenbacker (1890–1973). Rickenbacker downed 22 German planes and four observation balloons. Rickenbacker flew for the 94th Aero Pursuit Squad, known as the "Hat in the Ring" squad because its insignia depicted a hat with a circle around it. His success as a fighter pilot was due not only to skill and courage, but also to his dedication. He often flew voluntary "lone-wolf" missions on his own time, just cruising around for enemy planes.

It was while Rickenbacker was on one such volunteer solo mission that he encountered a group of seven German planes—two that were taking photographs and five others protecting the first two. Despite being outnumbered seven to one, Rickenbacker attacked, downing two of the planes and scattering the rest. For this feat of bravery, he was awarded the Congressional Medal of Honor.

Before entering the war, Rickenbacker was a champion auto racer. After the war, he became president of a commercial airline. He reenlisted to serve during World War II and was on board a B-17 bomber that crashed in the South Pacific while on a secret mission in October 1942. He and six others survived 24 days at sea in a life raft before being rescued. He went on to write several books narrating his exploits.

The Big One, Revisited

In many respects, World War II was the remake, 30 years later, of World War I. Military dictators in Germany, Italy, and Japan were launching aggressive attacks on other nations and, despite a widespread desire to stay out of it, the United States was eventually drawn in and helped turn the tide of a long and bloody war. The decisive event that propelled the country into battle was the bombing of Pearl Harbor, Hawaii by the Japanese on December 7, 1941.

The Home Front

Like many sequels, World War II was bigger, longer, and more spectacular than the original. It was waged from North Africa to the North Atlantic to the Far East. And soldiers weren't the only ones involved. The civilian war effort mobilized practically everyone, kids included, in drives and volunteer programs to conserve food and raw materials. Patriots across the country bought war bonds and went without meat on certain days of the week in order to do their share for the war effort. Women joined the civilian workforce as never before to replace the men who were fighting overseas, thanks in part to Rosie the Riveter, who appeared on posters intended to encourage women to take on jobs ordinarily reserved for men.

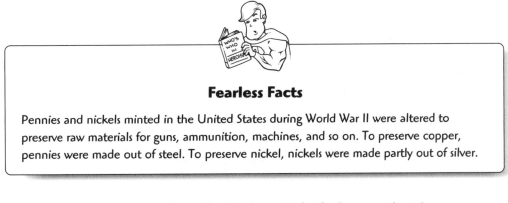

Fearless Facts

Pennies and nickels minted in the United States during World War II were altered to preserve raw materials for guns, ammunition, machines, and so on. To preserve copper, pennies were made out of steel. To preserve nickel, nickels were made partly out of silver.

Unfortunately, patriotism at home had its hysterical side. Japanese-Americans were widely suspected of sympathizing with the enemy and suffered persecution as a result. Approximately 70,000 Japanese-American citizens were forced to leave their homes and enter internment camps, where they lived throughout the war. Amazingly, despite being denied their constitutional rights, Japanese-American men in internment camps were subject to the draft. Many who refused to fight for the country that put their families in concentration camps were sent to jail as draft resisters.

Worthy Words

Go for broke is a gambling expression that means "bet everything you have." This was the motto of the 422nd Regimental Combat Team comprised of Japanese-American soldiers. This was the most heavily decorated regiment in U.S. history, awarded 18,143 decorations, including a Congressional Medal of Honor and 3,600 Purple Hearts. Many of these decorations were awarded posthumously and presented to parents who were confined in internment camps for Japanese-Americans.

Go for Broke

Many Japanese-Americans, however, not only went to war, but also volunteered without having to be drafted. Many served in the Pacific in the Military Intelligence Service where their knowledge of Japanese proved valuable in translating intercepted messages from the enemy. More famous, however, are the Japanese-Americans who fought in Europe and northern Africa. Segregated into their own regiment—the 442nd–they became the most heavily decorated regiment of the war and in U.S. military history.

The 442nd was assigned to combat in Africa, then Italy, and then France, suffering heavy casualties all the way. In France they rescued the "lost battalion" of World War II. This was a Texan unit of some 200 soldiers who became separated and surrounded by German troops. In addition to the many other medals and awards the 442nd earned in combat, they were made "honorary Texans" for their heroic rescue effort. The soldiers of the 442nd were fearless fighters whose combat motto was *"go for broke."* This motto became the title of a 1951 movie telling their story.

Among the heroes of the "go for broke" unit was Captain Daniel Inouye. Two weeks before the end of the war, in April 1945, Inouye was in combat in France. He had just pulled the pin out of a hand grenade and was about to throw it when he was hit in the right elbow by an exploding shell. The explosion didn't take Inouye's forearm off completely, but left it dangling by a few strands. For all practical purposes, however, his right forearm was gone. Yet his right fist, no longer usable but attached and dangling from his shattered elbow, still clutched the hand grenade which was about to go off.

Inouye grabbed the hand grenade with his left hand and threw it just in time. It exploded in the face of the German soldier who had shot him. He then fought his way back to his bunker, shooting with his left hand. Years later, he was elected to the U.S. Senate from his home state of Hawaii. He became a nationally recognized figure in the late 1980s while serving as chairman of the U.S. Congressional Iran-Contra Committee investigating the conspiracy to trade arms to Iran in exchange for support for the revolution in Nicaragua.

Another hero of the 442nd is Private Sadao Munemori. While his outfit was trapped inside a shell crater by machine-gun fire, he volunteered to go out of hiding and succeeded in taking out two enemy machine-gun nests with hand grenades. He had just returned safely to the crater when a live grenade was thrown in among the

American soldiers. He dove on the grenade, covering it with his body just as it exploded. For his heroism, he was awarded the Congressional Medal of Honor.

Fearless Facts

At the start of World War II, women doctors were not accepted into the U.S. military despite a shortage of qualified doctors. At the same time, women nurses were routinely accepted. Dr. Emily Barringer led a committee of the American Medical Women's Association attempting to reverse this policy. Her efforts bore fruit in April 1943 with the passage of the Spackman Bill, enabling women doctors to serve.

Audacious Audie Murphy

Although the most decorated U.S. military unit was the 422nd, the most decorated American is Texas-born World War II hero Audie Murphy (1924–1971) who received 33 decorations, including the Congressional Medal of Honor, by the end of the war (all this before reaching the age of 21). After the war, Murphy became a movie star, appearing in 44 feature films including the 1955 blockbuster *To Hell and Back*. That film was based on his autobiography of the same title; in the film, Murphy recounts his war experiences.

Murphy won his Congressional Medal of Honor for his heroic acts of January 1945 as a platoon leader in the 15th Infantry Division. The division was faced with the job of holding the line against six German tanks and 250 enemy infantry troops. Murphy's 15th was fighting with two tank destroyers, but both of them had been taken out of the action by tank fire. It looked as though the Germans would push their way through.

Murphy, however, had other ideas. He grabbed a .50-caliber machine gun and mounted it on top of a burning tank destroyer. While shooting at the advancing enemy, he called for artillery fire and directed missile launches. In this way, he single-handedly held off the six tanks and 250 soldiers until reinforcements arrived. He leapt off the destroyer just as it exploded.

After the war, actor James Cagney saw Murphy's picture on the cover of Life magazine and invited him to Hollywood to try his hand at acting. Murphy got his first starring role in 1949 in the film *Bad Boy*. The film was about a juvenile delinquent who thinks he killed his own mother. Murphy later settled into a niche in Hollywood as a star of

Heroic Shorts

44,000 Native Americans served in World War II and 40,000 more took on war-related jobs on the homefront. This is a disproportionately high level of participation given the total number of Native Americans living at the time. In the 20th century, five Native Americans were awarded the Medal of Honor—three for action in World War II and two in Korea.

Some 400 Navajo were recruited by the Marines to serve as "Code Talkers" who sent messages in Navajo code that could not be deciphered by the Japanese. The idea to use Navajo as a code came from Philip Johnston, a World War I veteran who grew up on a Navajo reservation as the son of a missionary. He proposed the Navajo language as a code—ideal because it is complex and has no written alphabet. The Navajo Code Takers were instrumental in the success of the U.S. Marines in the Pacific, sending hundreds of secret messages with high levels of accuracy.

westerns, although he made war films as well. He even played himself in the movie, *To Hell and Back* (1955). In addition, he was a successful songwriter.

Murphy succeeded as a movie star and songwriter despite ongoing difficulties with post-traumatic stress syndrome, or shell shock. He was active in promoting awareness of this little-known condition at a time when most veterans were reluctant to talk about the darker side of their experiences. After his death in 1971 in a plane crash, he was buried in Arlington National Cemetery, where his tomb has been the second most visited grave site after that of John F. Kennedy.

Old Blood and Guts

One of the most flamboyant of World War II war heroes is General George Patton, an expert on tank warfare and leader of American tank divisions in northern Africa, Italy, and France. He conducted himself with great pride, demanding respect and securing the admiration of his men through his insistence on discipline as well as through his stylish leadership. He had his general's star painted on his helmet and wore ivory-handled revolvers in his belt and walked with the swagger of someone who was proud to be a soldier.

Patton took command of a tank corps that had suffered demoralizing losses at the hands of "the Desert Fox," German General Erwin Rommel at Kasserine pass in Tunisia. Patton built morale in his men by insisting on strict adherence to army hygiene and dress codes and by having his officers lead attacks from the front, rather than from the rear where it was safer. He also gave fiery pep talks that steeled his men for battle and earned him the nickname "Blood and Guts" Patton.

Patton's sometimes theatrical style worked and his tanks rolled on to numerous victories throughout the course of the war. He was such a war hawk that he seemed to hate to see the bloody struggle come to an end. In fact, after the Allied victory, Patton proposed rearming the Germans and leading them to war against the Soviet Union! The 1970 movie *Patton*, based on the general's military career, won seven Oscars, including best picture. George C. Scott also won an Oscar for his portrayal of Patton.

General Douglas MacArthur. (Rutgers University Special Collections and Archives)

"I Shall Return"

Douglas MacArthur (1880–1964) was a general during World War II and the Korean War who became famous for his flamboyance as well as his success. His father was a hero of the Civil War who fought for the Union. The two MacArthurs are the only father and son to win the Congressional Medal of Honor. Douglas MacArthur graduated from West Point in 1903 and later fought in World War I where he was wounded three times. It was then he began sporting his trademark scarf and riding crop into battle. In 1930 he became the youngest man ever appointed army Chief of Staff. In 1941 he took

Towering Tips

Don't assume that the demanding leadership style practiced by General Patton works for everybody. He had no patience for what he considered laxness in duty and once had to make a public apology for slapping a soldier for cowardice.

Worthy Words

The name **G.I. Joe**, was used during the war, before Hasbro came out with the first action figures, to refer to the typical American soldier. The initials, "G.I." stand for Government Issue and applied to all the equipment and supplies used by American soldiers, who were themselves known as G.I.'s.

command of the U.S. forces in the Far East. He was stationed in Bataan but was ordered to leave when the Japanese bombed Pearl Harbor. This was when he uttered the famous words, "I shall return." And eventually, he did return.

He represented the U.S. as Supreme Commander of Allied Forces at the Japanese surrender on September 2, 1945, and became the military governor of Japan from 1945–1950. He later commanded U.N. forces in Korea, implementing the Inchon offensive against the North Koreans, forcing them to retreat. When the alliance between China and North Korea solidified, MacArthur advocated war with China so strongly that President Truman, who didn't want war with China, relieved him of command in April of 1951. Nevertheless, he received a hero's welcome on coming home.

War Games

World War II was such a popular war among Americans that soldiers in general were honored as heroes in the public imagination. Countless war movies glorifying the soldier and his calling were made during the war and in the years following. (The Spielberg blockbuster *Saving Private Ryan* is a recent example.) And gratitude to the nation's fighting men on the part of their wives and sweethearts gave rise to the baby boom as children were conceived in unprecedented numbers during the post-war years!

And, as the baby boomers grew to be old enough to play with toys, many, many little boys were given action figures to play with modeled after the typical American World War II soldier. In fact, Hasbro's *G.I. Joe* was the first action figure ever marketed, and it was hugely popular. It provided a generation of youngsters the opportunity of pretending to follow in the heroic footsteps of the previous generation. G.I. Joe later became a comic book series and an adventure cartoon series.

The Least You Need to Know

➤ Both World Wars required civilian sacrifices on the home front as well as great loss of life of enlisted men in combat.

➤ The "lost battalion" of World War I held out for a week without food and supplies behind enemy lines.

➤ The 442nd "go for broke" Japanese-American regiment is the most decorated unit in U.S. military history.

➤ Audie Murphy won 33 medals by the age of 21 before going on to become a movie star.

➤ General George "Blood and Guts" Patton inspired a movie based on his life that won seven Oscars, including best picture.

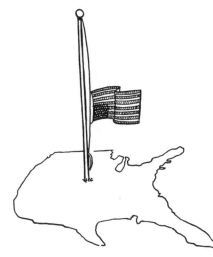

Interests Abroad, Outrage at Home

The morale of the U.S. military was riding high in the wake of World War II. America emerged as one of only two global superpowers—and the only one based on democratic principles. Many believed that America had the duty to use its military strength to protect the free world from the encroachment of communism much as it had used its military strength against Nazism and Fascism during World War II.

So, as the southeastern country of Vietnam struggled to establish itself as an independent nation after decades of colonial rule, the United States became involved, working to prevent the communist North Vietnamese leader Ho Chi Minh from taking over. As it turned out, this was no easy task. Ho Chi Minh's opposition in South Vietnam consisted mainly of a few rich, westernized leaders in the cities. The poor, rural South Vietnamese had little stake in the effort to defeat communism. In fact, many sided with Ho Chi Minh, seeing him as a liberator of their country—much as Americans see George Washington.

The U.S. government poured larger and larger amounts of money and increasing numbers of troops into Vietnam, but was unable to contain the Viet Cong soldiers loyal to Ho Chi Minh. Tensions turned to war, and the war escalated and dragged on, becoming increasingly unpopular with American citizens. Many felt that the war was unjust and the American government was in the wrong. Many also felt that the United States couldn't win. And many were horrified at the loss of human life on both sides. As a result, Vietnam war heroes often failed to capture the hearts of Americans back home. Instead, leaders of the anti-war movement emerged as heroes, denouncing the war and defying the government.

Quagmire

The Vietnam War was the longest and most humiliating of our nation's armed conflicts. U.S. military involvement began in 1950 when the government provided assistance to the French, who were attempting to quell Ho Chi Minh. A peace agreement would not be signed until 1973, and even then the peace wouldn't hold until 1975 when South Vietnam surrendered and Americans fled from Saigon.

Fearless Facts

Prior to the Vietnam War, the United States actually defended Ho Chi Minh in his struggle for independence against Japan. When the French took control of Vietnam from the Japanese, Ho Chi Minh continued his struggle against the French and the United States sided against him.

Bad Vibes

Public disgust with the war stemmed from many factors and grew as the fighting dragged on. Here are some of the more important items on the grudge list of those opposed to the war:

➤ About 58,000 Americans lost their lives fighting in Vietnam. Despite this high cost, few Americans felt the war was important to the national interest.

Fearless Facts

The memorial in Washington known as The Wall is inscribed with the names of all those killed or missing in action in the Vietnam War. It was designed by sculptor Maya Ying Lin and unveiled on Veteran's Day, 1982.

➤ Many felt the war was unjust as it became clear that most Vietnamese sided with Ho Chi Minh. It seemed the U.S. military effort to contain communism wasn't based on democratic principles or the will of the Vietnamese themselves.

➤ Many felt the war was unwinnable, given the limited objectives of the U.S. military. In actuality, the war was a restricted war. No one wanted to start a full-scale war involving the communist giants, China and the Soviet Union. Avoiding the kind of aggressive action that would set off World War III also meant, in effect, that the U.S. military was pulling its punches, afraid to deliver a knockout blow.

➤ Many Vietnamese citizens were killed in the war, often at the hands of U.S. troops who mistook them for guerrilla troops or suspected them of aiding the enemy. It became evident at home that some American soldiers were guilty of atrocities against innocent civilians as entire villages were wiped out, including women and children.

➤ Reluctance on the part of Americans to serve in the war divided the country in many ways. Civil rights leaders complained—justifiably—that wealthier whites had an easier time avoiding the draft and, as a result, the soldiers who were sent to fight were disproportionately poor and minority members.

➤ As opposition to the war increased, the government went to increasingly great—and objectionable—lengths to generate support. Officials disseminated lies about the progress and purpose of the war. Meanwhile, peaceful anti-war leaders were demonized as radical troublemakers and convicted in highly publicized trials of instigating riots.

➤ As it became clear that the war was not vital to the national interest and that the United States would not win, U.S. leaders—notably President Nixon and Secretary of Defense Robert McNamara—prolonged the war in the interest of saving face. Many saw this as an inadequate reason for sacrificing American lives.

All in on Getting Out

These listed concerns and other objections fueled the largest and most diverse anti-war movement in history, including participants from all races, classes, and generations. Resistance was based on moral, political, and sometimes religious reasons, and spread so widely that it dovetailed with the broader countercultural revolution of the 1960s. This revolution stressed peace, love, freedom, and the questioning of authority and "the establishment."

Groups opposed to the war included minorities, women, Catholics, college students, communists, and even veterans of the war. Famous public figures of all kinds actively opposed the war, suffering official censure and sometimes imprisonment for their actions. These opposition figures included Dr. Martin Luther King, Dr. Benjamin Spock, Rev. William Sloane Coffin, singer Joan Baez, and actress Jane Fonda.

Activists who opposed the war believed that the government and military were wrong in their policies and practices. Many stood up for their beliefs by defying the government, risking arrest and imprisonment. Some were also subject to smear campaigns on the part of the government and the police who wanted to discredit war resisters as selfish, unprincipled disruptive radicals. Of course, many who defied the government were draft dodgers who simply did not want to fight in Vietnam and some were troublemakers who just wanted to stir up sedition at home. But many were spurred by loftier ideals and sacrificed their own freedom and comfort for their convictions.

Peace Roster

Here's a list of some notable anti-war activists:

➤ Among the first anti-war activists were Catholic priests Daniel and Philip Berringer, who helped found an anti-war organization called the Catholic Peace Fellowship. Their moral and spiritual opposition to the war incited them to break the law by helping young men evade the draft while making a statement at the same time. They incorporated symbolism in their resistance efforts by destroying draft papers with napalm, a deadly chemical used in the war, and by dumping blood on them. They succeeded in galvanizing support for resistance and in clogging up the administrative pipeline through which young Americans were drafted. For their efforts, they were arrested and sentenced to six years in prison.

➤ Another group actively involved with resisting the war was the Black Panther Party, a civil rights group whose purpose was to promote black power. Founder Bobby Seales, leader Stokely Carmichael, and Education Minister Eldridge Cleaver organized and led anti-war demonstrations and spoke out against the injustice of the war. Cleaver was arrested for his actions and served a prison term. His experiences are described in his famous book *Soul on Ice*.

➤ Ruden Salazar was a reporter for the Los Angeles Times who wrote progressive articles on Latino issues. Salazar was present at the Chicano Moratorium of August 29, 1970. This was the largest Mexican-American anti-war rally. Rioting broke out in the wake of the demonstration, and Salazar was shot in the head and killed by a policeman with a tear-gas gun while sitting in a bar. Despite Salazar's prominence, there were no inquiries into the killing.

Heroic Shorts

Tom Hayden was married to actress Jane Fonda, who was among dozens who registered opposition to the war by visiting Hanoi, the capital of North Vietnam, where she made speeches opposing U.S. policy on Hanoi radio. In particular, she accused the United States of spreading lies against the Vietnamese communists by saying they tortured American POWs. Many who supported the government were outraged by Fonda's actions, regarding her as a traitor to the country that made her rich and famous. Among these was a former serviceman named James Clinton. Clinton was so obsessed with what he took to be Fonda's treachery that he began doing research to find out why so many American citizens went to Hanoi. He wrote to about 100 of them and conducted interviews. In the course of his research, he gradually came to believe that the U.S. government was wrong in continuing the war and that anti-war activists did the right thing in going to Hanoi. He collected and published these interviews in a book called *The Loyal Opposition* (University Press of Colorado, 1995).

231

Towering Tips

Beware of those who try to sew enmity in order to gain support for their cause. Officials in the Bush administration exaggerated antagonism between Vietnam soldiers and anti-war activists, claiming that returning soldiers were often spat upon by overzealous peaceniks. The purpose of the rumors was to forestall opposition to the Persian Gulf War by appealing to Americans to stand behind U.S. troops!

➤ College students were among the most active and ardent of those opposed to the war. Marches, sit-ins, draft-card burnings, and other demonstrations were planned and staged on college campuses throughout the country. Perhaps the most prominent student leader was Tom Hayden, co-founder of Students for a Democratic Society. Hayden helped organize the infamous protest held outside the Democratic National Convention in Chicago in 1968, in which 12,000 police, 7,500 Army personnel, and 6,000 National Guardsmen confronted some 5,000 protesters. Violence erupted with TV cameras on hand to record the struggle for the evening news. Hayden and six other leaders of the protest were arrested for conspiracy to start a riot. Hayden was one of five of the so-called Chicago Seven to be convicted. All five appealed the conviction and won.

➤ Many of those who opposed the Vietnam War were themselves involved in the U.S. military, including veterans and enlisted men. Some famous examples were the Fort Hood Three—Texas G.I.s James Johnson, David Samas, and Dennis Mora—who refused to go to war, calling it unjust, immoral, and illegal. Mora spoke at a press conference announcing the three's refusal to fight. Shortly afterward, all three were arrested by federal agents, court-martialed, and sentenced to two years in prison.

➤ Among the vets who opposed the war was Green Beret Master Sergeant Donald Duncan, a member of Veterans for Peace, comprised of vets who opposed the Vietnam war. After serving in Vietnam himself, Duncan campaigned against the war by publishing articles and giving lectures across the country

Peace Leader

Perhaps the most prominent of the many anti-war groups of the 1960s was the National Mobilization to End the War in Vietnam (MOBE) led by longtime pacifist David Dellinger. Dellinger spent time in prison for refusing to serve in World War II. At the time, he could have avoided service by remaining in Yale Divinity School, but he didn't want his religious studies to function as an excuse for his pacifism. So he quit divinity school and was imprisoned for refusing to go to war.

Years later, as a leader of the movement to oppose the Vietnam War, he worked to forge alliances among of all kinds of anti-war groups. He respected that different people within the movement had different attitudes toward the war and toward demonstrating against it, so he mediated among various leaders and organized rallies that would enable participants to choose whether to demonstrate legally or to defy the law through acts of civil disobedience.

For example, he helped organize a rally in Washington D.C. held in 1967 in which 100,000 people gathered at the Lincoln Memorial in peaceful protest of the war. After the rally, he urged the crowd to disperse and warned them of the dangers of participating in a plan to surround the Pentagon and block the entrances to the building on all sides. In this way, he tried to prevent people from becoming swept up in a frenzied mob. The more radical—and illegal—march on the Pentagon was led by the more militant anti-war activists, Jerry Rubin and Abbie Hoffman.

Unlike many anti-war activists, Dellinger opposed violence of any kind, and worked to prevent demonstrators from rioting senselessly. Yet, he was arrested and charged with conspiracy to incite riot in the wake of the violence at the Democratic National Convention in Chicago in 1968. He was one of five of the Chicago Seven to be convicted and believed he and other anti-war leaders were made scapegoats for the riots.

Fearless Facts

David Dellinger claims that while in prison he prevented a fellow inmate from being stabbed and sexually assaulted by telling the would-be assailants they would have to stab him first.

Paper Trail

Wrongdoing on the part of the United States prompted many to take a heroic stand in defiance, including some who worked for the government. One government worker who risked the consequences of causing deep doo-doo to hit the fan was Daniel Ellsberg, an ex-Marine who had access to a secret report on the war that came to be known as the Pentagon Papers. This was a highly classified history of the war that had been commissioned by the Department of the Defense, revealing a pattern of deception practiced by the government in concealing military actions in Vietnam from the American people.

Ellsberg was convinced the war was wrong and believed it should stop. In addition, he opposed the continuing spread of misinformation on the part of the government with regard to the war. So, in 1971, he leaked the Pentagon Papers to the *New York Times*, fueling public outrage against the war and the government. Ellsberg was arrested and indicted for espionage.

Because he committed a crime in releasing government secrets to the public, Ellsberg faced a long prison sentence. Yet, he exposed the government in acts of deception, so many Americans supported him. To turn the tide of popular sentiment against him and discredit him somehow, government spies broke into the office of Ellsberg's psychiatrist in search of information that could damage him publicly. The break-in was detected, however, and, as a result, the charges against Ellsberg were dismissed.

Inner Reaches

Amid the spread of mounting disillusionment with the U.S. government, growing numbers rejected not only the cause of the war, but also the "establishment" and all it stood for—conventional ideas about what is important in life, how to behave, and even how to think. Thus the anti-war movement was part of a larger social upheaval in which a generation of Americans expressed serious doubts about many of the values held by their parents. One of the biggest philosophical heroes of this generation was Dr. Timothy Leary (1920–1996), a psychologist who quit his teaching post at Harvard University to experiment with LSD.

Fearless Facts

Timothy Leary had an unpleasant run-in with "the establishment" as a cadet at West Point while being unofficially punished for an incident involving alcohol. Everyone at the military academy was to avoid speaking to him. Irrationally, this unofficial policy continued for months and began to interfere with morale among the other cadets. Finally, Leary agreed to drop out of the academy on the condition that the honor committee in charge of his case announced his innocence.

As a psychologist at Harvard, Leary conducted research into the effects and potential uses of a hallucinogenic drug called psilocybin, found in certain mushrooms. Leary believed the drug could be useful in expanding consciousness and developing the potential of the mind. He was interested in the beneficial effects of the drug and found it useful in helping ex-convicts adjust to life out of prison and in helping them stay out. He also took the drug himself, together with his students, to learn more about it. Despite his success, he met with opposition to his work from those who feared harmful effects of the drug.

After being pressured into the choice of either giving up his research or leaving his post at Harvard, he decided, in 1963, to continue his work on psilocybin without academic support. Shortly afterward, Michael Hollingshead, a British philosophy student who had heard about Leary's work, contacted him. Hollingshead introduced Leary to a new drug called LSD that had been synthesized by Dr. Albert Hoffman of Switzerland. The new drug, like psilocybin, was hallucinogenic, but was much more potent.

Leary became a spokesman for the use of LSD as a consciousness-raising tool, believing it could transform society for the better. He wrote manuals for LSD users with instructions on how to use the drug safely and how to get the most out of it. And he coined the famous countercul-ture slogan "tune in, turn on, drop out." Thou-sands of Americans followed Leary on his quest for higher consciousness through experimentation with LSD.

Towering Tips

Few people these days continue to regard experimentation with drugs as an acceptable means of expanding consciousness. Instead, drugs are widely regarded as among the worst of social ills. In fact, drug abuse—especially heroin—was a serious problem for many soldiers in the Vietnam War who sought escape through drugs and developed addictions.

While returning from a vacation in Mexico in 1966, Leary and his daughter were arrested for possession of a few dollars worth of marijuana. Leary was tried and sen-tenced to 30 years in prison. For someone committed to expanding the limits of his consciousness, the prospect of being confined behind bars was intolerable, so he fled to Sweden and lived as a refugee from U.S. law. During this time, he made friends with some of the biggest rock-and-roll heroes of all time, including John Lennon and Jimi Hendrix. Their experiences with LSD became a source of inspiration for their music.

Closing the Gulf

Ultimately, the Vietnam War proved impossible to justify. It had the beneficial result of making U.S. leaders cautious in undertaking the Persian Gulf War which, in contrast to the interminable Vietnam, lasted only 45 days, from January to March 1991. Almost half a million troops from the United States, France, The United Kingdom, Egypt, Syria, Saudi Arabia, and Kuwait combined forces against Iraq, resulting in 244 fatal Allied casualties. Of these, 146 American lives were lost.

The war garnered enough approval from the American public for two heroes to emerge: the smart and battle-ready Norman Schwarzkopf, and the straightforward, statesmanly Colin

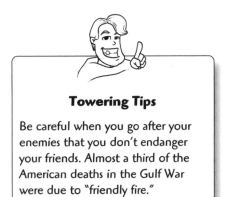

Towering Tips

Be careful when you go after your enemies that you don't endanger your friends. Almost a third of the American deaths in the Gulf War were due to "friendly fire."

Heroic Shorts

Another heroic Vietnam vet who went on to become active in politics was James Stockdale, a Navy pilot who flew over 200 missions before being shot down. He survived the crash, but was badly injured and taken as a prisoner of war. He was the high-ranking officer at his POW camp and did his duty by encouraging his fellow prisoners to follow the U.S. military code of conduct. Among other things, the code of conduct required POWs to refuse to give away military secrets. This proved especially difficult for Stockdale and his men because they were tortured for information. Stockdale spent seven years in prison as a POW, much of the time in solitary confinement. He communicated with other prisoners by tapping on the walls in code. After the war he was awarded the Congressional Medal of Honor. In 1992 he ran as the Independent Party vice-presidential candidate along with Ross Perot.

Powell. Both served in Vietnam before they became heroic Gulf War generals. Both helped to engineer a swift and decisive victory.

Stormin' Norman

Named for his father, a general in World War I and World War II., H. Norman Schwarzkopf Jr served two tours of duty in Vietnam, where he earned many decorations, including the Distinguished Service Medal. He remained in the military after the war and was promoted to general in 1978. Ten years later he became head of the U.S. High Command.

When plans were being hatched to retaliate against the Iraqi invasion of Kuwait, Schwarzkopf wanted to serve as a field general rather than send troops into action from behind a desk. In this respect, his style hearkens back to General George "Blood and Guts" Patton, for whom combat had an almost religious significance. Schwarzkopf made a famous Patton-like remark at a speech he gave at West Point Military Academy in which he referred to "armchair generals" as "military fairies." He is known to have had a Bible at his command post with a military camouflage cover.

Yet Schwarzkopf isn't a typical arrogant war hawk. He is a devoted fan of opera and ballet and speaks fluent French and German. His softer side is evident from the cover of his autobiography, *It Doesn't Take a Hero* (Bantam Books, 1992), on which he is pictured with tears brimming in his eyes. (Whatever it was that caused his deep sadness wasn't his book deal, which earned him $5.5 million!)

Schwarzkopf became a hero for his role in planning and leading "Desert Storm," the successful invasion of Iraq that led to the Gulf War victory. The Iraqis were expecting an attack on their forces in Kuwait. Schwarzkopf surprised them by sending troops into Iraq itself, farther to the north. The deceptive attack resulted in the quick surrender of large numbers of Iraqi soldiers. Those who didn't surrender were killed with technologically advanced and superior firepower.

Stormin' Norman, as he became known in the press, was a big hit with the public, who registered a whopping 93% approval of his actions in the wake of the war. Approval has remained high despite criticism from some veteran activists for not acting more forcefully to protect U.S. troops from exposure to chemical weapons and for not being more open about the problem of exposure after it occurred. Toxic chemicals may have sickened some 100,000 troops when an Iraqi munitions dump was destroyed.

Top Brass

General Colin Powell is a universally respected military man and was one of the government officials in charge of the Gulf War. Like Schwarzkopf, he was decorated for service during two tours of duty in Vietnam. He went on to serve as National Security Advisor to President Reagan starting in 1987. Two years later he was promoted to four-star general and became chairman of the Joint Chiefs of Staff. This is the highest military post in America, and Powell is the first and only black man to have held it. (His parents were Jamaican immigrants who moved to Harlem, where Powell was born.)

Towering Tips

The Bush administration strove to emphasize concern for U.S. troops in the Gulf as a means of deflecting critical attention away from questioning the war's legitimacy. Thousands of Americans took the hint and displayed yellow ribbons symbolizing support for U.S. troops. The responsiveness of the American public to sentimental appeals in time of war is satirized in the film *Wag the Dog,* starring Robert De Niro and Dustin Hoffman.

Powell was in charge of planning and directing the invasion of Panama as well as the Gulf War. He enjoys tremendous popularity with the public and has been courted by both the Democrats and Republicans to run for president. He retired from the military in 1993.

The Least You Need to Know

➤ The Vietnam War was the longest in U.S. history, costing 58,000 American lives.

➤ Opposition to the war was a major part of the countercultural revolution of the 1960s, in which "the establishment" was regarded with deep suspicion.

➤ Anti-war activists included civil rights groups, communists, veterans, religious pacifists, and college students.

➤ Generals Norman Schwarzkopf and Colin Powell became heroes of the Persian Gulf War years after serving in Vietnam.

Part 4
Rights Stuff

Wars don't last forever, and when they're over, the best thing to do is to go back to the business of trying to live peacefully. The battle for human rights, on the other hand, never ends; it has to be re-fought again and again to preserve freedom and justice for all. That's why heroic human rights leaders are important—not only for their accomplishments, but as role models for those who face similar struggles.

The great Indian patriot Mahatma Gandhi, for example, served as a role model for black civil rights leader Martin Luther King and Chicano labor leader Cesar Chavez. Each of them, in turn, has served as a role model for countless more people. These and other great human rights heroes have done such an impressive job that it is often tempting to think their achievements have ended the need for further work and vigilance. The fact is, though, that history isn't over yet. And as long as people continue to act in selfishness and ignorance, it will take continued heroic efforts to set things right.

Sadly, there's a common tendency among many people to think badly of those who are struggling and have a hard time fitting in. It's a way—a cheap way—of feeling good about ourselves, because it provides reassurance that we are somehow better than others. This feeling lies behind most of the prejudice and arrogance that have led to so much of the world's injustice. It takes great wisdom and courage to resist this tendency and to side with those who need help and persuade others that the deck is unfairly stacked against them. This heroic task lies at the basis of the ongoing struggle for human rights.

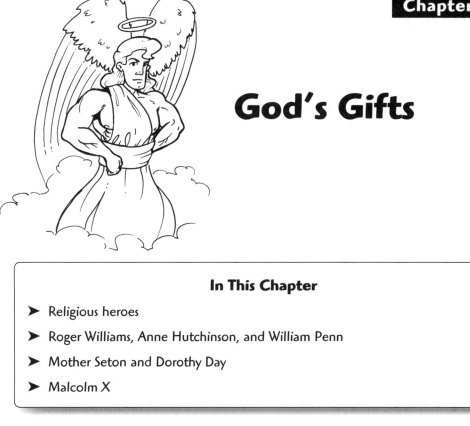

Chapter 18

God's Gifts

In This Chapter

➤ Religious heroes

➤ Roger Williams, Anne Hutchinson, and William Penn

➤ Mother Seton and Dorothy Day

➤ Malcolm X

There has always been something quintessentially heroic about those who live their lives in accordance with their religious convictions. It's hard not to admire people who dedicate themselves to unselfish purposes; and for centuries, religion has supplied a higher cause for heroic souls who are less concerned with looking out for number one than they are with God, moral goodness, and their fellow human beings. By obeying the promptings of religious faith, they set an example for everyone, regardless of belief.

America has been a particularly fertile nesting ground for religious heroes, thanks to the country's tradition of religious freedom that has helped define our national character from the beginning. Religious dissidents came here to escape the constraints imposed on them in their homelands, making America a bastion of religious tolerance. Among the important ideals on which the United States were founded was the separation of church and state—freedom of the individual to hold his or her own religious beliefs independently of the laws of the land.

In America, in other words, the government doesn't have the right to mess with people's beliefs. Of course, this way of doing things didn't just happen without hard work on the part of some especially committed individuals. And, as with other kinds of freedom, the need to keep working for religious freedom continues even after it becomes recognized in the law books.

Faith Haven

The tradition of religious freedom in America had its beginnings in the colonies, where pilgrims came in search of a place to worship according to their beliefs. They left England during a time of growing dissent and repression. Fortunately for Americans, some of the most ardent and influential Puritans checked these problems at the door when they came to the New World. Among the most famous colonial defenders of religious freedom and tolerance are Roger Williams, Anne Hutchinson, and William Penn.

Fearless Facts

Among the many groups, in addition to English Puritans, who came to the New World to escape religious persecution were Catholics from England, Huguenots from France, Jews from Portugal, and Presbyterians from the Scottish Highlands.

Promised Land

Among the first defenses of religious freedom and toleration to be written in America came from a disaffected English preacher named Roger Williams (1603–1683). Williams was unhappy with Anglicanism—the state religion of England—especially because it was against the law to practice other religious beliefs. Catholics and Jews were fiercely persecuted as enemies of the crown. Sectarian (Puritan) Protestants had a tough time as well. They were forced to attend Anglican services and pay taxes in support of the Anglican clergy. Growing resentment on the part of the Puritans against the state religion fueled the British Civil War, which culminated in the beheading of King Charles I in 1649.

Williams himself started out in England as an Anglican priest, but left the priesthood and the country because the rules of Anglicanism didn't mesh with his own beliefs. Like many English Puritans, he sailed for America hoping to find a less-restrictive religious environment and arrived in Plymouth in 1631. Yet he continued to be unhappy with the way the colonial government imposed religious rules and he spoke out against them. He argued that civil laws should not interfere with personal conscience. He said, in effect, that legislating faith would defeat the purpose of faith.

Roger Williams. (Rutgers University Special Collections and Archives)

Williams believed that faith was one of the most important aspects of religious life, and that the way to be a truly religious person was to have faith. He thought that if the government went around telling people what to believe, personal faith would be undermined. This idea is common sense among religious Americans today, but it was a radical idea in Williams' time. Williams tried to set up democratic rule in his church, and for this heinous crime he was tried in court and banished from the colony.

Cast out from Massachusetts, he made friends with the Naragansett Indians and obtained land from them for a colony of his own, which later became the state of Rhode Island years after Williams got a charter to set up his own colonial government. Meanwhile, he wrote and published pamphlets arguing for religious freedom and tolerance. Sectarians such as Baptists and Quakers who had trouble finding acceptance in England and the other colonies found a peaceful place to practice their beliefs in

243

Towering Tips

You're more likely to get other people to think the way you do by tolerating the beliefs of those you disagree with than by assailing them. This shows good sense and opens the way for reasonable dialog.

Williams' new colony. True to his ideals, Williams upheld the religious rights of all who moved there, even though he ardently disagreed with some of them.

Many Quakers, for example, made their home in Rhode Island, despite the fact that Williams was outraged by their tendency to place relatively little importance on the Bible. He challenged the Quaker leader, George Fox, to debate the issue, and published a pamphlet criticizing Fox and his beliefs. He insisted, however, that the question should be decided by each individual rather than by a code of civil laws. The terms of Williams' own religious faith changed through the years. In 1639 he became a Baptist, but later joined the Seekers. Although his own beliefs changed, he remained committed to the universal right of individual belief.

Heroic Shorts

Among Anne Hutchinson's supporters was Mary Dyer, who, like Hutchinson, was forced to move from Massachusetts to Rhode Island with her family in 1638. Dyer later traveled to England, where she converted to Quakerism and returned to the New World to spread her newfound convictions. A zealous and persistent advocate of Quakerism, she was arrested and exiled from Massachusetts three times. After she returned and was arested a fourth time in 1660, she was hanged.

Inner Spirit

Unlike Roger Williams, Anne Hutchinson (1591–1643) did not come to the New World on a religious pilgrimage, but as the wife of a merchant. Once in America, however, she became heavily involved in religion and the religious debates that occupied so much of the time and attention of the colonists. She arrived in Massachusetts Bay Colony in 1634 and soon won the gratitude of her neighbors for nursing the sick.

She aroused enmity, however, when she began preaching ideas that conflicted with the established church. Her message was that each individual can have a direct sense of God and that this personal experience was the most important aspect of religion. In contrast, conventional morality and rules were far less significant. She succeeded in persuading a group of followers—including some ministers of the church—of the value of her ideas, but this only angered the church leaders, who felt her approach to religion was dangerously subjective.

Like Williams, Hutchinson stood trial for her unorthodox beliefs and her insistence on spreading them around. She made an impressive showing at her trial, responding to her accusers with logic and humor, but sealed her own fate near the end when she claimed that God would destroy all who opposed her! She was banished from the Bay Colony in 1637 and excommunicated from the church for heresy. She moved to Rhode Island briefly before settling in New York, where Indians killed her. The Hutchinson Parkway, named after her, runs by the rock where she died.

Penn Is Mightier Than the Sword

Another founder of a colony that later became a state was the Quaker leader William Penn (1644–1718), founder of Pennsylvania and its capitol, Philadelphia (the "city of brotherly love"). Unlike most Puritans, Penn came from a privileged background. His father was a British naval hero with connections to royalty. Penn went to Oxford to study in preparation for a life as a British gentleman. But he picked up the Puritanical fever that was going around and found himself suspended from school for his beliefs.

Penn joined the Quakers in 1667 and became active in the sect, going on missions to Holland and Germany to try to win new converts and to spread the Quaker ideal of "the light within"—a direct inner connection to God. At this time, he had no plans of founding a colony in America. That happened later, after he got an offer of land in the New World from King Charles II. It seemed that the King owed money to Penn's family and Penn inherited the payment. Instead of money, the King offered Penn his own colony in the New World. (Ironically, Penn later returned to England and served time in debtor's prison.) So, in 1681 Penn set sail for Pennsylvania.

He wanted his colony to be an exemplary Christian society, premised on the Quaker belief that respects the godly aspects inherent in all people. In 1862 he helped draft the Pennsylvania Frame of Government, which defended individual freedom, particularly the freedom to practice religious faith according to individual choice. In the process of setting up his colony, he became known for dealing fairly with the Indians.

Towering Tips

The first U.S. rabbi to be born in America was Gershom Mendes Seixas (1746–1816). Rabbi Seixas founded charitable organizations, raised money to found synagogues, and promoted Jewish participation in civic affairs of the newly formed United States. Seixas's father immigrated from Portugal and came to New York City where Seixas grew up and was appointed Rabbi of Congregation Sherith Israel in 1768. In 1776, when the British were advancing on the city, Seixas and most of his congregation moved away. During these years he supported the revolutionary cause. In fact, his brother Abraham was an officer in the Revolutionary Army. Seixas founded a new congregation in Philadelphia before returning to New York City in 1784. Soon after the war, while in Philadelphia, Seixas fought against a rule requiring members of the Philadelphia Assembly to affirm their belief in the New Testament. The rule defied the Constitution and would have prevented Jews from serving in the Assembly.

William Penn. (Rutgers University Special Collections and Archives)

He conducted extensive negotiations with the Delaware Indians, who lived on the land he acquired for his settlement. In return for title to the land, he gave the Delaware a fair price (1,200 pounds) and set aside an ample tract for their use. Unfortunately, although Penn abided by the treaty, white leaders who came after did not and eventually dispossessed the Indians. But the Indians remembered Penn's integrity. When they made war on white settlers in Pennsylvania, they spared the Quakers, regarding them as peaceful and fair.

God's Workers

Protestants have always emphasized the importance of personal faith as a key to salvation. In contrast, Catholics have tended to stress action, or "good works," as a means to personal salvation. Therefore, it's no surprise that the Protestant religious heroes—including the Puritans Williams, Hutchinson, and Penn—are known for their advocation of religious toleration and freedom, which promote the development of individual faith, while Catholic heroes are known for their work in helping others. Two outstanding Catholic luminaries from different periods of American history are Mother Elizabeth Seton and Dorothy Day.

Mother Knows Best

Elizabeth Bayley Seton (1774–1821) started off as an Episcopalian, married, and had five kids. Tragedy struck, which changed her life. While vacationing in Italy in 1803 with her husband,

Towering Tips

Look for William Penn making friends with the Indians in the background of the famous painting by colonial painter Edward Hicks called *The Peaceable Kingdom*. The name of the painting refers to God's peaceful kingdom promised in scripture in which "the lamb will lie down with the lion," and the painting itself depicts this utopian ideal. Of course, the symbolism of animals getting along peacefully suggests that human beings should live peacefully with one another, too. It was Penn's hope, in founding Pennsylvania, to start a government where people could live together peacefully.

he died, leaving her virtually alone in an alien country. Italian Catholics, whose sympathy and friendship not only consoled and strengthened her, but also made a profound impression on her as well, succored her in her grief.

Two years later, after long reflection back in the States, she decided to convert to Catholicism. Not surprisingly, her Episcopal priest was opposed to the idea. Unfortunately, many of her friends turned from her as well and she went through a difficult time as a widowed mother. She hung on, however, and dedicated herself to her new calling as a charitable Catholic, starting a school for girls and, later, a convent.

Her school in Baltimore was the first free Catholic school in the country. Later, in 1809, she started a new religious order, the American Sisters of Charity. At this time, she took holy vows of poverty and chastity. She continued to teach and stressed the

*Mother Elizabeth Seton.
(Dictionary of American
Portraits)*

importance of education in classes and in her writings and translations. Over a century after her death, in 1959, she was declared venerable by the Catholic Church. She was beatified in 1963 and canonized (declared a saint) in 1975. She remains the only Catholic Saint born in the United States. Her feast day is September 14.

A Great Day

Dorothy Day (1897–1980), another Catholic hero, was, like Mother Seton, not born Catholic. She converted in 1927 after spending years as a socialist. She went to jail in 1917 for demonstrating for women's suffrage at the White House. She also worked as a reporter for the socialist paper *The Masses*, which opposed World War I. As a result, several editors of the paper were charged with sedition. Day was not arrested, but she remained a committed pacifist throughout her life. She also read extensively and developed a keen sense of social justice. Her concern for the poor and the socially displaced entered into her decision to join Catholicism as she became involved with Catholic charities.

Fearless Facts

Although she is known today as a devout Catholic and committed pacifist, Day carried on a four-year relationship with an atheist and anarchist who, when she got pregnant, insisted she have an abortion. Catholic Church doctrine doesn't support either of those activities.

Day found a way to promote good works in print as well as in person when she started the newspaper *The Catholic Worker* in 1933. She continued to write a column for her paper until her death 47 years later. Her paper and her work supported the homeless and jobless and other poor people. She also defended civil rights and protested against nuclear arms. In fact, she staged yearly protests against air-raid drills held in New York City, for which she was arrested and jailed in 1956, 1957, and 1959. She opposed the drills because they suggested that nuclear war is socially acceptable.

Fearless Facts

Day's paper, *The Catholic Worker*, was a big success when it came out in 1933 during the early years of the Depression. Three years later, however, it lost two thirds of its readership for condemning the Fascist regime of Spanish dictator Francisco Franco during the Spanish Civil War. Franco defended the Catholics and Spain and for that reason alone was popular with Catholics in America.

Throughout her life, she never entirely abandoned her socialist ideas, but supported trade unions and cooperative farms. She encouraged people to help themselves through faith and social action by volunteering to join in collective good works. She provided the inspiration for starting six communal farms and 40 shelters for the needy. And she was jailed at the age of 75 for picketing on behalf of farmers' rights. She continued her work all her life and died at a homeless shelter that she ran. Many Catholics have suggested that Day should be made a saint. In 1982, her stance on pacifism was officially accepted as consistent with Vatican II.

The X-Man

Islam has played a special role in the history of black civil rights in America, providing a religious focus and rationale for black empowerment. As black Muslims have pointed out, Christianity was preached to American blacks when they were slaves. For this reason, some have seen Christianity as a white man's religion and have embraced Islam as a religion native to the Middle East and Africa and therefore more suited to promoting black power on non-white terms. These blacks have joined into an American sect known as the Nation of Islam. The single most powerful exponent of the Nation of Islam as a means of black empowerment was Malcolm X (1925–1965), who successfully persuaded tens of thousands of blacks to embrace the Islamic faith. In fact, Malcolm's status as a hero extends beyond the Islamic religion. Millions of blacks of all faiths look to him as one of the greatest American heroes of all time.

Set Free in Prison

Malcolm X was born Malcolm Little in Oklahoma, the son of a poor farmer who was killed by whites in an unjust act of racial hatred. He grew up in poverty, first with his eight brothers and sisters in Oklahoma and later in Boston where he moved to stay with relatives. There he turned to crime, and was known in the street as Detroit Red. At the age of 21, in 1946, Malcolm was arrested and given 10 years for burglary. He wound up serving six years of his term before being paroled. In the meantime, he went through some important changes.

A cell mate told him about the teachings of Elijah Mohammed, an African-American convert to Islam who said that blacks had their own history independent of whites and that blacks owed loyalty not to the United States, but to the Nation of Islam. This message made a big impression on Malcolm, and he began to understand the hardships he had experienced as stemming from white oppression; moreover he came to believe that Islam could help black Americans overcome this oppression.

Fearless Facts

Elijah Mohammed, the founder of the Nation of Islam, was born Elijah Poole, the son of a Baptist minister. He believed that, because of their special history, blacks owed no loyalty to the United States. In keeping with his beliefs, he refused to serve in World War II and spent time in prison as a result. Boxing hero Muhammad Ali, a convert to the Nation of Islam, refused to serve in the Vietnam War for the same reason. As he explained it, "No Vietnamese ever called me 'nigger.'"

Malcolm converted to Islam in 1947 while in prison and changed his last name to X. The name-change signified a spiritual and a political awakening. He saw his original family name as coming from white slave owners, so he rejected it along with their religion. The X stands for ex-slave and ex-Christian. Inspired to develop his new understanding of oppression, Malcolm X read everything he could get his hands on in prison. He read the entire dictionary and copied entries. And, by the time he was let out of prison, he had read every book in the prison library.

Nation Builder

After getting out of prison, he met with Elijah Mohammed and set to work starting up Muslim temples across the country. He started small, but worked devotedly, preaching on street corners and starting the paper *Mohammed Speaks* in his basement. To make sure the message spread, he assigned quotas to everyone who sold the paper. He became a prominent Muslim minister and eventually became the second highest leader of the Nation of Islam behind Elijah Mohammed.

Thanks to Malcolm X's efforts, the Nation of Islam grew exponentially from 50,000 to 500,000. He spoke for blacks in ways that no one else was able to do. He disagreed with Martin Luther King, who favored racial integration. Malcolm X believed, in contrast, that blacks had to achieve empowerment on their own, separate from whites. He also disagreed with King's stand on non-violence. Although Malcolm X did not advocate violence, he taught that blacks should defend themselves when attacked "by any means necessary."

By the 1960s, Malcolm X emerged as a leading figure in America's black consciousness movement. He frequently made the news and was greatly in demand as a public speaker. Meanwhile, prominent blacks converted to Islam, most notably Muhammad Ali (formerly Cassius Clay) and Kareem Abdul-Jabbar (formerly Lew Alcindor).

Fearless Facts

Malcolm X's widow, Betty Shabazz, accused Louis Farrakhan of complicity in her husband's assassination. Her daughter, Qubillah Shabazz, was later a suspect in a plot to murder Farrakhan.

251

Malcolm X had a falling out with Elijah Mohammed in 1963. The following year, he broke with the Nation of Islam and was replaced by Louis Farrakhan. Despite his disaffection with the Nation, he remained a committed Muslim. He traveled to Africa and Asia, making a pilgrimage to Mecca in keeping with the teachings of Islam. The experience broadened his sense of the Muslim faith and he came to appreciate its importance as a religion of many races.

On February 21, 1965, Malcolm X was shot in New York City while giving a speech. The reason for the assassination remains a mystery. Some have suggested that he was murdered by members of the Nation of Islam for opposing their leadership. Others blame the death on a conspiracy between the New York City police and the FBI who may have regarded him as a political threat.

The Least You Need to Know

➤ Roger Williams was kicked out of Massachusetts Bay Colony for trying to set up a democratic church bureaucracy. He later founded Rhode Island on the principle of religious tolerance.

➤ William Penn founded Pennsylvania as a "holy experiment" in tolerant and peaceful government. He is one of the few white settlers to have made and abided by fair treaties with the Indians.

➤ Mother Elizabeth Seton was the first Catholic saint to be born in the United States. She founded the first free Catholic school.

➤ Dorothy Day combined progressive ideas of social justice with Catholic faith and good works to launch the Catholic Worker Movement.

➤ Malcolm X attracted thousands of converts to the Nation of Islam as a means of black empowerment.

Standing Tall

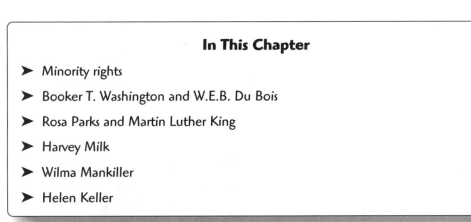

In This Chapter

➤ Minority rights

➤ Booker T. Washington and W.E.B. Du Bois

➤ Rosa Parks and Martin Luther King

➤ Harvey Milk

➤ Wilma Mankiller

➤ Helen Keller

Starting with the English colonists in the seventeenth century, waves of immigrants have come to America. You've probably been told already that they came in search of freedom and opportunity and you've also probably heard that they found these things. In fact, people say all the time that freedom and opportunity are what America is all about—especially for immigrants who are willing to work for their share of the American Dream.

What they don't always say, however, is that Americans have always been afraid that there might not be enough of the American Dream to go around. It often happens, as a result, that certain groups try to get it all to themselves or at least keep certain other groups from getting their fair share. Prejudice and discrimination set in as people try to convince themselves that they belong while another minority does not. And they develop stereotypes, practice intimidation tactics, and even pass unjust laws to keep others from encroaching on what they see as their territory—whether it's their part of town, their social status, or their system of so-called democracy.

Fortunately for the American Dream, there have always been people of all colors, nationalities, and backgrounds willing to fight for real democracy. Historically, the longest and most difficult struggle in achieving equal rights has been fought by African Americans, but other groups have fought—and keep fighting—important battles as well.

Lifting the Bootstraps

Not all those who stand up for their rights and the rights of their people do so defiantly to bring about immediate justice. Some civil rights heroes have worked long and patiently for gradual change. The advantage of this strategy is that it's safer and more peaceful and can also accomplish other goals in addition to justice, such as economic empowerment. This is the course taken by Booker T. Washington (1856–1915), who fought racism against recently freed black slaves by helping to show how productive blacks could be in the post–Civil War American economy.

School Days

Like his contemporary, Frederick Douglass, Washington was born into slavery, the son of an unknown white father. After the Civil War and emancipation, he moved with his family to Malden, West Virginia where he worked as a houseboy for a woman from Vermont who taught him to read. In 1872 he entered the Hampton School for Blacks, where students without money could work their way through.

Booker T. Washington.
(Dictionary of American
Portraits)

The school was founded and run by ex-Union General Samuel Armstrong with the help of the American Missionary Association. Its purpose was to educate poor blacks so that they could go on to learn skills to help rebuild the shattered economy of the South. The students led a regimented life and were taught, along with their courses, to stand up straight, behave politely, and work hard. Booker T. Washington became a model student who fully understood and believed in what Armstrong was trying to do. He graduated in 1875 and gave a commencement speech that was later printed in the *New York Times*.

After graduation, he worked briefly as a waiter in a resort hotel before returning to his hometown of Malden to teach. Then, in 1879, he was invited back to Hampton School as a teacher. Two years later, General Armstrong recommended him to head the new Tuskegee Institute, a college for black future teachers. Under Washington, the school quickly grew in size and importance. The curriculum stressed vocational training, because it was Washington's belief that practical skills would prove the most useful for blacks in improving their situation.

Money First, Justice Later

This situation was not simply due to widespread poverty and ignorance. Southern whites were generally resentful about the fall of the Old South and took their resentment out on the freed slaves. Terrorism, including cross burnings and lynchings, was routine. The response Washington advocated was not for blacks to stoop to the level of their oppressors, but for them to remain committed to self-improvement, rather than get caught up in a racial war they had little hope of winning. He made a speech at the International Exposition of 1893 in Atlanta in which he said that blacks and whites could best make progress by working separately. By avoiding racial disputes and

Heroic Shorts

While Washington was working to promote black vocational education during the late decades of the nineteenth century, immigrants were pouring into the industrial cities of the North in search of jobs in mills and factories. Working conditions were often brutal and pay was often bad. The labor supply was so plentiful that employers could usually dictate the terms of employment. Many who could not get work were left out in the cold. To combat this problem, Jane Addams (1860–1935) opened Hull House in Chicago, a famous settlement house that welcomed anyone who needed a place to go—the poor and unemployed, battered wives, and anyone else who had been displaced by big city life. Hull House has come to epitomize Addams' lifelong humanitarian efforts on behalf of the needy. Her work expanded during World War I to embrace a commitment to world peace. After the war, she was a representative at the Women's Peace Conference held in Zurich, Switzerland in 1919. Shortly afterward, she became the first president of the Women's International League for Peace and Freedom and was named "honorary president for life" when she resigned in 1929. She also helped to found the American Civil Liberties Union in 1920. In 1931 she was awarded the Nobel Peace Prize.

working to rebuild, the country could gradually solve its racial and economic problems.

Washington was successful in advancing the prospects of southern blacks both as a teacher and a promoter of black education. His tact and integrity helped him get financial support for Tuskegee from wealthy northerners, including Andrew Carnegie and Henry Ford, and also won him considerable political power, which enabled him to promote black industry and education still further. And he advanced a practical philosophy of empowerment that has made him one of the big heroes of black history.

Towering Tips

Booker T. Washington, although a great black leader with tremendous talent and energy who succeeded in helping blacks in many ways, operated much like a political boss, maintaining power by doing favors for people in exchange for support. While his ideas appealed to many white people, he attracted black followers by using his power to help them. And he expected loyalty in return!

Professor Protest

Not everyone agreed with Washington's plan for black people. Most notably, W.E.B. Du Bois, the black teacher, writer, and co-founder of the NAACP, took issue with Washington, arguing that segregation was a barrier to black advancement. Washington continued to believe that blacks needed to be economically strong before they would be fully respected by whites and that, although the laws requiring racial segregation were unjust, they did not prevent blacks from improving themselves. In contrast, Du Bois thought that whites were to blame for oppressing blacks and that the oppressive practices should be protested rather than silently endured.

While Washington attracted a big following from Tuskegee in the South, Du Bois criticized his ideas and organized a group of black intellectuals in the North who met regularly at Niagara Falls starting in 1905. They came to be known as the Niagara Movement. The group issued declarations of protest against segregation and terrorism against blacks. They stressed, contrary to Washington, that whites were responsible for the oppression of black people and that whites should work to end it. Meanwhile, he started newspapers for black people to promote awareness of civil rights issues and foster a positive black national identity.

Many white people, too, became convinced of the value of Du Bois' arguments. In 1909, several white sympathizers joined with him to create the National Association for the Advancement of Colored People (NAACP). The organization became a major legal and public supporter of black civil rights throughout the twentieth century.

Fearless Facts

For the first decade of its existence, the NAACP was run almost entirely by whites with the significant exception of W.E.B. Du Bois. This changed when James Weldon Johnson took charge of the organization in 1920. A former diplomat, Johnson greatly augmented the power and prestige of the organization with whites and blacks alike. Under Johnson, the NAACP began winning court cases on behalf of black people whose rights had been violated.

Star Reporter

Life was extremely hard for many blacks for many decades following emancipation—especially in the South, where they often faced poverty and racial hatred. Many were the victims of terrorism. Lynchings were not uncommon. One African-American hero who denounced this form of terrorism was Ida B. Wells, a school teacher turned activist who wrote for the *Memphis Star* newspaper.

While a teacher on a train to Memphis, she was told to leave her seat and move to a blacks-only car. When she refused, the conductor grabbed her and she retaliated. She later sued the railroad and won. The decision, however, was overturned on appeal.

As a teacher, she had first-hand experience with the inadequate education offered to black children. She wrote a series of articles complaining of this. She wrote more articles after three of her friends were lynched, denouncing the atrocities. Because of her articles, published in the *Memphis Star*, the newspaper office was destroyed by white terrorists and the paper was closed.

Wells went on to make speeches around the country and in Europe complaining about the lynchings. In 1898, she helped form a delegation to the White House to take up the issue before President McKinley. Wells was a member of the NAACP and the Negro Women's Club. In addition, she marched for women's suffrage and worked with Jane Addams to oppose segregation in schools.

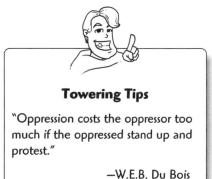

Towering Tips

"Oppression costs the oppressor too much if the oppressed stand up and protest."

—W.E.B. Du Bois

On the Bus

Despite the successes of the NAACP, segregation laws remained in force in many states a full century after the birth of Booker T. Washington. One such law in Alabama required black bus passengers to give up their seats to white passengers if the driver told them to. On December 1, 1955, four white passengers got on a crowded bus in Montgomery, Alabama. The driver told four black passengers to give up their seats. Only three of them did so.

The black passenger who refused to give up her seat was Rosa Parks, a housekeeper and seamstress who did volunteer work for the Montgomery Voter's League and the Youth Council of the NAACP. Instead of giving up her seat, she made a statement that will live forever in the history of civil rights: "No!" The driver stopped the bus and called the police, who arrested Rosa Parks. She was later released on bail.

The little incident sparked outrage in the Montgomery black community, dramatizing the racial injustice blacks in America had been dealing with since the inception of the nation. Community leaders, including church ministers, met to discuss how to handle the situation. Among them was the minister of Montgomery's Dexter Avenue Baptist Church, the Reverend Dr. Martin Luther King.

Heroic Shorts

One of many heroic black civil rights leaders of the 1960s was Fannie Lou Hamer, who took part in the movement as a "Freedom Rider"—traveling through the South on a bus to places that enforced segregation laws and publicly breaking them. (Such laws, although federally illegal, were widely practiced at the time.) For her heroic actions, she was arrested and beaten in prison, suffering permanent eye and kidney damage. She also worked to encourage blacks to register for the vote after being fired from her job for attempting to register herself. Her efforts helped bring about the Voting Rights Act of 1965, prohibiting unfair tests that were used to deny the vote to blacks.

King and Country

Martin Luther King (1929–1968) is the most beloved civil rights hero in America. He is remembered for his dedicated, nonviolent struggle to end segregation in America and has come to represent the ideal of a just and peaceful American society for all races. And he wrote and spoke eloquently in support of this ideal. His writings include *Why We Can't Wait, Strength to Love, From Chaos to Community,* and the famous "I Have a Dream" speech. His birthday is celebrated as a national holiday and he is recognized all over the world as a symbol of nonviolent activism for the cause of racial justice.

King encouraged blacks to respond to the Rosa Parks' arrest peacefully and helped organize a boycott of the bus company whose unjust policies set off the incident. The boycott was a big success, because most of the company's passengers were black and they were eager to make their feelings known and willing to walk or carpool to work for the sake of the boycott. It continued for 382 days, despite anger and resentment on the part of some whites who threw rocks at carpoolers.

Still worse, a bomb exploded on King's front porch. Fortunately neither King nor any of his family were hurt, but an angry crowd gathered outside. Many called for revenge for the bombing, but King spoke to them, urging a peaceful, and even loving, response. His commitment to nonviolence stemmed from the Christian gospels, in which Jesus teaches his followers to "turn the other cheek" when someone strikes them, and from the great Indian civil rights leader Mahatma Ghandi.

Fearless Facts

Many black civil rights leaders disagreed with King's policy of nonviolence, most notably Malcolm X, Stokely Carmichael, and H. Rap Brown.

Building the Dream

At last the boycott ended successfully when the Supreme Court ruled that segregated policies on interstate transportation were illegal. King continued to speak out and demonstrate for civil rights and against segregation. He encouraged blacks to vote and join the NAACP. He led a march on Washington in 1957 to end segregation. Although it was attended by some 25,000 people, the demonstration had little immediate effect. Segregation laws remained in force around the country: Blacks were denied the use of many public and private facilities including restaurants, clubs, drinking fountains, washrooms, and housing.

In 1963, King led a group of demonstrators to Birmingham, Alabama, where racism was as deeply entrenched as anywhere in the country. Americans across the country were outraged at the news that King and his followers were brutalized by Birmingham police. The event

Heroic Shorts

Thurgood Marshall (1908–1993) was the first black man to become a Supreme Court Justice, serving from 1967–1991. He was the great-grandson of a slave and class valedictorian at his graduation from Howard Law School in 1933. As a lawyer he represented many civil rights activists in court and, in 1938, worked as a lawyer for the NAACP. He won 29 of the 32 major cases he took on for the group and set important legal precedents in laws effecting desegregation.

helped awaken the country to the reality and injustice of racism. Later that year, on August 28, King organized a second march on Washington to end segregation. This was attended by more than 10 times the number at the march of 1957—more than a quarter of a million people gathered in front of the Lincoln Memorial.

At his march King gave his famous "I Have a Dream" speech, describing his vision of interracial brotherhood in America. This second demonstration, which crowned almost a decade of courageous action for his cause, bore fruit. King's speech was printed in papers around the country and public support for civil rights ran high. The following year saw the passage of the Civil Rights Act, which outlawed racial segregation. The same year, King was awarded the Nobel Peace Prize and became the award's youngest recipient at the age of 35.

Of course, the passage of the Civil Rights Act did not bring an end to racism. The plight of blacks in the many big-city ghettoes was so bad that rioting broke out across the country in Los Angeles (Watts), Chicago, Detroit, Cleveland, Newark, and New York. Racial violence was widespread throughout the 1960s. King denounced the violence while continuing to work for racial justice. In 1968, he went to Memphis, Tennessee to demonstrate in support of striking garbage collectors. While standing on the balcony of his hotel room at 6:00 p.m. on April 4th, King was shot by James Earl Ray.

Fearless Facts

Martin Luther King is commemorated on postage stamps from many countries, including the United States, Mexico, Paraguay, Haiti, the Virgin Islands, Samoa, Benin, Cameroon, Congo, Yemen, Ghana, Mali, Niger, Dahomey, Rwanda, Liberia, and India.

Grade A Milk

The black civil rights effort has served as a model for many minority groups seeking justice in America, including gays and lesbians. In fact, awareness that the struggle for justice of any minority is a common one was a key to the success of gay rights leader Harvey Milk (1930–1978). He is said to be the first openly gay man to hold public office in the United States. Milk was a Wall Street stock analyst who realized that he wanted to become active in politics and support gay rights. So, he moved to San Francisco's gay Castro district and launched his political career from a storefront office that he shared with a camera shop.

Milk ran for the San Francisco Board of Supervisors, but failed in his first bid, in part because many people in his district were straight and didn't particularly care to elect a gay supervisor. In a subsequent campaign, Milk changed people's minds by mobilizing gays in support of other local minority causes. Gays boycotted Coors beer in support of a local union strike, and rallied in support of the rights of local Chinese-Americans. Meanwhile he was an outspoken advocate of gay rights, encouraging gay men to acknowledge their sexuality. Thanks to Milk's efforts, the San Francisco City Council passed the Gay Rights Ordinance making it illegal to fire an employee on account of sexual preference.

Milk had a political rival named Dan White who was a staunch conservative. Bewildered and frustrated by Milk's political success, White assassinated Milk on November 27, 1978 and went on to use his gun on George Moscone, the Mayor of San Francisco. That evening, Milk's many supporters held a candlelight vigil. Singer and lesbian activist Joan Baez attended and sang "Amazing Grace" through a megaphone.

At his trial, Dan White's lawyers brought out the famous "Twinkie" defense, claiming that White's judgement was impaired as a result of eating too much junk food. The tactic evidently went over pretty well, because the court handed down a surprisingly light sentence for the murder of two prominent public officials: seven years, eight months in prison. The gay community of San Francisco was outraged and rioted at the news in May 1979.

Los Cinco de MAYO

Other minority leaders who have studied the black civil rights movement as a model for their own cause are the Chicano (Mexican American) organizers known as Los Cinco, "The Five," who founded the Mexican American Youth Organization (MAYO) in Texas in the 1960s to combat discrimination. Los Cinco began as a group of friends who met to drink beer and talk about politics and the problems Chicanos were facing. Gradually the bull session turned into a study group as the friends began to read and discuss history and political theory. This was the beginning of a influential Chicano civil rights movement that combated deeply entrenched problems including institutionalized racism in schools, police brutality, and labor discrimination.

The five charter members of MAYO were Jose Angel Gutierrez, Juan Patlan, Ignacio Perez, Mario Compean, and Willie Velasquez. One of the group's biggest accomplishments was to promote Chicano voting in Texas, which resulted in the election of many Chicano officials in predominantly Chicano areas. In fact, the group started up a Chicano political party, La Raza Unida (United People) Party. The

Towering Tips

Look for the movie based on Milk's story, an Oscar-winning documentary, *The Life and Times of Harvey Milk* (1984).

Heroic Shorts

Maggie Kuhn (1905–) founded the group that became known in the press as "the Gray Panthers," devoted to fighting prejudice and policies harmful to the elderly. A long-time labor and civil activist, she worked to unionize women clerical workers during the Depression and later wrote and edited for the magazine, *Social Progress,* put out by the Presbyterian Church. She was active in improving conditions for the elderly even before her forced retirement at the age of 65 in 1970 and was also an outspoken critic of the Vietnam War. She cooperated with Ralph Nader to work for nursing home reform and demonstrated against the American Medical Association for putting profit above quality in medical care. She testified before a congressional committee on aging in 1977.

group also organized student boycotts to improve education at schools in Chicano neighborhoods.

Despite their success in organizing Chicanos and promoting their civil rights and political awareness, not all Chicano political leaders approved of MAYO. Some felt the group's leaders were too unwilling to compromise with the established political structure. One of MAYO's original members, Willie Valasquez, left the group, partly because he felt the Chicano movement would make more progress by being less confrontational. Velasquez played a leading role in forming the Southwest Voter Registration Project, continuing to work for Chicano awareness, but adopting a more conciliatory stance toward the Anglo community. In 1995, seven years after his death, Velasquez was awarded the Medal of Freedom for his efforts on behalf of Chicano civil rights and education.

Chief Wilma

A heroic civil rights leader of Native Americans is Wilma Mankiller (1945–), who became the first female chief of the Cherokee. Starting in 1983, she served as assistant chief to chief Ross Swimmer, who moved on to become head of the Bureau of Indian Affairs before completing his term as elected chief. After that, Mankiller was elected as chief for the following two terms, 1987 and 1991. She has been has working for Indian rights, Cherokee self-rule, and the unification of the divided Cherokee nation since years before she took office.

Mankiller first became involved in Indian rights in the 1960s when Indians attempted to reclaim possession of Alcatraz Island, which was once used as a federal prison but had been abandoned by the U.S. government in the 1950s. The effort stemmed from the discovery in a clause in the Treaty of Laramie, signed back in 1868, specifying that Indians could reclaim federal land that was no longer used. So a group of Indians camped out on the island, claiming it as theirs! Mankiller helped out from the mainland, collecting food and supplies.

The event whetted Mankiller's appetite for civil activism on behalf of her people. In 1985 she was named "Woman of the Year" by *People* magazine. Later, as Cherokee chief, Mankiller worked out an agreement with the U.S. government for Cherokee self-rule. In addition, she worked to reunite the Cherokee nation, which was split up during the nineteenth century during the forced migration westward from their original homeland. In 1987 she organized and chaired a conference for Cherokee reunification.

Light in the Darkness

One of the most inspiring civil rights activists of all time is Helen Keller (1880–1968), the legendary deaf and blind writer and spokesperson for many causes—including women's voting, labor rights, birth control, venereal disease, and the rights of the blind. Her most heroic feat, however, was overcoming her deafness and blindness in learning to communicate, write, and finally speak, thanks to the teaching of her lifelong friend and helper, Anne Sullivan. Keller tells their story in *The Story of My Life* (1902). The story has been dramatized by the play and Oscar-winning movie *The Miracle Worker*.

Helen Keller lost her sight and hearing in a disease suffered in infancy when she was 19 months old. Anne Sullivan later taught her to communicate through sign language and eventually taught her to write and talk, enabling her to get an education. She wrote of her experiences while enrolled in Radcliffe College, where she graduated in 1904 and attracted attention to her accomplishments through her book.

Heroic Shorts

Elie Wiesel (1928–) survived his experience as a prisoner in a German concentration camp to become a leading critic of the holocaust and of atrocities related to war. Interred with his father in the Buchenwald camp, he witnessed his father's death. His mother and younger sister perished at Auschwitz. His novelistic memoir *Night* (1960) relates the events of his imprisonment, raising a subject that most people—Jews and gentiles alike—were ignoring or trying to forget. Known internationally as "a modern Job" and "the conscience of the holocaust," he became a U.S. citizen in 1963. In 1978 he was named chairman of the Holocaust Memorial Council by President Carter. The following year he visited Thailand and Cambodia to help refugees and to draw attention to the atrocities being committed.

She drew on her notoriety when promoting various liberal causes. One was workers' rights. In 1909 she joined the Socialist Party and later joined the Industrial Workers of the World (the Wobblies) and supported labor hero Joe Hill. She was also active in women's rights. She promoted women's voting rights and birth control and supported the heroic birth control advocate Margaret Sanger. In addition, she spoke out against venereal disease, a taboo subject few were willing to talk openly about. Yet, as she said, silence only furthered the spread of the disease.

Helen Keller. (Dictionary of American Portraits)

She also worked to improve the lives of the blind, serving on the Massachusetts Commission for the Blind and later as a spokesperson for the American Federation for the Blind. Meanwhile, she became an internationally noted lecturer with speaking engagements that included a trip to Japan. During World War II she toured military hospitals in support of Allied troops. For her many achievements, she was awarded the Medal of Freedom—the highest honor that can be conferred on a civilian.

The Least You Need to Know

➤ Booker T. Washington and W.E.B. Du Bois espoused conflicting philosophies of black empowerment. Washington emphasized economic improvement, whereas Du Bois stressed social justice.

➤ Rosa Parks set off the black civil rights movement of the 1960s, led by Martin Luther King, when she refused to give up her seat on a bus to a white person.

➤ Harvey Milk, the first openly gay man to be elected to political office, was shot by a political rival in San Francisco.

➤ As chief of the Cherokees, Wilma Mankiller worked for Cherokee self-rule and unification.

➤ Helen Keller overcame deafness and blindness to become a world-renowned writer, speaker, and spokesperson for social issues.

Chapter 20

Wonder Women

In This Chapter

➤ Susan B. Anthony, Elizabeth Cady Stanton, and Lucretia Mott

➤ Margaret Sanger and the birth control movement

➤ Betty Friedan and NOW

Women in America have made themselves a force to be reckoned with by organizing for the sake of women's rights and for the sake of justice, freedom, and humanity. Of course, these ideals are important for their own sake, but the question of how women should act in promoting them has been hotly debated since colonial times. Throughout American history, many have been reluctant to see sexual equality as a good thing, but have regarded it as a threat to other values. For years, the efforts of a relatively few committed and courageous women in pursuit of sexual equality have seemed—to a majority of people—like willful, unreasonable attempts to rock the boat.

Ever since its beginning in 1848, the women's movement in America has been faced with the challenge of showing that equality for women is not a recipe for disaster, but a means of achieving justice, freedom, and humanity—ideals that even the movement's worst enemies of both sexes respect. Traditionally, men have been in charge of pretty much everything and have taken credit for almost all the accomplishments of the human race. But of course, things go wrong. The women's movement got its start in America as women tried to lend a hand to help with some of the more serious social problems facing the country.

Heroic Shorts

A notable nineteenth-century advocate for women's rights, temperance, abolition, and Jewish-Americans was Ernestine Rose (1810–1892), a Polish immigrant who became a well-known speaker for these causes, often working together with Susan B. Anthony, Elizabeth Stanton, and Lucretia Mott. For 10 weeks she carried on a debate in print with the editor of *The Boston Investigator* who published anti-Semitic opinions.

Too often, however, women found that their help was not appreciated and the concerns they shared with men were left unresolved. At the same time, women began seeing that sexual inequality had a lot to do with these other problems. They came to see that social power for women could have positive results for society in general, so they spoke out for women's rights despite fierce opposition. Only recently has sexual equality come to be widely regarded as a good thing for its own sake as women finally begin to take a significant share of the credit and responsibility for the way the country works. This is largely the result of the heroic women who have stood up and spoken out for a chance to make a difference.

Common Causes

The women's movement in America had its roots in two other nineteenth-century movements in which women were active in large numbers: temperance and abolition. Well before the outbreak of the Civil War, many joined together to denounce the evils of alcohol, which they thought responsible for a number of social problems including poverty, wife beating, and child neglect. At the same time, abolition was gaining momentum, fueled by the serial publication, starting in 1851, of Harriet Beecher Stowe's *Uncle Tom's Cabin*, which dramatized the brutality and injustice of slavery.

Those most responsible for the women's movement all had ties to temperance and abolition. Their call for freedom for the slaves and sobriety for everyone was not simply idealistic, but was based on practical concern for society. Slavery fostered cruelty among slave owners and alcohol fostered irresponsibility. Both failings took a toll on society in general and on women in particular who, because of their dependent position, could be easily victimized by cruel and irresponsible men.

Many women involved in abolition and temperance came to appreciate the need for women's rights as a result of these other movements. They argued that women should have the right to divorce their husbands if they were cruel or irresponsible, should have the right to own property independently of their husbands, and should have better employment opportunities. Chief among these activists were Susan B. Anthony (1820–1906), Elizabeth Cady Stanton (1815–1902), and Lucretia Mott (1793–1880). Through their efforts against alcohol and slavery, they came to see both that women suffered unfairly as a result of male vice, and that women's contributions to society were undervalued and discouraged. So, they gradually widened the focus of their social activism to include women's rights.

Elizabeth Cady Stanton.
(Dictionary of American
Portraits)

The Start of Something Big

Mott and Stanton were active in the abolitionist movement and met in London in 1840, where they took part with other abolitionists at an anti-slavery meeting. The women at the meeting were at first refused entrance and later permitted only to observe sitting in the balcony. Frustrated and offended by the experience, the two went on to organize the first Women's Rights Convention, held in Seneca Falls, New York in 1848. Mott was a leading speaker at the meeting, which was attended by both men and women.

Mott's husband, James Mott, who was familiar with parliamentary procedure through his experience as an abolitionist, chaired the convention. The participants drew up a Declaration of Sentiments, which was modeled after the Declaration of Independence. It called for increased property rights for women, better employment opportunities, and the vote. Many of those attending, including Stanton, resisted adding voting rights to the list of demands, thinking it was too soon to call for such a drastic change. Mott, however, persuaded them of the importance of the vote to the women's movement and it was added to the list.

This convention was the first of many that came to be held around the country. As the movement spread, it had a polarizing effect and created a backlash. A few meetings met with opposition and some had to be canceled or rescheduled as a result of mob violence. More commonly, the meetings were simply ridiculed as "hen conventions" and the participants derided as addled eccentrics.

*Lucretia Mott.
(Dictionary of
American Portraits)*

Founding Mothers

Mott and Stanton continued to work for abolition until after the Civil War, becoming public figures both for their efforts to end slavery and for their commitment to women's rights. After the war, they organized the National Women's Suffrage Association, attempting to secure voting rights for women. The group's first meeting was held in 1866, when Mott was 73, with Stanton serving as the group's first president. Mott was also active in promoting peace. Her husband, James Mott, was president of the Pennsylvania Peace Society. Lucretia took over as president when he died in 1868.

Mott was generally recognized as the elder stateswoman of the women's movement in the late decades of the nineteenth century. She enjoyed an honored place at the thirtieth anniversary meeting of the Women's Rights Convention held in 1878. At the time, women's rights still had a long way to go, but the movement was in full swing and had succeeded in placing important demands on the table. Mott and Stanton were largely to thank for the growth of the movement, attracting followers through their persistent efforts and their talents as public speakers.

Susan B. Anthony.
(Dictionary of American
Portraits)

Fearless Facts

Lucretia Mott was creative and practical in fulfilling her traditional responsibilities of a woman while expanding the possibilities held out by that role. She played hostess to many noted intellectuals and personalities of her day, for example, including John Quincy Adams, John Greenleaf Whittier, Ralph Waldo Emerson, and Sojourner Truth. So as not to miss out on any of the after-dinner conversation while doing dishes, she brought a wash basin to the dinner table and washed up while participating in the conversation.

Sue B.

Lucretia Mott was a Quaker who grew up believing that divine spirit resides in all people. This notion helps explain her unusual self-confidence as well her social activism. In the Quaker meetings she attended, in contrast to the religious services of other groups, anyone who wanted—including women—could stand up and talk about

Heroic Shorts

An early feminist who put up with more than her share of public ridicule was Amelia Bloomer, who, in 1851, spoke out against the confining and cumbersome hoop skirts currently in fashion among middle-class women. She rightly complained that they restricted women's movement to the extent that were prevented from doing many useful things. In their place, she advocated "bloomers," long Turkish-style pants fastened around the ankles and worn underneath a loose-fitting skirt. Although many women—notably Elizabeth Stanton and Susan B. Anthony—chose to wear bloomers, they were widely laughed at as outlandish.

whatever he or she felt like. Topics addressed could be religious, of course, but also social concerns such as slavery and drunkenness. Mott often spoke at Quaker meetings, so it seemed natural to her that she and other women ought to "have a voice" in public affairs as well. The idea carried over into her efforts for women's rights.

Another outspoken Quaker who believed in temperance and abolition and who became a leader in the women's rights movement was Susan B. Anthony. She was a schoolteacher who became a Unitarian after her father was ousted from her Quaker group and a black man was denied a place at one of the meetings. Like Mott and Stanton, Anthony was active in temperance and abolition as well as women's rights. She served as secretary of the Daughters of Temperance Society in New York and later, during the Civil War, was an outspoken critic of slavery. She became well known for her public speaking on abolition. Her abolitionist views were so extreme that she was burned in effigy in Syracuse. But it is as a tireless organizer and advocate of the women's rights movement—and particularly women's suffrage—that she is best remembered.

Down by Law

At an early age, Anthony came to be outraged that married women were not allowed to own property independently of their husbands. Starting in 1854, she traveled around New York State collecting 6,000 signatures for a petition calling for property rights for women. She also formed an informal partnership with the older Elizabeth Cady Stanton. Stanton sometimes wrote speeches that Anthony delivered at women's rights meetings. Sometimes the two spoke together.

Anthony's early attempt to achieve property rights for women met with ridicule in the New York State legislature. She continued her efforts, however, and, in 1860, appeared before the state legislature together with Stanton, demanding property rights for married women, the right to sue in court, and equal guardianship over children. The speech was a huge success and met with the approval of the legislature, which passed the Married Women's Property Bill. Sadly, the act was watered down two years later.

In the wake of the Civil War, as voting rights for blacks were being debated, Anthony became convinced of the fundamental importance of women's suffrage. She and Stanton founded the American Equal Rights Association to promote voting rights for women and blacks. Former abolitionist men took over the organization and directed it exclusively toward voting rights for blacks, so Stanton and Anthony left the group to

Fearless Facts

A Welsh woman named Hester Vaughan became pregnant by her employer, who then fired her and tried to cover up the incident. Unemployed and without income, she was kicked out of her lodgings and delivered her baby without a home. After the child died, she was arrested, convicted of the child's murder, and sentenced by an all-male jury to be hanged. As a woman, she was not legally entitled to speak in her own defense at her own trial. Thanks to protests led by Susan B. Anthony and Elizabeth Stanton, Vaughan was pardoned by the governor of Pennsylvania and later returned to Wales.

form the National Women Suffrage Association. Meanwhile, in 1868 she started up a women's rights journal, *The Revolution*. She also became active in women's labor issues. She became the first president of the Workingwoman's Central Association, which advocated equal pay for women and encouraged working women to unionize.

In the early 1870s, women began to argue that the Fifteenth Amendment to the Constitution, which guaranteed black Americans the right to vote, also legally applied to women. The argument was based on the wording of the amendment, which said "persons" born in the United States were citizens and could vote. Inspired by this idea, Anthony and a group of women went to the polls in New York and simply voted.

None of the officials at the polls were prepared for the unprecedented appearance of women, so no one stopped them. Shortly afterward, however, Anthony was arrested for violating voting laws.

While awaiting trial, Anthony delivered lectures and rallied support for her cause—and her case. In fact, she elicited so much sympathy in her county that the district attorney moved her trial to another jurisdiction where he could be more certain of a verdict of guilty. Anthony was convicted and fined for illegal voting, but simply refused to pay.

Towering Tips

Pay your debts! People will respect you and, besides, it's good for the economy. This is what Susan B. Anthony did after going $10,000 in the hole with her journal, *The Revolution*. She was praised in the papers for meeting her financial obligations under circumstances where most businessmen would have declared bankruptcy.

The Lecture Circuit

Anthony remained a dedicated advocate of women's suffrage, lecturing tirelessly all across

Towering Tips

Keep in mind that injustice effects everyone. Susan B. Anthony demonstrated this point by explaining why male teachers did not enjoy the social status they deserved. She pointed out that women were allowed to be teachers but were barred from becoming doctors, ministers, and lawyers, thereby fostering the misguided social attitude that female teachers were less intelligent than males in exclusive professions! In a later incident, an abolitionist asserted that Anthony was not qualified to speak out against the injustices of marriage since she was not married herself. She responded by saying that he must not be qualified to speak out against slavery since he was not himself a slave!

the country, much as she had for other causes—temperance and abolition. It is estimated the she gave an average of 85 lectures a year during her 60-year career as an activist. And she continued working into her 80s! Over the years, she gradually won many opponents over to her cause, and many of those who opposed her were compelled to admire her integrity, intelligence, poise, and commitment.

An indication of the degree of difficulty Anthony faced in her life-long struggle for women's rights is the fact that women's suffrage was not written into law until the passage of the Nineteenth Amendment in 1920, 14 years after her death. It took the following generation to assimilate and act on her efforts. To this day, she is the only woman aside from Lady Liberty to have been portrayed on U.S. currency—the Susan B. Anthony dollar coin.

Gaining Control

Susan B. Anthony saw that the vote was necessary for women to achieve political equality. Years later, Margaret Sanger (1883–1966) saw that birth control was necessary for women to achieve social equality. She spearheaded America's birth control movement and suffered persecution and imprisonment for her cause. Much like Anthony and the women's vote issue, Sanger saw birth control as an important right in itself as well as means of improving the lives of women and benefiting society in general.

Guilty Secrets

Sanger was ahead of her time in promoting birth control in America, since most Americans were too prudish to talk openly about sex, even as a social and health issue. In contrast, birth control was already legal in many countries of Europe as Sanger was working to promote it in America. Prudishness, however, was only one aspect of the silence and opposition toward birth control. Birth control was actually legal for men in special cases, to prevent the spread of disease.

As a result, men could get condoms legally for use with mistresses and prostitutes, especially if they were wealthy or well connected. But this was a matter left up to male doctors and their male patients. Women, on the other hand, were denied the legal right to birth control, even if they were sick, worn out, or impoverished from having children. Eventually, however, the practical need for birth control emerged so clearly and urgently that Sanger was able to make people listen and change their minds.

Bringing Something to the Party

Sanger worked at a hospital as a nurse-in-training. She got involved in socialism through her friend and future husband, Bill Sanger, with whom she attended socialist meetings. At those meetings, she came into contact with labor leaders Eugene Debs and Bill Haywood. Eventually she joined the Socialist Party, finding an appreciative audience for her ideas about the relations between sex and reproduction and society—ideas formed in response to observations she made as a nurse.

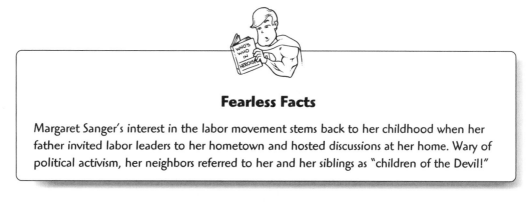

Fearless Facts

Margaret Sanger's interest in the labor movement stems back to her childhood when her father invited labor leaders to her hometown and hosted discussions at her home. Wary of political activism, her neighbors referred to her and her siblings as "children of the Devil!"

Editors of the journal *The Socialist Call* invited her to contribute a regular column on health and reproduction called "What Every Mother Should Know." The column was a big success, so Sanger started up a second column called "What Every Girl Should Know." An advance notice for this column said the first installment would be about sexually transmitted diseases—a subject widely considered socially taboo. The column was censored by order of the post office.

An Ounce of Prevention

Sanger continued to work for socialism. She testified in a court hearing about the poor health of the children of textile workers who were on strike. She also worked for New York City's Visiting Nurse's Association, providing health care for the poor. Many poor women she visited were burdened by children they could not afford to care for properly. They often asked Sanger for a safe means of preventing unwanted pregnancy. Contraception, however, was against the law. Doctors and nurses who distributed birth control could be jailed. What's more, the only reliable means of birth control known to doctors in America at the time was the condom. There was no safe, reliable birth control for women, legal or otherwise.

In 1913, Sanger sailed to France, where contraception and abortion were legal, in search of knowledge. She found that social conditions among the poor were much better than in America, largely as a result of contraception and abortion. Poor families had fewer children and, as a result, were better able—both physically and economically—to care for those they had.

On returning to the United States, Sanger founded the National Birth Control League to spread her message to doctors, politicians, and the public. She also started up a magazine called *The Woman Rebel*, which had a broad feminist focus and denounced unfair legal practices as well as capitalism, organized religion, and marriage. The magazine's first issues were banned by the post office, but were distributed in secret anyway.

Fearless Facts

An anti–obscenity law signed into effect under the Grant administration empowered postal inspectors to open sealed mail and censor or confiscate anything they deemed obscene, including Margaret Sanger's publications on how to prevent venereal disease! Later, under the same law, her writings on birth control were confiscated. Later still, the government itself published in pamphlet form an article on venereal disease it had censored previously, distributing them to soldiers overseas during World War I.

Trying Times

Shortly afterward, Sanger was arrested and charged with sending obscenity through the mail. The mainstream press sided against her. While she awaited trial, she arranged to have a booklet printed called *Family Limitation*, which described the birth control techniques she learned in France. The booklet included detailed illustrations. Printer after printer refused the job before she finally found one who would do it in secret.

Her efforts delayed her trial preparations, so she requested a postponement; her request was denied. Against her lawyer's advice, she refused to plead guilty, wanting to expose the injustice of the laws she broke. But, as she did not have adequate time to prepare her defense, she fled the country rather than stand trial. She sailed to England using a forged passport. There she found the support of like-minded medical professionals who persuaded her to renounce socialism to concentrate fully on birth control and to improve her image with the public. From England she traveled to Holland where, because of the nationally supported system of birth control clinics, the maternity death rate was lower than anywhere else in the world. She studied Dutch birth control techniques before returning to America to face trial.

In her absence from the United States, her booklet *Family Limitation* became an underground success. All over America, people were coming to realize the personal and social benefits of safe birth control. Socialist journalist John Reed persuaded her to pose for a photograph with her two sons, looking tranquil and maternal, to dispel her reputation as a radical agitator. Popular sympathy for Sanger and her cause increased. On the day of her trial, the courtroom was mobbed with supporters. The trial was postponed and later her case was dismissed.

From Clinic to Clink

During the following year, 1916, Sanger went on a tour giving lectures throughout the country to drum up support for birth control clinics. She and some of her followers were arrested in Portland, Oregon while handing out copies of *Family Limitation* at a public meeting. As they were taken to jail, hundreds of other women followed and demanded to be arrested too! More and more people began to see the obscenity laws as out of date.

After her lecture tour, Sanger decided to open her own birth control clinic, even though it meant defying the law. She was unable to find a doctor willing to risk imprisonment, but she had the help of her sister, a registered nurse named Ethel Byrne. They had difficulty finding a landlord who would rent them space for their clinic, but eventually moved into two rooms in a Brooklyn slum, Brownsville. Sanger and her sister printed up handbills in English, Yiddish, and Italian advertising the clinic and its services. On the day they opened, dozens of women were waiting in line.

After 10 days of continuous work at the crowded clinic, the police busted them. Sanger spent the night in jail, paid bail, returned to the clinic, and resumed work. She was arrested a second time, and the police ordered the landlord to evict them for creating a public nuisance. While awaiting trial, she appealed for support from the New York Medical Society, but was denied. Sanger claimed the society, run by male doctors, wanted to reserve contraception for men but deny it to women as a means of preserving sexual control.

Heroic Shorts

Socialist journalist John Reed (1887–1920) covered the Russian Revolution of 1917 for American newspapers, worked for the Bureau of International Revolutionary Propaganda, and helped found the Communist Party in America. His book on the Bolshevik Revolution, *Ten Days That Shook the World* (1919), came to be used as a history textbook in the Soviet Union. The Soviets regarded him as a hero and, upon his death, buried him outside the Kremlin in Moscow's Red Square. The movie *Reds* (1981), directed by and starring Warren Beatty, is based on Reed's life and his relationship with free-thinking feminist Louise Bryant, played by Diane Keaton. The film includes interviews with real-life acquaintances of the famous journalist. It won Oscars for direction and cinematography.

Towering Tips

Speaking out for others can be a great thing, but helping others speak for themselves can be even better. Margaret Sanger's influential book *Mothers in Bondage* (1928) is a collection of 500 of the many letters she received telling of the hardships faced by mothers unable to control their own pregnancies.

Ethyl Byrne, Margaret's sister, was tried and convicted to 30 days in a workhouse. Hoping to attract attention to the cause, she went on a hunger strike, prepared to die for the sake of women's birth control rights. After going more than four days without food, she was wrapped in a blanket and force-fed a concoction made of milk, eggs, and brandy, becoming the first American woman ever to be force-fed in jail.

Despite support from dozens of women, both rich and poor, at her trial, Sanger was also convicted and sentenced to 30 days in prison. Claiming she was a political prisoner rather than a criminal, she refused to submit to the standard procedures for finger printing and physical examination. While in prison, she shared her knowledge of birth control with other female convicts.

Off the Hook

Upon her release, her fellow inmates cheered her as she left. Supporters were on hand in the streets and sang the *Marseilles*, the national anthem of the French Revolution, as a show of encouragement for the birth control revolution. Sanger continued her efforts by publishing *The Birth Control Review* and by revising and continuing to distribute *Family Limitation*. Meanwhile, she appealed her conviction for distributing contraception. Although the ruling was upheld, the appeals court decided to allow doctors to give birth control to women for health reasons, making birth control clinics legal.

Sanger continued to write, lecture, and organize for the birth control movement. Her book *Motherhood and the New Race* (1920) became a best-seller. She was invited to lecture in Japan and also lectured in the Middle East. And she organized the first National Birth Control Conference in the United States. Although she continued to face heated opposition, the press, the public, and the medical community grew increasingly supportive. At last, in 1936, the American Medical Association accepted birth control as a legitimate medical procedure for all who choose it. In 1942, Sanger was named honorary president of the Planned Parenthood Federation.

Success for NOW

A legislative watershed of the women's movement in America was the Equal Rights Amendment, which was first proposed in Congress in 1923. The ERA called for "equality of rights under the law" for women. The amendment was not passed by Congress until nearly 50 years later. In 1971 it was approved in the House and the following year, in the Senate. Still, the amendment failed, because the required three fourths of the states failed to ratify it. Ratification failed again in 1982, falling short by just three states.

Despite the failure of ERA, the 1960s and 1970s ushered in tremendous gains for the women's movement as women demanded equal rights in the work place and battled against widespread sexual discrimination. A tremendous catalyst for these gains was provided by Betty Friedan, author of *The Feminine Mystique* and founder of the National Organization for Women.

Disturbing Stats

While working as a freelance writer of magazine articles, Friedan was asked by Smith College (for women) to prepare a questionnaire for the class of 1941, about to attend its 15-year reunion. The purpose of the questionnaire was to find out about the uses they made of their college education. Not surprisingly, the questionnaire revealed that the overwhelming majority of respondents were housewives. What was surprising to Friedan at the time was that most revealed they were dissatisfied with their lives as mothers and homemakers. And most blamed themselves for their unhappiness in these stereotypical roles. The happy homemaker was a feminine ideal that many women felt themselves unable to live up to.

Sensing she was on to an important discovery, Friedan wrote up the results of her survey and submitted them to women's magazines. Her findings were rejected by *McCalls* and *Redbook* for being too bleak. *Ladies Home Journal* agreed to accept it only if they could change the conclusions so as to present a misleadingly positive picture and perpetuate the happy homemaking myth. Friedan refused and decided to publish her findings as a book instead of an article.

The result was *The Feminine Mystique* (1964), which argued that the domestic roles accepted by most American women were inherently unsatisfying. Instead, she recommended more professional training and employment for women and cautioned against early marriage. For working mothers, she called for maternity leave and childcare. Too often, women were fired from their jobs—as Friedan was herself—when they left to have children.

Heroic Shorts

Shirley Chisholm (1924–) was a political leader and civil rights activist for women and African Americans. After years spent running a nursery school, she joined the Seventeenth Assembly District Democratic Club and began working for greater representation in government for black people and women. In 1960 she founded the Unity Democratic Club to promote African-American candidates and, in 1964, was elected herself to the New York State Assembly. Four years later she became the first black woman to be elected to the U.S. House of Representatives. In 1972 she ran for president in the Democratic primaries. In 1984 she founded the National Political Congress of Black Women, and in 1993 she was appointed ambassador to Jamaica.

Lady Libber

Friedan's book quickly became a controversial bestseller as Friedan continued to denounce social injustice against women. She complained about the ways women were portrayed in the media as less intelligent and important than men. And she spoke out against sex discrimination in hiring practices, pointing out that classified ads for high-paying jobs often specified "male" applicants while low-paying jobs specified "female." And she denounced the virtual absence of women in high positions in the important fields of law, government, and medicine.

In 1966, she organized the National Organization for Women (NOW), serving as president until 1970. NOW defended the rights of women in the workplace by filing legal suits against businesses that practiced sex discrimination. Gradually, NOW became a major political force, winning important legal battles and influencing legal and government policies to help women compete for jobs.

Working with NOW as well as independently, Friedan worked to promote women's equality in virtually every aspect of public life. In 1969 she started the National Abortion Rights Action League. She founded the National Women's Political Caucus in 1971 together with Gloria Steinem and Bela Abzug. She worked with the banking industry to eliminate discrimination so that women could obtain loans and mortgages. And she became a college professor at Temple, Yale, and Queens College, teaching about the women's movement and promoting women's studies in the curriculum.

The Least You Need to Know

➤ The women's movement in America can trace its roots to the temperance and abolition movements.

➤ Elizabeth Cady Stanton, Lucretia Mott, and Susan B. Anthony were outspoken in the cause of women's rights in the nineteenth century.

➤ Margaret Sanger dedicated her life to promoting birth control in America and eventually succeeded in getting birth control accepted as a legitimate medical practice.

➤ Betty Friedan founded the National Organization for Women after writing the best-selling feminist milestone *The Feminine Mystique*.

Chapter 21

Hard Work

In This Chapter

➤ Heroic labor leaders and heroic lawyers

➤ Samuel Gompers and the AFL

➤ Eugene Debs, Bill Haywood, and the Wobblies

➤ Mother Jones and Joe Hill

➤ Louis Brandeis and Clarence Darrow

➤ Cesar Chavez and the UFW

Like it or not, work is the single most important thing in the lives of most Americans. It not only pays the rent and puts food on the table, but it also keeps the country humming. And work has special importance in American history because it forms the basis of economic opportunity that makes freedom and equality possible. After all, most people like to think of America as a place where anyone who is willing to work hard can be successful. It is working people who have made America a leading industrial nation and, as a result, a leading world power.

Throughout much of the history of working life in America, workers have had a hard time reaping the benefits of their own hard work. "Big business" and entrepreneurs got rich while labor wore itself out trying just to stay afloat. Despite their hard work, most working people remained poor and found little opportunity to rise above their circumstances. Many were immigrants who faced discrimination and prejudice.

Compounding the problem has been the tendency on the part of the "haves" to think they deserve their success while the "have nots" deserve their humble circumstances. Middle- and upper-class society is often complacent about the plight of the working poor. The poor, in turn, face special difficulties when trying to speak for themselves, since they are quickly suspected of trying to make trouble. It's hard to get respect when you start out in life at the bottom of the ladder.

Although it often goes unappreciated in the post-industrial America of today, the labor movement has been crucial in making this country what it has become by promoting the health, prosperity, freedom, and dignity of working people. In the face of hardship, class prejudice, and repression from business and government, workers have organized together to improve their lives. In the process, many of their leaders emerged as heroes of the working class.

The Roller of Big Cigars

During the early years of American industrialism in the wake of the Civil War, workers had little control over their own lives. Terms of employment depended mostly on whatever seemed most profitable to employers, who often treated labor as a disposable resource. Low pay, hazardous and unhealthy job conditions, long hours, no benefits, and no job security made many workers worse off than slaves, with little hope of improving their lives other than to organize into unions.

The leading union organizer of the country during the early years of the labor movement was Samuel Gompers (1850–1924), who promoted causes most of us today think of as basic quality-of-life issues for workers: higher wages, shorter hours, and safer conditions. He did this by spearheading the American Federation of Labor, a national alliance of trade unions that put pressure on government to pass legislation in support of workers. Gompers served as AFL president from 1886 to 1924.

Gompers was born in London and attended the Jew's Free School before becoming a shoemaker's apprentice at an early age. At age 10, he switched vocations to cigar making. At 13 years old, he immigrated to New York City with his family and the following year joined the cigar maker's union. A skilled worker and valuable employee, Gompers also spoke out bravely in the interests of his fellow workers, who made him president of the Cigar Maker's local union at the age of 25.

During this time, Gompers became involved in other organizations for workers and gained exposure to the socialist ideas that appealed strongly to many of his fellow union leaders and labor organizers. Many believed that workers' rights could not be adequately recognized and upheld under capitalism and advocated a workers' revolution. Gompers, in contrast, developed a policy, which he upheld throughout his lifetime, of economics over politics. He believed that the role of unions should to promote the economic prosperity of workers through democratic processes within the capitalist system.

*Samuel Gompers.
(Dictionary of
American Portraits)*

Hoping to spread awareness of labor issues and influence government to pass legislation in support of workers, Gompers helped to found the Federation of Organized Trades and Labor Unions, which met every year to develop and propose better labor practices. Gompers was especially interested in promoting limits for child labor and mandatory schooling for working children as well as an eight-hour workday for everyone. Sadly, the organization lacked the power to exert much of an effect on government and Gompers became frustrated with it.

In 1886, he helped found the American Federation of Labor, which became the leading organization of unions in the country. As AFL chief he lobbied Congress, negotiated strike settlements, and built union membership and strength. His strategy was to work for limited gains for labor within the democratic process rather than for a wholesale, revolutionary shift of power to the laborers as many other labor leaders called for. Even so, many corporate leaders accused him of interfering with free enterprise and often resisted even the most basic changes in the direction of workers' rights. On the other hand, the more radical labor leaders accused him of pandering to business by not taking a more aggressive stand against the system. He is remembered today, however, as a committed and practical organizer who set the standard for union leadership for the twentieth century.

Wobbly World

Other famous labor leaders of the late nineteenth and early twentieth centuries were more radical than Gompers was; they thought that workers' rights would not be adequately recognized in a capitalist society. The most prominent of these were Eugene

Worthy Words

Members of the Industrial Workers of the World were known as **Wobblies**. One story says the name got started when an Asian worker pronounced "I.W.W." as "eye wobble wobble." Another possibility is that the word preexisted the start of the organization as a pejorative term and was taken on as a badge of working-class pride. Critics of the movement jokingly suggested the initials stood for "I Want Whiskey."

Debs (1855–1926) and "Big" Bill Haywood (1869–1928), who founded the Industrial Workers of the World, informally known as the *Wobblies*. This was a union, open to workers in all trades, which had the stated purpose of overthrowing capitalism and replacing the government with a system run by the workers.

Of course, Debs and Haywood got into serious legal trouble for their radical views, serving jail sentences for sedition and conspiracy. But they were zealous defenders of workers' rights at a time when workers faced especially difficult circumstances. They organized thousands of working people into unions and organized many strikes on their behalf. And they won admiration from their followers and enemies alike for their courage and conviction.

Workin' on the Railroad

Debs became the leading socialist in America in the years just before the turn of the century. He started out as a railroad worker and became a union leader, eventually starting the American Railway Union in 1893. The following year he led a strike against the powerful Pullman Car Company, which had just cut wages. The railroad industry was vital to the nation's business, and those who ran it made huge fortunes and had tremendous pull in government. So, the federal government sided with management and outlawed the strike.

Debs persisted in leading the strike, despite a court order to go back to work. He was arrested and sent to jail for six months. In prison he came to believe that big business and government had formed an unholy alliance and that, in order for workers' lives to improve, a revolution was necessary. So he joined the Socialist Party and became its most prominent member, running for president five times on the Socialist Party ticket. In 1905, he joined with Bill Haywood in founding the I.W.W.

Debs, Haywood, and the Wobblies encountered powerful opposition from business and government, yet they continued to fight and organize for their cause. They encountered especially difficult times at the start of World War I, when government was cracking down on anyone who stood in the way of the war effort. The I.W.W. not only opposed the war, but continued to organize strikes. Debs was arrested as a war resistor and sent to federal prison for many years.

Prison didn't stop him from running for president as a socialist. In fact, he got close to a million votes while in jail. Even so, the party strength was ebbing as most Americans rallied behind the war effort. Debs remained in prison until he was pardoned by President Harding in 1921.

Eugene Debs. (Dictionary of American Portraits)

Down in the Mines

The other co-founder of the I.W.W., Bill Haywood, was a charismatic leader who led a hard life and developed a reputation as a fighter and tough guy. He got his start as a miner—perhaps the most dangerous of all industrial jobs. Haywood was only three years old when his father died in a mining camp. Despite the danger, Haywood started mining himself at the age of nine to support his mother. He later quit mining for a while to become a cowboy; he couldn't get enough work, however, so he returned to mining.

With good reason, he felt trapped in a dangerous and undesirable field, so he joined the Western Federation of Miners in 1893 just as the union was getting started. He was active in the union and gradually assumed leading positions as secretary and president of the local union before joining the national board of directors in 1900, where he served as secretary and treasurer. Meanwhile, he served as editor for the union's magazine.

Bill Haywood led some especially hard-fought mining strikes for better working conditions, which were violently suppressed. He responded

Towering Tips

For a taste of what miners' lives were like back in the early days of the labor movement, check out the John Sayles film *Matewan* (1987) about union organizing among West Virginia miners in the 1920s.

Bill Haywood posed for his portrait in profile to hide the fact that he lost an eye in a childhood accident. (Dictionary of American Portraits)

by endorsing violence on the part of strikers. His fight-back policy combined with his talents as a fiery speaker won him many ardent admirers as well as bitter enemies. The defeat of the union in the strikes made him determined, with the help of Debs, to organize the I.W.W.—a still more powerful union. Haywood became chief of the union in 1915.

Meanwhile, he organized hundreds of strikes and helped establish hundreds of local I.W.W. branches. The union was most successful in the West, especially among miners and lumberjacks, but also had a strong following among textile workers in the Northeast. Haywood was arrested in 1917 for conspiring to assassinate the governor of Idaho, who had called out federal troops to suppress striking miners.

Thanks to the brilliant work of his famous attorney, Clarence Darrow, Haywood was acquitted. He continued as a leading labor activist until he was arrested again in 1917 for leading strikes that interfered with the war effort. This time he was convicted and, while awaiting appeal, jumped bail in 1921 and escaped to the Soviet Union, where he hoped to flourish under socialism. He accomplished little under the Soviet government, but the Russians recognized his activism in the cause of workers when he died. Half of his cremated remains were buried in Moscow, and the other half were sent back to the United States for burial.

Still More Left

In addition to its famous co-founders, the I.W.W. had other legendary members as well, including Mary Harris "Mother" Jones and Joe Hill, who are remembered for their commitment to workers' rights. Mother Jones is perhaps the most beloved American labor leader of all time. Her career as a workers' rights activist began long before the founding of the I.W.W. and continued after the peak years of Wobbly influence. She organized and supported striking workers, and demonstrated and made speeches on behalf of them and their children. She was especially active in opposing child labor. In fact, in her later years she often referred to all work-

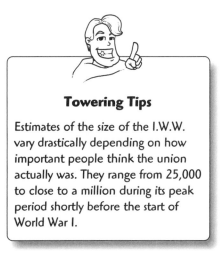

Towering Tips

Estimates of the size of the I.W.W. vary drastically depending on how important people think the union actually was. They range from 25,000 to close to a million during its peak period shortly before the start of World War I.

ing people as her children, thus earning the nickname Mother Jones. (A well-known leftist magazine is named after her and uses her reputation as a feisty hell-raiser to help convey its image.)

Mother Knows Best

Mary Harris Jones was born in Cork County, Ireland, the daughter of a railroad worker, and immigrated to America at the age of five. She worked as a schoolteacher and later as a dressmaker before marrying an ironworker and having four children, all of whom died in an outbreak of yellow fever. With her family gone, she returned to dressmaking and gradually became involved in the labor movement, eventually winning fame for her staunch support of coal miners.

She organized miners' unions in West Virginia and later traveled to Colorado to support striking coal miners. She also demonstrated with railroad workers and copper miners out west. In the following years, she traveled back and forth between Colorado and West Virginia whenever trouble broke out, leading strikes, speaking out for miners, and getting herself arrested on several occasions.

She witnessed the infamous Ludlow Massacre of April 1914, when federal troops fired on striking miners in Colorado to force them back into the mines. Troops remained stationed at Ludlow to keep the mines open for many months afterward. Mother Jones stirred up resentment by raising a public outcry in response to the massacre. She also testified at a congressional inquiry into the killings. She went on to join striking garment workers in New York City, later participated in a nationwide steel strike, and worked with textile unions in the South and East.

It was through the textile industry that she became involved with the child labor problem. Outraged by the industry's exploitation of children, she led a children's march to the home of Teddy Roosevelt. Meanwhile, throughout the early decades of the twentieth century, she traveled around the country to speak or demonstrate for labor. She remained active in support of workers into her 90s.

Big Hill

Joe Hill (1882–1915) is remembered as the unofficial songwriter and poet of the workers' movement. He wrote many songs about the plight of workers during his time, many of which were humorously modeled after other well-known songs. He led a short, troubled, unsettled life, filled with fighting, wandering, and stealing, as well as organizing unions. He was born in Sweden and named Joel Haaglund, changing his name to Joe Hill after coming to America as a teenager. After arriving in America, he traveled around in search of work. He became a Wobbly in 1910 and grew committed to the cause of working people.

Fearless Facts

Joe Hill fought in the Mexican Revolution on the side of the peasants led by Pancho Villa. Many American socialists were interested in this conflict, which was covered by the famous American socialist journalist, John Reed.

Hill was an outspoken radical and made many enemies. He was seriously beaten up in an argument over free speech and carried scars from the fight the rest of his life. He was equally combative as a union organizer, making such a name for himself that he was blacklisted all over the West. Employers refused to hire him on account of his reputation as a union agitator.

Unable to get enough work, Hill turned to crime for his livelihood. He was arrested in January 1914 for killing a grocery store owner and son. Many believed he was framed for the murder on account of his Wobbly activism. In a highly controversial trial, he found guilty and sentenced to death. Despite calls for his release by his supporters, he was executed by firing squad in November 1915. His last words were surprisingly unpoetic for a man who had become famous for writing songs and poems. He said, "Don't waste time in mourning. Organize."

Legal Eagles

Workers had few allies to help them in their struggle for better lives. Ironically, the American ideals of freedom and independence usually meant that employers were free to do whatever they wanted with their employees and could act independently of laws that might require them to improve working conditions. Government, in other words, tended either to stay out of labor disputes or side with big business. This is one reason many labor activists became desperate and sometimes worked outside the law.

Fortunately for the labor movement, not everyone was against the workers. Two of the greatest trial lawyers in history—Clarence Darrow and Louis Brandeis—took up their cause in court on a number of important cases. By defending workers at a time when most of the powerful people in law, government, and business were against them, Darrow and Brandeis helped generate awareness of the plight of labor and won important legal decisions.

Watching Out for the Little Guys

Louis Brandeis (1856–1941) was a brilliant trial lawyer who became rich and famous in his practice specializing in business law. He became concerned with the labor problem and came to

Heroic Shorts

Among those who were most active in the attempt to get Joe Hill out of jail was Elizabeth Gurley Flynn, (1890–1964), a Wobbly spokesperson and activist who became known as "the Rebel Girl" because of a song by that title written about her by Hill. She spent time in jail herself for her union activities. A defender of free speech, she called attention to the sexual exploitation of female inmates by police and prison guards in a jail in Spokane, Washington. She later joined the Communist Party and, later still, did jail time for protesting the Korean War.

believe that existing laws were inadequate to decide labor issues fairly. Meanwhile, unlike many successful people, he reached a point at which he felt he was rich enough and decided to give something back to society by taking on cases others didn't want without charging a fee. He often defended people who needed talented defense but who couldn't afford to hire a good lawyer—including poor working people. In this way, he earned a reputation as "the people's lawyer."

Brandeis grew up in Louisville, Kentucky. His parents were middle-class Jews who had immigrated from Prague. They sent Louis back to Europe to be educated in Germany before he entered Harvard Law School, where he graduated at the top of his class at the age of 21. As he developed his sympathy for workers' rights, he took on a case in 1907 that later became famous between the state of Oregon and Oregon businessmen who opposed the state law limiting the work day for women workers to 10 hours.

Brandeis argued in defense of the law. Those who opposed it claimed it was unfair for the state to interfere with the policies of business. Brandeis defended the law not through the usual means of appealing to legal precedent, but by showing how harmful it was for the health, safety, and morale of workers to work such long days. He gathered evidence from medical records and from factory inspectors' reports in preparing the famous "Brandeis Brief." Although the brief went on for over 100 pages, only two pages were concerned with citing legal precedent. The rest was based on statistics about workers' lives.

Brandeis not only won the case, but also called attention to the difficult conditions facing workers everywhere. As a result, courts became more likely to look sympathetically at cases involving workers' rights. Meanwhile he continued to devote his legal skills to the cause of workers' rights. In 1910 he took on the job of mediating a labor dispute between striking garment workers and their employers in New York City. With Brandeis supervising negotiations, the disputants worked out a mutually satisfactory agreement. The negotiation marked an early success in the history of collective bargaining.

Many of the garment workers involved in the dispute were Jewish immigrants. Working with them inspired Brandeis to promote Jewish nationalism as a Zionist. He joined the Zionist Movement in America and soon became a leading member. The aim of the movement was to build a Jewish homeland in Palestine. Brandeis lectured, organized, and raised funds for the movement, arguing that the Zionist mission was an extension of the American ideals of freedom and patriotism for the Jews.

Meanwhile, Brandeis, who had supported Woodrow Wilson's campaign for the presidency, was appointed to the Supreme Court. He supported Wilson's policies of setting guidelines for business and industry. Brandeis consistently offered minority opinions as a Supreme Court Justice, disagreeing with the other, more conservative judges on many social issues. He ruled in favor of regulations for business and legal protection for organized labor. He argued, for example, that picketing should be considered a form of free speech, protected by the First Amendment.

Attorney for the Damned

Clarence Darrow (1857–1938) won fame as an attorney in some spectacular cases involving some especially hard-to-defend clients, including Bill Haywood and Eugene Debs. In fact, he thought of himself as the "attorney for the damned." He was a staunch defender of freethinking and was bitterly opposed the death penalty. He was both proud and grateful that none of his clients were sentenced to death.

Darrow was philosophically inclined to defend even the most depraved criminals. Although he believed in social justice, he disagreed with the concept of free will. Instead, he thought human actions—including crimes—were understandable reactions to life experiences. In defending notorious clients, he emphasized the circumstances leading up to the crime while picking apart unreasonable assumptions built into standard trial practice. In this way, he managed to avoid a death sentence for the infamous child murderers, Leopold and Loeb.

Darrow's freethinking played an important part in the legendary "Scopes Monkey Trial" of 1925 in which a high school teacher was brought to court in Tennessee for teaching the theory of evolution. But it was as a defender of workers' rights that Darrow asserted his concern for social justice. His first important effort on behalf of workers came in 1893 in the wake of the Haymarket Square rioting.

Fearless Facts

The famous "Scopes Monkey Trial" was dramatized in the play *Inherit the Wind* by Jerome Laurence. The movie version of the play came out in 1960 with Spencer Tracy playing Henry Drummond, the fictitious character representing Clarence Darrow.

Amid a tense period of labor unrest, industrial workers in Darrow's hometown of Chicago met in Haymarket Square, but their meeting was broken up by police. Someone threw a bomb into police ranks before shooting broke out on both sides. Seven men were scapegoated for the incident, including known anarchists arrested because of their reputation as radicals rather than evidence linking them to the killings. Three were hanged. Darrow petitioned the governor, who was a former law partner of Darrow's, to pardon the others. Thanks to Darrow, their lives were saved.

Darrow went on to become a renowned champion of labor unions in court battles. In 1894, he quit his highly paid job as a corporate lawyer to defend Eugene Debs, who was indicted for illegal striking. In 1902 he defended miners during a nationwide anthracite coal strike. His most famous labor case was the murder trial of Bill Haywood, who was accused of conspiring to assassinate the governor of Idaho, Frank Steunenberg.

Steunenberg sided with business during the bitter labor struggles between miners and their employers that frequently erupted in violence. He called in federal troops to suppress strikers and force them back to work. After someone set off an explosion in some company buildings, dozens of union members and sympathizers were taken captive and held without trial. In effect, Steunenberg declared martial law in order to quash the strikes. Investigations into the murder uncovered a conspiracy implicating Haywood. Haywood was acquitted, thanks to Darrow, who persuaded the jury that evidence linking him to the crime was circumstantial.

Heroic Shorts

Oliver Wendell Holmes Jr. (1841–1935) was a Supreme Court Justice from 1902 to 1932, where he became known as "the Great Dissenter," because his opinions were often in the minority. He championed many liberal causes, including free speech, explaining his reasons with clarity, force, and eloquence. Despite his committed political views, he remained a proponent of laws that reflected the views and desires of the people. His father was a famous writer and physician.

Heroic Shorts

Bert Corona (1918–) has been a heroic advocate for Mexican immigrants. He worked on the Civil Rights Commission until 1967, when he resigned as a result of his feeling that the commission was racist and failed to do enough for Mexicans and Mexican-Americans. He defended undocumented workers and was a prominent leader of *La Hermandad Mexicana Nacional* (the National Mexican Brotherhood). He helped many Mexican immigrants gain U.S. citizenship and fought against the unstated U.S. policy of alternately exploiting or excluding Mexican workers depending on the economic situation in America.

Down on the Farm

Thanks in good part to the union activists and the lawyers who defended them, industrial working conditions have improved considerably since the days of the most bitter and violent labor battles. Of course, disputes still take place, but few question the right of workers to form unions and bargain or strike for what they think is a fair deal. Even so, some workers have continued to face hardship as a result of poverty and prejudice when attempting to improve their lives. Most notable among these are Chicano (Mexican-American) migrant farm workers.

Migrant farm workers have struggled to unionize and gain collective bargaining leverage in dealings with the growers who employ them. For years, moving from place to place has made it difficult to improve their lives, leaving them at the mercy of their employers, who have been able to hire them cheaply and on an as-needed basis. The difficulty is compounded by the fact that illegal and temporary Mexican immigrants have often been willing to work even more cheaply.

The difficulties of migrant farm workers continue, but they have succeeded in forming the United Farm Workers Union, thanks to its dedicated founder, Chicano labor leader Cesar Chavez (1927–1993). Chavez successfully led the UFW in one of the longest strikes in history. And he is especially admired as a heroic labor leader for his lifelong adherence to a policy of nonviolence inspired by Mahatma Ghandi and Martin Luther King.

Putting Down Roots

Chavez' grandparents immigrated to the Arizona Territory from Mexico in the late nineteenth century and built a farm, which prospered until the depression hit. When Cesar was 10 years old, his parents were forced to sell the farm for a fraction of what it was worth. Like many struggling ex-farmers of the dust bowl days, he and his family moved to California in search of work. Chavez remained a migrant farm worker all his life, except during World War II when he served in the Navy.

Unfortunately, when the depression ended for most Americans, it never seemed to go away for the migrant farm workers. Constant traveling around after low-paying jobs made it difficult to get a good education or save money to invest in a farm or other business. It was a hard, exhausting, dead-end lifestyle. Not only were they often forced to accept work for inadequate pay, but they were often overcharged for food and supplies by their employers, who made extra money selling them things they needed while on the job.

A way out opened up for Chavez in 1952 when he joined the Community Service Organization. He became an active member, recruiting more workers for the organization, helping them register to vote, providing legal assistance and, of course, help with labor negotiations. Eventually, however, Chavez came to think that the Community Service Organization wasn't going far enough in organizing workers, so he quit in 1962 and formed the National Farm Workers' Association with Dolores Huerta, which later became the United Farm Workers' Union.

A Striking Difference

In 1965, with the support of the AFL-CIO, the NFWA began what turned into a five-year strike against the entire California grape-growing industry, which was especially exploitative of migrant farm workers. The strike had significance not only as a labor struggle, but as a civil rights struggle as well, since so many farm

Towering Tips

Dolores Huerta (1930–) co-founded the Farm Workers' Association with Cesar Chavez. This organization later became the United Farm Workers' Union. Huerta served as the union's vice president during the early 1970s and organized boycotts and strikes and lobbied legislators on behalf of farm workers. Like Chavez, she worked with the Community Service Organization in Stockton, California before founding the union. She has continued to work for labor despite being seriously injured at a peaceful demonstration in 1988, where she was clubbed by police.

workers were Chicano. Americans all over the country boycotted grapes in support of the strike. The United Auto Workers' Union helped out with financial support. Chavez emerged as a consciousness raiser, advocating peaceful protest in pursuit of civil and economic empowerment. He led a march of 300 miles (from Delano, California to the state capital in Sacramento) that got national attention.

By 1970, most of the grape growers gave in and signed contracts with the UFW, marking one of the most significant labor victories in American history. Chavez went on to lead other strikes aimed at getting higher pay and better working conditions for farm workers. During the 1980s, Chavez became concerned that pesticides used in grape growing were leading to high rates of cancer among farm workers and their families. He organized the union in protest of the pesticides and went on a hunger strike, going without food at the age of 61 for 36 days.

Former presidential candidate Jesse Jackson pledged support for pesticide protest. In fact, Jackson was only one of many famous political figures who registered support for Chavez during his long career. Others include Hubert Humphrey, Eugene McCarthy, and Robert F. Kennedy, who referred to Chavez as "one of the heroic figures of our time."

The Least You Need to Know

➤ Samuel Gompers, founder of the American Federation of Labor, set a precedent for union activism within the capitalist system.

➤ Eugene Debs and Bill Haywood of the Wobblies advocated a socialist revolution.

➤ Mother Jones and Joe Hill became legendary Wobblies after immigrating to America in hopes of a better life.

➤ Louis Brandeis and Clarence Darrow became famous attorneys, devoting their legal talents to the defense of workers and labor leaders.

➤ Cesar Chavez successfully led one of the longest labor strikes in American history against the California grape-growing industry.

Chapter 22

Life and Limb

In This Chapter

➤ Health and safety heroes

➤ Helen Taussig and cyanosis

➤ Jonas Salk and the polio vaccine

➤ Rachel Carson and *Silent Spring*

➤ Linus Pauling and the test ban

➤ Ralph Nader and *Unsafe at Any Speed*

One of the best ways to become a hero is to save a life. An even better way is to save many lives. A select handful of twentieth-century Americans have become big heroes by figuring out ways to save lives on a large scale—either by developing new life-saving medical procedures or by calling attention to widely unrecognized life-threatening problems. Americans will be eternally grateful for their achievements even though many of them have been surrounded by controversy.

The first approach—making medical breakthroughs—involves lots of hard work mastering scientific knowledge and bringing medical techniques to new levels. This can be risky business, since so many human lives depend on a safe, effective outcome. At times there can also be intense competition with rivals in the field. But there is also much-needed public and private support involved, since few reasonable people would stand in the way of a possible solution to a health crisis.

The second approach—alerting people to problems they weren't aware of—is very different, since it often involves getting branded as a crank and a troublemaker. Most people don't like to hear about how things can go wrong, especially if they are part of the problem. So you have to stand up to the opposition while persuading people that you understand what's wrong better than the "experts" in government and industry who, too often, are more concerned with their own success and public image than the general good.

Baby Steps

Perhaps it's not surprising that among the most admired figures in the field of medicine are those who have developed new ways of healing chronically sick children. Many people instinctively feel that young lives are especially worth saving and that illnesses fatal to children are especially terrible. As a result, two heroes who conquered children's illnesses are remembered with special gratitude: Jonas Salk, who developed a vaccine for polio; and Helen Taussig, who invented a surgical procedure to cure cyanosis.

All Heart

A common, and usually fatal, congenital disease afflicting thousands of children was cyanosis, or blue baby syndrome, caused by a heart disorder that prevented the blood from getting an adequate supply of oxygen (resulting in a bluish color of the babies afflicted with the disease). Until just over 50 years ago, there was no cure for the condition. Heart surgery was rarely practiced. Most blue babies simply died in childhood; some were kept alive in oxygen tents. Many came to the Harriet Lane Pediatric Clinic where Dr. Helen Taussig first got the idea for a surgical procedure that would help them.

Fearless Facts

Shortly after surgery for blue babies became available, citizens in Baltimore opposed to vivisection (surgery inside the chest cavity on live patients) petitioned to have it stopped. Taussig appeared in court with several of her former patients who had been cured as a result of the procedure. The petition was roundly defeated.

Helen Taussig (1898–1986) was the daughter of a Harvard economics professor. She studied at Radcliffe before transferring to the University of California at Berkeley.

She returned to Harvard to study medicine, but transferred to Johns Hopkins in Baltimore, in part because at the time Harvard did not give medical degrees to women. There she specialized in cardiology. Completing her degree, she became director of the Harriet Lane Pediatric Clinic.

Feeling Blue

Many doctors referred cyanotic children to the clinic simply because there was little anyone could do for them. The disease was incurable and usually resulted in death. As the number of blue-baby patients in her clinic increased, Taussig became painfully aware of the need of a cure. Therefore, she designed a procedure for shunting blood around the weakened area of the heart to the lungs where it could load up on oxygen.

She brought her idea back to her old stomping grounds at Johns Hopkins University, where she persuaded a surgeon named Albert Blalock to help her develop it. They worked out a technique for taking part of an artery from one arm and using it as a sidetrack in the heart. Dr. Blalock performed the procedure for the first time in November 1944 on an 11-month-old girl who had spent her life confined in an oxygen tent. The operation was successful and the patient turned from blue to pink as her blood soaked up a healthy supply of oxygen for the first time.

Fearless Facts

Albert Blalock, who helped develop the procedure for operating on blue babies, was assisted by an African American named Vivian Thomas, who performed hundreds of trial runs of the operation on dogs in order to make sure it would be safe for humans.

The procedure turned out to be safe and effective, and thousands of blue babies came to Johns Hopkins from all over the world to have it performed. Dr. Taussig became famous and was appointed to a professorship at Johns Hopkins in 1959.

Taussig continued to work for the health of children. In the early 1960s, a drug known as thalidomide was available without a prescription for the prevention of nausea. It was used by many pregnant women who subsequently gave birth to children with serious birth defects. Taussig was one of the first people in the United States to learn of the problem. A colleague in Germany, where many thalidomide babies had been born, told her about the problem there. Acting independently, Taussig traveled to Germany to find out what was going on and to witness the harm caused by the drug. She later testified to the dangers of thalidomide before a Senate committee in the United States.

In 1965, Taussig became the first female president of the American Heart Association. She was one of the first to realize that heart disease could begin during infancy as a result of overly fatty foods. She died in an auto accident at the age of 88.

A Shot in the Arm

For decades, one of the most serious health hazards was the crippling (and often deadly) poliovirus, which broke out periodically in epidemics around the country. The disease was especially rampant among children, although adults were susceptible as well. Among those afflicted was Franklin Delano Roosevelt who, although unable to walk far without crutches, got elected president for four consecutive terms of office. Thousands of others were more severely paralyzed or killed by the disease.

Fearless Facts

The March of Dimes started out as a fund raising campaign to help fight polio. The original "poster children" were young polio victims who were selected every year to be photographed for the campaign.

Towering Tips

Be careful when preparing and administering killed virus vaccines that the viruses you are using really are killed. During the early years of inoculation with the Salk vaccine, serum improperly prepared by Cutter Laboratories including live viruses infected 204 people with polio, resulting in 150 cases of paralysis and 11 deaths!

The search for a cure continued for decades as medical science made gradual advances. Three types of the virus were discovered in 1931 by Australian Sir Macfarlane Burnet. In 1949 a group of American scientists—John Enders, Thomas Weller, and Frederick Robbins—figured out how to grow the poliovirus in the laboratory, making it easier to study. They were awarded the Nobel Prize for this achievement in 1954. At last, in 1952, Dr. Jonas Salk discovered a vaccine against polio using strains of each of the three kinds of virus that had been killed. Subsequent tests on animals proved the vaccine was safe and effective. Salk further demonstrated its safety by injecting it into himself.

Salk (1914–1995) attended New York City College and New York Medical School before taking a job in medical research at the University of Michigan. During World War II, Salk worked on vaccines against the flu. After the war, he moved to Pittsburgh to study polio with financial support from the National Foundation for Infantile Paralysis, which was founded in part by President Franklin D. Roosevelt. There he developed the vaccine.

Use of Salk's vaccine was approved by a Vaccine Advisory Committee formed to review the vaccine, despite intense opposition by Dr. Albert Sabin (1906–1993), who for years had been working on his own cure for polio. Sabin claimed that a killed virus vaccine such as Salk's would not work permanently, but would require repeated inoculations. An intense personal animosity developed between the two. Sabin believed passionately in his own cure for polio— a live virus vaccine prepared from carefully cultured strains. But Sabin's vaccine wasn't ready, and the public was eager for a cure.

In retrospect, the conflict between Salk and Sabin can be seen as a healthy, if overheated, personal rivalry. By the time Sabin was ready with his vaccine, Salk's treatment was already widely in use in the United States. So, Sabin tested his cure in the Soviet Union in 1959. (He was born in pre-Soviet Russia and immigrated to the United States to study medicine.) The tests were successful and, two years later, Sabin's treatment was licensed for use in the United States. Both Sabin's and Salk's vaccines were safe and effective, but Sabin's turned out to be cheaper and easier to administer, so it came to be adopted as the standard inoculation.

In countries that have put Salk's and Sabin's vaccines into use, polio has been virtually wiped out. Salk spent much of his later years involved in AIDS research.

Heroic Shorts

Another baby-saving hero was Mary Breckinridge (1881–1965), the pioneering midwife who founded the Frontier Nursing Service in order to meet the medical needs of new mothers in rural areas. Breckinridge and her corps of nurses stayed at outposts in rural Kentucky starting in the mid-1920s. When called for, they traveled on horseback to provide assistance—usually in delivering newborn babies. During the first years of its existence, Breckinridge funded the organization out of her own pocket. It later became the American Association of Nurse-Midwives.

Nature Calls

Most people weren't aware of pollution as a major health hazard until well into the 1960s when it started to become clear that industrial wastes and by-products could ruin the environment and make people sick. And even then, the problem wasn't obvious. It took some sensitive and sensible observation and writing on the part of Rachel Carson, a talented writer and researcher, to wake people up to the first large-scale industrial health and environmental crisis in America. The crisis was due to the deadly effects of the widely used pesticide DDT.

Heroic Shorts

Rachel Carson is often said to be America's first environmental activist. Arguably, however, the distinction belongs to Henry David Thoreau (1817–1862), the independent thinker and writer of *Civil Disobedience* (1849) and *Walden* (1854). Thoreau believed in the transcendental importance of nature and argued against the tendency to conform thoughtlessly to the rules of society and government. His ideas about peaceful protest inspired the great Indian revolutionary Mahatma Ghandi, who in turn inspired great American heroes such as Martin Luther King and Cesar Chavez.

From Ocean Spray to Bug Spray

Rachel Carson (1907–1964) attended Pennsylvania College for Women in Pittsburgh, where she majored in zoology before earning a masters in biology from Johns Hopkins. Her main interest was ocean life and she did research at the Woods Hole Marine Biological lab in Massachusetts. She later taught at Johns Hopkins and the University of Maryland, but also devoted much of her time to writing and publishing personal observations about the ocean. Her dual interest in the ocean and in writing led to a job with the Fish and Wildlife Service in Washington D.C. writing for a radio program on ocean life.

She held the job during the depression and used her income to support her mother and two nieces. In her spare time, she wrote an article on the ocean for *Atlantic Monthly*, which was so well received, she expanded it into her first book, *Under the Sea-Wind* (1941). Her second book, *The Sea Around Us* (1951), quickly became the top-selling book in the country. The success of this book enabled her to devote herself to writing full time.

Meanwhile, through her job at the Fish and Wildlife Service, she became familiar with growing evidence of the dangers of DDT. Ever since World War II, DDT had been used extensively to kill insects that carried disease—most notably fleas carrying typhus and mosquitoes carrying malaria. It was inexpensive, easy to use, and effective; so it became widely used by industry and government. Only a few scientists had reservations about its safety. Carson was one of them and she wanted to make the public aware of the dangers. As early as 1945, she proposed an article on DDT to *Reader's Digest*, but the idea was turned down.

In addition to scientific studies, which were suppressed by the chemical industry, some alarming incidents occurred. An acquaintance of Carson's complained that many birds disappeared from her property after a DDT spraying in 1957. Shortly afterward, some Long Island residents asked the government not to go ahead with a planned spraying in their area. Their request was denied. The government saw nothing wrong with DDT and felt it should be used to control disease-carrying insects. Yet, DDT continues to be toxic long after it is sprayed and becomes concentrated as it passes from insects to the birds and other animals that eat them.

For the Birds

So, Carson began working on a book to alert the public of the danger. She published her book, *Silent Spring*, in 1962. Even before the book was published, it elicited an ardent response. She had already published portions of it in the *New Yorker*. Makers of DDT condemned the work as unreliable and alarmist and claimed that DDT was necessary to curtail the spread of disease and to ward off crop failure caused by insects. Readers around the country were convinced, however, and chimed in with Carson's outcry against the pesticide.

Silent Spring, named for the eerie absence of birdsong in springtime that results from DDT sprayings, became a bestseller and prompted government investigations into the deadly chemical. Her efforts led to the first major ecological victory on the part of scientists and citizens concerned about the environment. Now that concern for the environment has become a leading priority of many Americans, her work continues to seem important. She was awarded the Presidential Medal of Freedom in 1980, 16 years after her death.

> **Towering Tips**
>
> There's always the danger that people in positions of responsibility—in business or government, for example—will mistakenly assume that what is good for them is good for everybody and will fail to see whatever harm they may be causing. On the other hand, there's the danger that eccentric crackpots claiming to be concerned about the good of all will cause trouble and interfere with conscientious efforts of responsible people to do their jobs. The best way to tell the difference is through thorough research and careful weighing of the issues, combined with an honest evaluation of your own interests and motives. This is no easy task, but it's an important one if democracy is to work!

Bombs Away

Finding a solution for problems that cause widespread disease and death is certainly heroic, but so is preventing such problems. We can all be glad that, so far, the world has not been destroyed by nuclear holocaust. Of course, it's hard to say whether the actions of any one person can be held responsible for the survival of the world. There are many, however, who think that Linus Pauling, the Nobel Prize-winning chemist and peace activist, deserves our thanks for his efforts to stop the proliferation of nuclear weapons.

Linus Pauling (1901–1994) was a chemistry professor at Stanford University. He is widely regarded as one of the most brilliant scientists of the twentieth century. He used his scientific prominence to promote awareness of the dangers of nuclear weapons. He was horrified at the nuclear bombing of Hiroshima and Nagasaki during World War II, and thought that too many Americans failed to understand just how catastrophic a nuclear war would be.

Fearless Facts

During the 1950s, the government and many public schools fostered the idea that nuclear war would be less than catastrophic in many ways, including drills for responding to nuclear attack. School children were instructed to crouch under their desks with their heads down. We now know such an action would be perfectly useless against toxic nuclear fallout. These drills were later parodied by humorous instructions for crouching in order to kiss your butt goodbye!

Part of his concern came from his knowledge, as a scientist, of the incredibly deadly and devastating nature of nuclear radiation. At the same time, his interest in world peace was shared by his wife, Ava, who was a committed peace activist. As a famous scientist, Pauling was able to get many of her ideas across to the public more effectively than she could herself.

During the post-war years, Pauling spoke out against nuclear weapons. He also opposed the suppression of free speech and was openly critical of Senator Joseph McCarthy, who fueled national paranoia by launching tirades against the evils of communism. Many in government took Pauling's attacks on nuclear arms as evidence that he was a communist sympathizer and saw him as a potentially dangerous radical. As a result, Pauling was denied the right to obtain a passport to travel overseas to attend scientific conventions—a routine and important part of the job of being a scientist!

Twice Pauling was asked to appear before a congressional committee, where he insisted he was not a communist. He wasn't anti-American, he was simply pro-peace. Although for years he was prevented from traveling overseas, he rallied many of his fellow scientists in support of peace. He gathered 11,000 signatures from scientists all over the world in support of a ban on nuclear bomb testing. In addition, he drafted a resolution setting forth terms for a test ban treaty between the United States and the Soviet Union and sent a copy to President Kennedy and another copy to Soviet Prime Minister Kruschev.

Pauling's impressive act of reason and determination bore fruit. In 1963, America and the Soviet Union agreed to a partial test-ban treaty that included a number of provisions called for by Pauling's resolution. That same day, October 10, Pauling was selected to receive the Nobel Peace Prize for his anti-nuclear efforts. This was Pauling's second Nobel Prize. He was awarded the first in 1954 for his work on explaining the chemical bond. He is the first person ever to receive two unshared Nobel Prizes.

Fearless Facts

Pauling was a single-minded and hardworking science student since at least as far back as high school, where he refused to take a civics class since he felt it was unnecessary and because he wanted more time to study science. As a result, his high school withheld his diploma. Even so, the brilliant student had no trouble getting into college. And, almost 50 years later, his high school finally decided to give him the diploma—after he had already been awarded his second Nobel Prize!

Pauling went on to pursue interests in health and medicine. He discovered that sickle cell anemia was caused by a genetic defect. He also made what was, at the time, controversial claims about the health benefits of vitamin C. He claimed that high doses of vitamin C could help prevent many diseases from colds to cancer. Although many thought he had gone off the deep end, most scientists have come to believe he was right!

Looking Under the Hood

It sometimes happens that people who seem like troublemakers turn out to be heroes. This was true of Linus Pauling, who found himself in conflict with the government over his stance on nuclear testing. It's also true of Ralph Nader, who elicited the resentment of the automobile industry for claiming that many cars were unsafe to drive. As with Pauling, a little antagonism didn't stop Nader from spreading his message and convincing people that important changes were in order. His success helped him become the leading consumer advocate in America.

Ralph Nader (1934–) began thinking about democracy and citizenship at an early age, thanks to his parents (who came to America from Lebanon, started a bakery and restaurant, and had stimulating conversations around the dinner table about civics and society). Nader went to Princeton University to study government and economics before attending Harvard Law School, where he edited the Harvard Law Review. While in law school, he did a study of deficient safety in cars that he published in the leftist paper *The Nation*.

He went on to set up his own law practice. Meanwhile he developed the article on automotive safety into his famous book, *Unsafe at Any Speed* (1965). The book argued that automakers didn't pay enough attention to safety when designing cars. Focusing on a General Motors sports car, the Corvair, Nader said, for example, that the car had a poorly designed rear suspension that increased the car's likelihood of rolling over in an accident.

Heroic Shorts

Ralph Nader can be seen as carrying on the proud American tradition of "muckraking." The original muck-rakers were journalists of the late nineteenth and early twentieth centuries who published books and articles on corporate greed and corruption, drawing attention to the social costs borne most heavily by the lower classes. One leading muckraker was Ida Tarbell (1857–1944), who became famous for attacking John D. Rockefeller and Standard Oil, which enjoyed an obscenely profitable monopoly. Her book on the subject prompted a federal investigation into the company. Tarbell was also a peace activist. After interviewing Italian dictator Benito Mussolini, she warned the world of the ascent of Fascism in Italy.

General Motors was not pleased about Nader's book and set out to discredit him. They hired private detectives to dig up any embarrassing secrets he might have. Their scheme backfired, however, because the detectives were found out and GM was obliged to apologize to Nader in front of the Senate—on national TV! Footage of GM executives humbling themselves before the scruffy lawyer catapulted Nader to fame.

Nader's book and lobbying efforts resulted in laws requiring tougher auto-safety standards. In the following years, Nader made citizen and consumer advocacy a way of life. He widened his scope of activity to include other kinds of product safety: the environment, foods, drugs, the water supply, banking, government, care of the elderly, and care of mental patients. He did this with the help of a task force—fellow lawyers and law students he recruited to help research dangers to citizens and abuses of power.

The task force became known in the press as "Nader's Raiders," as the group's efforts gave rise to increased government regulation, corporate responsibility, and consumer awareness. Among the many organizations the group helped to start is the Public Interest Research Group. Although Nader provided direction and impetus for the task force, he avoided taking credit for the work of its members, who wrote articles in their own names and spoke at press conferences pertaining to their projects. The responsibility and independence of the members of his task force is in keeping with Nader's belief that private citizens should be more active and aware of what is going on and have more of a say in things. Conversely, Nader believed those in positions of power should be held accountable for their actions.

Nader deplored cronyism and secrecy in bureaucracy and was instrumental in getting the Freedom of Information Act passed. This legislation guarantees to private citizens and reporters the right to have access to government documents, including fatality statistics and other studies that could indicate problems with big business or government. And Nader has continued to write articles for magazines and papers on many subjects of public concern. In 1996, Nader made a bid for president as the Green Party candidate in the national primaries.

Late Bloomer

Nader has worked against the tendency of powerful business and government people to use that power for their own advantage by shirking their responsibilities toward those with less power. It sometimes happens, however, that someone in a position of power uses it for unusually good purposes. This is what former president Jimmy Carter has tried to do with the prestige and influence he has won by having been elected president of the United States. Even—and especially—after leaving office, Carter has used his political clout in an effort to solve some of the most serious problems around the world. You might say Carter takes a global perspective on health and safety issues.

Towering Tips

Don't let your failures prevent you from making the most of your successes. If you fail to impress the nation with your machismo as a leader, you may still be able to make a difference as a wise, kind, caring, and energetic worker for important causes!

Jimmy Carter (1924–) came from a peanut-farming family in Georgia, where he became state governor before being elected president in 1976. As president he mediated the Camp David Accords in 1978 between Anwar Sadat and Menachim Begin, the leaders of Egypt and Israel—countries that had long been engaged in bitter conflict. The 13-day conference led to the signing of a treaty the following year. He also worked out the terms for the SALT II nuclear limitation treaty between the United States and the Soviet Union.

A major blight on Carter's presidency occurred in the wake of the Iranian revolution in which revolutionaries took hostages from the U.S. embassy in Iran. Carter seemed to take the hostage crisis personally, but was unable to resolve it during his one term in office. A daring attempt to rescue the hostages by helicopter failed in disaster. The crisis greatly diminished Carter's popularity with voters, who elected Ronald Reagan at the following election. Yet even as a lame-duck president, Carter continued to work for release of the hostages. Ironically, they were set free the day Carter left office.

Although Carter often failed to project the image of a strong leader, he had proven himself as a great peacemaker, and he put his reputation to good use after leaving office. In 1982 he founded the Carter Center for monitoring and working out solutions for global problems. The center has worked, for example, to curtail the nuclear weapons program in Korea, forge the Dayton accords between warring Bosnians and Serbs, limit exploitation of child labor in Pakistan, and fight disease and house refugees in Africa. Carter is the only U.S. president to become a hero after leaving office, using his political experience and acquaintance with world leaders to resolve military conflicts, protect human rights, and promote economic stability all over the world.

The Least You Need to Know

➤ Helen Taussig developed a surgical procedure for curing cyanosis, or "blue baby" syndrome.

➤ Jonas Salk developed the first vaccine for polio.

➤ Rachel Carson inaugurated the environmental movement with her book *Silent Spring*, about the hazards of DDT.

➤ Linus Pauling won two Nobel Prizes: the first for chemistry and the second for peace. His work helped bring about a nuclear test ban treaty between the United States and the Soviet Union.

➤ Ralph Nader has been the country's leading consumer advocate since his book *Unsafe at Any Speed*, which exposed inadequate safety standards in the auto industry.

➤ Jimmy Carter used his experience and connections as a former president to help solve global problems after leaving office.

Part 5
Good Shows and Good Sports

Many heroes are admired for their important accomplishments and many are admired for their qualities: their prowess, skill, talent, and style. Although we may sometimes lose sight of important accomplishments, Americans have a special passion for heroic qualities, and so we showcase them in films, concerts and recordings, and sporting events. As a result, the hero worship of the nation's stars and celebrities is a favorite national pastime.

In a way, this sort of hero worship provides an escape from the concerns of everyday life. The hero worship transforms these concerns and helps us overcome them. And it allows us to feel part of something bigger than we are and to share feelings with others like us all across the country whom we've never met. After all, one of the best ways to make friends in a strange town is to find people who admire the same actors, musicians, and sports stars as you.

Arguably, it's part of every star's job description to be a hero—to do admirable things most people can't do and do them in a special way. Of course, this includes just about every famous sports figure, actor, and musician! This last section focuses on the celebrities who have made the biggest marks as athletes and entertainers.

Chapter 23

Class Acts

In This Chapter

➤ Actor heroes

➤ Humphrey Bogart and Katherine Hepburn

➤ Jimmy Stewart and John Wayne

➤ Paul Robeson and James Dean

➤ Clint Eastwood

➤ Christopher Reeve and Gilda Radner

Americans have always placed great importance in their acting heroes. Hollywood is an especially American institution that, in fact, reflects the importance to Americans of heroism in general. No other industry has put so much effort into the portrayal of heroism. The importance of this project continues to prove itself again and again all over the world.

Acting heroes can be heroes in more ways than one. Not only may they have heroic personal lives, but they also adopt heroic personas on stage and in movies. It often happens with the greatest actors that their personalities reinforce their performances. This can produce the kind of stage and movie magic that makes for classic films and shows.

Of course, the kinds of heroes actors become depends on qualities admired by their audiences. These qualities have a way of changing across generations, so the greatest actors at any one time reflect something about the ideals of their fans. As a result, the

Worthy Words

You know you have a true American icon when his name gets used as a slang term decades after his death. The expression **"to bogart,"** which means to keep something for oneself rather than share it, originally was used in 1970s and 1980s counter-culture to criticize people who didn't want to share marijuana cig-arettes ("Don't bogart that joint"). The idea is not that Humphrey Bogart represents selfishness, but that he almost always had a cigarette dangling from his mouth in keeping with his dark, streetwise image.

heroism portrayed by actors may draw on popular dreams and desires as well as personal vision. Thus, the characteristics of Hollywood heroes can tell us a lot about ourselves as Americans.

In addition, there is yet another aspect of the heroism of some actors. A few have won admiration by using their fame in support of social causes, devoting some of the energy and charisma that made them famous to promote awareness of real-life dramas so that every-one can work toward a happy ending.

The Bogey Man

A leading candidate for the favorite Hollywood actor of all time became legendary for his unique persona: soulful yet cynical, tough yet sensitive, independent yet sympathetic, worldly-wise yet with a heart in the right place. Humphrey Bogart (1899–1957) was the quintessential serious dramatic actor during the golden age of Hollywood from the late 1930s into the 1950s. He has become a complex American icon, representing the subtle power of remaining in control and true to oneself in a foolish and impetuous world.

The Good Bad Guy

Before launching his acting career, Bogart served in the Navy during World War I. At this time, he injured his upper lip, leaving a scar and the slight speech impediment that helped make him so distinctive an actor. After the war, he acted on Broadway and later, in the 1930s when talking films began coming out, he moved to Hollywood to try screen acting—along with many other aspiring actors of the time.

Lacking the wholesome good looks of the typical screen and stage hero, but having a self-confident, streetwise aura, Bogart was typecast as a gangster in plays and early films. Getting his first big break, he played gang leader Duke Mantee in the Broadway play *Petrified Forest* (1935). He reprised the role and became noticed as a star-quality actor when the play was made into a Hollywood movie in 1937.

In many of his later films, he played the hero he seemed not to be in his early career, giving the concept his own particular spin. Bogart's most famous roles have been dark, reluctant heroes, preferring to stay unnoticed and in the background, but coming through in a crisis by doing the right thing, however difficult. It is the sense of unself-ish wisdom garnered from hard experience rather than mere courage or moral righ-teousness that makes Bogart's characters so appealing. In fact, the slang term *"bogart,"* used to refer to selfish behavior, is misleading, since it comes from an actor who generally played unselfish characters.

Among Bogart's most famous films is *The Maltese Falcon* (1941) in which Bogey plays Sam Spade, the famous detective invented by Dashiell Hammett. Thanks to his knowledge of criminal motivation, Spade unravels a web of unholy alliances and double-crosses. Meanwhile he manages to blend streetwise grittiness with international sophistication to play a convincing character who always knows what's going on.

Here's Lookin' at You, Kid

Bogey's most legendary role is cafe owner Rick Blaine in the Oscar-winning film *Casablanca* (1942). Blaine is a cynical businessman who just wants to survive and stay out of trouble in Nazi-occupied Casablanca until an old flame calls on him to help her escape to America with her French Resistance husband. With nothing to gain but poignant regrets about what might have been, Blaine risks his life and his cafe to help his ex-girlfriend. Of course, she falls in love with him again and is reluctant to get on the plane, but he does the right thing and says goodbye.

Bogey as Rick Blaine is a hero who understands the world's evil and foolishness—this is what enables him to be so helpful—and he has learned to put up with these problems. In the end, however, he resists the temptation to be evil or foolish himself. He seems not to be an especially moral person; he has adapted to his sinister surroundings to the point of blending in with them. As the drama unfolds, however, he emerges as an exceptionally good man, tolerating all kinds of human weakness and taking courageous risks to make things better for others.

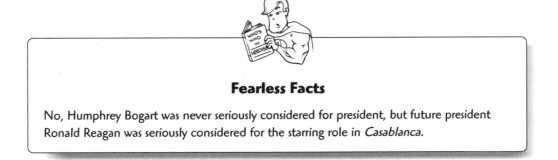

Fearless Facts

No, Humphrey Bogart was never seriously considered for president, but future president Ronald Reagan was seriously considered for the starring role in *Casablanca*.

Bogart won an Oscar for his starring role in *The African Queen* (1951), in which he romances Katharine Hepburn. In addition to his many silver-screen love interests, he had a number of real-life romances as well, marrying four times. His fourth marriage was to Lauren Bacall, who played opposite Bogart in several films, including *To Have and Have Not* (1945), *The Big Sleep*, (1946), and *Key Largo* (1948).

Leading, Leading Lady

The most widely admired Hollywood actress of all time is Katharine Hepburn (1909–), whose long career bespeaks her uncommon energy, good sense, and intelligence.

Brilliantly talented in both comic and dramatic roles, she garnered a record-breaking 12 Oscar nominations and 4 Oscars for best actress. She won three of these when she was past the age of 60.

Her father was a surgeon and her mother was active in the women's movement and a supporter of birth-control hero Margaret Sanger. Hepburn won her first Oscar for *Morning Glory* (1933) and has been attracting fans ever since with her films and her self-assured, witty personal style. She has had romances with the famous millionaire Howard Hughes and actor Spencer Tracey, with whom she co-starred in nine movies in the 1940s through the 1960s.

In addition to her Oscars, she is an Emmy-winning TV actress and has won the Golden Palm at the Cannes Film Festival. Her last Oscar was for *On Golden Pond* (1981). She wrote and published her memoirs, aptly entitled *Me* in keeping with her unapologetic self-assurance.

A Wonderful Life

One of the best-loved Hollywood actors of all time is Jimmy Stewart (1908–1997). Like Bogart, Stewart became legendary for playing unlikely and reluctant heroes. Unlike Bogey, however, Stewart's characters tend to be wholesome and down to earth. Stewart's just-plain-folks is more than just an act, since he was known to be modest and unassuming in private life as well as on the screen.

Stewart tended to play characters who believe in common decency, patriotism, and esprit de corps. Much about Stewart's life reflected these values as well. He was an avid Boy Scout in his youth. He went to Princeton University to study architecture before becoming a Broadway performer. For a time while he was just starting out, he shared living quarters with future fellow actor Henry Fonda.

He interrupted his acting career to enlist in the armed forces in 1941 before the United States entered World War II. He was a noted pilot and bomb-squad commander, flying 20 combat missions and earning the Flying Cross. By this time, he had already become a movie star, having won an Oscar for *The Philadelphia Story* (1940).

Fearless Facts

Jimmy Stewart's hometown-hero quality is more than just an act. His Oscar for *Philadelphia Story* was displayed in the family hardware store in Indiana, Pennsylvania for many years.

Stewart's most famous role is regular-guy George Bailey, the head of a small-town mortgage and loan company in Frank Capra's heartwarming film *It's a Wonderful Life* (1946). Bailey's responsibilities to the company, his family, and his neighbors prevent him from pursuing his life-long dream of exploring the world. What's worse, he becomes embittered and suicidal when, through no fault of his own, his company gets into financial trouble. Fortunately, an angel appears and shows him what the town would have been like if he had never been born.

His supernatural glimpse of a squalid and brutal world without enough good, solid, honest, and responsible people like him gives him a fresh perspective on his life and helps him appreciate the outpouring of support he gets in the end from his family, friends, and neighbors. The movie's lesson about the importance of building ties with others by living up to social responsibilities succeeds magnificently, thanks in large part to Jimmy Stewart's ability to infuse humanity into his role. His portrayal of an ordinary, yet special, person in small-town America seems effortless.

Stewart made over 75 films in his long career, often playing average people with exceptional convictions, as in another Capra film, *Mr. Smith Goes to Washington* (1939). Here Stewart plays an unlikely senator who fights government corruption with simple, but infectious enthusiasm for democracy.

The Duke

A movie hero who has often been imitated but never duplicated is man's man John Wayne (1907–1979), star of dozens of war and cowboy movies who achieved legendary stature by playing slow, strong, and steady he-men. John Wayne commands respect as the sort of man who is used to putting up with hardship and knows how to tell others what to do. Even as a young actor, he conveyed an aura of seasoned experience combined with gritty determination.

Fearless Facts

John Wayne was born Marion Morrison, getting his stage name as a young actor from an agent who didn't think Marion was the right name for his character. His nickname, "Duke" stems from childhood, when young Marion had an Airedale terrier named Duke. The boy and his dog were often seen together and people started calling the Airedale "Big Duke" and the future actor "Little Duke."

Heroic Shorts

Since the days of silent film, acting legend Gary Cooper (1901–1961) was for many, the embodiment of ideal manliness. Tall, strong, and handsome, his image incorporated rugged courage, kindness, and a sense of duty and responsibility. His father was a prosperous lawyer with a ranch in Montana, where Cooper grew up. He later used his experience with horses to good advantage starring in cowboy films. He made one of his best films, *High Noon* (1951), quite late in his career, after winning an Oscar for his starring role in *Sergeant York* (1941). Cooper started off as a screen actor back in the days of silent movies, playing opposite the famous leading ladies of cinema, including Clara Bow. At the end of his career, he received an honorary Oscar for his distinguished career.

In keeping with his no-nonsense image, John Wayne never planned on an acting career before becoming an actor. A talented football player in high school, he went to the University of Southern California on a football scholarship. It just so happened that the radio-cowboy personality Tom Mix was a big USC football fan who worked out a deal with the coach for tickets to the games in exchange for behind-the-scenes jobs in show business for the players. Wayne got work as a prop man.

It was while working as a part of the production crew that Wayne became acquainted with director John Ford, who recommended him to fellow director Raoul Walsh for a part in the epic western *The Big Trail* (1930). Wayne took to his role as a young pioneer like he was born for it, and went on to make over 150 movies, including several for John Ford—notably the state-of-the-art western drama *Stagecoach* (1939), in which he played Ringo Kid.

In fact, *Stagecoach* was a major breakthrough in Wayne's career. Although, prior to making the film he was getting plenty of work as an actor, his only parts were in B-movies. These were low-quality films that didn't enable Wayne to make a name for himself as a great actor. With *Stagecoach*, however, he emerged as a star and went on to make many more war and cowboy action dramas. He won an Oscar for *True Grit* (1969) as a one-eyed alcoholic U.S. marshal on the trail of a murderer.

One of his last roles was in *The Shootist* (1976), in which he played a dying gunman. The film takes on added poignancy in light of the fact that Wayne had been diagnosed with cancer while making it. He died three years later, requesting an epitaph for his tombstone of the kind you might see carved in a marker on Boot Hill: *Feo, Fuerte, y Formal*, which is Spanish for "Ugly, Strong, and Dignified." These words, however fitting, do not appear on his monument.

Rebels—With and Without Causes

Social rebellion is often associated with civil rights activism. One of the best ways to work for justice is to carry out projects, including plays and movies, critical of the things wrong with society. Rebellion is also often associated with being young. Many young people who have just recently reached adulthood lash out against the values and lifestyles of their parents in an attempt to deal with the world on their own terms.

Two legendary American actors, although very different from one another in most respects, typify each of these approaches to rebellion. They are Paul Robeson and James Dean.

In Black and White

The multitalented and widely admired African-American Paul Robeson (1898–1976) became an actor, singer, and civil rights worker after an impressive academic and athletic career in college followed by a law degree. The son of a runaway slave, he attended Rutgers University on scholarship were he made Phi Beta Kappa and was class valedictorian. He also earned 15 varsity letters in baseball, basketball, football, and track. He went on to graduate from Columbia Law School and found work at a law firm, but quit when a white secretary refused to take dictation from him because he was black.

He took up stage acting and won acclaim in London for his portrayal of Shakespeare's *Othello* before appearing in movies. A notable early success is the silent film *Body and Soul* (1924), in which Robeson plays two roles: an evil preacher and his good brother. Many of his subsequent films, including *Proud Valley* (1939) and *Native Land* (1942), deal with civil rights issues. He sang the classic song "Ole' Man River" in the 1936 film version of the Broadway musical *Showboat*. Robeson himself was active in the cause of civil rights, labor, and peace. He donated the proceeds from one of his plays to German-Jewish refugees in 1933.

Paul Robeson appearing in Othello. *(Rutgers University Special Collections and Archives)*

His activism got him into trouble with the U.S. government. After speaking against the Cold War, he was called to appear before a congressional committee where he was accused of Communism. In 1950 he had his passport revoked.

End of the Road

Still another acting icon is James Dean (1938–1955), who stands apart from other great actors in achieving legendary status in such a short time before his untimely death. His stature as an actor rests on only three major motion pictures, *East of Eden* (1955), *Rebel Without a Cause* (1955), and *Giant* (1956), which was released after his death. His tragic death in a car accident at the peak of his young career seems to underscore the searching turbulence of the characters he played. He projected a restless dissatisfaction that spoke powerfully to a new generation—a generation just beginning to feel rebellious in response to the conformity and complacency that dominated middle-class life in the 1950s.

Dean played characters who were sensitive, misunderstood, and looking for more than they had. *Rebel Without a Cause*, about a young man whose troubles no one is able to fully understand, is most distinctively characteristic of this image. Dean sought adventure in real life as a race car driver. He was on his way to a race he had entered in Salinas, California in his Porsche Spyder when he crashed into a car that pulled out suddenly into the highway. After his death, he got his second Academy Award nomination for *Giant*. (He got the first for *East of Eden*.)

Feeling Lucky

John Wayne, a leading guy-hero of his generation, exhibited many of the qualities that men of his day admired, despite the fact that he also exhibited less-admirable traits in his films as well, including stubbornness, ornery-ness, and cussedness. Of course, such minor imperfections only give a hero character, making him easier for ordinary people to identify with. And, to an extent, these foibles are actually good things insofar as they help the hero get done whatever needs doing.

The outstanding guy-hero of the following generation took cussedness to an extreme, winning adulation from millions of young men as an over-the-top, R-rated action star. This is Clint Eastwood (1930–), whose icy ruthlessness and controlled brutality as Dirty Harry sent chills of excitement down the spines of moviegoers. Yet over the course of his long and productive career, Eastwood has displayed depth and variety in his acting that his many imitators cannot approach.

Fearless Facts

In addition to his starring roles in dozens of movies, Clint Eastwood has directed over 20 films.

A Bad Good Guy

Eastwood struggled for years as a young actor landing only bit parts—often playing cowboys simply because he looked good in western outfits. His big break came with his chance to play Rowdy Yates on the TV series *Rawhide*, which was a hit for many years in the early 1960s. Eastwood had the opportunity to enjoy a comfortable career in television like dozens of other competent actors who are remembered, if at all, for a single TV role.

Instead, Eastwood took the chance of branching out. While on vacation from *Rawhide*, he traveled to Italy to do campy western films with director Sergio Leone. Called "spaghetti westerns," because of their saucy Italian flavor, these films combine adventure and drama with a tongue-in-cheek, arty self-awareness. All at once they explored, glorified, and parodied the myths of masculinity and the cowboy. Eastwood made a perfect spaghetti-western star, playing his parts with an air of ironic detachment that contributed both to the subtle humor of the films and to the mystique of his heroic character.

A Fistful of Dollars (1964) was followed by *For a Few Dollars More* (196) and *The Good, the Bad, and the Ugly* (1966). Eastwood emerged as an actor totally in control of his work, keeping his cool in the midst of cinematic violence and elevating meanness to an art form. In the wake of the spaghetti-western craze, he went even further in the direction of controlled, cocksure meanness in *Dirty Harry* (1971), playing a policeman who grows disgusted with bureaucratic and legal protections afforded to criminals and takes the law into his own hands.

Dirty Harry introduced a theme that has become a staple of action movies ever since. Portraying the legal and police system as too soft, the film glorifies the hard-guy hero who can look degenerate scum in the face and blow it away. Eastwood, in a famous opening scene, goes so far as to do this while chewing on the last bite of the hotdog he had for lunch!

Fearless Facts

Clint Eastwood is not opposed to government and bureaucracy in real life. In fact, he has served as mayor of Carmel, California.

Branching Out

Clint Eastwood became legendary as the quintessential meaner-than-the-bad-guy good-guy. This type of hero, of course, is controversial because it sacrifices the moral values of compassion and fair play for the sake of cheap thrills. It also refutes the long-cherished belief that good can triumph over evil only by being better than evil. Although Eastwood made this type of hero famous, he is not just a one-trick pony. He has acted successfully in roles in which he displays feelings more subtle than icy nastiness, most notably in *Unforgiven* (1992), a film he directed himself.

Unforgiven is about a veteran hired killer who has seen—and survived—the tragedies that result from the outlaw's way of life. After years of going straight, he takes on one more job in order to make enough money so that he can retire for good. The movie is gripping for its own sake and also works as a poignant reflection on Eastwood's career as a hard-guy action hero. It won four Oscars, including best picture.

Grace Under Fire

Some actors seem heroic because of the way their careers seem to parallel their private lives. Others are heroic because of their ability to carry on with their careers despite suffering personal calamities. Stellar examples are Christopher Reeves (1952–) and Gilda Radner (1946–1989). Reeves won acclaim and admiration for his work both before and after a horseback riding accident that left him paralyzed. Gilda Radner carried on with her career as a beloved comedian after being diagnosed with ovarian cancer.

Superman

Christopher Reeve became a major star for playing the title role in *Superman* (1978). He made the character modest, likable, and good, without sacrificing the mysterious excitement inherent in superheroism. While making three sequels as the popular pulp superhero, Reeves remained a classy-enough actor to pull off a major part in the standout Merchant Ivory costume drama *Remains of the Day* (1983), as well as starring roles in numerous other films.

His career suffered a significant (but only temporary) setback after a riding accident in May 1995. An avid English-style horseback rider, Reeves was urging his horse over a gate. The horse balked and Reeves was thrown from the saddle. His foot got caught in one of the stirrups, and he landed hard on his head and fractured some vertebrae, leaving him paralyzed and unable to breathe. Fortunately, he received immediate medical attention that saved his life, although he has since been confined to a wheelchair.

Since the accident, he has continued to act and also direct. He has also become active in promoting awareness of paralysis. He has hosted the Paralympics in Atlanta, for example, and has also served as chairman of the American Paralysis Association. He also spoke at a Democratic National Convention and started up the Christopher Reeve Foundation to support research and legislation for the disabled.

Meanwhile, he narrated the Emmy–award-winning HBO documentary *Without Pity: A Film About Abilities*, profiling the lives of several disabled people. And he gained national attention for his big acting comeback as star of a made-for-TV remake of *Rear Window* (1998). The original Hitchcock film starred Jimmy Stewart as an amateur detective in a wheelchair. As a paralytic, Reeves brought a dose of realism to the role that heightened the drama.

Heroic Shorts

While male action heroes are a dime a dozen these days, female action heroes are relatively few and far between. The outstanding woman of heroic action movies is Sigourney Weaver (1949–), who made an unprecedented mark as a do-or-die fighting female in the sci-fi nail-biter *Alien* (1979). She shines in the role of space explorer embroiled in psychological and physical battle with the grossest space creatures ever to burst their slime-covered selves out of the bodies of ordinary-looking fellow crewmen. She has reprised the part in numerous sequels and has also turned in a monumental performance as the female lead in Roman Polanski's *Death and the Maiden* (1994), for which she received critical acclaim. She was born Susan Alexandra Weaver and changed her name at age 14 to Sigourney after a character in F. Scott Fitzgerald's novel *The Great Gatsby*.

Tumor and Humor

Gilda Radner was an Emmy–award-winning comedian and star of the popular TV show *Saturday Night Live*, where she became famous for her many comic roles including Emily Litella, Rosanne Rosanna-Danna, and Baba Wawa, her spoof of TV journalist Barbara Walters. After five seasons with *Saturday Night Live* (1975–1980), she did Broadway shows and films. She married actor/director Gene Wilder, with whom she co-starred in several films, the last of which was *Haunted Honeymoon* (1986).

In October 1986, she was diagnosed with ovarian cancer. Despite her fatal illness, she kept up her comic spirits and wrote a serio-comic book about her medical experiences called *It's Always Something*. After her death, in keeping with her wishes, Gene Wilder founded Gilda's Club, a social club and support service for people with cancer.

Funny Fellow

Perhaps the best loved and most widely admired American comedian is Bill Cosby (1937–), whose wise and gentle humor has appealed to black, white, young, old, the rich, and the not-so-rich, for nearly four decades. A native of Philadelphia, Cosby began his career as a standup comedian in nightclubs before breaking into television. As co-star of *I Spy* (with Robert Culp), Cosby won three Emmy Awards for best actor. He went on to star in many popular TV shows, including *The Bill Cosby Show* (1969), *Cos* (1976), *The Cosby Show* (1984), and *Cosby* (1996). As you can tell by these titles, Cosby himself is the main attraction in his shows.

Meanwhile, Cosby has continued to perform standup comedy. In fact, he has put out numerous albums of his comedy routines, for which he has won five Grammies. And Cosby has other talents in addition to comedy. He has recorded albums as a jazz musician and written bestselling books, including *Fatherhood*, *Childhood*, and *Time Flies*. He has also written stories for children. He received his Ph.D. in education from the University of Massachusetts in 1977.

The Least You Need to Know

➤ Humphrey Bogart became legendary for playing reluctant, worldly-wise heroes.

➤ Katherine Hepburn garnered a record-setting 12 Oscar nominations and 4 Oscars.

➤ John Wayne broke into show business through his USC football coach.

➤ Clint Eastwood became a controversial hero for playing good guys who were even meaner than the bad guys.

➤ Gilda Radner's legacy continues through Gilda's Club, founded to help people cope with cancer.

Top of the Charts

How does a musical figure become a legend? By forging his or her own way, by challenging the status quo, by years of vision and achievement. Legends inspire listeners to start piano lessons, to try singing at an open-microphone club, to practice the trumpet, to write a first song, to pick up a guitar, to dance in front of a bathroom mirror with a hairbrush as a stand-in for a microphone.

Of course, for nearly two centuries before the era of television, America sang. Americans thrilled to the marches of John Philip Sousa, the show tunes of Rodgers and Hammerstein, the instant classics of Irving Berlin, the classically driven pop of George Gershwin, and the witty ditties of Cole Porter. There was swing and Dixieland, jazz and big-band music, with superstar bandleaders and sidemen: Artie Shaw, Glenn Miller, Louis Armstrong, Benny Goodman, Bix Beiderbecke. Thousands came out to see and hear contralto Marian Anderson, entertainer Al Jolson, vocal stylist Billie Holiday, crooner Bing Crosby, jazz great Ella Fitzgerald, and many others. Here, however, we're going to look at the people who helped to make rock 'n' roll—a distinctively American music—great.

Fearless Fact

Are teen idols heroes? To many American teens and preteens, absolutely. But once you get a little older, you realize that Ricky Nelson, Fabian, the Monkees, Shawn and David Cassidy, Leif Garrett, New Kids on the Block, and Hanson are more cute than hero-worthy. Plus, you find out that, behind the *Teen Beat* posters, these guys weren't exactly Boy Scouts. Well, maybe Hanson.

On the Tube

But only in the media age, when we could see musicians in action, did the whole package come together. With *American Bandstand*, the 33-$\frac{1}{3}$ rpm LP, and pop-music radio coming of age, musical developments began arriving much faster, and it became harder to keep up. New heroes emerged—some faded quickly; others stuck around. It's the latter that we recognize as legends: Those who produced timeless music.

The Originals

When the Rock 'n' Roll Hall of Fame opened for business in 1986, two of the initial inductees were, arguably, the true architects of rock and roll. Chuck Berry and Little Richard have always insisted that they were the ones who got the whole thing started, and they may both be right.

In early songs like "Maybellene," Berry played country guitar licks over an R&B rhythm, singing without the gospel-tinged soul that characterized most black singers at the time. His "white" singing was the reason, he said, that his songs crossed over to the regular pop charts! Berry's songs are simple but elegant, and in them you can hear the foundation of the decades of rock 'n' roll to come. Indeed, it became common practice for up-and-coming rock bands to master classics such as "Sweet Little Sixteen," "Rock and Roll Music," "Roll Over Beethoven" and "Johnny B. Goode." You've probably heard one of your favorite bands (such as the Beatles) performing a Berry song.

And the songs are so well constructed that they're practically timeless. That's Berry's 1964 hit "You Never Can Tell" playing during the John Travolta–Uma Thurman "twist" scene in *Pulp Fiction*. It sounds nostalgic yet utterly contemporary.

Little Richard Penniman took a different tack from Berry. Playing piano instead of guitar, he pounded out boogie-woogie rhythms and sang with as much passion as he could muster, ending vocal lines with near-screams, as in his 1957 "Lucille." His first hit, "Tutti Frutti," entered the charts in December 1955, announcing itself with the unforgettable "Awopbopaloobopalopbamboom!" The song was a hit, but Richard suffered a terrible insult when, only a month later, a limp rendition of "Tutti Frutti" by Pat Boone (the epitome of white-bread soullessness to black entertainers of the time) ended up placing higher and staying in the Top 40 twice as long. Richard got the last laugh, though—Boone's take is remembered as only a joke.

> **Towering Tips**
>
> At the end of the 1985 movie *Back to the Future*, Michael J. Fox (purportedly from the present) entertains a crowd of 1955 prom-goers with a rendition of "Johnny B. Goode," starting with the famous two-string guitar riff. What better song to introduce people to rock 'n' roll?

Hail to the King

There's never been an icon—in music or any-where else—like Elvis Presley. Chuck Berry and Little Richard may have enunciated the basic vocabulary of rock 'n' roll, but Elvis Presley brought it into American everyday language. If his waggling hips shocked parents in the 1950s, his heartfelt ballads made them sigh.

Elvis began as a country singer and drew notice when he mixed in R&B stylings. His first real recording, "That's All Right (Mama)," drove audiences wild, especially when he performed it with dramatic, sliding-across-the-stage hip swivels. Signed to a major label, he recorded a remarkable series of singles. In 1956 alone, Elvis had five Number 1 hits (lasting a total of 25 weeks of the year), all of which are still classics: "Heartbreak Hotel," "I Want You, I Need You, I Love You," "Don't Be Cruel," "Hound Dog" and "Love Me Tender." He kept it going the next year with "Too Much," "All Shook Up," "Teddy Bear," and "Jailhouse Rock."

It wasn't only Elvis' recordings that got attention, though. His national TV debut, complete with lascivious gyrations, outraged the adult audience and gave the singer some desirable notoriety. For some time after that, TV producers insisted on showing Elvis from the waist up only; typically, then, in mid-song the studio audience would begin shrieking maniacally while folks watching at home could only guess at what was going on.

The singer began starring in movies, none of which were very good, but most of which were commercially successful. In 1958 he began a two-year stint in the Army. When he returned, he took on a more mature, adult-oriented persona. The hits kept coming—"Stuck on You," "It's Now or Never," "Are You Lonesome Tonight?"—but Elvis would never again be the rebel that had blown away American radio listeners and TV viewers.

He cranked out countless films, and most of his records were soundtracks. While he continued to have Top 40 hits every year until his death (107 in all), the songs stopped

323

reaching the Number 1 spot, and then even the Top 10. One exception was 1969's great "Suspicious Minds," recorded not long after a triumphant TV special.

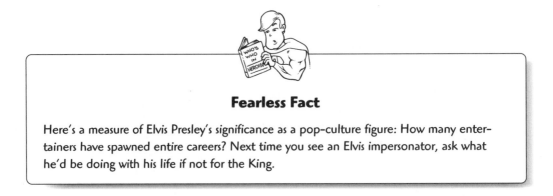

Fearless Fact

Here's a measure of Elvis Presley's significance as a pop-culture figure: How many entertainers have spawned entire careers? Next time you see an Elvis impersonator, ask what
he'd be doing with his life if not for the King.

In the 1970s, Elvis became far more a showman than a musician, but even then he set a standard for pomp and glitz. Long after his records stopped topping the charts, his Las Vegas shows were legendary. His trademark lip curl and bashful "Thank yuh ver' much" made their way into pop culture, along with his Brylcreemed pompadour.

A handful of hardcore fanatics insist the King faked his 1977 death and is living anonymously in some small town, but don't believe it. To quote the signature post-concert announcement: "Elvis has left the building."

All Funked Up

After success with singles in 1956 and 1958, James Brown hit his stride in 1960, beginning an unbroken streak of hits that lasted 15 years. Two years later, a raw and unreserved full-length album, *Live at the Apollo*, established Brown as a prophet of American black music. And in 1964, he shifted in a new direction—one that would have a dramatic impact on pop music to come.

Brown's new sound reconfigured songs, downplaying melody and lyrics and doing away with standard verse-chorus-verse arrangements. It brought him instant pop-chart success. He released the instant classics "Papa's Got a Brand New Bag," "I Got You (I Feel Good)," and "It's a Man's Man's Man's World" in quick succession, and all went Top 10. The evolution continued with songs such as "Cold Sweat" and "Get Up (I Feel Like Being a) Sex Machine," which often consisted of little more than extended jams based on a single repetitive riff, with Brown wailing and screaming and a horn section offering occasional tight blasts. The groove was the entire point.

Considering Brown's radical shift, and the impossibility of humming or singing along with the songs, it's perhaps surprising that he continued to enjoy chart hits. But a popular part of the package was Brown himself, an incredibly dynamic dancer and stage presence who earned the nickname of "the Hardest-Working Man in Show Business." And with his 1968 hit "Say It Loud—I'm Black and I'm Proud," he crystallized his place as the leading figure in black music.

After the mid-1970s, Brown was bumped off the charts by the emergence of disco, a preponderance of tighter, briefer funk songs on the radio, and the fact that his recordings were less and less vital. He had a huge comeback hit in 1986 with the jingoistic "Living in America," from *Rocky IV*, but went downhill soon after that: He was arrested after an interstate car chase, charged with various crimes (drugs, firearms, assault), and sentenced to six years in prison. Released after 26 months, he has continued to have trouble with the law.

But his influence is greater than ever. The all-groove-no-melody hip-hop and rap of the 1990s is completely indebted to Brown's sound, and any number of recordings have sampled his drumbeats and trademark whoops. More than that, Brown's stretching of the standard of acceptability in pop music has had an impact on music of all genres. He has truly become "the Godfather of Soul."

Worthy Words

An **icon** is not the same as a hero. An icon symbolizes an idea or event; a hero, on the other hand, maintains his or her own personal integrity. Take two prime examples: singers Janis Joplin and Jim Morrison, whose legends have grown immeasurably since their drug-induced deaths, both at age 27. Considering their self-destructive behavior, which tossed away years of potentially great work, they're about the worst role models imaginable. Cool, sure. Heroes? Not to most.

True Confessions

Pick up just about any album by a female singer-songwriters of the '80s and '90s, and read the liner notes. More often than not, there'll be a thank-you to Joni Mitchell. Canadian Mitchell (who's spent most of her musical career based in Los Angeles), one of the finest songwriters and performers of the '70s, was a pioneer in both musical style—she used unusual open tunings and was one of the first to integrate jazz and pop—and writing, setting the standard for introspective lyricism. She first came to prominence through others' versions of her songs: Tom Rush recorded "Urge for Going" and "The Circle Game," and Judy Collins did "Michael from Mountains" and hit the Top Ten in 1968 with "Both Sides Now."

Mitchell's singing and performance developed with her first three records, sparse and lovely collections of pretty songs showcasing her guitar, piano, and soprano voice. A single off her *Ladies of the Canyon* album, "Big Yellow Taxi," came close to the Top 40. But it was her fourth record, Blue, that broke through to a wider public, displaying a new level of honesty in confessional songwriting. Without sentimentality, Mitchell cuts close to the bone—her own—in examining her life and relationships. As a definite product of the singer-songwriter era, *Blue* remains a landmark record, one adopted by new waves of listeners each year.

Towering Tips

In Janet Jackson's 1997 single "Got 'Til It's Gone," that's a sample of Joni Mitchell singing a line from her 1970 song "Big Yellow Taxi." The original song is a wry plea for environmental sanity: "Don't it always seem to go/You don't know what you've got till it's gone/They paved paradise and put up a parking lot."

After the brilliant *For the Roses*, Mitchell had her greatest commercial success with 1974's upbeat *Court and Spark*, which used a jazz band to add a light touch to her songs. On the strength of hits "Help Me" and "Free Man in Paris," the album rose to No. 2 on the charts and brought a new sensibility and sophistication to the pop music of the day.

But it was the next two records—seen as a letdown at the time—that may prove Mitchell's most enduring legacy. For 1975's *The Hissing of Summer Lawns*, she brought in real jazz musicians and expanded her arrangements to make them more layered and diffuse, while her lyrics became more poetic and less direct. It was a far cry from the acoustic singer-songwriter material of only a few years earlier, and the album received a mixed critical reception (though it sold well), but *Hissing* is, in retrospect, perhaps her most imporant album. Her magnificent 1976 release, *Hejira*, strips down most songs to just guitar, voice and fretless bass, experimenting with chordal structure and narrative lyricism.

Over the next few years, Mitchell delved deeper into jazz—too deeply for most fans—and lost the support of radio. Her work in the '80s was erratic, hurt by her increasingly husky voice (wrecked by chain-smoking), but in the '90s she's made something of a comeback, releasing well-received albums that, while not commercial blockbusters, are worthy additions to her marvelous catalog.

National Anthems

It's not just great songs on the radio that make us fans of music—it's also great artists. It adds to a song to know about the person singing, to know what album that artist released last year, and to know what he or she might release next year. The superstars of pop music are what keep us listening.

Behind the Shades

You would have to search far and wide to find two people less handicapped by their disabilities than Ray Charles and Stevie Wonder, pianists whose blindness has always been seen as more a trademark or character trait than as a handicap. Their careers are an inspiration not only to those struggling with disabilities, but to us all; and their music has brought joy to five decades of listeners.

In his early 20s, Charles began developing a gospel-inflected style of playing and singing that came to fruition in his 1954 hit "I Got a Woman," which evoked the fervor of the Baptist church and an R&B sensuousness. In the next several years, he

produced a number of thrilling hits ("This Little
Girl of Mine," "Don't Let the Sun Catch You
Crying," "Drown in My Own Tears"), topping it
off with his 1959 call-and-response triumph
"What'd I Say," a classic still in the repertoires of
any number of bar bands.

In the first two years of the 1960s, Charles
refined his style and built on his earlier success
with more-polished tracks like "Georgia on My
Mind" and the rousing "Hit the Road, Jack."
Then he began experimenting with other genres,
primarily country music, and slipped a bit into
the adult-contemporary niche. While his later
work has always been interesting, it has never

Towering Tips

All you do-it-yourselfers with guitars
and four-track tape recorders in your
living room, check out Prince's
debut album, *For You*. He wrote all
the songs and played all the
instruments—while still in his teens!

again captured the exhilaration of those 1950s songs. Even so, Charles has remained a
formidable, lively presence, and his raspy voice—a model for white blues/rock artists
like Eric Burdon and Joe Cocker—is still a joy to hear, even in TV commercials.

When America first heard Stevie Wonder, his voice hadn't yet changed. Billed as "the
12-Year-Old Genius," Wonder dazzled listeners with blasts of chromatic harmonica in
"Fingertips (Part 2)," a 1963 single that eventually sold a million-plus copies. Over the
next decade, after puberty had its way with the singer's vocal cords, Wonder had
success with such singles as "Uptight," "I Was Made to Love Her," "For Once in My
Life," "My Cherie Amour," and "Signed, Sealed, Delivered."

Finally, in late 1972, Wonder broke through with the album-buying public, using his
flexible voice, unerring melodic sense, and multi-instrumental prowess. (He was one of
the first black artists to make extensive use of the synthesizer.) His album *Talking Book*
rose to Number 3 on the strength of two divergent Number 1 hits: the breezy "You Are
the Sunshine of My Life" and the funky "Superstition." The latter, dark and driving,
heralded the direction of Wonder's greatest 1970s recordings, which addressed social
and political issues while staying relentlessly catchy. He was prepared to use his music
to describe and comment on the political and social landscape of America. Wonder
made Nixon the subject of "You Haven't Done Nothin'"; he captured the American
urban drama in "Living for the City"; and he paid reverent tribute to Duke Ellington
with the song "Sir Duke."

Wonder remains a towering figure—instantly recognizable and supremely talented. As
the featured performer at the Super Bowl XXXIII halftime show, in January 1999,
Wonder performed a nifty tap dance—no mean trick for a man who's been blind since
birth!

Lady Soul

Aretha Franklin's father was a Baptist preacher, and she started out singing gospel. At
18, she signed to Columbia and began recording secular pop: eight albums in seven

years, everything from light jazz to new soul. None of her work met with much success. But in 1966, frustrated, she joined Atlantic Records and set out in a new direction. Her first attempt, "I Never Loved a Man (The Way I Loved You)," showcased Franklin's remarkably rich voice in a new setting, with a lively rhythm section. Dazzled listeners sent the single to the pop Top 10, and Atlantic rushed to record the rest of the album. Her next single, a cover of Otis Redding's "Respect," was enough to secure Franklin's title as the "Queen of Soul."

Enjoying her first mainstream success, and with the backing of top-notch musicians, Franklin gained confidence and turned in a career's worth of classics in a year's time: "Dr. Feelgood," "Chain of Fools," "Baby I Love You," "(You Make Me Feel Like) A Natural Woman." They're songs that continue to get airplay and attention three decades after their release, and are still recognized as some of the finest tracks of soul music ever produced.

Franklin followed her astonishing success with "The House That Jack Built," the dynamic, self-penned "Think" and a definitive version of Burt Bacharach and Hal David's "I Say a Little Prayer," but she seemed to have lost some focus, and indeed she would never again record music as vital as those 1967–1968 songs. The durability of her fantastic early recordings, however, kept her from obscurity, and she has remained a figure of soulful, feminine strength to generations. Her records from the 1960s remain tremendously important and influential—a blueprint for how soul music can sound.

Towering Tips

The next time you hear Bruce Springsteen's rousing anthem "Born in the U.S.A.," listen closely to the lyrics—they're hardly as upbeat and pro-America as many casual listeners seem to think. President Ronald Reagan actually attempted to use the song for his 1984 reelection campaign, but he desisted when Springsteen complained publicly and swore allegiance to civil rights and environmental causes.

Born in New Jersey

In Bruce Springsteen, blue-collar Americans found a voice—a rock star who sang about his car, his girl, and his job. Honing his craft in the New Jersey club scene, Springsteen composed articulate rock songs that managed to speak directly to working-class listeners while being artful enough to satisfy those hoping for a prophet. His first two albums, brilliantly written but erratically performed and produced, sold slowly but steadily, aided by his relentless touring.

And then, in 1975, Springsteen released *Born to Run*, a landmark album that landed him simultaneously on the covers of *Time* and *Newsweek*. Still considered the quintessential American rock album, *Born to Run* is full of evocative anthems such as "Thunder Road," "Tenth Avenue Freeze-Out," "Backstreets," and the stunning title track. His following albums showed a musical and emotional maturing that his fans continued to feel spoke directly about their lives and experiences.

Material Girl

Madonna Louise Veronica Ciccone has been an integral part of the pop landscape since 1982, setting trends and riding them just long enough to find the next one, reinventing herself whenever necessary, convenient, or just interesting. Whether her bubblegum recordings will stand the proverbial test of time is an open question— "Vogue" and "Open Your Heart" aren't exactly "Smoke Gets in Your Eyes" or "Desperado"—but she will live on as a major figure in American pop culture.

Through vivid videos, elaborate stage shows, and the 1991 documentary *Truth or Dare*, Madonna has offered a colorful example to follow (or disdain). Always a few months ahead of her time, she has made a practice of catching the public off-guard. When the world caught up to her once-naughty "Like a Virgin" routine, she produced *Sex*, an oversized, silver-toned, $50 volume of salacious photos that booksellers kept shrink-wrapped and on a high shelf behind the counter.

For a full decade, between 1983 and 1992, every one of Madonna's singles save one (1989's "Oh Father") went Top 10—more than two dozen of them, beginning with "Lucky Star" and "Borderline" and going all the way to "Erotica." In between were 10 Number 1 hits, making her one of the most successful pop artists in history. Key to Madonna's longevity is her capacity for reinvention, for catching trends (such as vogueing), moving on, and through it all maintaining a solid, recognizable identity. If all the clothing changes have seemed more than a little calculated and manipulative, at least it's done with a cheeky wink.

In recent years, nearing her 40th birthday, she has seemed less inclined to shock. After a number of minor film roles and a stint on Broadway, she landed the lead in the 1996 movie *Evita*. And even if her thin voice was but a shadow of that of Patti LuPone (who played the title role on Broadway), Madonna at least proved herself worth taking seriously onscreen. She has accomplished more than making the world safe for girls to wear their underwear on the outside—she's shown by example what a strong woman is capable of.

The Folk-Song Army

Some artists have used songs to change not just the world of music but society in general. There's a long history of political music, of songwriters who have devoted their lives to making the world a better place.

He Had a Hammer

Woody Guthrie died in 1967, and Pete Seeger turned 80 in May 1999—and yet the two are as vital as ever, by virtue of their legacy. Separately and together, the fathers of folk music tried to create a music of the people, a music larger than themselves, and by so doing enriched American life beyond measure.

Guthrie started out in the 1930s playing guitar at union meetings and migrant labor camps, writing songs such as "Pastures of Plenty" and "This Land Is Your Land" along with charming children's songs such as "Car Car" (which your parents might have sung to you in your car-seat way back when). Although his songs weren't exclusively political, they all meant to capture something of ordinary Americans' feelings.

In 1940, Guthrie met banjo player Pete Seeger, and the two brought together what would become a true musical movement. Guthrie wrote a captivating autobiography, *Bound for Glory*, in 1943, and after World War II ended (he served in the merchant marines), he made an extensive series of recordings for the Folkways label, ensuring its survival. He also made time to write columns for pro-union newspapers before his slow death, in 1967, from a degenerative nerve disease.

Seeger had spent years traveling the country, learning songs from workers and farmers, before he hooked up with Guthrie and the folk community. He had an immediate impact on music and society, writing songs such as "If I Had a Hammer" and even becoming a mainstream success with the popular quartet The Weavers. The anti-Communist paranoia of the late 1940s got the openly left-wing Seeger blacklisted, but he continued to play concerts abroad and to speak out on free speech and civil rights issues.

His presence today remains vital not only because of the effects of his activism—in 1968 TV audiences saw him perform his anti–Vietnam War song "Waist Deep in the Big Muddy" on *The Smothers Brothers Comedy Hour*—but because of the songs he wrote, among them "Where Have All the Flowers Gone" (a hit for the Kingston Trio) and "Turn, Turn, Turn" (a hit for the Byrds). His rewrite of "We Shall Overcome" transformed it from an obscure gospel tune into a worldwide anthem. Seeger recorded more than 50 albums, including a few with Woody Guthrie's son Arlo (himself famous for "Alice's Restaurant" and "City of New Orleans"), and some instructional banjo records. And he's still going: His most recent release appeared in 1996.

Changing the Times

In his late teens, Bob Dylan (born Robert Zimmerman) read Woody Guthrie's memoir, *Bound for Glory*, and everything changed for him: He learned every Guthrie song he could, took on the singer's romantic hobo persona, and adopted an Oklahoma twang. He learned to play harmonica while strumming the guitar, and took New York by storm when he arrived in 1961, at age 20, and began playing folk and blues standards in a distinctively rough-hewn voice. On his first album, released in early 1962, "Song to Woody" (one of just two original songs) was a heartfelt tribute to his muse.

After that record, Dylan began writing prolifically and brilliantly, bringing a then unheard-of degree of literacy to popular music. Many of his early songs were politically charged and lyrically powerful: "Blowin' in the Wind," "Masters of War," "A Hard Rain's a-Gonna Fall," "The Times They Are a-Changin'." Dylan's sparse, raw arrangements (usually just voice, guitar, and harmonica) weren't exactly radio-friendly, but plenty of smoother-sounding artists—most notably, Peter, Paul and Mary—popularized versions of his early songs, and throughout the 1960s and 1970s, Dylan's songs would become standards in his and others' hands.

In 1964, Dylan's music turned introspective and openly poetic—as close to high art as pop had come—and the next two years proved to be his peak. His 1965 album *Bringing It All Back Home* shocked many with its full rock-band arrangements, but it was his first huge popular success. That fall he brought out the monumental six-minute single "Like a Rolling Stone," proving that songs longer than three minutes could indeed be hits.

If Dylan had stopped recording then—and after a 1966 motorcycle accident, he actually did for a while—he would still be hailed as one of the few most important figures in rock history. But over the past three decades, he has gone through a number of transformations that have proven prescient and influential. Over the years, Dylan's albums and live performances have become erratic and unpredictable, and his nasal voice hasn't gotten much easier on the ears. He is, however, always interesting and occasionally spellbinding. His impact on music—and on American culture—is incalculable.

Heroic Shorts

Bob Dylan wasn't the only folksinger inspired by Woody Guthrie's life and work. After college, Texas songwriter Phil Ochs moved to New York and became active with the left-wing activist folk movement. His overtly political songs rivaled Dylan's in their effectiveness (if not in language), adding a strong dose of wry humor. Ochs's 1964 debut, *All the News That's Fit to Sing*, was hailed as the opening shot from a major new talent, pushed along by Joan Baez's well-received cover version of his wistful "There but for Fortune."

Ochs recorded two more significant albums in the next year and a half: *I Ain't Marching Anymore* and *Phil Ochs in Concert*—both full of songs that directly targeted southern racists ("Here's to the State of Mississippi"), farmers who exploited migrant workers ("Bracero"), wishy-washy Democrats ("Love Me, I'm a Liberal"), and pro-war politicians ("Draft Dodger Rag"), among others. Although Ochs's spare, guitar-and-vocal records didn't make the U.S. charts, they were highly influential and popular within a certain set.

The Voice

At 18, Joan Baez dazzled the 1959 Newport Folk Festival with her clear soprano and striking renditions of classic ballads; a few years later she was America's "queen of folk." She became inextricably linked with Bob Dylan due to an early joint tour, a highly publicized romance and Baez's many renditions of his songs. But she struck out in her own direction, becoming deeply involved with the antiwar movement. She twice found herself in jail after peace rallies, married an antiwar activist who went to prison for resisting the draft (they divorced four years later), and even recorded an album, symbolically, in North Vietnam.

Baez also made an impact with her own, introspective compositions, most notably "Diamonds and Rust," an evocative account of her affair with Dylan. And her 1974 album Gracias a la Vida celebrated her Chicano heritage. Since 1971, when she had a hit with a version of the Band's Civil War song "The Night They Drove Old Dixie Down," Baez's commercial success has been sporadic. Yet she remains a major concert draw and a powerful voice for social justice.

Unsung Heroes

Just about any artist who has released an album, whether on a major label or a tiny independent, is a hero to someone. If you're a real music fan, you almost certainly have a handful of favorite bands that stubbornly remain unknown to the general public, despite your best efforts. But artists whose albums don't sell many copies aren't necessarily unimportant. It's often said of the first Velvet Underground album: "It only sold 10,000 copies, but everyone who bought it formed a band."

The artists who follow didn't have much commercial success in the United States, but they were major influences on the bands you all know. They're the kind of artists who inspire comments like, "They changed my life."

Sure, the basic vocabulary of rock was written by Chuck Berry and Little Richard, but we're not still all listening to "Johnny B. Goode" and "Tutti Frutti"; and the reason is that later musicians added to that language. These artists, in different genres, changed the face of today's music.

➤ Memphis quartet Big Star released only two records during its lifespan, and those albums suffered from distribution problems and sold practically nothing. But the band, founded by singer/songwriters Chris Bell and Alex Chilton, ex-frontman of the Box Tops (that's him, at 16, singing "The Letter!") became legendary, and its recordings presaged the resurgence of power pop in the '90s. Despite the albums' pathetic sales, they were heard by any number of people who went on to make records of their own, inspired by Big Star's Beatlesque melodies and harmonies, layered over a tough backbeat. The Bangles and the Searchers covered "September Gurls," and the Replacements even immortalized the band in "Alex Chilton" ("I never travel far/without a little Big Star").

➤ The Velvet Underground, founded in late 1965, introduced the world to grunge rock a quarter century before Nirvana. Playing songs by guitarist Lou Reed, the Velvets never had anything resembling a hit in the United States or abroad, but the quartet's Andy Warhol–produced debut, *The Velvet Underground and Nico*—featuring the groundbreaking drug dronefest "Heroin," the S&M tribute "Venus in Furs" and the lovely "Femme Fatale"—remains a touchstone for many modern musicians. Modern indie bands like Luna, the Jesus and Mary Chain, and My Bloody Valentine pick up directly where the Velvets left off, but you can hear the influence of the band (and of Reed's distinctive talk-singing) in David Bowie, R.E.M., and much of today's alternative music.

➤ Born Chester Arthur Burnett, the singer known as Howlin' Wolf helped create Chicago blues and influenced a generation of blues-mad rockers with his presence and his songs. A huge man with a hoarse voice, he began to record in the mid-1940s, bringing a raw, Mississippi Delta sound to the blues. In the 1960s, he reached a large white audience courtesy of the Rolling Stones and the Yardbirds, who took every opportunity to enthuse about Wolf and recorded versions of his songs. He died in 1976 without ever having a hit single or album. His best-known songs—"Back Door Man," "Sitting on Top of the World," "Smokestack Lightning," and "Killing Floor"—will live forever: They were widely covered by artists from Cream to the Doors and remain standards in rock and blues repertoires today.

Fearless Fact

Robert Johnson recorded only 29 songs in his short lifetime, all in two sessions (seven months apart), and no one knows much about him. But those 29 songs include a handful of much-covered classics ("Crossroads," "Dust My Broom," "Sweet Home Chicago"), and Johnson's bottleneck guitar style was a major influence on the Delta bluesmen who followed him.

➤ In his mid-20s, John Lee Hooker moved from Mississippi to Detroit and began playing in blues clubs. In 1948 he made an album featuring his unusual open-tuned electric guitar and bluesy voice, the first of dozens he would record over the next five decades. Through the 1950s, Hooker built a faithful R&B following, and he expanded his audience to young whites with appearances at folk clubs and festivals. As the years went on, more and more blues and rock artists (acoustic and electric) spoke of Hooker's influence. At the age of 74, Hooker finally broke through with 1989's *The Healer*, whose list of guest artists was testimony to Hooker's appeal: Carlos Santana, Bonnie Raitt, Robert Cray, and Los Lobos. And he's not through; he recorded well-received albums in 1995 and 1997.

➤ While listeners embraced John Lee Hooker's spare guitar-and-vocal sound, it was Muddy Waters (born McKinley Morganfield) who made loudly amplified blues cool. It was his recordings of songs like "King Bee," "Hoochie Coochie Man," "I Got My Mojo Working," "Baby Please Don't Go" and "I Just Want to Make Love to You" that directly inspired scores of blues rockers. In the 1960s, artists such as Eric Clapton, Mike Bloomfield, Steve Winwood, and Johnny Winter praised Waters to the skies; the Rolling Stones even took their name from a Waters' song. Even after his fame became widespread, Waters never had a hit song or album, but his importance to modern rock is undeniable.

The Ax-Men

The guitar—particularly the electric guitar—has been the dominant instrument of the second half of the twentieth century, and it has spawned a singular type of virtuoso: the guitar hero. Plenty of players, most hard rockers, have earned the title: Steve Vai, Deep Purple's Ritchie Blackmore, Ozzy Osbourne's sideman Randy Rhoads, the Edge of U2, Joe Satriani, Jeff Beck, Steve Howe of Yes, Rush's Alex Lifeson, Duane Allman, Metallica's Kirk Hammett, Slash of Guns 'N' Roses, Pink Floyd's David Gilmour . . . the list goes on and on.

Jazz and fusion have their own special breed—Stanley Jordan, Al Di Meola, Allan Holdsworth, Larry Carlton, Django Reinhardt, George Benson, John McLaughlin. And if a blues guitarist is good enough to be a success, he's probably good enough for the title, as players such as B.B. King, Kenny Wayne Shepherd, Robert Cray, Stevie Ray Vaughan, and Mike Bloomfield have discovered.

But the higher appellation, guitar god, belongs to just four men: Jimmy Page, Jimi Hendrix, Eric Clapton, and Eddie Van Halen. Check the guitar magazines: One of this quartet winds up on the cover of each magazine at least once a year. You'd be forgiven for assuming that Hendrix was still alive and that Page's band Led Zeppelin was still recording albums. While Clapton and Page helped bring blues into the mainstream of American pop, melding it with other genres, it's Hendrix and Van Halen who have had the greater impact on rock and rock guitar.

Don't Try This at Home

By the time he recorded his first album, *Are You Experienced?*, the Seattle-born Hendrix had perfected a guitar style that combined virtuosic blues-based playing with a wildly ambitious sense of songwriting and a heretofore-unheard mastery of effects and feedback. In the three-plus years before he died in his sleep at just 27, Hendrix completely revolutionized the guitar—and, as a songwriter, left behind a number of pieces that still startle with their power, including "Purple Haze," "The Wind Cries Mary," "Castles Made of Sand," "Little Wing," and "Voodoo Chile."

It was onstage that Hendrix had perhaps the biggest impact. He could be a mesmerizing showman, writhing orgiastically, destroying instruments and amplifiers to get the desired noises, playing behind his back and with his teeth. In one of his most famous concerts, Hendrix concluded his set at the 1967 Monterey Pop Festival—his U.S. debut!—by squirting lighter fluid on his still-plugged-in guitar, setting it ablaze, and smashing it against his amplifiers. Captured on film, the performance solidified the guitarist's image as raw and untamed, a view that sells short his awesome technical abilities.

No Peeking

When a young Eddie Van Halen was working to perfect his revolutionary two-handed tapping technique, he would turn his back to the audience—just in case someone out there was looking to steal his style. No one did, and when his band, Van Halen, released its debut album in 1978, it set the rock world on its ear. Several years later, all manner of would-be guitar heroes were imitating Van Halen's technique, sometimes effectively (although more often just self-indulgently), but never topping the master.

And Eddie had moved on to explore new sounds, new styles, always setting the pace. Even as the band has changed lead singers from goofy, bombastic David Lee Roth to journeyman Sammy Hagar to, recently, the underwhelming Gary Cherone, Van Halen has stayed at the forefront of guitar groups.

Not to Mention . . .

So where are the women? It's a sad fact that guitar heroes have always been men—but that doesn't mean women haven't made a major impact. Nancy Wilson of the Seattle group Heart blew away crowds by simply being an aggressive, hard-strumming woman in a hard-driving rock band. While most of her guitar work is rhythm playing (an exception: the great acoustic intro to "Crazy on You"), she was a hero to a generation of young women guitarists who were inspired to strap on Stratocasters and Les Pauls.

In the '90s, Ani DiFranco has captured much attention for not only her politically charged songwriting but her astonishing acoustic attack, a tuneful amalgam of picks and strums and harmonics, bolstered by press-on nails and electrical tape. DiFranco, in only her mid-20s, is too prolific to have put together a single topnotch record—as of early 1999, she's released 10 full-length albums, plus a double-live set—but 1994's *Out of Range* and 1995's *Not a Pretty Girl* feature jaw-dropping acoustic and electric guitar work.

The Least You Need to Know

➤ Chuck Berry and Little Richard invented the language of rock 'n' roll . . .

➤ But Elvis Presley had a bigger impact on America.

➤ Hip-hop started with James Brown back in the 1960s.

➤ Bob Dylan is part of the protest-song tradition that began with Woody Guthrie.

➤ Many of the artists who inspired other musicians had little commercial success.

Chapter 25

Giants of the Game

In This Chapter

➤ The quintessential heroes

➤ Stars of the game

➤ Obstacles overcome

Baseball players are both life sized and larger than life. Unlike the 320-pound linemen increasingly dominating football fields, unlike the seven-footers who propel themselves through the air above basketball courts, baseball players are frequently of average stature. Sure, imposing physical specimens abound, but there's plenty of room for pudgy, medium-height guys who, out of uniform, wouldn't look out of place in the local YMCA locker room.

This may be one of the reasons why most Americans have fantasized, at one time or another, about playing the sport, in the sun, under the appreciative gaze of thousands of adoring fans. It all looks so easy, as though it were just chance that you aren't the one playing second base in this year's World Series. (If you had just spent a few more afternoons with dad catching fly balls ....)

But put a bat in the hands of a Kirby Puckett, for instance, and the difference between mere mortals and baseball gods becomes immediately apparent. And it's obvious why we invest so much of our hopes and dreams in the men who play baseball.

The Founding Fathers

In every great American institution, from the presidency to major league baseball, certain figures play key roles that seem to move history along. When we think of the narrative sweep of baseball, these are the players who come to mind first.

Worthy Words

Where does the word **jock** come from? Not from where you might think. It's from the word jockey, which dates back to 1670, describing a competitive horse racer. The shorter form didn't show up until 1826—and jockstrap, slang for an athletic supporter, came into usage six decades after that.

A Diamond Among the Roughnecks

Before Christy Mathewson, professional baseball was somewhat disreputable, seen as an unrefined game played by blue-collar ruffians—an only slightly unfair characterization of the players of the sport. But then, the first golden boy of American sport came on the scene, and everything changed. In the intelligent face and commanding performance of Mathewson, America saw its first baseball hero.

Born in 1880 in Pennsylvania, Mathewson attended Bucknell University, where he starred in baseball and football and was class president, a respected student, and a checker champion. In keeping with his growing storybook legend, he married his college sweetheart. When he told his mother (who had hoped her overachieving son would become a minister) that he planned to play pro baseball, she made him promise to never play on a Sunday. He never did.

But Mathewson's image would have carried little weight if he hadn't been such good player. In 1903, his second full season with the New York Giants, he won 30 games and lost 13, using a pitch he called a "fadeaway" (later dubbed a screwball). And then he got better, winning 33 and 31 the next two years. In the 1905 World Series, he put on perhaps history's finest exhibition of pitching, throwing three complete-game shutouts in only six days, allowing a total of 14 hits and one base on balls.

Dubbed "the Christian gentleman" by sportswriters because of his elegance and patrician virtue on and off the field, "Matty" was the king of baseball at just 25. He took on some of the trappings of royalty: He was aloof toward fans and teammates, keeping others at a slight distance. For some reason, that only added to his appeal. He was the first ballplayer to be worshipped by boys and men, the first whom mothers hoped their sons would look up to and emulate.

All the Way Homer

If Christy Mathewson infused baseball with a much-needed shot of class, Babe Ruth made the game fun. And more than anyone, he deserves credit for rescuing the game from the disaster of the 1919 Black Sox scandal (in which seven players on the favored

Chicago White Sox threw the World Series to the Cincinnati Reds).

Ruth began his professional career just before Mathewson's retirement and became, first, the league's best left-handed pitcher and, next, the greatest batter in history. As a role model, Ruth was disastrous—a prodigious drinker, carouser, and womanizer. But he did as much for the game of baseball as Mathewson did: He brought it to life. The "Sultan of Swat" was the ideal hero for America in the Jazz Age.

Starting out with the Boston Red Sox, he was the league's best left-handed pitcher; when he moved to the outfield, he became the game's most dynamic hitter. After less than three full seasons at the plate, Ruth had hit more career home runs than anyone else. And he showed a flair that packed 'em into the ballpark: In the season after the Boston team sold Ruth to the New York Yankees (in a misguided deal that still makes Red Sox fans weep), attendance in New York doubled.

Heroic Shorts

Even off the diamond, Mathewson proved himself an incomparable American hero. In the middle of World War I, he resigned as manager of the Cincinnati Reds and enlisted in the Army Chemical Warfare Division. When he accidentally inhaled some poison gas, he damaged his lungs, contracted tuberculosis, and died seven years later—on the opening day of the 1925 World Series.

Ruth went on to have the most storied career in baseball history, rewriting the record books as the centerpiece of a Yankees lineup that today is still considered the finest ever. He hit for average and power, repeatedly topping his own home-run marks. His 1921 numbers—59 homers, 177 runs scored, 171 RBIs, a .378 average, and a never-surpassed .846 slugging average—represent the greatest season any batter has ever had and ushered in an era when power hitters ruled supreme.

Fans knew from the sports pages of Ruth's giant appetites, but they often weren't told the details or true stories: For instance, the barrel-chested "Bambino" was a regular at whorehouses around the country. In 1925, he came down with a severe case of syphilis and gonorrhea and had to be hospitalized, but the story that America heard was that he had overeaten (a lie all too easy to believe).

If we had known everything about Ruth at the time, if sportswriters hadn't been so chaste and protective, would he still be the hero he was and is? Probably. His smile was wide and genuine, and he indisputably brought the game to life, bringing joy to baseball and to sports in general.

The Rock

Even in media-crazed New York, it took people a long time to notice the man who batted behind Babe Ruth. Lou Gehrig was quiet and retiring, whereas Ruth was boisterous and gregarious—Gehrig didn't make headlines, or friends, as easily as his teammate. His home runs were line drives rather than Ruth's towering shots. But eventually baseball, and all the world, realized what a treasure Gehrig was, and today he is considered as heroic a figure (the closest thing to a saint) as American sports has produced.

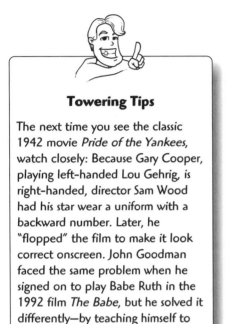

Towering Tips

The next time you see the classic 1942 movie *Pride of the Yankees*, watch closely: Because Gary Cooper, playing left-handed Lou Gehrig, is right-handed, director Sam Wood had his star wear a uniform with a backward number. Later, he "flopped" the film to make it look correct onscreen. John Goodman faced the same problem when he signed on to play Babe Ruth in the 1992 film *The Babe*, but he solved it differently—by teaching himself to hit and throw left-handed.

The legend begins like this: On June 2, 1925, Yankees first baseman Wally Pipp complained of a headache and was replaced by the rookie Gehrig—who then stayed in the lineup until May 2, 1939. Dubbed "the Iron Horse," Gehrig was the immovable cornerstone of the Yankees' "Murderers' Row" team of 1927–1928 and the next decade. (Wally Pipp, incidentally, was traded to Cincinnati.)

Gehrig was just about the best hitter in baseball, with the possible exception of Ruth. In 1927, his 47 home runs were more than any player in history besides Ruth, and he topped his teammate in average, hits, and RBIs. But until Ruth left the Yankees, Gehrig's colorless efficiency kept him in shadow. And even then it wasn't easy for him to step into the limelight. The day that Gehrig set a record by hitting four home runs in a single game was also the day that Giants manager John McGraw chose to announce his retirement, and that was the lead story the next day.

In 1938, as a young centerfielder named Joe DiMaggio was becoming a full-fledged hero in his own right, Gehrig's performance began to slip. When he showed up for spring training the following season, it was obvious that something was seriously wrong: Although just 35, and always in top physical condition, Gehrig moved like an old man, with shuffling feet and sluggish reflexes. He took himself out of the Yankee lineup after 2,130 consecutive games—a record that stood for 56 years—and checked into the Mayo Clinic. Doctors gave Gehrig just two years to live.

Worthy Words

Lou Gehrig's disease is the common name of amyotrophic lateral sclerosis, a progressive, fatal neuromuscular disorder that the Yankee star was diagnosed with in 1939 and died from in 1941.

On July 4, 1939, the Yankees held "Lou Gehrig Appreciation Day," and the man famous for not saying much delivered a heartbreaking farewell speech. "Fans, for the past two weeks you have been reading about a bad break I got," he told his former teammates and 62,000 onlookers, his voice echoing through the stadium. "Yet today I consider myself the luckiest man on the face of the earth." Less than two years later, Gehrig died, and the Yankees retired his number 4, the first man to be so honored.

Grace Under Pressure

Only a couple of years after Babe Ruth left baseball, Yankee fans caught a glimpse of the game's next great universal hero, the one who would supplant Lou Gehrig as the leader of the team and the sport. For two years, Joe DiMaggio had torn up the Pacific Coast League in San Francisco; and in 1936, the 21-year-old began to dominate the majors. He racked up breathtaking statistics, and his team was, of course, the best in the game.

But there was something different about "Joltin' Joe." He was shy, or maybe just snobbish, and was a dignified hero in the Christy Mathewson mold—the very picture of elegance and nobility. He spoke as little as possible, avoiding fans and controversy. In his off hours, he hobnobbed with celebrities in exclusive nightclubs, where his presence would be noticed but his fiercely guarded privacy would be respected.

DiMaggio won three Most Valuable Player awards, but his truly immortal moment came in 1941, when he began a consecutive-game hitting streak that obliterated all previous streaks, totaling 56 games with at least one hit. After being stopped by only a marvelous fielding performance by Cleveland third baseman Ken Keltner, he hit in another 16 straight.

Fearless Fact

In 1978, Pete Rose of the Cincinnati Reds made a serious run at Joe DiMaggio's record 56-game hitting streak, finally setting a National League mark with 44 straight games. Rose, nicknamed "Charlie Hustle," had long been a fan favorite for his aggressive play and relentless hitting, and most were happy when Rose finally topped Ty Cobb's record of 4,191 career hits. But he demolished any possibility that he would be considered a timeless baseball hero when, in 1989, he was permanently banned from the sport for betting on games—including those in which his team had played.

Even after his playing days ended, DiMaggio remained in American hearts and minds. It only added to his mystique when he married bombshell Marilyn Monroe three years after his retirement. They divorced after only nine months together, but he always remained close to her, and since her death he has had roses regularly delivered to her grave.

Forty-eight years after his 56-game streak, DiMaggio remains big news: His death on March 8, 1999, let loose an outpouring of national grief.

Heroic Shorts

It's immediately obvious that the lion's share of American baseball heroes played for the New York Yankees. Why so many great players from this one team? One reason is that, before every team had regular nationally televised games, the teams that played in New York—the media center of the country and the world—got news coverage. Also, Yankee Stadium, with 62,000 seats, was regularly filled with enthusiastic fans; in comparison, the 1935 St. Louis Browns drew a season total of 80,922 attendees. For stars in the 1950s, a decade during which the Yankees won 8 of 10 American League pennants, getting recognized was particularly difficult.

Superstars

They're the reason we watch, the reason we stay interested, the reason we care. Without the game's great stars, baseball becomes a blur of unfamiliar names, meaningless statistics, and repetitive action. These are the names you know—or, at the least, should know.

Look at Me—I Can Be Centerfield

Eventually, even the great Joe DiMaggio began to slip, and the Yankees were prepared, with a kid waiting to take over. His name was Mickey Mantle, and he was nothing like the smooth, polished Joltin' Joe; Mantle played with fire and exuberance, swinging the bat with abandon, even striking out in spectacular style. Mantle was a blond hick from Oklahoma who dazzled fans with blazing speed and prodigious home-run hitting from both sides of the plate. He racked up tremendous numbers that would have been far higher if he hadn't been plagued with injuries throughout his entire career.

Despite the Yankees' dominance (beginning in 1949, the team played in 14 World Series in 16 years), the other New York teams got plenty of attention too. As with the Yankees, the success of the Brooklyn Dodgers and New York Giants depended in large part on their charismatic centerfielders.

The Dodgers had the classy power hitter Duke Snider, who in 1955 led his team to its first-ever World Series victory—after seven ultimately fruitless pennant wins—by leading the league in RBIs and winning Sporting News Player of the Year honors. For the decade of the 1950s, Snider totaled far more homers and RBIs than either Mantle or Willie Mays, but it was his consistency that amazed. In the five seasons from 1953 to 1957, he hit between 40 and 43 home runs each year.

And the Giants had Mays, a marvelous hitter who quickly became a fan favorite for his pell-mell base running (his cap usually flew off as he rounded second base) and his outfield play. For balls hit in front of him, "the Say Hey Kid" used the "basket catch," snaring flies with a casual flick of the glove. He was able to run down pretty much anything else: His most famous catch, in the 1954 Series, was an impossible over-the-head grab made while running full-tilt toward the centerfield fence—after which he wheeled and made a perfect throw to the infield.

When Baseball Came Back

In 1994, a strike aborted the season and even killed the World Series for the first time in 90 years. Interest in the game began to wane for the first time in memory. With headlines about exorbitant salaries still fresh in our minds, we began to see players as greedy and spoiled. Even baseball-card values, which had reliably soared every year for more than a decade, sagged.

But it all came back in 1998, when we got to see sports heroes at their finest, as Sammy Sosa and Mark McGwire made people fall in love with baseball again. In their race to top the single-season home-run record—and each other—they set a marvelous example for how competitors can compete cheerfully, with dignity and respect for each other and for the game they're playing. Although McGwire ended up the victor, with 70 dingers, Sosa's 66 won him the league's MVP award.

And then there was Cal Ripken Jr. Of all baseball's records, a few, like Joe DiMaggio's hitting streak, are deemed unbreakable. Somehow, players find ways to surpass even those. At the top of the list expected to last forever was Lou Gehrig's streak of 2,130 consecutive games. And yet when, on Sept. 6, 1995, Ripken came out for his 2,131st straight game, it seemed only right. And he wasn't through: On June 14, 1996, Ripken even topped the world record for consecutive games, held by Japanese third baseman Sachio Kinugasa of the Hiroshima Carp, who played every Central League match from Oct. 19, 1970 to Oct. 22, 1987. Ripken didn't sit out a game until 1998, ending his streak at 2,632.

Of course, Ripken has been more than just tireless. He was twice named MVP, has played in 16 straight All-Star games (as of 1998), has hit more home runs than any shortstop in history, and holds or shares 11 major-league fielding records. But it's as an example of consistency and steadfastness that he's an American hero.

You Don't Own Me

Back in the 1880s, when pro baseball was just getting started, team owners devised a way to maintain control over their players. It was called the *reserve clause*, and it bound ballplayers for life to the team that originally signed them. Unless a team decided to trade, sell, or release a player, he was stuck. Unlike just about any other worker in the United States, players had no freedom to quit and work for someone else. And until Curt Flood decided in 1969 to challenge the reserve clause, no significant player had been willing to put his career on the line to take on the system.

Flood had spent a dozen years in the St. Louis Cardinals outfield, hitting .293 and winning seven Gold Glove awards for fielding excellence. After the 1969 season, the Cardinals traded him to the second-division Philadelphia Phillies, who offered him a more-than-respectable $100,000 for the next year. He refused to uproot his family, and filed suit against the league management and all 24 team owners, demanding the

Towering Tips

If you've ever wondered why some superstars stuck with one mediocre ballclub for their entire careers, look no further than the reserve clause for explanation. The players didn't necessarily stay on those teams because they liked the fans so much—they had no choice.

reserve system be abolished. He wrote to baseball commissioner Bowie Kuhn: "I do not feel that I am a piece of property to be bought and sold irrespective of my wishes."

He sat out a year while his case dragged on and went to the Supreme Court. He moved out of the country, and finally accepted an offer to play for the Washington Senators. But his skills had atrophied, and he quit baseball after just 13 games. The Supreme Court decided against Flood, 5-3, leaving the reserve clause in place. But the system was weakened by the challenge. A few years later, two players appealed to an arbiter to be made free agents; those players won, thereby killing the reserve clause. It probably wouldn't have happened as soon without Flood's fight. In giving up his career for the sake of principles and the greater good of players' rights, he proved himself one of baseball's true heroes.

In the Shadows

➤ Hank Aaron made it to two World Series with the Milwaukee Braves, but he never became the well-known icon that, say, Willie Mays did. He played 23 seasons and was so consistently excellent that he was simply taken for granted. Aaron's name will forever be linked with the number 755—the number of home runs he hit, the most ever, the only one to top Babe Ruth's 714.

Just because fans of the 1950s and 1960s didn't pay much attention to Aaron's superlative achievements is no reason why we shouldn't, however. He deserves to be celebrated far more than he is.

➤ The acknowledged team leader of the 1979 champion Pittsburgh Pirates was slugging first baseman Willie "Pops" Stargell, who, at 39, had a middling season at the plate. But the baseball establishment recognized that Stargell's worth went far beyond his statistics, and he shared the Most Valuable Player award—one of the rare times when great leadership has been recognized as a quality as important as home runs.

➤ Roberto Clemente was the Pittsburgh Pirates' resident phenomenon for 18 years, a savage hitter with an astonishing throwing arm. He won four batting titles and a dozen Gold Glove awards, yet got little attention from the New York- and California-based press. He got his chance when Pittsburgh finally got into a World Series in 1971. Clemente was the MVP, and the Pirates won the Series. On the last day of the 1972 season, he reached the magic 3,000-hit plateau. Ten weeks later, an earthquake devastated Nicaragua, and Clemente volunteered to take food and medical supplies to survivors. The plane crashed into the sea; his body was never found. The Hall of Fame waived the standard five-year waiting period and inducted Clemente immediately—making him the first Latino player in the Hall.

Over Hurdles

To succeed, some great figures had to fight against tall odds, face virulent opposition, or make a point to maintain their integrity. What's particularly impressive is that they not only overcame the obstacles but flourished, creating a vital legacy. They're not merely inspirations to those who face similar hurdles, they're also heroes to us all.

Separate but Equal

By the time Branch Rickey and Jackie Robinson teamed up to integrate major-league baseball, African Americans had been banned from the game for six decades. Back in 1887, white superstar Adrian "Cap" Anson had refused to play on the same field as black players, and that was all the excuse that organized baseball needed. At first the restriction was set in writing; in later years, it would be informal but equally as binding. African Americans were forced to form their own teams, which staged games and tournaments on an irregular basis, whenever managers could coordinate dates and rent a field.

Into the mishmash of shifting teams and competition came Andrew "Rube" Foster, a talented pitcher who played 15-odd years for various Chicago-based black teams. After retiring from the mound around 1915, Foster became manager of the Chicago American Giants and began lobbying other team managers to bring more organization to black baseball. So, with five other teams, Foster formed the Negro National Baseball League in 1920. Three years later, six more teams got together to form the Eastern Colored League. For the first time, black baseball had regular schedules, and for four years in the '20s even held a Negro World Series between the two leagues. Foster had created an important institution, and when he died in 1930, some 3,000 people attended his funeral.

Without Foster, black baseball floundered and didn't settle until the mid-30s, until W. A. "Gus" Greenlee, the "numbers king of Pittsburgh," reorganized the Negro National League and started an annual all-star game. A decade later, the Negro leagues were in full swing. Thousands of fans came out to see stars like Buck Leonard, Josh Gibson, and Satchel Paige. Though the players yearned to be matched against white baseball's best, and certainly playing conditions on the road were nothing like the major leagues' comparatively lush accommodations, black baseball was something to be proud of: a collection of successful black-owned businesses that gave crowds what they wanted.

So while we should certainly celebrate Jackie Robinson's breakthrough, and the major leagues' finally opening their doors to African Americans, it's important to remember that integration meant the death of the Negro Leagues. With their passing, in the early '50s, went decades of history and a meaningful link between players and fans that would never be regained.

Strong Beliefs

Hank Greenberg was hardly the first Jew to play major-league baseball, but he was the most prominent during a particularly dire time in history for Jews in America and, especially, in Europe. As anti-Semitism rose in the United States and Adolf Hitler's power grew in Germany, the sad-eyed Detroit Tigers first baseman became a sign of strength for Jews at home and abroad.

Greenberg began making heads turn in 1934, batting in 139 runs. (The then-notoriously bigoted *Sporting News* noted that there "was little suggestion of the Jewish characteristics in his appearance, the nose being straight.") For Jews, though, his finest achievement was something he didn't do: On September 19, although the Tigers were nearing the climax of a tight pennant race, Greenberg sat out the game; it was Yom Kippur, the holiest day of the year for Jews. Fortunately, the Tigers finished seven games ahead of the pack. Four years later, Greenberg showed his power by hitting 58 home runs, nearly equaling Babe Ruth's then-record of 60. "As time went by," he recalled, "I came to feel that if I, as a Jew, hit a home run I was hitting one against Hitler."

Worthy Words

A **gentleman's agreement** is another name for a pact that's secured not by a contract but by the honor of those participating. In the case of baseball, the club owners and league management quietly agreed not to hire black players. In the 1940s, it wasn't just African-Americans who were discriminated against: The 1947 film *Gentleman's Agreement* (based on a Laura Hobson novel) depicts people in high society excluding Jews while insisting that they don't.

Thirty-one years later, America had become far more tolerant of its citizens' differences, and Jews were slowly recovering confidence after the Holocaust, but it was still a meaningful gesture when Los Angeles Dodgers superstar Sandy Koufax refused to pitch the first game of the 1965 World Series, which was scheduled for Yom Kippur.

As a 19-year-old, Koufax drew a (for the times) huge signing bonus from the Los Angeles Dodgers and, for six years, showed a powerful arm but little control. In 1961, he realized that he didn't have to throw the ball as hard as he could each pitch—and, just like that, he had control. Over the five seasons to follow, he absolutely dominated baseball, pitching four no-hitters and posting a total 111-34 won-lost record. And then, after the 1966 season, he became the first baseball player to hang up his spikes at the peak of his career, announcing his retirement due to the unbearable pain in his pitching arm. In 1972, his first year of eligibility, Koufax followed Greenberg into the Baseball Hall of Fame—the first Jewish players to be so honored.

The First

The story of Jackie Robinson is one of the most familiar in all of sports; it's told and retold not only because it's a great tale of triumph over evil, but also because, well, it's a great story. The tale has two heroes, almost equal in stature: one white, one black; one older, one young. It begins with crusading Brooklyn Dodgers general manager Branch Rickey, who decided in 1945 that the time had come to integrate baseball—and that, by being the first to bring talented African Americans aboard his team, he could give the Dodgers an edge on the field. To begin his experiment, he picked a star Negro League player, Jackie Robinson, and offered him a spot on the Dodgers' top farm team—if the volatile infielder promised to "turn the other cheek" when facing racist abuse. Robinson agreed, led the AAA league in hitting, and came up to the Dodger club in 1947—the first black man to play major-league ball in the twentieth century.

He encountered immediate resistance from his new team. Several players signed a petition insisting that they would never play on the same field as an African American. Manager Leo Durocher rejected their bigotry in no uncertain terms, however, and Robinson took his place at first base. Spectators and opposing teams showered him with epithets, but he held his temper and pressed on.

Heroic Shorts

Less than three months after Jackie Robinson made his debut as a Brooklyn Dodger, 23-year-old Larry Doby pinch-hit for the Cleveland Indians, thus integrating baseball's American League. Like Robinson, Doby first met with resistance from teammates and abuse from fans, but won them over with stellar performance.

The Indians may have been integrated early on (in 1948, Doby and the legendary Satchel Paige helped the team to the World Series), but the American League was far slower to sign up black players than its National League counterpart. It cost the AL teams dearly: Not only did they deprive themselves of the Negro League's rich talent pool, but for years afterward black players gravitated toward the NL teams on which their heroes had starred.

And in short order, he changed the game of baseball for good. First of all, Robinson brought black fans to the ballpark—not only to Brooklyn's Ebbets Field, but to every stadium the Dodgers played in. (The ring of cash registers, more than issues of social justice, was key to ending segregation in baseball.) And second, Robinson showed white America a new way to play baseball. He sped up the pace, beating out bunts for hits and running the bases so aggressively that he often disrupted the pitcher's concentration (and the game).

At the season's end, Robinson won the first-ever Rookie of the Year award, and he had sparked Brooklyn to come within a game of winning its first World Series. Two years later, Robinson hit .342 and was the National League's MVP, leading Brooklyn to another pennant.

Over the next several years, the club owners one by one began to back out of their "gentleman's agreement" to keep African Americans out of the big leagues. Hank Aaron, Ernie Banks, Monte Irvin, and Don Newcombe all came up, along with Frank Robinson, Roy Campanella, and Willie Mays. Giving the lie to racists' insistence that black players couldn't make it in the pros, African Americans (beginning with Jackie Robinson's 1949 award) won 9 of 11 straight MVPs in the National League—at a time when only a relative handful were even in the big leagues!

Robinson, who had been a relatively old rookie at 27, retired a decade later, destined to be remembered as a hero not just of baseball but of America. Together, he and Branch Rickey had struck a resounding blow against segregation and racism.

Don't Call Him Handicapped

Of all the men who've had to overcome obstacles to succeed in sports, few have faced a handicap like pitcher Jim Abbott, who was born without a right hand.

As a boy, Abbott developed and perfected his glove transfer: He balances his glove on the end of his right arm as he delivers a pitch and then, as part of his follow-through, slips his left hand into his glove. He even learned how to hit with power when at the plate.

A high school superstar, Abbott performed brilliantly at the University of Michigan and for the United States national team, becoming the first baseball player ever to be given the Sullivan Award, honoring the nation's top amateur athlete. The California Angels signed him and sent him directly to the big leagues.

Fearless Fact

There's actually a bit of precedent for Jim Abbott's playing: during World War II, when many stars headed overseas and ballclubs were desperate for players, Pete Gray played outfield for the St. Louis Browns during the 1945 season. He hit just .218 in 77 games, an unimpressive record . . . except for the fact that Gray had no right arm! He fielded fly balls surprisingly effectively, however—catching the ball, quickly tucking his glove under the stump of his missing limb, and throwing it.

Against the pros, Abbott struggled somewhat his first two seasons before racking up a solid 18-11 record in 1991. After an uneven 1992, he headed to the New York Yankees, where he pitched two middling seasons, highlighted by a September 1993 no-hitter.

He left baseball after a disastrous 1996 season. But his story isn't over yet. In a come-back appearance against the unstoppable 1998 Yankees, his old team, Abbott put in six decent innings and won the game.

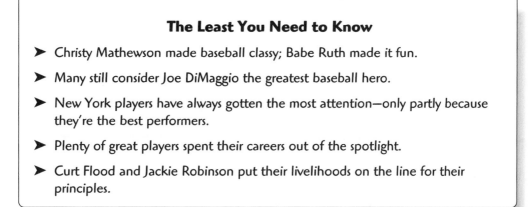

The Least You Need to Know

➤ Christy Mathewson made baseball classy; Babe Ruth made it fun.

➤ Many still consider Joe DiMaggio the greatest baseball hero.

➤ New York players have always gotten the most attention—only partly because they're the best performers.

➤ Plenty of great players spent their careers out of the spotlight.

➤ Curt Flood and Jackie Robinson put their livelihoods on the line for their principles.

Chapter 26

On the Ball

In This Chapter

➤ Gridiron giants

➤ Through the hoop

Sports heroes show us competition at its best. In life, we all fail, deal with unfairness, and occasionally win—but we don't do it in front of millions of people. The magnifying glass of the fans and the press is what makes athletes' achievements larger than life. But almost none of us go through life alone, which is why team sports serve as a metaphor for the way we live.

Behind the Masks

Football has almost as much claim on being America's national game as baseball does; it's been played professionally almost as long, and its TV audiences routinely top those for baseball games. So why has the sport produced fewer heroes? Several reasons:

➤ Careers are shorter (on average, just three and a half years), leaving fewer players with long, stellar records of consistent stardom.

➤ Americans have always been taken with rags-to-riches narratives, with stories of players making it from the fields (or the projects) straight to the big time. In football, as in basketball, the vast majority of players graduated from college, so only very rarely do players become instant stars "out of nowhere," from Midwest farms or urban ghettos.

> ➤ More than anything, it's that players' personalities are buried underneath layers of padding and equipment—and that football is far more of a team sport than baseball, in that any one performer is utterly impotent without the cooperation of his teammates. There's no equivalent of the home run in football, or of the no-hitter.

But as in baseball, there's often that one big play that changes the game, the play that dashes the hopes of half the fans and brings a cheer to the throats of the other half. Football history is packed with thrilling finishes, come-from-behind rallies, once-in-a-lifetime receptions and interceptions, and game-breaking runs and returns—often in weather so bad that everything shuts down except the game.

Here Comes the Red

In the mid-1920s, America was in love with sports, and Harold "Red" Grange ruled football—college football, that is. Playing for the University of Illinois, Grange was America's most famous player. Sportswriter Grantland Rice nicknamed him "the Galloping Ghost" and picked him for his All-America team three consecutive years. In one 1924 game, against Michigan State (which was on a 20-game winning streak), Grange returned the opening kickoff 95 yards for a touchdown, and then turned three more long runs into touchdowns—in the next 12 minutes. Later in the game, he scored again and even passed for a sixth touchdown.

Fearless Fact

Arguably, no man has had as much impact on the game of football as Chicago Bears coach George Halas. After founding the Bears in 1920, Halas made his team into a winner by scouting far and wide for players and holding the first daily practice sessions. He was an architect of league rules, and even of how the league divisions were arranged. His career spanned the decades between Red Grange (whom he signed) and Walter Payton (whom he drafted). He **was** pro football.

In 1925, when pro football was struggling to attract fans and attention, the Chicago Bears signed Grange to a contract, and he led the team on a 19-game, two-month tour of American arenas, bringing football to cities that had never seen pro games. *Sports Illustrated* later called the tour "the 66 days that made pro football." And Grange continued to star as a professional: He was a cornerstone of the championship Bears of 1932 and 1933.

Winning Isn't Everything

Vince Lombardi is one of the only coaches in sports history to overshadow his players. When people think of the Green Bay Packers of the 1960s, the powerhouse team that captured the first two Super Bowls, it's Lombardi's name that usually first comes to mind rather than running backs Jim Taylor or Paul Hornung, or even quarterback Bart Starr.

Fearless Fact

Every city fortunate enough to have a resident NFL franchise would argue that its fans are more passionate and loyal than any other's. But that honor truly belongs to the supporters of the Green Bay Packers—they actually own the team. In 1923, to stem a financial crisis, the team was formally incorporated; stockholders paid $25 a share and were required to purchase six season tickets.

Lombardi spent nine years at the Packers' helm. The season before his arrival, the squad won just 1 game of the 12-game season; two years later, he got the team into the NFL championship game. The following season, 1961, Green Bay crushed the New York Giants 37-0 in the championship—the first of five that Lombardi would lead his team to.

In early 1968, Lombardi stepped down to become general manager of the Packers and, the next year, took over the head-coach spot of the Washington Redskins. But after one season, in 1970, he fell ill and died of cancer. Before that year's Super Bowl, the silver championship award was officially named the Vince Lombardi Trophy.

If anything, Lombardi has become more famous in the decades since his death: His inspirational, take-no-prisoners aphorisms are frequently quoted by businesspeople to rally the troops. A few examples:

➤ "It's not whether you get knocked down, it's whether you get up."

Towering Tips

Although the aphorism "Winning isn't everything—it's the only thing" is usually attributed to 1960s Packers coach Vince Lombardi, he never said it. His actual quote was, "Winning isn't everything, but wanting to win is." Who really uttered the famous "only thing" phrase? College coach Red Smith.

➤ "Football is a great deal like life in that it teaches that work, sacrifice, perseverance, competitive drive, selflessness, and respect for authority is the price each and every one of us must pay to achieve any goal that is worthwhile."

➤ "If you'll not settle for anything less than your best, you will be amazed at what you can accomplish in your lives."

➤ "I firmly believe that any man's finest hour, the greatest fulfillment of all that he holds dear, is that moment when he has worked his heart out in a good cause and lies exhausted on the field of battle victorious."

Got Your Backfield

Jim Brown had played just nine seasons when, in the middle of filming *The Dirty Dozen* in London, he abruptly called a press conference to announce his retirement from football. The proclamation stunned the football world—after all, Brown was only 30 and was at the top of his game, the greatest running back in history. The previous season he had scored 17 touchdowns, won his third MVP award, and scored three touchdowns in the postseason Pro Bowl. He had added to his career-rushing yardage—already the most in history.

But Brown wanted to make a bigger difference in the world than adding to his records and making more films (although he's found time to act in nearly two dozen of them). In the years since leaving football, he's worked tirelessly to help inner-city youths, attempting to break up gangs and make black communities self-sufficient. His Amer-I-CAN program operates on the front lines, advocating education. "I was no role model," he told a group of Clevelanders waiting in line for autographs a few years back. "I was just a football player. The greatest tool that God gave me was my mind."

Brown set rushing records so high that it took an unusually talented and determined running back to break them. It took Walter Payton. Nicknamed "Sweetness," Payton spent his career with mediocre Chicago Bears teams; he didn't get into a Super Bowl until his twelfth season and therefore played largely out of the spotlight. In one game, Payton gained a still-record 275 rushing yards, and the Bears won the match only 10-7. But the world took notice when the compact (5'10", 202 pounds) halfback broke Jim Brown's career record for rushing yardage (and kept going). In his 13 seasons, during which he missed just one game, Payton gained a total of 16,726 yards

Heroic Shorts

Although he made it to the NFL Hall of Fame for his seven brilliant seasons, Chicago Bears halfback Gale Sayers will live forever in football fans' minds for another reason as well: his rivalry and friendship with Brian Piccolo, a teammate who slowly succumbed to cancer. Sayers memorialized Piccolo in his autobiography *I Am Third*, which was adapted into a well-received TV movie that was produced (starring Billy Dee Williams as Sayers and James Caan as Piccolo) in 1971, called *Brian's Song*.

rushing. He retired holding eight NFL and 27 Bears records, leaving memories of one of the best all-around players in football history. (He even threw eight touchdown passes!) And fans recalled a diligent, determined, classy athlete seemingly immune to the pitfalls of ego. "I'm not a role model. I'm just Walter Payton," he said, echoing Brown's sentiments. "If kids see some good in me they can utilize and emulate and make their lives better, so well and so good. But they have to realize I'm human just like anybody else. I'm capable of making mistakes."

See You Next Year

College football players come and go, but coaches are forever—or at least that's the way it seems sometime. The greatest of all, Paul W. "Bear" Bryant, came to the University of Alabama to helm the Crimson Tide in 1958. He retired a quarter-century later the winningest coach in major college-football history.

Bryant—who won his nickname by wrestling a bear—was an all-Arkansas player in high school and played for Alabama, taking on an assistant-coaching position after graduating in 1935. After stints at Maryland, Kentucky, and Texas A&M (he took the teams at the last two to conference titles), he returned to Alabama and turned the football program into a powerhouse, producing the nation's top-ranked team year after year. His teams won national championships in 1961, 1964, 1965, 1973, 1978, and 1979, and Alabama was selected to play in 24 bowl games in Bryant's 25 years. "Bear" retired in 1982 with a lifetime record of 323 wins, 85 losses, and 17 ties—the best record in college football history.

Heroic Shorts

Considering the months when the NFL holds its season, perhaps the sport's true heroes are the fans who turn out for the games in all weather. In the epic Green Bay match on the last day of 1967, when the Packers met the Dallas Cowboys on a day that the Wisconsin temperature dropped to −13°, the field's 750,000-volt heating-coil system died, leaving the playing surface frozen solid. It came down to a tough decision: With 16 seconds remaining on the game clock, trailing by three points, and Green Bay on the two-foot line, coach Vince Lombardi called for a touchdown attempt rather than a near-certain field goal that would have tied the match and sent it into overtime. Quarterback Bart Starr sneaked across the goal line, and the final score was 21-17.

"I was thinking of the fans," Vince Lombardi said later. "I couldn't stand to think of them sitting in those cold stands for an overtime period."

Nothing but Sky

Joe Montana of the San Francisco 49ers is revered not only because he was perhaps the greatest quarterback of all, but because he was so good for so long: Montana was football's leading passer in 1981, 1984, 1985, 1987, and 1989. When Montana joined them, the team had run up a 2-14 record for the second straight season. In his third year (his first full one as a starter), he took the team to a 13-3 mark (the best in team history) and an eventual Super Bowl victory.

Three years later, the 49ers had developed into a dynasty in the making, winning 15 games against just one loss. In Super Bowl XIX, Montana was matched against Miami's Dan Marino, who had just set season records for yardage and touchdowns, and won with an MVP performance, leading San Francisco to a 38-16 victory. And in 1989, Montana racked up possibly the best season ever by a quarterback, setting a record for QB rating and leading the 49ers to a 55-10 Super Bowl blowout.

Fearless Fact

49ers quarterback Joe Montana (and his successor, Steve Young) had help in his quest for passing records and Super Bowl victories: wide receiver Jerry Rice, who owns more records than anyone in NFL history, including career receptions, touchdowns, yardage, consecutive games with a reception, season yardage, as well as most of the Super Bowl receiving records.

But the three Super Bowl MVP awards and sky-high QB ratings won't live as long in fans' memories as Montana's finest moment: what's come to be known as "The Drive." In Super Bowl XXIII, the 49ers were behind 16-13 with just over three minutes remaining on the game clock—and 92 yards to go to the Cincinnati goal line. In a dozen plays, under unbelievable pressure, Montana methodically moved his offense down the field, passing nine times (eight of them completions). The last one, with less than 40 seconds on the clock, was a game-winning touchdown pass.

Fearless Fact

Three days before Superbowl III, brash New York Jets quarterback Joe Namath made a public promise: "I think we'll win it; in fact, I'll guarantee it." Most people snickered: The Jets, representing the upstart American Football League, were 18-point underdogs against the Baltimore Colts. But Namath made good, leading his young team to a 16-7 win. That January 1969 game was enough to secure the quarterback a place in football history.

On Top of the Heap

John Elway is one of football's best-known and most likable figures, with a stupendous throwing arm and an infectious smile, and sportswriters took the Denver Broncos' back-to-back Super Bowl victories in 1998 and 1999 as a chance to laud Elway as a great quarterback, even "the game's greatest quarterback." He's not, of course—his career QB rating is 26th on the all-time list, and his achievements don't come close to those of Johnny Unitas, Bart Starr, Joe Montana, Sammy Baugh, Steve Young, or even Dan Marino. But certainly Elway is a genuine hero to many (particularly Denver fans), and a symbol of triumph, of coming back from defeat. And that should be enough for anyone.

Follow the Bouncing Ball

A basketball court is smaller than most sporting arenas, and there's no plastic sheet, as in hockey, protecting fans from flying balls, bodies, and blood. The players wear less than those in other sports, too, and since many of them are giants (so to speak), there's more of them exposed: skin, sweat, elbows, tongues (in Michael Jordan's case). All this gives basketball fans a feeling of closeness: These guys are right there. Their on-the-court feats of athleticism are undisguised, and the best players deserve the adulation they're given.

The Tall Guy

George Mikan is one of those rare sports figures who was so dominating that rules were introduced specifically to cut down his advantage. In 1944, Mikan, a 6'10" center at DePaul University, made a practice of standing beneath the DePaul basket and batting away opponents' shots, and the NCAA was forced to ban "goaltending." It didn't even slow him down: He was a three-time All-American and led the nation in 1945 and 1946. In a game against Rhode Island State, he scored 53 points—more than the entire RI team.

In the pros, he led his teams to championships (before the NBA became the one professional basketball league) seven of his eight years in the game. With the Minneapolis Lakers, he led the NBA in scoring four times and rebounding twice, and played in the league's first four All-Star Games. When the Associated Press polled members, George Mikan was voted far and away the greatest basketball player of the first half-century.

Hey Coach!

In 1960, the Boston Celtics put on the court a starting five who would all end up in the Hall of Fame. In fact, three players who weren't even good enough to be in the starting lineup would one day be enshrined as well. (Imagine a baseball team in which every one of the eight starting players was a future Hall-of-Famer!) Small wonder that the Celtics were practically unbeatable: The team won eight straight NBA championships between 1959 and 1966, a string never equaled by any team in any sport, professional or amateur.

With so much playing talent, how important was the coach? Crucial. Arnold "Red" Auerbach was responsible not only for assembling the ingredients for the team's dominance but for combining those ingredients in the ideal way.

When given Bob Cousy, a ball-handler and passer such as basketball had never seen, Auerbach developed a fast-break offense that sped up the game and made it infinitely more exciting. (It's tough to imagine a time when there was no such thing as the fast break, but there was—for decades.) When the coach got defensive genius Bill Russell on the squad, he worked up an aggressive team defense that shut down the opposition. And when he finally decided to retire to become the Celtics' general manager, he chose Russell to succeed him—a controversial choice that proved brilliant.

Fearless Fact

Women's basketball may have gone professional only in the last couple of years, but amateur players have thrilled fans for decades. The standout: Nera White, who was named the sport's MVP 10 times by the Amateur Athletic Union between 1955 and 1969. In 1957–1958, she led the U.S. team to the World Basketball Championship in Rio de Janeiro, where she earned another MVP award.

Big D

Bill Russell's lifetime per-game scoring average was just half of that of Wilt Chamberlain, his chief rival—yet he's generally considered to have been the greater player. It's a tribute to Russell's awesome defensive skills and to his on-the-court leadership ability. (It didn't hurt that, in head-to-head matchups, Russell usually shut down his larger opponent.)

Russell rose to fame from an unusually inauspicious start: He didn't make his high school team as a sophomore and never scored more than 14 points a game as a senior. But at the University of San Francisco, he became a defensive star and team leader, guiding USF to two national championships and 60 consecutive wins his last two years. On the 1956 Olympic team, he led the U.S. team to gold-medal victory. With the Boston Celtics, he led the team to 11 championships in 13 years, including an unprecedented eight consecutive titles.

Russell's main contribution to the game was to show how a superior defense can be almost as exciting to watch as a great offense—and how the best player isn't necessarily the one who racks up the highest numbers. His teammates and opponents evidently agreed: Russell won five MVP awards.

Fearless Fact

Talk about life after basketball! Bill Bradley helped the United States win an Olympic gold medal in 1965, was the No. 1 pick in the entire draft that year, became a key player on the great 1970s New York Knicks, and was named to the NBA Hall of Fame. And then he retired, ran for the U.S. Senate, became a highly respected statesman—and is campaigning for the presidency in 2000.

Throughout his championship years, Bill Russell's chief rival was Wilt "The Stilt" Chamberlain, a player so dominating that, while at the University of Kentucky, he prompted a rule change on inbound passes—his 7-foot-1 height and leaping ability gave him too much of an advantage.

Playing with professionals, Chamberlain was just as impressive, leading the NBA in scoring his first seven seasons and making the slam-dunk famous. During the 1961–1962 season, he averaged 50.4 points a game. (By way of comparison, Michael Jordan's highest average was 37.1.) On March 2, 1962, against the New York Knicks, Chamberlain scored 100 points, 27 more than any other player has ever scored in a game. The Philadelphia center also led the league in rebounding 10 times and set a record with 55 rebounds in a single 1960 match.

Incidentally, when Chamberlain's second autobiography, *A View From Above*, was published in 1991, he became famous for yet another astonishing statistic: the number of sexual partners he's had. Although he hasn't kept precise figures, he said, he's slept with close to 20,000 different women. In the book, he hastened to explain that, as far as he knew, all 20,000 were single at the time—after all, he believes in the sanctity of marriage. No kidding.

Fearless Fact

For nine straight years, Oscar Robertson was named first-team All-NBA; he ended his career holding records for lifetime assists and scoring average for a guard. But "the Big O" helped change basketball even more off the court: In 1970, he filed a class-action suit on behalf of NBA players that led, in 1975, to the abolishment of "the option clause" and a revision of the college draft. No longer would a player be bound to a single team for life.

Reach for the Sky

Combing the defensive skills of Bill Russell and the offensive power of Wilt Chamberlain, Kareem Abdul-Jabbar was so good for so long that he seemed to have always been the NBA's dominant center. As a teenager, Lew Alcindor (he changed his name in 1971 for religious reasons) led his New York City team to 71 straight victories. In three years on the UCLA varsity, he took the team to an 88-2 record, bringing home three consecutive NCAA championships. He was even named MVP of the NCAA tournament all three years!

He bagged a record total of six MVP awards, and got to play on another basketball dynasty when the Lakers drafted Earvin "Magic" Johnson in 1979.

Abdul-Jabbar's tremendous defensive skills got him named to the NBA's All-Defensive Team 11 times, and *Sports Illustrated* found 28 opportunities to put him on the cover during his 20-season career. When he finally retired, in 1989, he owned career records for games and minutes played, points scored, and blocked shots, as well as for all-time leading playoff scoring.

In addition to writing two autobiographies, Abdul-Jabbar authored a 1996 volume titled *Profiles in Black Courage*, intended to teach schoolchildren about heroic African-Americans in U.S. history. "Who are kids' heroes today? What lessons do they have to teach?" Abdul-Jabbar asked in February 1998. "When

Towering Tips

You can catch Kareem Abdul-Jabbar in a small but hilarious role in the 1980 comedy *Airplane!,* in which he pokes fun at his image as one of America's most recognizable celebrities. The basketball Hall of Famer has had parts in seven other films, including *Game of Death* (he studied martial arts with Bruce Lee for years), *Fletch, Troop Beverly Hills,* and *Slam Dunk Ernest*—impressive largely because there aren't many casting opportunities for seven-footers!

I asked this of kids, I was not surprised to learn that their heroes were mainly high-profile athletes and entertainers. Virtually none I spoke to knew anything about African-Americans of other eras or the history of our people in this country." It's a tremendous credit to the man that he recognizes the limitations of holding up athletes as our most important heroes.

Magic Tricks

The NBA had produced plenty of topnotch players and exciting games, but basketball didn't catch on with most American sports viewers until two players arrived on the scene to add a burst of excitement. The friendly rivalry between the Lakers' Earvin "Magic" Johnson and the Celtics' Larry Bird drew thousands of new fans, and the league capitalized on the players' star value.

As a college sophomore, Johnson led Michigan State to the NCAA championship (beating Larry Bird's Indiana State team), and he skipped the last two years of school to enter the NBA draft, in which he was the top pick overall. Once on the Los Angeles Lakers, Johnson shone, and the team—anchored by Kareem Abdul-Jabbar—became a powerhouse, winning the NBA championship his rookie season and four more times in the next eight years. Johnson's brilliant passing and fine shooting won him three MVP awards and nine straight All-NBA First Team nominations.

But it was Magic's boyish exuberance that made him an idol—his wide smile brought real joy to the game, and he became a household name even among non-viewers. When he abruptly retired in 1991, announcing that he had the AIDS virus and would devote his life to helping stop the spread of the disease, he was the recipient of a widespread outpouring of goodwill.

Fearless Fact

Before there was "Air Jordan," Julius Erving ruled the skies. Nicknamed "Dr. J" while a college star, he played a flamboyant, aggressive game, leaping high and seeming to float; as an offensive force, he was virtually unstoppable. He ended his 16-year career (including five years in the American Basketball Association) first in career steals, third in points—and first in memorable nicknames.

Johnson had a great debut season, but he didn't win Rookie of the Year honors, because Larry Bird chose that same year to enter the NBA. The Celtics had fallen since the Bill Russell days, sinking to a 29-53 record in the 1978-1979 season. The next year, Bird's first, he led a dramatic turnaround, taking the Boston squad to a 61-21 mark and leading the team in scoring, rebounding, steals, and minutes played. The next season, the Celtics won the NBA championship.

Over the seasons to come, Bird became known throughout the country for dramatic, hustling, clutch play—he was a great passer and scorer, capable of taking over a game by himself, a leader who inspired his teammates to excel. The league took notice in a big way: Bird was twice runner-up for the MVP award before winning it three consecutive times. In 1985–1986, he led the Celtics to a 67-15 record and the championship, and he was deluged with honors: league MVP, MVP of the finals, *Sporting News* Man of the Year, and the Associated Press Male Athlete of the Year. Bird retired in 1992, hobbled by back injuries, but he left an indelible mark on the sport and remains one of basketball's most celebrated figures.

The Air Up There

Is Michael Jordan the greatest player in NBA history? It's an easy case to make: five times MVP, eight times All-NBA Defensive First Team, the highest career-scoring average, and leader of the fabulous Chicago Bulls, champions each of Jordan's last six seasons. And unlike Wilt Chamberlain, who similarly dominated the NBA in his early career but for years couldn't get his team to a championship, Jordan has always rushed to give credit to his coach, teammates, and competitors; only rarely was he accused of hot-dogging at the expense of his team.

But Jordan's value exceeds his leadership of the Bulls—for his 13 seasons, he was basketball's key marquee player, picking up where Magic Johnson and Larry Bird left off. His soaring style of play influenced an entire generation of up-and-comers on schoolyards and NBA courts alike. Attendance and TV ratings leaped when Jordan was playing; he kept interest in the game going even when fans of other sports were being turned off by high salaries and bratty behavior.

Fearless Fact

In the era of Magic Johnson and Larry Bird, Cheryl Miller of the University of Southern California managed to make headlines of her own. In 1986, *Sports Illustrated* named her the best player—male or female—in college basketball, and she became the first college basketball player to be named a *Parade* All-America four straight years.

One sign of Jordan's charisma is that most Americans haven't tired of seeing his friendly face—his shaved head and earring instantly recognizable—despite its ubiquitous presence on TV screens and billboards. Certainly he's spent more time on television than any other player, both as competitor and corporate pitchman—most prominently for Nike, which has emblazoned Jordan's image on every blank public surface in the United States. Dozens of fans around the world with time on their hands have added to the saturation by putting up Web sites with photos and tributes to their hero.

The Least You Need to Know

➤ Before Red Grange, the only football America cared about was collegiate.

➤ Footballers like Jim Brown and Walter Payton broke records with their skills and tried to help others with their minds.

➤ Bill Russell deserves credit for making basketball defense fun.

➤ Magic Johnson, Larry Bird, and Michael Jordan are the reason why basketball is all the rage.

Chapter 27

Going It Alone

In This Chapter

➤ Tennis champions

➤ Kings of clubs

➤ Heroes of the ring

➤ On the track

In most individual sports—like boxing, golf, and tennis—the stars are competing for themselves, not for some larger goal or team. They have no one but themselves to catch them when they falter or to bolster their flagging spirits. When these athletes win matches, their victories are personal. Some competitors bring glory not just upon themselves but upon their sport and their country. For that, we recognize them as real heroes.

Aces

Before World War I, American sports fans didn't care much for tennis. It was seen as a game for effete bluebloods and polite, stuffy Europeans. Until 1920, when a new hero began to dominate the game, most people viewed tennis as a leisure sport completely alien to their workaday lives. Now, of course, it's played casually by millions of Americans—and at a world-class level by a very few.

A Real Man

During the 1920s, a decade that would become known as the Golden Age of Sport, tennis had a superstar to rival baseball's Babe Ruth and boxing's Jack Dempsey. "Big Bill" Tilden didn't win his first U.S. championship until 1920, at the advanced age of 27. Once he started winning, however, he didn't stop, capturing six national singles championships in a row.

But more than simply taking home a lot of trophies, Tilden had a huge impact on the game in two ways:

➤ Tilden was an extraordinary student of tennis, making it a science; and his efforts paid off in his books about the game, which taught the fundamentals of winning tennis to any number of players who followed him.

➤ Tilden's outsized personality (although always gentlemanly, he was explosive and flamboyant on and off the court) brought drama and masculinity to tennis. Sometimes Tilden would actually lose the first two sets of a match so that he could come back and win as an underdog! Tilden inspired "red-blooded" American he-men to take an interest in tennis tournaments. (Ironically, if the 1920s' public had known of Tilden's long-concealed homosexuality, they might have felt differently about him.)

In 1949, the Associated Press asked sportswriters to rank the best athlete of the first half of the century. Tilden received more than twice the votes of anyone else, including Babe Ruth.

The Match to End All Matches

In 1937, after spending the winter studying the game (particularly his backhand), American tennis star Don Budge was well-nigh invincible, winning nearly every match he competed in. He was even given the coveted Sullivan Award, bestowed upon the country's outstanding amateur athlete. No other tennis player before or since has won the award.

On July 30, 1937, Budge won what is still considered history's greatest match, and in the process secured his place as a hero of the sport and of the nation. He was paired against a close friend, Germany's Baron Gottfried von Cramm, the world's No. 2–ranked player, behind Budge. To heighten the drama, the event was the finals of the Davis Cup—then the most prestigious tournament in tennis—and the match was played on Wimbledon's hallowed Center Court. Britain's Queen Mary attended. So many Americans tuned in via radio that stock-market sales slumped during the game.

To add a last bit of tension, just before the start of play, Cramm got a good-luck call from none other than Adolf Hitler—although the German player was no fan of the Nazis.

The two battled back and forth, breaking each other's serve. Cramm held on to win the first set 8-6, and the edged ahead in the next. Cramm took the second set 6-5, leaving the American one set away from losing the match and his No. 1 ranking.

Budge eked out a 6-4 victory in the third set. Cramm fell behind in the fourth set and eventually dropped it. In the final game of the fifth set, Budge managed to take the set 8-6 after the two had rallied, switching leads and stretching the game out to a total of 18 points. Budge served for match point, and after trading several shots, he hit a return on a dead run, crashed down on the sidelines—and looked up to see the ball just catch the corner of Cramm's court.

At the net, Cramm told Budge, "This was absolutely the finest match I have ever played in my life. I'm very happy that I could have played it against you, whom I like so much. Congratulations." Then the two threw their arms around each other to conclude the epic contest—after which Budge brought the Davis Cup back to America for the first time since 1927. (For a thrilling play-by-play account of the match, look up Budge's 1969 autobiography, *A Tennis Memoir*.)

Fearless Facts

Between 1909 and 1943, Hazel Hotchkiss Wightman won a total of 43 national championships in singles and doubles, but her greatest significance was in her role as the "Queen Mother of American tennis," as she was once dubbed. Wightman introduced to the game a new, aggressive style of women's play, and she personally coached dozens of up-and-comers who went on to be the best women players of the 1940s and 1950s.

Winning a Place

Tennis is one sport in which women's competition draws as much attention as men's does. If female champions still can't quite keep up with the sheer power of the top men in tennis, they're clearly great athletes regardless—and are often more fun to watch. Of all the best players of the last half century, a handful stand out:

➤ At age 15, only a year or so after she first picked up a tennis racket, Althea Gibson won the New York State black girls' singles tennis championship, and spent the next eight years working toward earning an invitation to the U.S. Tennis Championship at Forest Hills, New York. The club had hosted the annual match for 35 years before blacks were permitted to play there. Finally, grudgingly, Gibson was invited in 1950 and made headlines by nearly beating defending champion Louise Brough. Seven years later, she hit the big time, capturing the women's singles title at Wimbledon (as the first African-American to play there), the U.S. Women's Clay-Court singles title, and the U.S. Open; the Associated Press named her Woman Athlete of the Year. New York gave her a ticker-tape parade, and Mayor Robert Wagner told her, "If we had more women like you, the world would be a better place." The next year, Gibson repeated as Wimbledon and national champion—and then, since tennis championships then offered glory but little money, she retired.

➤ Today, Billie Jean King is best known for her highly publicized "Battle of the Sexes" match, but she was the world's best women's tennis player for an entire decade beginning in 1966. Winning headlines for her aggressive play as well as her outspoken advocacy of women's equal treatment in tennis, she captured a half dozen Wimbledon titles, along with four U.S. Opens. In 1975, after winning Wimbledon, she retired from singles competition—prematurely, she later decided regretfully—although she continued to play doubles, winning the Wimbledon title an incredible 10 times! Today she coaches the U.S. Federation Cup team, plays on the Virginia Slims Legends Tour, owns a World Team Tennis franchise, and recently began a foundation to promote equal opportunity outside sports.

➤ Through both her genial personality and her phenomenal play, Chris Evert helped turn women's tennis into the popular TV sport it is today. In a 10-year stretch, Evert played in nine U.S. Open finals, winning six of them, along with seven French Opens and three Wimbledon titles. Demonstrating the same charisma that has made her a successful broadcast commentator, she became a crowd favorite and later a worldwide celebrity: A 1991 poll found her the nation's best-known athlete, male or female. Doubtless, though, she'd prefer to be remembered less for her 1980s popularity than for being the first player to win 1,000 singles matches and for finishing her career with a .900 winning percentage, the highest in pro tennis history.

➤ At the U.S. Open, shortly before her nineteenth birthday, Martina Navratilova defected to the United States from Czechoslovakia because of that government's manipulation of her tennis career. It took several more years for her to vie for the No. 1 position, and she won her first Wimbledon singles championship against Chris Evert—ironically, her frequent doubles partner. Navratilova became a U.S. citizen in 1981 and celebrated by winning six straight Wimbledons, along with nine other Grand Slam tournaments. Her last big win was at Wimbledon in 1990, although by then the determined star got as much attention for her never-denied homosexuality as for her play—and became a role model in the gay community as well the athletic.

Battle of the Sexes

Bobby Riggs was out to stir up trouble. In 1973, the sexual revolution was in full swing and Women's Lib was a hot topic. Riggs, a tennis champion back in 1939 and since then the self-proclaimed "king of male chauvinist pigs," publicly challenged America's top women players to a match. He insisted that he—although two decades past his prime—could beat any woman on the court, and thus prove male superiority.

At first, the 55-year-old Riggs looked as though he had made his case: He took on and badly beat No. 1–ranked Margaret Court, 6-2 and 6-1. He set about goading his next victim, 29-year-old Billie Jean King, into another match. The result was the most famous match in tennis history.

King had long been an unofficial spokeswoman for women's tennis. In 1970, at a time when tournaments routinely awarded women winners far less prize money than men, she and other top competitors rebelled by simply refusing to play. King helped organize a separate women-only tournament, sponsored by Virginia Slims; that tournament continues to this day. The following year, she and other women players brought signs demanding "Women's Liberation" to the Wimbledon tournament.

On September 20, 1973, 30,000 onlookers (still a record) piled into the Houston Astrodome, including scores of men wearing T-shirts declaring, "I am a male chauvinist pig." An estimated 40 million TV viewers watched. Going along with the media-driven circus atmosphere, King was carried into the stadium on an Egyptian litter borne by bare-chested men; Riggs arrived in a rickshaw pulled by scantily clad women. She presented him with a small pig, while he gave her a giant lollipop.

Then "The Battle of the Sexes" began, with King a 5-2 underdog. "As I sat in the locker room waiting to vomit," she told *Newsweek* on the event's 25th anniversary, "I kept thinking this was not about a tennis match, this was about social change. I had to win."

Indeed she did, in straight sets: 6-4, 6-3, 6-3.

The Brats

For more than a decade in the '70s and '80s, Jimmy Connors and John McEnroe were far and away the best American tennis players; along with women like Chris Evert and Martina Navratilova, they helped make tennis a popular, glamorous sport and inspired any number of schoolkids to pick up the sport. McEnroe in particular ranks among history's greatest players.

But they hardly deserve to be called heroes. While Connors and McEnroe set new standards for ability and on-the-court performance, they dragged down the genteel game with shocking displays of disrespect and out-and-out rudeness, including screaming and flinging their racquets when unhappy about a linesman's call.

For examples of their petulance and foul-mouthed abusiveness toward referees, fans and opposing players, you'll have to look elsewhere—few of their incivilities are fit to be printed here. Connors deserves special mention for introducing to the game both the loud grunt and the practice of interminably bouncing the ball before serving.

No one ever said that sports stars have to be saints—if they were, the world of athletics would be a lot duller than it is. But we also don't have to honor those who dishonor their sports—and themselves.

Fearless Facts

Arthur Ashe had been an outstanding tennis player in his day, the first African American to be named to the Davis Cup team and the first black man to take titles at the U.S. Open, Australian Open, and at Wimbledon. But his life took on larger significance in 1992, when he went public with the fact that he had AIDS, enduring his misfortune with the same gentlemanly dignity and grace he had shown as a player. For the strength of his character, Ashe was named 1992 Sportsman of the Year by *Sports Illustrated* (less than a year before he died).

Beginning of a New Era

Affable, articulate, and astonishingly talented, Pete Sampras makes an appealing role model. His aggressive, serve-and-volley style of play keeps viewers glued to the set, and his upbeat manner has helped bring to a welcome end the "roughneck era" of men's tennis—exemplified, among American players, by the crudeness of John McEnroe and Jimmy Connors.

At 19, Sampras was the youngest player ever to win the U.S. Open, and the next year he helped the U.S. Davis Cup team win that championship, leading a wave of young American stars to begin to dominate men's tennis. In 1993, Sampras slammed more than 1,000 aces—the most ever in a single season—on the way to winning Wimbledon and the U.S. Open. Early the next year, he took the Australian Open, making him the first player in a quarter century to win three Grand Slam tournaments in a row. After winning his fifth Wimbledon title, he ended the 1998 season ranked No. 1, the sixth straight year—a streak unmatched by anyone in tennis history.

Hot Links

Golf is a sport that almost anyone can—and sometimes it seems as though everybody does—play (not well, necessarily, but play). But the fact that so many Americans are golf-course weekend warriors only makes us appreciate the top pros more: It's not as easy as it looks! (Most casual golfers seem to have enough trouble just finding matching outfits to wear on the course.)

Although golf was invented in the British Isles in the fifteenth century, it didn't make its way to our shores until 1887. Even then, we didn't get a real golf hero until the 1920s, when a young man named Bobby Jones, a full-time student and part-time golfer, began an astonishing winning streak. In 1928, Jones won the U.S. Open, U.S. Amateur, British Open, and British Amateur—and then retired at age 28. He remained a major influence on the game, making instructional films that were shown at country clubs across America in the 1930s, and, more important, co-designing the Augusta National Golf Club, where the Masters is held.

Fearless Facts

We're all taken with stories of adversity overcome, which is one reason why golfer Ben Hogan was so widely popular in his prime. In 1948, the taciturn Hogan announced himself as the sport's next big thing by winning the U.S. Open, shooting a record score. But in February 1949, a bus smashed head-on into Hogan's car, injuring him so badly he didn't play another tournament for nearly a year. And Hogan's grim intensity and relentless practicing paid off: He completed his comeback by winning the 1950 U.S. Open, dragging himself around the course, his legs wrapped in elastic bandages. He won the tournament in 1951 and 1953 as well, tying Bobby Jones's record of four Open victories.

The Other Babe

There's never been a female sports role model on the scale of Babe Didrikson Zaharias, one of the greatest women golfers ever. And golf represents only the tip of the iceberg for this versatile, charismatic athlete.

In 1932, she pulled off a legendary stunt: She entered the National Amateur Athletic Union track meet and competed in eight of the competition's 10 events, winning the 80-meter hurdles, baseball throw, shot put, broad jump, javelin, and high jump, setting three world records in the process. All that in one afternoon! In that year's Olympic Games, she won two gold medals.

In 1938, she gave golf her full attention and quickly became a superstar. Dazzling the press and fans with flair and audacity: "I am out to beat everybody in sight, and that's just what I'm going to do," she said; she won a career total of 31 professional tournaments and 51 amateur events. In 1946 and 1947, she won 17 consecutive events.

Even after being diagnosed with cancer of the intestine and of the lymph nodes, she kept going. In 1954, she entered 18 tournaments and won five—including her third U.S. Open title, which she won by a still-record 12 strokes. But the illness was too much for her, and she died in September 1956 at the age of 45.

Zaharias' story was filmed as *Babe*, a well-regarded 1975 TV movie starring Susan Clark, adapted from Zaharias' autobiography, *This Life I've Led*.

Friendly Rivals

Since Jack Nicklaus turned pro in 1961, he has won 18 major tournaments, by far more than any other golfer, and a total of 56 PGA tournaments—at least one a year for a 17-year stretch. But his influence on golf is far more than just being its best player for longer than anyone else: Through his rivalry with Arnold Palmer, he helped attract a wider audience to the sport. For the first time, golfers became household names among even those who wouldn't be caught dead enduring a televised tournament.

Palmer had been the greatest star of the late 1950s, a colorful, hard-swinging player who made an instant impression with his competitiveness and naked emotions. He drew legions of fans, who dubbed themselves "Arnie's Army," and thereby attracted much more money to the sport.

When Nicklaus began to overtake Palmer as the sport's top competitor, the "Army" was openly resentful of the younger man, but the two players eventually became close friends, and Nicklaus' charisma won them over. The "Golden Bear" has remained golf's leading figure for an amazingly long time, spanning generations of fans. In February 1999, Nicklaus underwent hip-replacement surgery and missed the Masters for the first time in four decades. The previous year, at age 58, he tied for sixth at the tournament.

And his legacy is ensured in more ways than records: Nicklaus has also become one of golf's leading course designers, leaving his mark on greens and sand traps around the world.

From Bottom to Top

Lee Trevino and Chi Chi Rodriguez may not be the most accomplished golfers to swing a nine-iron, but they're among the best loved. As the sport's most prominent Latinos, they helped break down color barriers in popular perceptions of golf. With college golfing programs churning out more and more already trained performers, they provide a last link to a time when most golfers rose from obscure beginnings. And as entertainers, they enlivened a game that for decades was overly somber and straight-laced.

Trevino, born to a poor Hispanic family in Dallas (he never knew his father and was raised by his grandfather), joined the PGA Tour in 1967 and quickly made a splash, beating Jack Nicklaus in the 1968 U.S. Open. After that tournament, he joked, "I may buy the Alamo and give it back to Mexico." It was the first of 27 tournaments (including six majors) that Trevino won before retiring to the broadcast booth in 1982 and the Senior Tour in 1989, where the "Merry Mex" dominated play for several years.

Rodriguez grew up in a tin-roofed shack outside San Juan, Puerto Rico. At the age of nine, he began caddying for 25 cents a round at an old country club across the road and became obsessed with golf—he would slip onto the course at night and practice his stroke by whacking a crunched-up tin can with a tree limb.

Worthy Words

The PGA—Professional Golfers Association, of course—was founded in 1916 along with the first tournament dedicated to professional golfers only. In 1980, PGA officials recognized the commercial potential of tournaments featuring "living legends" of golf, and launched the Senior Tour, for golfers over 50.

After serving in the Army and finding financial backers, Rodriguez joined the PGA Tour, playing for 25 years and winning eight tournaments, at which point he joined the far more lucrative Senior Tour. But it's the golfer's outlandish personality (upon making birdies, he launches into a bullfighter routine) and generosity, more than his performance, that has made him so admired. His foundation for troubled youths in Florida has raised more than $1 million, and he delights in involving kids in the game of golf.

Into the Woods

Golf needed a Tiger Woods. After decades in which attention focused on particular charismatic players, the game was languishing, in the popular view if not actually on the links. Bursting on the scene with unprecedented vitality, Woods represented something genuinely new in golf—a fresh image of youth and energy. He was also the highest-profile non-white player in the sport's history, and his mixed-race heritage (his mother calls him "the universal child") made him a powerful symbol to the fast-growing number of Americans with mixed ancestry.

Born at the end of 1975, Woods grew up a golf prodigy: He first made local news by winning a Pitch, Putt, and Drive competition at the age of three, against rivals who were 10 and 11. He continued to dominate amateur matches through his teen years, winning a never-before-seen three consecutive U.S. Amateur Tournaments. Three days after capturing the third, he announced he was turning pro and signed endorsement contracts worth some $60 million.

The endorsements brought immediate controversy, not only because of the extraordinary amount of money involved but because the tone of the first TV commercial played off Woods' ethnicity, beginning with a voice-over: "There are still courses in the U.S. I am not allowed to play because of the color of my skin." Many didn't approve of the ad's harsh tone; it even sparked an entire episode of *Nightline*.

Fearless Facts

It's unclear whether, in fact, there are still American courses where Tiger Woods is banned because of his skin color. For a very long time, golf was unquestionably a white man's game: Until 1960, the PGA's constitution limited membership to whites; the organization's by-laws were changed only when challenged by the State of California. The Masters, the sport's most prestigious tournament, didn't invite an African-American to play until 1975.

Distractions aside, Woods, now playing against the world's best, continued winning, topping the $1 million mark in winnings after only nine tournaments. That year, 1996, *Sports Illustrated* named him "Sportsman of the Year" and *Newsweek* put him on the cover. And in April 1997, at his first Masters Tournament, Woods broke new ground in two ways: He won by 12 strokes, the widest margin ever; and he became the first non-white to win the tournament.

And because tough competition is good for both interest in a sport as well as for the players themselves, golf fans should rejoice that, in 1998, another personable young golfer, David Duval, came seemingly out of nowhere to challenge Woods for supremacy in the sport, actually outplaying and outearning him for the year. Fans should be salivating at the prospect of a lively rivalry that could last decades.

Kings of the Ring

Back when fighters made a profession of duking it out inside a ring, in eighteenth-century England, boxing was called "The Noble Art of Self-Defense." We've come a long way from those days to the pay-per-view Atlantic City and Las Vegas bouts of the 1990s. Boxers today seem less noble than those of the past: After decades of likable, articulate champions who were genuine role models in and out of the ring, the most prominent and naturally talented boxer of the last 15 years is thuggish heavyweight Mike Tyson, who has come to symbolize the sport.

But boxing has hardly seen its last days: It's only a matter of time before another charismatic fighter rises to restore the sport's dignity. And boxing, like other sports, can draw upon a glorious history studded with heroic he-men.

The Great Black Hope

On December 26, 1908, black boxer Jack Johnson met heavyweight champion Tommy Burns in Sydney, Australia, and beat him so badly that many whites publicly called for a "great white hope" to defeat the new champ, whom they deemed "arrogant."

Ex-champ Jim Jeffries was convinced to come out of retirement and take on Johnson, and when he was similarly trounced, white fans were incensed. Mobs nationwide rioted against African-Americans, with 19 deaths in all.

Towering Tips

There aren't many boxing-themed pop songs, but here's one to check out: Chicago rockers Styx led off the band's 1978 album *Pieces of Eight* with a bombastic number titled— what else?—"Great White Hope."

When the violence died down, the National Sporting Club held a "Great White Hope Tournament" to find a boxer to unseat Johnson. Their choice, Jim Flynn, lost badly, and that was the end, for the next quarter century, of white versus black championship bouts—in 1913, New York and California prohibited mixed-race matches, and white heavyweight contenders (including the great Jack Dempsey) began to refuse fights with African-Americans.

In 1937, Joe Louis met and defeated James Braddock in Chicago; since then, black boxers have held the heavyweight title most of the time. The term "great white hope" has stayed alive, used without irony—but, fortunately, also without malice—every time a white challenger steps into the ring for a championship bout.

Saved by the Bell

In the great sports decade of the 1920s, while Babe Ruth ruled baseball, Jack Dempsey was the king of the ring. His fearsome reputation came not only because of his attacking style, but also because of an aggressive publicist, who built up Dempsey as the "Manassa Mauler" and got his client as much newspaper ink as possible.

Dempsey won the heavyweight title in July 1919 by beating the hulking Jess Willard in three rounds. He remains most famous for two of boxing history's most notable bouts, one of which he lost.

In 1923, Dempsey found himself matched against Luis Angel Firpo, a large Argentinean who had used his great strength (though minimal boxing skills) to win several victories in America. Promoters rented the huge Polo Grounds stadium in New York and packed in 82,000 spectators. From the opening bell, the fight was sheer mayhem: Dempsey knocked Firpo down seven times in the first round alone, but the challenger got up each time to strike back, once knocking Dempsey through the ropes and completely out of the ring and into a row of sportswriters. In the second round, Dempsey managed to knock his opponent unconscious, apparently the only way to keep him down.

Towering Tips

Boxing has been a part of well over 120 non-documentary movies, far more than any other sport. Among the classics are these: *Raging Bull*, with Robert De Niro as middleweight Jake LaMotta; *Somebody Up There Likes Me*, with Paul Newman as middleweight Rocky Graziano; and the fictional movies *The Champ*, *Requiem for a Heavyweight*, and, of course, all the *Rocky* movies.

It was the champion's last fight for three years, because no "worthy" challenger could be found. (Like many other heavyweights, Dempsey refused to box African-Americans.) He was out of shape when he finally took on Gene Tunney and lost. A year later, a rematch took place in front of 105,000 spectators in Chicago. In the seventh round, Dempsey knocked down Tunney and was on the verge of victory. He hesitated before moving to a neutral corner and therefore gave his opponent an extra few seconds in the 10-count. Tunney got to his feet and held on to win, but Dempsey got the cheers when he left the ring.

To the Rescue

Much as Babe Ruth had rescued baseball after the 1919 Black Sox scandal, Joe Louis helped save boxing. By the early 1930s, the sport had hit a low point, controlled largely by gamblers who manipulated the outcome of fights. Louis, the "Brown Bomber," emerged as a instant hero to black Americans—and, eventually, to whites as well.

On Sept. 24, 1935, Louis, then a rising star, met former heavyweight champ Max Baer in Yankee Stadium in front of 95,000 people and knocked Baer out in four rounds. Almost two years later, Louis got a shot at the heavyweight title (because champion Jimmy Braddock was reluctant to fight German challenger Max Schmeling). Louis knocked out Braddock in the eighth round and became the first black heavyweight champ since Jack Johnson lost the title in 1915.

But the most important fight in Louis' career came a year later, June 22, 1938, when Louis took on Schmeling (for the second time). The German boxer was never a Nazi himself but, to Americans, served as a convenient stand-in for the white supremacy of Hitler's Germany. When Louis destroyed Schmeling, knocking him out after just two minutes and four seconds of the first round, he became a hero to all Americans.

Louis had many more bouts and retired as undefeated world heavyweight champion in March 1949, after nearly a dozen years as champ—longer than any boxer, in any weight class, has held a title. But the Schmeling match remained Louis' crowning achievement, when the Brown Bomber, in just over two minutes, managed to unite all Americans.

The Man with the Mouth

While Joe Louis fit perfectly America's need for a strong, dignified hero, Muhammad Ali was equally indicative of his times, the turbulent 1960s and 1970s. Born Cassius

Clay in Louisville, Kentucky, he made a name for himself not only with his undeniable speed and power, but also with his brashness, becoming perhaps the most charismatic athlete since Babe Ruth.

As a teenage amateur in 1960, Clay captured the national Gold Gloves heavyweight title and the Olympic light-heavyweight gold medal. He won his early pro fights, in four or five rounds, usually as he had loudly predicted before the matches, inventing clever rhymes on demand about forthcoming bouts.

Clay set his sights on champ Sonny Liston and publicly taunted him—to his face!—for months. At the weigh-in, he arrived screaming, "Float like a butterfly, sting like a bee," a phrase that became a trademark. When they finally met in the ring, in February 1964, he beat Liston when the champion failed to come out for the seventh round. The two fought again 15 months later, but one thing had changed: Clay, influenced by Malcolm X, had become a Black Muslim and had changed his name to Muhammad Ali. In the ring, Liston fared no better: With a quick, light punch, Ali put the former champion down for the count inside of 60 seconds of the first round. (Liston insisted afterward that he had thrown the fight, and replays lend some support to his claim.)

Fearless Facts

At first, many sportswriters, fans, and even boxers refused to use Cassius Clay's new Muslim name. Heavyweight Ernie Terrell was one of those who didn't acknowledge it, and when the newly christened Muhammad Ali met Terrell in February 1967, he spent the entire fight—a victory, of course—shouting, "What's my name? What's my name?" Ali's successful defense of his adopted name paved the way for others to make similar choices: when Lew Alcindor changed his name to Kareem Abdul-Jabbar in 1971, he faced little resistance.

When the Vietnam War came, Ali was classified 1-A, but he refused to be inducted, claiming an exemption on the grounds that he was a Muslim minister. He was indicted for draft evasion and sentenced to five years in prison, but the sentence was suspended (the U.S. Supreme Court eventually ruled in Ali's favor). He was stripped of his title and announced his retirement.

In March 1971, he set out to regain the title and, more than three years later, captured it in 1974 from George Foreman in Zaire (the so-called "Rumble in the Jungle," documented in the 1996 film *When We Were Kings*). Then came his third fight with Joe Frazier, the so-called "Thrilla in Manila" (documented in the 1996 film *When We Were Kings*), which Ali won in 14 rounds. At 36, Ali capped off his career with a dramatic pair of fights, losing a split decision to 22-year-old Leon Spinks and then beating Spinks seven months later to regain the heavyweight title for an unprecedented third time.

In recent years, Ali has remained an icon of American sports, as his struggle with Parkinson's disease has raised questions in many minds about the brutality inherent in boxing and the lasting brain damage a long career can inflict—it's particularly heart-breaking to see this smart, articulate man crippled.

Man Versus Track

Track-and-field events are the purest exhibitions of athleticism, with virtually no equipment, except for shoes or skates, and sometimes—as in the case of swimmers—not even that. It's just one man or woman going all out, relying on no one else.

Fearless Facts

Jim Thorpe entered the 1912 Olympics with a reputation as America's greatest all-around amateur athlete, and he didn't disappoint—winning gold medals in the decathlon and the pentathlon. But when it was discovered that he had once played professional baseball, he was forced to give back his medals. Seventy years later, after Thorpe had died, his name was restored to the record books.

Despite the entry of money into the Olympic Games in recent years (not to mention the bribery scandals tainting the 2002 Salt Lake City Winter Games), most competitors still hold to the Olympic creed: "The most important thing in the Olympic Games is not to win but to take part, just as the most important thing in life is not the triumph but the struggle. The essential thing is not to have conquered but to have fought well."

That's Showing Him

Jesse Owens first made headlines in 1935, when he entered an intercollegiate track meet and set four world records—in the broad jump, 100-yard dash, 200-yard dash, and 220-yard hurdles—all in less than an hour! But his moment of immortality came the following summer at the Berlin Olympics. Under the wrathful gaze of Adolf Hitler, who had pledged to make his Olympics a demonstration of whites' natural superiority, Owens captured a record total of four gold medals: in the broad jump, 100-meter dash, 200-meter dash, and 400-meter relay.

Back home, New York threw a ticker-tape parade for the star. At a Waldorf-Astoria reception in his honor, though, Owens found that his medals—won in the name of his country—didn't mean as much as he had hoped: The hotel's policy of segregation obliged him to take a freight elevator to his own reception.

The Comeback Girl

Wilma Rudolph was about the least likely track hero imaginable: She was born with polio and, as a toddler, could barely use her left leg. Her mother and three siblings massaged her leg daily, and she wore a steel brace until age 11. In 1956, as a junior in high school, she made the Olympic team and won a bronze medal as part of the U.S. relay squad, but she vowed to return and excel. In the 1960 trials, she set a world record in the 200-meter dash and qualified in the 100-meter race as well. At the Rome Games, she won gold medals in both, plus the relay event, becoming the first American woman to win three gold medals.

When she returned home, she met with President Kennedy, spoke at banquets, and attended a parade in her hometown—the first integrated event in the history of Bethlehem, Tennessee. Rudolph went on to work with the Job Corps, taking a break to help with Operation Champion, a 1967 federal program intended to help train star athletes from urban ghettoes. In 1977, she published her autobiography, *Wilma*, which was made into an uninspired TV film starring Cicely Tyson and Shirley Jo Finney as Rudolph.

Going the Distance

It wasn't long ago that women weren't allowed to officially run marathon races; the Boston Marathon banned women competitors until 1972. Joan Benoit Samuelson deserves a good deal of the credit for creating interest in women's long-distance races. She was a college senior when she won the 1979 Boston Marathon, in what was then the fastest time ever for an American woman. Samuelson took the opportunity to

Worthy Words

Those who win decathlons and heptathlons are usually considered the finest all-around athletes. What's involved? Heptathlons, a women's Olympic event only since 1984, consist of seven events: 100-meter hurdles, high jump, shot put, 200-meter and 800-meter runs, long jump, and javelin throw. Decathlons, around since 1912, include the following: 100-meter, 400-meter, and 1,500-meter runs; 110-meter high hurdles, javelin and discus throws, shot put, pole vault, high jump, and long jump.

lambaste the Olympic Committee, which didn't offer women runners any race longer than 1,500 meters. "I think women can do anything they want, at any distance," she told a reporter.

But the Olympics wouldn't offer a marathon for women until 1984 (in which she took home the gold), so Samuelson coached at Boston University and competed in national races, setting new records for the half-marathon, marathon, and 10-mile race. In 1983, she won Boston again, this time in just two hours, 22 minutes, and 24 seconds, a new world record—and 13 minutes faster than she had run the course four years earlier.

She ran in Boston again in 1985, topping her own time and setting an American record that still stands. She then eased off on competing, choosing to spend more time with her family, and decided against trying out for the 1988 and 1992 Olympic teams. But lately she's gotten more involved: In 1998, at age 41, Benoit ran the Boston race—against competitors half her age or younger—and placed 12th.

Doing It for Themselves

If you were confused in the mid-1980s about Florence Griffith Joyner and Jackie Joyner-Kersee, you weren't alone: The two track stars both attended UCLA, trained under Bob Kersee, competed in sprints, were related to champion jumper Al Joyner, and won medals in the 1984 and 1988 Olympics. And since they were as glamorous as track stars get, they were showered with attention.

Joyner-Kersee, sister of Joyner and wife of Kersee, won a basketball scholarship to UCLA but gave up the sport in favor of the heptathlon after winning a silver medal in the 1984 Games. In 1987, she won the heptathlon and long jump at the world championships; and the next year, she won Olympic gold in the heptathlon, setting a new world record, and in the long jump, setting a new Olympic record. And four years later, she again won the heptathlon.

Like her counterpart, Griffith Joyner, wife of Al Joyner, Joyner-Kersee won a silver medal in the 1984 Games, in the 200-meter dash. It was at the 1988 Olympics that she made a tremendous impression, however, winning three golds and a silver—although much of the notice she got focused on her colorful, one-leg-exposed outfits.

Into the Water

A disproportionate number of American sports heroes have come from competitors in Olympic swimming and diving:

➤ Johnny Weissmuller captured American boys' imaginations with gold medals in the 1924 and 1928 Games—before winning the hearts of female moviegoers as the star of dozen *Tarzan* films.

➤ At the age of 11, Florence Chadwick won her first swimming race, a six-mile "rough-water swim." After 19 years of racing, she turned professional, appeared in the movie *Bathing Beauty*, and began training to swim the English Channel. In 1950, she became the first woman to swim the Channel in both directions.

➤ By taking home a record seven golds in the 1972 Games, mustachioed swimmer Mark Spitz stirred the pride of American Jews who would be traumatized by the terrorist massacre of Israeli athletes only a few days later.

➤ Greg Louganis dominated diving in the 1984 and 1988 Olympics only to announce, a few years later, that he was proudly gay, adding depth to his athletic achievements.

➤ At age 16, swimmer Janet Evans won three gold medals in the 1988 Games—and followed that with a gold and silver four years later. Evans, the only female swimmer ever to win back-to-back Olympic and World Championship titles (in the 800-meter freestyle), owns three world records.

The Least You Need to Know

➤ Bill Tilden, a 1920s superstar, made tennis safe for American men.

➤ In the "Battle of the Sexes," Billie Jean was King.

➤ Jack Nicklaus is the reason why channel-surfers keep running across golf tournaments.

➤ Joe Lewis restored integrity to the sport of boxing.

➤ Before Joan Benoit Samuelson, women marathoners weren't taken seriously.

Storied Pages

Clinton, James W. *The Loyal Opposition: Americans in North Vietnam, 1965-1972*. University Press of Colorado, 1995.

Dorson, Richard M. *American Folklore*. Chicago: University of Chicago Press, 1959.

Fishwick, Marshall. *The Hero, American Style*. New York: David McKay Company, 1969.

King, Peter. *Football: A History of the Professional Game*. New York: Sports Illustrated, 1997.

Kennedy, John F. *Profiles in Courage*. New York: Harper and Row, 1955.

Murphy, Edward F. *Heroes of World War II*. Presidio Press: Novato, CA, 1990.

Reynolds, Richard. *Super Heroes: A Modern Mythology*. Jackson: University Press of Mississippi, 1995.

Rowbotham, Sheila. *A Century of Women: The History of Women in Britain and the United States*. New York: Viking, 1997.

Savage, Candace. *Cowgirls*. Berkeley: Ten Speed Press, 1996.

Schwarzkopf, Norman and Peter Petre. *It Doesn't Take a Hero*. New York: Bantam Books, 1992.

Shay, Frank. *Here's Audacity: American Legendary Heroes*. Freeport, NY: Books for Libraries Press, 1930, reprint, 1967.

Ward, Geoffrey C. and Ken Burns. *Baseball: An Illustrated History*. New York: Alfred A. Knopf, 1994.

Waters, Frank. *Brave Are My People: Indian Heroes Not Forgotten*. Santa Fe: Clear Light Publishers, 1993.

Wecter, Dixon. *The Hero in America: A Chronicle of Hero Worship*. Ann Arbor: University of Michigan Press, 1963.

Honor Roll

The chapters in this book jump around among various periods in history, so here's a chronological list of heroes to help you place them in time.

Hiawatha (c1100–1150) was the legendary unifier of the original five tribes that became the Iroquois nation.

Captain John Smith (c1580–1631) was an English colonist who came to Jamestown, Virginia; he may have made up the story that he was saved from execution by Pocahontas.

Squanto (c1585–1622) was the Native American who acted as teacher and interpreter for the *Mayflower* pilgrims and brokered a treaty between them and the Wampanoag Indians.

Anne Hutchinson (1591–1643) was banished from Bay Colony for her liberal religious views. Indians later killed her.

Pocahontas (c1595–1617) was a Native American who married colonist tobacco grower John Rolfe and sailed to England where she was introduced to royalty.

Roger Williams (1603–1683) was kicked out of Massachusetts Bay Colony for trying to set up a democratic church bureaucracy. He later founded Rhode Island on the principle of religious tolerance.

William Penn (1644–1718) founded Pennsylvania as a "holy experiment" in tolerant and peaceful government. He is one of the few white settlers to have made and abided by fair treaties with the Indians.

Benjamin Franklin (1706–1790) was an inventor, printer, and patriot who secured invaluable military and financial assistance as a diplomat to France.

Pontiac (1720–1769) was an Indian war chief who organized an uprising and fought on the side of the French in the French and Indian War.

George Washington (1732–1799) refused exhortations to assume power as a military dictator years before being elected as the nation's first president.

Daniel Boone (1734–1820) helped open up the wilderness of Kentucky to early settlers. By the time of his death in 1820, Boone was admired in Europe and idolized in America.

Paul Revere (1735–1818) rode out into the night in April 1775, to warn the colonists that British troops were on the move.

Thomas Paine (1737–1809) was a writer whose revolutionary pamphlets inspired those who sided with the American Revolution.

Thomas Jefferson (1743–1826) wrote the Declaration of Independence (1776), drawing on the political philosophy of English thinker John Locke.

Molly Pitcher (1754–1832) carried water for soldiers and filled in to man a cannon when her husband was wounded in the Revolutionary War.

Andrew Jackson (1767–1845) was a noted Indian fighter who became the first president to be elected despite major opposition from Congress.

Tecumseh (1768–1813) was an Indian chief who served as a British general in the War of 1812.

Meriweather Lewis (1774–1809) and **William Clark** (1770–1838) led the first expedition across the country and reached the Pacific in November 1805.

Mother Elizabeth Seton (1774–1821) was the first Catholic saint to be born in the United States. She founded the first free Catholic school.

Davy Crockett (1786–1836) was a frontiersman and Indian fighter who died at the Alamo.

Sacagawea, (c1794–1880) hired on by Lewis and Clark as an interpreter, was neglected in her time but is remembered today as one of the biggest heroes of the expedition.

Sojourner Truth (1797–1883) was a freed slave who worked for the underground railroad and spoke against slavery and for women's rights.

John Brown (1800–1859) was an abolitionist who led the raid on Harper's Ferry, where he was captured and later executed.

Robert E. Lee (1807–1870) was the leading Civil War general for the South, and was known for his brilliant and daring military tactics.

Jefferson Davis (1808–1889) was president of the Confederate States during the Civil War.

Abraham Lincoln (1809–1865) passed the Emancipation Proclamation in 1863 to make good a threat to rebel states that unless they ceased their opposition to the Union he would free their slaves.

Kit Carson (1809–1868) was an explorer and Indian fighter who became an early pulp-fiction hero.

Elizabeth Cady Stanton (1815–1902) spoke out for women's rights, abolition, and temperance.

Frederick Douglass (1817–1895) was a former slave, abolitionist, writer, and statesman.

Susan B. Anthony (1820–1906) was outspoken in the cause of women's rights, including the right to vote.

Harriet Tubman (1820–1913) was a leading figure in the underground railroad.

Clara Barton (1821–1912) was the founder of the American Red Cross; she got her start as a nurse in the Civil War using medical supplies she collected herself.

Geronimo (1823–1909) was an Apache chief who eluded capture for years as a raider.

Stonewall Jackson (1824–1863) was a Civil War general for the South who got his nickname for refusing to give ground in battle.

Mother Jones (1830–1930) was a radical labor activist who supported strikers and demonstrated against child labor.

Sitting Bull (1831–1890) was a Sioux medicine man who helped Crazy Horse defeat General Custer at the battle of Little Big Horn in 1876.

Andrew Carnegie (1835–1919) was a leading industrialist, millionaire, and philanthropist who built the Carnegie steel empire.

George Custer (1839–1876) was a flamboyant cavalry officer who was defeated by Crazy Horse and Sitting Bull at Little Big Horn.

Crazy Horse (1842–1877) was the Sioux chief who defeated Custer at Little Big Horn.

Buffalo Bill (1846–1917) was a showman who glorified and exaggerated his accomplishments as a buffalo hunter, scout, and Indian fighter.

Thomas Edison (1847–1931) opened workshops and had dozens of assistants working under him, producing and perfecting inventions.

Samuel Gompers (1850–1924) was the founder of the American Federation of Labor and set a precedent for union activism within the capitalist system.

Eugene Debs (1855–1926) was a labor leader and presidential candidate on the Socialist ticket five times.

Robert Peary (1856–1920) led the first expedition to reach the North Pole, arriving in April 1909.

Booker T. Washington (1856–1915) came to stand for economic empowerment for blacks and accommodation to segregationist whites as head of the Tuskegee Institute.

Louis Brandeis (1856–1941) was an attorney who devoted legal talents to the defense of workers and labor leaders.

Clarence Darrow (1857–1938) was an attorney who defended high-profile and controversial clients, including labor leaders Bill Haywood and Eugene Debs.

Teddy Roosevelt (1858–1919) led the Rough Riders in their famous charge up San Juan Hill in the Spanish American War.

Annie Oakley (1860–1926) was a sharpshooter who starred in Buffalo Bill's Wild West show.

John J. Pershing (1860–1948) was appointed by President Woodrow Wilson to command the Allied Expeditionary Forces in World War I.

Henry Ford (1863–1947) introduced mass production as a way of making the automobile cheap and practical.

George Washington Carver (1864–1943) invented hundreds of new uses for peanuts in an effort to improve the economy of the poor South.

Wilbur (1867–1912) and **Orville** (1871–1948) **Wright** discovered the ability to measure air pressure on moving objects, enabling them to accomplish what many authorities believed was impossible.

Bill Haywood (1869–1928) helped found the Wobblies (Industrial Workers of the World) and advocated a socialist revolution.

Will Rogers (1879–1935) was a cowboy, vaudeville star, radio personality, and homespun philosopher.

Joe Hill (1879–1915) became a legendary Wobbly poet and songwriter after immigrating to America in hopes of a better life.

Helen Keller (1880–1968) overcame deafness and blindness to become a world-renowned writer, speaker, and spokesperson for social issues.

Christy Mathewson (1880–1925) brought a touch of class to baseball in the early part of the century—and proved himself one of history's finest pitchers.

Margaret Sanger (1883–1966) dedicated her life to promoting birth control in America and eventually succeeded in getting birth control accepted as a legitimate medical practice.

General George "Blood and Guts" Patton (1885–1945) inspired a movie based on his life that won seven Oscars, including best picture.

Richard Byrd (1888–1957) was an aviator as well as an explorer; he is credited with being the first person to fly over the North Pole.

Captain Eddie Rickenbacker (1890–1973) downed 22 German planes and four observation balloons during World War I to become the leading American flying ace.

Dwight D. Eisenhower (1890–1969) assumed command of the Allied forces during World War II and planned the invasion of Normandy on D-day.

Bill Tilden (1893–1953) was America's first tennis superstar, and his play (as well as his books about the sport) inspired thousands to become fans and participants of the game.

Babe Ruth (1895–1948) began his career as a dominating pitcher and ended it as the best hitter, and greatest star, that baseball would ever know.

Jack Dempsey (1895–1983) was the greatest heavyweight boxer of the 1920s, securing everlasting fame with a pair of high-profile bouts.

Paul Robeson (1898–1976) was a singer and actor who promoted civil rights and organized labor.

Amelia Earhart (1898–1937) perished in the attempt to become the first person to fly around the world at the equator.

Humphrey Bogart (1899–1957) became legendary for playing reluctant, worldly-wise heroes.

Linus Pauling (1901–) won two Nobel Prizes—the first for chemistry, and the second for peace. His work helped bring about a nuclear test ban treaty between the United States and the Soviet Union.

Charles Lindbergh (1902–1974) was the first person to fly solo across the Atlantic from New York to Paris, in May 1927.

Lou Gehrig (1903–1941) batted right behind Babe Ruth in the Yankees' lineup, and terrified pitchers for well over a decade—but he's best remembered for playing in 2,130 consecutive games.

Red Grange (1903–1991) was the greatest football player of the 1920s; he toured the United States in 1925, creating widespread excitement for professional play.

Rachel Carson (1907–1964) inaugurated the environmental movement with her book *Silent Spring*, about the hazards of DDT.

John Wayne (1907–1979) broke into show business through his USC football coach.

Hank Greenberg (1911–1986) was a source of pride to Jews—and all Americans—during World War II, slamming home runs as a rebuke to Adolf Hitler.

Rosa Parks (1912–) set off the black civil rights movement of the 1960s, led by Martin Luther King, when she refused to give up her seat on a bus to a white person.

Woody Guthrie (1912–1967) wrote "This Land Is Your Land" and about 1,000 other songs. His son Arlo carries on his music-of-the-people tradition.

Vince Lombardi (1913–1970) coached the Green Bay Packers to victory in the first two Super Bowls, but is best known for his motivational aphorisms.

Jesse Owens (1913–1980) will forever be remembered for his spectacular performance in the 1936 Berlin Olympics, where he won four gold medals and shamed his Nazi hosts.

Jonas Salk (1914–1995) developed the first vaccine for polio.

Joe DiMaggio (1914–1999) was one of baseball's most graceful players, and a three-time MVP. His greatest achievement was hitting in 56 straight games during the 1941 season.

Babe Didrikson Zaharias (1914–56) began as a gold-medal Olympic track star and all-around athlete; later she became one of the greatest women golfers.

Joe Louis (1914–1981), the "Brown Bomber," held the heavyweight title for a dozen years and helped save boxing by restoring integrity to the sport.

Muddy Waters (1915–1983) recorded passionate blues that heavily influenced a generation of rockers such as Eric Clapton and the Rolling Stones.

Jackie Robinson (1919–1972) stepped over baseball's color line, becoming the first African-American to play major-league ball in the twentieth century.

Pete Seeger (1919–) has spent his life campaigning for social justice, writing songs such as "If I Had a Hammer" and "Where Have All the Flowers Gone?"

John Glenn (1921–) was the first American astronaut to orbit the Earth, in February 1962. He later became the oldest man to travel in space (at 77 years old in October 1998).

Audie Murphy (1924–1971) won 33 military medals by the age of 21, before going on to become a movie star.

Lee Iacocca (1924–) reversed the fortunes of the ailing automaker Chrysler, through personal appeals and guarantees in an effective series of TV ads.

George Mikan (1924–) was basketball's first dominant big man, and the greatest player of the first half of the century.

Jimmy Carter (1924–) used his influence as a former president to help solve global problems after leaving office.

Malcolm X (1925–1965) attracted thousands of converts to the Nation of Islam as a means of black empowerment.

Chuck Berry (1926–) fused country and R&B to lay the groundwork for the rock 'n' roll of the 1960s, and wrote a series of classic songs that, even today, are inimitable.

Cesar Chavez (1927–1993) successfully led one of the longest labor strikes in American history against the California grape-growing industry.

James Brown (1928–) invented a groove-based rhythmic style that lives on in today's hip-hop music, and earned himself a reputation as "the hardest-working man in show business."

Martin Luther King (1929–1968) was the preeminent civil rights leader, advocating nonviolent resistance to racial discrimination.

Neil Armstrong (1930–) became the first person to walk on the moon, in July 1969.

Ray Charles (1930–) is a blind singer and pianist who made his mark in pop-music history with "What'd I Say" and "Hit the Road, Jack"—and has since gone on to produce nearly four decades of recordings.

James Dean (1931–1955) became legendary after starring in three films and dying in an auto accident.

Mickey Mantle (1931–1995) was one of baseball's most feared hitters and, as a switch-hitter, a threat from both sides of the plate. A fair-haired crowd favorite, he led the Yankees during some of their most glorious years.

Elizabeth Taylor (1932–) is a legendary actress who has been married eight times to seven husbands. On top of all this, she developed her own line of perfume and started her own foundation for AIDS research.

Roberto Clemente (1934–1972) piled up 3,000 hits and earned a reputation as the game's best-fielding outfielder before dying in a tragic plane crash.

General Norman Schwarzkopf (1934–) led U.S. forces in the Persian Gulf War.

Ralph Nader (1934–) has been the country's leading consumer advocate since his book *Unsafe at Any Speed* was first published. The book exposed inadequate safety standards in the auto industry.

Bill Russell (1934–) made defensive play into an art, but he truly excelled as a team leader, taking the Boston Celtics on an unprecedented winning streak.

Jim Brown (1936–) played nine years in the NFL, during which time he broke every rushing record—and then left pro football at the height of his career.

Colin Powell (1937–) was chair of the U.S. Army Joint Chiefs of Staff during the Persian Gulf War.

Curt Flood (1938–1997) sacrificed his career for the sake of his principles, directly challenging baseball's longstanding "reserve clause" in 1969.

Jack Nicklaus (1940–), by being both a charismatic personality and the most consistent golfer over the long term, brought millions of new fans to his sport.

Wilma Rudolph (1940–1994) overcame polio to become the first American woman to win three gold medals at the 1960 Olympic Games.

Bob Dylan (1941–) brought narrative poetry to folk-rock music and recorded some of the century's greatest albums. His nasal voice and harmonica are unmistakable.

Aretha Franklin (1942–) has been the "Queen of Soul" since the late 1960s, when she set the music world on its ear with "Respect," "A Natural Woman," "Chain of Fools," and other classics.

Muhammad Ali (1942–) got public attention for his quick-witted braggadocio and impromptu rhymes; he received admiration for his unstoppable power.

Jimi Hendrix (1942–1970) didn't live to see the tremendous impact his innovative guitar work would have on future legions of ax-men.

Joni Mitchell (1943–) set new standards for melodic lyricism and jazz-pop fusion, becoming a hero to two generations of aspiring singer-songwriters.

Billie Jean King (1943–) was a dominating tennis player, but she's best remembered for winning the famous 1973 "Battle of the Sexes" match against Bobby Riggs.

Wilma Mankiller (1945–) worked for Cherokee self-rule and unification as chief of the Cherokees.

Kareem Abdul-Jabbar (1947–) won six MVP awards during his long basketball career, ending up as the top scorer and rebounder of all time.

Sally Ride (1951–) became the first American woman launched into space, in June 1983.

Christopher Reeve (1952–) has acted and directed in numerous productions and worked to promote treatment and awareness for paralysis victims after becoming paralyzed in a riding accident.

Nancy Wilson (1954–), the in-your-face rhythm guitarist of the band Heart, showed thousands of women that they could be credible rock stars.

Joe Montana (1956–) ended his career widely considered the greatest quarterback in football history, leaving fans with memories of breathtaking clutch performances.

Magic Johnson (1959–) turned millions of casual basketball viewers into real fans with his spectacular play and exuberant disposition.

Cal Ripken Jr. (1961–) has been a landmark in the Baltimore Orioles infield since 1981. He began a consecutive-game streak the next year that lasted 16 years, and a record-setting 2,632 games.

Jim Abbott (1967–) has been a great inspiration by becoming a successful big-league pitcher despite being born with only one hand.

Index

N

403

Y-Z

When You're **Smart** Enough to **Know** That **You** Don't Know It All!

*For all the ups and downs you're sure to encounter in life,
The Complete Idiot's Guides give you
down-to-earth answers and practical solutions.*

Personal Business

The Complete Idiot's Guide to Assertiveness
ISBN: 0-02-861964-1
$16.95

The Complete Idiot's Guide to Business Management
ISBN: 0-02-861744-4
$16.95

The Complete Idiot's Guide to New Product Development
ISBN: 0-02-861952-8
$16.95

The Complete Idiot's Guide to Dynamic Selling
ISBN: 0-02-861952-8
$16.95

The Complete Idiot's Guide to Getting Along with Difficult People
ISBN: 0-02-861597-2
$16.95

The Complete Idiot's Guide to Great Customer Service
ISBN: 0-02-861953-6
$16.95

The Complete Idiot's Guide to Leadership
ISBN: 0-02-861946-3
$16.95

The Complete Idiot's Guide to Marketing Basics
ISBN: 0-02-861490-9
$16.95

The Complete Idiot's Guide to Office Politics
ISBN: 0-02-862397-5
$16.95

The Complete Idiot's Guide to Project Management
ISBN: 0-02-861745-2
$16.95

The Complete Idiot's Guide to Starting a Home Based Business
ISBN: 0-02-861539-5
$16.95

The Complete Idiot's Guide to Successful Business Presentations
ISBN: 0-02-861748-7
$16.95

The Complete Idiot's Guide to Freelancing
ISBN: 0-02-862119-0
$16.95

The Complete Idiot's Guide to Changing Careers
ISBN: 0-02-861977-3
$17.95

The Complete Idiot's Guide to Terrific Business Writing
ISBN: 0-02-861097-0
$16.95

The Complete Idiot's Guide to Getting the Job You Want
ISBN: 1-56761-608-9
$24.95

The Complete Idiot's Guide to Managing Your Time
ISBN: 0-02-862943-4
$18.95

The Complete Idiot's Guide to Speaking in Public With Confidence
ISBN: 0-02-861038-5
$16.95

The Complete Idiot's Guide to Winning Through Negotiation
ISBN: 0-02-861037-7
$16.95

The Complete Idiot's Guide to Managing People
ISBN: 0-02-861036-9
$18.95

The Complete Idiot's Guide to a Great Retirement
ISBN: 0-02-861036-9
$16.95

The Complete Idiot's Guide to Starting Your Own Business
ISBN: 0-02-861979-X
$18.95

The Complete Idiot's Guide to Protecting Yourself from Everyday Legal Hassles
ISBN: 1-56761-602-X
$16.99

The Complete Idiot's Guide to Surviving Divorce
ISBN: 0-02-861101-3
$16.95

The Complete Idiot's Guide to
Organizing Your Life
ISBN: 0-02-861090-3
$16.95

The Complete Idiot's Guide to
Reaching Your Goals
ISBN: 0-02-862114-X
$16.95

The Complete Idiot's Guide to
the Perfect Cover Letter
ISBN: 0-02-861960-9
$14.95

The Complete Idiot's Guide to
the Perfect Interview
ISBN: 0-02-861945-5
$14.95

The Complete Idiot's Guide to
the Perfect Resume
ISBN: 0-02-861093-8
$16.95

Personal Finance

The Complete Idiot's Guide to
Buying Insurance and Annu-
ities
ISBN: 0-02-861113-6
$16.95

The Complete Idiot's Guide to
Managing Your Money
ISBN: 1-56761-530-9
$16.95

The Complete Idiot's Guide to
Making Money with Mutual
Funds
ISBN: 1-56761-637-2
$16.95

The Complete Idiot's Guide to
Buying and Selling a Home
ISBN: 0-02-861959-5
$16.95

The Complete Idiot's Guide to
Getting Rich
ISBN: 0-02-862952-3
$18.95

The Complete Idiot's Guide to
Finance and Accounting
ISBN: 0-02-861752-5
$16.95

The Complete Idiot's Guide to
Investing Like a Pro
ISBN:0-02-862044-5
$16.95

The Complete Idiot's Guide to
Making Money After You
Retire
ISBN:0-02-862410-6
$16.95

The Complete Idiot's Guide to
Making Money on Wall Street
ISBN:0-02-861958-7
$16.95

The Complete Idiot's Guide to
Personal Finance in Your 20s
and 30s
ISBN:0-02-862415-7
$16.95

The Complete Idiot's Guide to
Wills and Estates
ISBN: 0-02-861747-9
$16.95

The Complete Idiot's Guide to
401(k) Plans
ISBN: 0-02-861948-X
$16.95

Lifestyle

The Complete Idiot's Guide to
Etiquette
ISBN0-02-861094-6
$16.95

The Complete Idiot's Guide to
Dating
ISBN: 0-02-861052-0
$14.95

The Complete Idiot's Guide to
Trouble-Free Car Care
ISBN: 0-02-861041-5
$16.95

The Complete Idiot's Guide to
the Perfect Wedding
ISBN: 0-02-861963-3
$16.95

The Complete Idiot's Guide to
the Perfect Vacation
ISBN: 1-56761-531-7
$14.99

The Complete Idiot's Guide to
Trouble-Free Home Repair
ISBN: 0-02-861042-3
$16.95

The Complete Idiot's Guide to
Getting Into College
ISBN: 1-56761-508-2
$14.95

The Complete Idiot's Guide to
a Healthy Relationship
ISBN: 0-02-861087-3
$17.95

The Complete Idiot's Guide to
Dealing with In-Laws
ISBN: 0-02-862107-7
$16.95

The Complete Idiot's Guide to
Choosing, Training, and
Raising a Dog
ISBN: 0-02-861098-9
$16.95

The Complete Idiot's Guide to
Fun and Tricks with Your Dog
ISBN: 0-87605-083-6
$14.95

The Complete Idiot's Guide to
Living with a Cat
ISBN: 0-02-861278-7
$16.95

The Complete Idiot's Guide to
Turtles and Tortoises
ISBN: 0-87605-143-3
$16.95

Leisure/Hobbies

The Complete Idiot's Guide to
Baking
ISBN: 0-02-861954-4
$16.95

The Complete Idiot's Guide to
Beer
ISBN: 0-02-861717-7
$16.95

The Complete Idiot's Guide to
Cooking Basics
ISBN: 0-02-861974-9
$18.95

The Complete Idiot's Guide to
Entertaining
ISBN: 0-02-861095-4
$16.95

**The Complete Idiot's Guide to
Mixing Drinks**
ISBN: 0-02-861941-2
$16.95

**The Complete Idiot's Guide to
Wine**
ISBN: 0-02-861273-6
$16.95

**The Complete Idiot's Guide to
Antiques and Collectibles**
ISBN: 0-02-861595-6
$16.95

**The Complete Idiot's Guide to
Boating and Sailing**
ISBN: 0-02-862124-7
$18.95

**The Complete Idiot's Guide to
Bridge**
ISBN: 0-02-861735-5
$16.95

**The Complete Idiot's Guide to
Chess**
ISBN: 0-02-861736-3
$16.95

**The Complete Idiot's Guide to
Cigars**
ISBN: 0-02-861975-7
$17.95

**The Complete Idiot's Guide to
Crafts with Kids**
ISBN: 0-02-862406-8
$16.95

**The Complete Idiot's Guide to
Fishing Basics**
ISBN: 0-02-861598-0
$16.95

**The Complete Idiot's Guide to
Gambling Like a Pro**
ISBN: 0-02-861102-0
$16.95

**The Complete Idiot's Guide to
Hiking and Camping**
ISBN: 0-02-861100-4
$16.95

**The Complete Idiot's Guide to
Knitting and Crocheting**
ISBN: 0-02-862123-9
$16.95

**The Complete Idiot's Guide to
Photography**
ISBN: 0-02-861092-X
$16.95

**The Complete Idiot's Guide to
Quilting**
ISBN: 0-02-862411-4
$16.95

**The Complete Idiot's Guide to
Yoga**
ISBN: 0-02-861949-8
$16.95

**The Complete Idiot's Guide to
the Beatles**
ISBN: 0-02-862130-1
$18.95

**The Complete Idiot's Guide to
Elvis**
ISBN: 0-02-861873-4
$18.95

**The Complete Idiot's Guide to
Understanding Football Like a
Pro**
ISBN:0-02-861743-6
$16.95

**The Complete Idiot's Guide to
Golf**
ISBN: 0-02-861760-6
$16.95

**The Complete Idiot's Guide to
Motorcycles**
ISBN: 0-02-862416-5
$17.95

**The Complete Idiot's Guide to
Pro Wrestling**
ISBN: 0-02-862395-9
$17.95

**The Complete Idiot's Guide to
Extra-Terrestrial Intelligence**
ISBN: 0-02-862387-8
$16.95

Health and Fitness

**The Complete Idiot's Guide to
Managed Health Care**
ISBN: 0-02-862165-4
$17.95

**The Complete Idiot's Guide to
Getting and Keeping Your
Perfect Body**
ISBN: 0-02-861276-0
$16.95

**The Complete Idiot's Guide to
First Aid Basics**
ISBN: 0-02-861099-7
$16.95

**The Complete Idiot's Guide to
Vitamins**
ISBN: 0-02-862116-6
$16.95

**The Complete Idiot's Guide to
Losing Weight**
ISBN: 0-02-862113-1
$17.95

**The Complete Idiot's Guide to
Tennis**
ISBN: 0-02-861746-0
$18.95

**The Complete Idiot's Guide to
Tae Kwon Do**
ISBN: 0-02-862389-4
$17.95

**The Complete Idiot's Guide to
Breaking Bad Habits**
ISBN: 0-02-862110-7
$16.95

**The Complete Idiot's Guide to
Healthy Stretching**
ISBN: 0-02-862127-1
$16.95

**The Complete Idiot's Guide to
Beautiful Skin**
ISBN: 0-02-862408-4
$16.95

**The Complete Idiot's Guide to
Eating Smart**
ISBN: 0-02-861276-0
$16.95

**The Complete Idiot's Guide to
First Aid**
ISBN: 0-02-861099-7
$16.95

**The Complete Idiot's Guide to
Getting a Good Night's Sleep**
ISBN: 0-02-862394-0
$16.95

The Complete Idiot's Guide to
a Happy, Healthy Heart
ISBN: 0-02-862393-2
$16.95

The Complete Idiot's Guide to
Stress
ISBN: 0-02-861086-5
$16.95

The Complete Idiot's Guide to
Jogging and Running
ISBN: 0-02-862386-X
$17.95

The Complete Idiot's Guide to
Adoption
ISBN: 0-02-862108-5
$18.95

The Complete Idiot's Guide to
Bringing Up Baby
ISBN: 0-02-861957-9
$16.95

The Complete Idiot's Guide to
Grandparenting
ISBN: 0-02-861976-5
$16.95

The Complete Idiot's Guide to
Parenting a Preschooler and
Toddler
ISBN: 0-02-861733-9
$16.95

The Complete Idiot's Guide to
Raising a Teenager
ISBN: 0-02-861277-9
$16.95

The Complete Idiot's Guide to
Single Parenting
ISBN: 0-02-862409-2
$16.95

The Complete Idiot's Guide to
Stepparenting
ISBN: 0-02-862407-6
$16.95

Education

The Complete Idiot's Guide to
American History
ISBN: 0-02-861275-2
$16.95

The Complete Idiot's Guide to
British Royalty
ISBN: 0-02-862346-0
$18.95

The Complete Idiot's Guide to
Civil War
ISBN: 0-02-862122-0
$16.95

The Complete Idiot's Guide to
Classical Mythology
ISBN: 0-02-862385-1
$16.95

The Complete Idiot's Guide to
Creative Writing
ISBN: 0-02-861734-7
$16.95

The Complete Idiot's Guide to
Dinosaurs
ISBN: 0-02-862390-8
$17.95

The Complete Idiot's Guide to
Genealogy
ISBN: 0-02-861947-1
$16.95

The Complete Idiot's Guide to
Geography
ISBN: 0-02-861955-2
$16.95

The Complete Idiot's Guide to
Getting Published
ISBN: 0-02-862392-4
$16.95

The Complete Idiot's Guide to
Grammar & Style
ISBN: 0-02-861956-0
$16.95

The Complete Idiot's Guide to
an MBA
ISBN: 0-02-862164-4
$17.95

The Complete Idiot's Guide to
Philosophy
ISBN:0-02-861981-1
$16.95

The Complete Idiot's Guide to
Classical Music
ISBN: 0-02-8611634-0
$16.95

The Complete Idiot's Guide to
Learning Spanish On Your
Own
ISBN: 0-02-861040-7
$16.95

The Complete Idiot's Guide to
Learning French on Your Own
ISBN: 0-02-861043-1
$16.95

The Complete Idiot's Guide to
Learning German on Your
Own
ISBN: 0-02-861962-5
$16.95

The Complete Idiot's Guide to
Learning Italian on Your Own
ISBN: 0-02-862125-5
$16.95

The Complete Idiot's Guide to
Learning Sign Language
ISBN: 0-02-862388-6
$16.95

The Complete Idiot's Guide to
Astrology
ISBN: 0-02-861951-X
$16.95

The Complete Idiot's Guide to
the World's Religions
ISBN: 0-02-861730-4
$16.95

**Look for the Complete Idiot's Guides at your local bookseller,
or call 1-800-428-5331 for more information.**

You can also check us out on the web at
http://www.mcp.com/mgr/idiot

alpha
books